Annual Editions: Psychology, 47/e

R. Eric Landrum

http://create.mheducation.com

ISBN-10: 1259657698   ISBN-13: 9781259657696

Contents

Detailed Table of Contents

B.F. Skinner at Harvard, Gregory A. Briker, *The Harvard Crimson*, 2014

In this retrospective piece about B.F. Skinner, his graduate school habits and freedom to conduct research at Harvard are discussed and examined.

Unit: Cognitive Processes

The Secret Life of Pronouns by James Pennebaker: What Do "I" and "We" Reveal about Us?, Juliet Lapidos, *Slate,* 2011

In this article, Lapidos reports on recent research that examines the role of pronouns as unexpected keys to communication. For instance, certain words, such as "nice" or "weird," are considered content words. However, this research focuses on function words, such as pronouns, articles, prepositions, and auxiliary verbs.

The Epidemic of Media Multitasking While Learning, Annie Murphy Paul, *The Brilliant Blog,* 2013

This author describes research suggesting that when students multitask during schoolwork, the learning is less effective and shallower as compared to studying with full attention. Other negative performance effects associated with multitasking, such as more time needed to complete assignments, more mistakes, and lower grades, have also been documented.

Pigeons, Like Humans, Can Behave Irrationally, Sandra Upson, *Scientific American,* 2013

Researchers are exploring the idea that if animals exhibit irrational behaviors (such as gambling), that commonality with humans may lead to some of the underlying brain mechanisms. Using pigeons in a laboratory, the researchers noted that pigeons make common reasoning mistakes similar to compulsive gamblers, such as the sunk cost fallacy.

"They are Happier and Having Better Lives than I Am": The Impact of Using Facebook on Perceptions of Others' Lives, Hui-Tzu Grace Chou and Nicholas Edge, *Cyberpsychology, Behavior, and Social Networking,* 2012

These researchers tested the hypothesis that Facebook users are influenced by easily recalled examples and that when reading positive content on Facebook, that positive content is due to the others' personality rather than situational differences that other people experience. The length of time that users have been on Facebook appears to be an important variable in explaining the impact that Facebook can have.

Cognitive Shields: Investigating Protections Against Dementia, Andrew Merluzzi, *APS Observer,* 2015

Researchers have recently indicated that over a lifetime, individuals can build a "cognitive reserve" which may serve as a protective factor from dementia. Multiple researchers in multiple laboratories are exploring different methods of encouraging individuals to build their cognitive reserve.

We Aren't the World, Ethan Watters, *Pacific Standard*, 2013

Using a game scenario where one player is given money that must be split with a second, anonymous player, both parties can keep the money if they both agree on the split. What researchers have found is that people from many cultures around the world do not react to this game scenario as Americans do, providing an important reminder that research findings based on American participants may not be universally generalizable.

Unit: Emotion and Motivation

Women at the Top: Powerful Leaders Define Success as Work + Family in a Culture of Gender, Fanny M. Cheung and Diane F. Halpern, *American Psychologist,* 2010

More and more women are emerging as leaders of businesses, industry, and national governments. The authors of this article raise the question about how women, who typically have strong family care responsibilities, become such influential and successful leaders. Based on cross-cultural research, the authors develop a leadership model to account for why women are able to make it to the top of their fields.

Self-Efficacy in the Workplace: Implications for Motivation and Performance, Fred C. Lunenburg, *International Journal of Management, Business, and Administration,* 2011

In this review paper, the author defines self-efficacy as the beliefs about one's ability to complete specific tasks, and then discusses four specific aspects or components of self-efficacy: past performance, vicarious experience, verbal persuasion, and emotional cues.

Post-Prozac Nation: The Science and History of Treating Depression, Siddhartha Mukherjee, *The New York Times,* 2012

Antidepressants, such as Prozac, are the third most common prescription drug in the United States. Patients with depression describe the relief provided by Prozac as transformative and like the lifting of a fog. The author describes several hypotheses for how Prozac works, including the correction of existing chemical imbalances in the brain. In some research circles, the key question has shifted from how Prozac works to does Prozac work?

Could Brain Scans Help Guide Treatment for OCD? Mary Elizabeth Dallas, *HealthDay,* 2015

About 2.5% of Americans are diagnosed with Obsessive Compulsive Disorder, and another 10% exhibit symptoms of OCD; that is, they have a lesser form of the illness. Although cognitive behavioral therapy has been useful as a short-term treatment for individuals with OCD, brain scan technology is currently being used to explore treatments that may have longer-term effectiveness.

Preface

Why does a student need to purchase a book that contains a collection of articles about psychology (the science of human behavior)? Why not just google the term and read what is available for free? I believe that is a fair question. Go ahead and Google "psychology" sometime—when I did this in September 2015, there were 264 million results—that's right, 264,000,000 web pages related to psychology. So I suppose with enough time you could identify (and read) some great articles about psychology, but I hope you have plenty of time for reading. Please also remember that not everything on the Internet is free—you'd have to pay per article to access some of the works provided in this book. Of course, to be fair, this book isn't free either—but with the curation of key articles completed for you and all the permissions fees paid on your behalf, we believe we've created a superior and readable resource that can help you better understand psychology, whether you're enrolled in an introductory psychology course or just looking to read more about a fascinating topic—our own human behavior—and what can be more fascinating than that?

Like any academic or professional discipline, psychology is filled with jargon and nuance—characteristics that are challenging for those new to any topic to absorb. For this reason, McGraw-Hill publishes *Annual Editions*— an anthology of current, clearly written, and highly understandable articles about psychology. The editorial staff at McGraw-Hill has designed *Annual Editions: Psychology* to meet the needs of lay people and students who are curious about psychological science and its applications. *Annual Editions: Psychology* provides a large selection of readable, informative articles primarily from popular magazines and newspapers. Many of these articles are written by journalists, but some are authored by psychologists. The articles for this volume are representative of current research and thinking in psychology. In fact, you'll see that the organization of the units and articles presented may follow quite nicely with the same order of topics and chapters you may be studying in an introductory psychology class.

This is a series that has been successful for quite some time. How do some articles get added to *Annual Editions: Psychology* whereas others are dropped? Were the articles that were dropped from the previous edition not very good? No, that's not the case at all! As new research emerges, a book like *Annual Editions: Psychology* allows both faculty members and students to stay abreast of current changes. So for some articles, it was time to update the work to more recent sources. McGraw- Hill also values instructor feedback highly, so sometimes an article on an important topic just didn't work out well when students are trying to read and comprehend the content. Results from instructor surveys were also instrumental in helping determine what should absolutely stay, and what areas might be updated; thus, it's good to keep filling out those surveys!

What would be the best way to get the most out of this book? Read it. Seriously—the book won't do you any good without reading it. As you read about the biological bases of behavior in your introductory psychology course, also read the similar content available to you in *Annual Editions: Psychology*. Concepts you may find difficult to understand from your textbook or from your instructor may become clearer to you once you read about the same topics when discussed by a knowledgeable journalist or the actual researcher. Read and engage with the articles provided in *Annual Editions: Psychology* and you'll be on your way to a better understanding of the science of human behavior—psychology, and the most fascinating topic of all—ourselves.

Editor

R. Eric Landrum is a professor of psychology at Boise State University, receiving his PhD in cognitive psychology from Southern Illinois University-Carbondale. His research interests center on the educational conditions that best facilitate student advancement. Eric is a member of the American Psychological Association, a fellow in APA's Division Two (Society for the Teaching of Psychology or STP). He served as STP secretary (2009–2011) and president (2014), and currently serves as president-elect of the Rocky Mountain Psychological Association.

Academic Advisory Board

Members of the Academic Advisory Board are instrumental in the final selection of articles for each edition of *Annual Editions*. Their review of articles for content, level, and appropriateness provides critical direction to the editors and staff. We think that you will find their careful consideration well reflected in this volume.

Elizabeth Athaide-Victor
Tiffin University

John Billingsley
Jr., American Intercontinental University

Stephanie Billingsley
Cincinnati State

Bernardo J. Carducci
Indiana University Southeast

Julie Carpenter
Paradise Valley Community College

Santiba Campbell
Bennett College

Sharon E. Chacon
Northeast Wisconsin Technical College

Daniel Dickman
Ivy Tech Community College

David Devonis
Graceland University

Thomas C. Davis
Nichols College

Carlos A. Escoto
Eastern Connecticut State University

Winona Fleenor
Virginia Highlands Community College

Jennifer Grewe
Utah State University—Logan

Kimberly Glackin
Metropolitan Community College—Blue River

Nicholas Greco IV
Columbia College of Missouri and Adler School of Professional Psychology

Bobby Hutchison
Modesto Junior College

Deborah Harris-Sims
University of Phoenix and Strayer University

Elizabeth Hammond
Columbus State Community College

Melodie Hunnicutt
University of South Carolina Beaufort and Midlands Technical College

Sheryl Hartman
Miami Dade College

Vivian Hsu
Rutgers University-New Brunswick

Elizabeth Jacobs
Glendale Community College

John Janowiak
Appalachian State University

Charles Kaiser
College of Charleston

James C. Kaufman
University of Connecticut

Jean Kubeck Hillstrom
New York City College of Technology, CUNY

Katherine Kipp
University of North Georgia—Oconee

Shaila Khan
Tougaloo College

Angela J.C. La Sala
College of Southern Nevada

Diana Lewis
Elms College

Hyoung Lee
University of Washington—Tacoma

Patricia Lanzon
Henry Ford Community College

Patricia Lindemann
Columbia University

Romney Landis
Weatherford College

Theresa Luhrs
DePaul University

Barbara Mcmillan
Alabama Southern Community College-Monroeville

Christopher McNally
John Carroll University

Eric Miller
Kent State University

Jamie Mahlberg
Rochester Community & Technical College

Jennifer McCabe
Goucher College

Margaret Miele
Fashion Institute Technology

Stephanie Moore
Northeast Mississippi Community College

Ticily Medley
Tarrant County College

Lorenz Neuwirth
College of Staten Island

Edward Raymaker
Eastern Maine Community College

Vicki Ritts
St. Louis Community College, Meramec

Carolyn Simoneaux
Urshan College

Colleen Stevenson
Muskingum University

Holly Schofield
Central Carolina Community College

Jason S. Spiegelman
Community College of Baltimore County

Laurence Segall
Housatonic Community College

Margaret Stanton
Valencia College

Mark R. Schweizer
Camden County College

Stephen P. Stelzner
College of Saint Benedict and St. John's University

Terry M. Salem
Lake Land College

Todd Steward
Sr., Pittsville High School

Loren Toussaint
Luther College

Bettina Viereck
University of Hartford

Heidi Villanueva
Virginia Union University

John E. Walsh
University of Colorado

Unit 1

UNIT

Prepared by: Eric Landrum, *Boise State University*

The Science of Psychology

Contemporary psychology is defined as the science of human behavior. Compared to other sciences (like chemistry or physics), psychology is a younger discipline. Some aspects of modern psychology are particularly biological, such as neuroscience, perception, psychophysics, and behavioral genetics. In fact, many of our recent advances in understanding, thinking, and behavior emerge from neuroscience—with examples of both men and women succeeding in this important field.

Modern psychology encompasses the full spectrum of human behavior, thought, and emotion. There is no aspect of human life that does not fall under psychology's purview. In fact, if you can think of a behavior, then there is surely a branch of psychology that focuses on the study of that behavior. From home life to the workplace to the athletic field to the church, synagogue, and mosque, psychologists seek to understand the causes of our behaviors and our thoughts. Some psychologists work to understand these behaviors simply for the sake of advancing new knowledge. Other psychologists take this new knowledge and apply it to improving the quality of everyday life. Still other psychologists focus exclusively on the most challenging problems facing the world today—war, hunger, poverty, sexual and other forms of abuse, drug and alcohol addiction, environmental change and global warming, and so on.

Psychologists work in varied settings. Many psychologists are academics, teaching and conducting psychological research on college and university campuses. Others work in applied settings such as hospitals, mental health clinics, industry, local, state, and federal government, and schools. Other psychologists work primarily in private practice in which they see clients for personal therapy and counseling sessions. Despite this diversity of settings, psychologists share a keen interest in understanding and explaining human thought and behavior. Psychologists receive rigorous training in their respective subfields of psychology. Undergraduates who are interested in becoming professional psychologists apply for and attend graduate school to receive specialized training. Some of these students earn their master's degree in psychology, whereas others go on to complete their doctorate (PhD or PsyD). For some subfields of psychology, such as clinical psychology, individuals must obtain a license to practice psychology. In this case, in addition to completing the graduate degree, the individual must also complete an internship in which he or she receives advanced and closely supervised training in the specialty.

Psychology is an incredibly diverse discipline that offers valuable insights into work, play, suffering, and love. It addresses many fascinating issues, dilemmas, and questions. Not only are individual psychologists successful in advancing careers, but psychologists on the whole continue to be successful in advancing our knowledge about human behavior. This unit offers you a glimpse at some of the pressing challenges that face psychologists in their work today and offers considerable insight into what you can expect from your study of psychology.

Article

Prepared by: Eric Landrum, *Boise State University*

Comprehensive Soldier Fitness and the Future of Psychology

MARTIN E. P. SELIGMAN AND RAYMOND D. FOWLER

Whom shall I send? And who will go for us?
And I said, "Here am I. Send me!"
                                        —Isaiah 6:8

Learning Outcomes

After reading this article, you will be able to:

- Explain the historical role of psychology within the U.S. Army.

- Evaluate how psychologists are using positive psychology to improve the mental health of U.S. soldiers.

The history of American psychology has been shaped by national need. This has been true of both the science of psychology and the practice of psychology. In this article, we look at past turning points and then describe why we believe that the Comprehensive Soldier Fitness (CSF) program is another such turning point.

In the past century, psychologists were among the first professionals to offer assistance to the nation. The work of psychologists in World Wars I and II helped to improve the effectiveness of the military, and it made enduring changes in psychology's identity and in the public recognition and acceptance of psychology.

Psychology in the United States was first recognized as an independent discipline in 1892 with the establishment of the American Psychological Association (APA). It began as a research–academic discipline with little interest in applications, and for the most part it remained so in its early years, with some notable exceptions. For example, two of the founders of American psychology were William James, who treated mentally ill patients with psychotherapy and medication, and Lightner Witmer, who established the first psychological clinic at the University of Pennsylvania in 1896 and is viewed as the founder of clinical psychology. But the first big leap into the application of psychology took place in the context of World War I.

In 1917, as war raged through Europe and American involvement seemed imminent, Robert Yerkes, a 40-year-old Yale professor of biopsychology and president of APA, proposed that APA help to create within the U.S. Army a psychology unit to select recruits and determine their duties. In a letter to the APA Council of Representatives, Yerkes (1918) wrote, "Our knowledge and our methods are of importance to the military service of our country, and it is our duty to cooperate to the fullest extent and immediately toward the increased efficiency of our Army and Navy" (p. 191).

A detailed plan was approved by the National Research Council and submitted to the Surgeon General of the Army. A unit was quickly established under the overall direction of Yerkes, who was commissioned a major. One group developed two new intelligence tests, the Army Alpha and the Army Beta, and administered them to more than 2 million soldiers. A second group interviewed and classified 3,500,000 soldiers and developed proficiency tests for military specialties.

The response of APA members to Yerkes's call for service was immediate. Although APA then had fewer than 300 members, Yerkes was able to compile a list of 150 psychologists who were willing to serve as civilian or uniformed psychological examiners, 24 of whom were available for service within a week. By the end of the war, several hundred psychologists were overseeing the work of several thousand men in personnel units throughout the military.

The effects of the program extended far beyond the military. Psychology, as a scientific and applied discipline, gained the recognition and support of the public, and psychological and educational testing centers were established in colleges and universities and in business and industry.

After the armistice, some of the participants in the Army program remained in military service to work in the 43 Army rehabilitation hospitals that had been established. Others left the service to develop tests for business and industry, but most returned to academic positions. Among those who served in the program were people who became the nation's leading psychologists, including J. R. Angell, E. K. Strong, E. G. Boring, Lewis Terman, E. L.Thorndike, L. L. Thurstone, and John B. Watson.

The attention given to psychology, and the increased number of academic programs, brought about a rapid increase in the number of psychologists. In the years following World War I, APA's membership grew tenfold, from approximately 300 members to 3,000. Doctoral production rose rapidly through the 1920s, and by the end of the decade, at least 35 universities had established doctoral programs, most of which included programs in applied psychology.

In 1939, as war again ravaged Europe, 50 psychologists met together to celebrate the 20th anniversary of their demobilization as members of the Army's Committee on Classification of Personnel. The meeting was attended by a representative from the Army Adjutant General's office, who drew attention to the worsening situation in Europe. Yerkes, representing APA, and Walter Bingham, representing APA's practitioner counterpart, began working to establish psychologists' roles in the coming war. Bingham was commissioned as a colonel, appointed chief psychologist for the Army, and given responsibility for personnel classification.

Yerkes, still vigorous as he approached retirement age but too old for military service, spent his time contacting high-level officials in the government and military to promote a broader role for psychology to include treatment, enhancement of morale, and training of military psychologists. By early 1941, he had drafted a comprehensive plan for the military that also aimed to transform the role of professional psychology. Yerkes wrote,

> Psychology must stand as a basic science for such universally desirable expert services as the guidance and safeguarding of an individual's growth and development, education and occupational choice, social adjustments, achievement and maintenance of balance, poise and effectiveness, contentment, happiness, and usefulness. (Yerkes, 1941, quoted in Capshew, 1999, p. 50)

Just six months after Pearl Harbor, there were over 100 psychologists working in Washington, DC. At the request of the Selective Service, a list of 2,300 psychologists qualified to help local draft boards determine the mental capacity of registrants was compiled, and efforts were made to ensure that some 1,500 psychologists eligible for the draft were placed in positions where their background and training could be utilized. Soon, hundreds of psychologists were spread throughout the military and in government agencies.

Personnel psychology in the military thrived in the war years, as it had in World War I. As psychologists developed many new tests of achievement, knowledge, and aptitude, the Army established the largest and most diversified testing program in history. Millions of tests were administered; for example, The Army General Classification Test (AGCT) was administered to 9 million men, one seventh of the U.S. male population.

At the start of World War II, clinical psychology, as opposed to personnel psychology, had little recognition in the military, and not much more in the wider world. Later in the war, psychologists began to serve in mental illness settings in the military, primarily because of the actions of psychiatrist William C. Menninger, newly appointed chief of neuropsychiatry. An acute shortage of psychiatrists led to the appointment of a chief clinical psychologist, the commissioning of 250 men who had experience in clinical psychology, and the establishment of permanent divisions of clinical psychology in the military services. By the end of the war, clinical psychology had become a full-fledged mental health profession, and the election in 1946 of Carl Rogers as the first clinical psychologist to be APA president confirmed its new status.

Building a productive relationship between psychology and the military was not without problems, but as the war drew to a close, both seemed pleased with the partnership. Surveys indicated that psychologists were more satisfied with their utilization in the military than were physicists, chemists, and geologists. And the military demonstrated its appreciation of the work of psychologists by continuing to recruit them: Demand for psychologists exceeded supply throughout the war (Napoli, 1981, p. 105). The Navy representative on the National Defense Research Committee said, "I believe that the application of psychology in selecting and training men, and in guiding the design of weapons so they would fit men, did more to help win this war than any other single intellectual activity" (Smith, 1948, quoted in Napoli, 1981, p 105). Psychology's contribution received praise from senior military officers and from the Army's chief psychiatrist, William C. Menninger, who foresaw a continuing role for psychologists in clinical work (Napoli, 1981, p. 106).

In 1946, the Veterans Administration, faced with an estimated 40,000 war casualties, launched a major program to fund training for new clinical psychologists. Subsequently, the National Institute of Mental Health and the U.S. Public Health Service provided millions of dollars in training and research grants to psychology graduate programs. The military services, especially the Navy, continued to fund psychological research. In the first 30 years after World War II, the federal government spent over $1.2 billion on psychological research, and over half of the members of APA received some government support (Napoli, 1981, p. 137).

Federal support through the military helped to build psychology into a major scientific discipline and profession and APA into the largest doctoral-level scientific society in the world. There are now approximately 3,000 psychologists in the Department of Veterans Affairs (VA) and over 1,500 serving in the military. And psychologists, with their research and applied work, continue to provide services to a wide spectrum of American society.

The Current National Need

The first author (Martin E. P. Seligman) was initially visited by Colonel Jill Chambers in August 2008 to discuss the problems of returning warriors, and this led to a meeting with U.S. Army Chief of Staff General George W. Casey Jr. and his advisers in the Pentagon in early December 2008. They outlined two sets of national needs and asked what psychology's response could be.

One national need was the unprecedented rates of post-traumatic stress disorder (PTSD), depression, suicide, and divorce among military personnel. Two facts stood out about this need: (a) The Army and the VA system were expending huge resources to treat these clinical issues, but their question was not how to provide more treatment but rather how to prevent these problems. (b) Related to this question was the identification of who was most at risk for PTSD: The Millennium Cohort Study found that the bottom 15% in mental and physical fitness accounted for 58% of the cases of PTSD (LeardMann, Smith, Smith, Wells, & Ryan, 2009). The other national need was for a resilient fighting force in our small, all-volunteer Army that would be capable of meeting the challenge of the persistent warfare and repeated redeployments that loom in the Army's future.

Seligman responded by suggesting that the human response to high adversity, such as combat, is normally distributed: On the left of the distribution are the minority who collapse—exhibiting what is called variously PTSD, depression, or anxiety. In the middle are the great majority who are resilient; they return to their normal level of functioning after a brief period of disruption. On the right-hand side of the distribution are those who grow: people who after adversity attain a higher level of functioning than they began with or, in other words, exhibit posttraumatic growth. The aim of any prevention program, Seligman suggested, should be to move the entire distribution toward growth. This aim would lower PTSD, increase resilience, and increase the number of people who grow.

Other important ideas, as well as a concrete plan, emerged from this meeting. The former Surgeon General of the United States, Richard Carmona, advised that civilian medicine was perversely incentivized: Of the $2 trillion the United States spends annually on health care, 75% goes into chronic disease and end-of-life care. In contrast, Army medicine is rationally incentivized—its mission is to produce health, not cure disease, and by producing health preventively, it will reduce later disease. This could be a model for civilian medicine.

The Surgeon General of the Army, Lieutenant General Eric Schoomaker, suggested constructively to General Casey that the program should not be part of his Medical Corps. Moving it from medicine to education and training would help remove any stigma and be much more in line with a universal training purpose. Seligman said that his model for preventive training was positive education: The Penn Resilience Program teaches teachers the skills of resilience and positive psychology, and the teachers then embed these skills into the teaching of their students. This reliably produces less depression and anxiety among the students (Seligman, Ernst, Gillham, Reivich, & Linkins, 2009). General Casey said that this model fits the Army's training process well: The teachers of the Army are the drill sergeants, and they would become the teachers of resilience and positive psychology. He further hoped that a successful demonstration of the effects of resilience training in soldiers and their families would provide a model for the civilian education of young people.

General Casey then set the new plan for Comprehensive Soldier Fitness into motion: It was assigned to education and training, under Brigadier General Rhonda Cornum, not to medicine. The four components detailed in this special issue of

the *American Psychologist* were fleshed out over the next three months: creating the Global Assessment Tool (GAT); creating self-improvement courses for the emotional, social, family, and spiritual fitness dimensions measured on the GAT; beginning to provide resilience training and positive psychology training throughout the Army; and beginning to identify and train master resilience trainers from Army personnel and civilian psychologists. These four components have involved dozens of psychologists over the past two years. We have worked in test creation and validation, in course creation, in writing and refining resilience and positive psychology training materials, and in serving as data analysts, as research designers, and as the trainers and facilitators of live courses with Army personnel. Of critical interest is the Soldier Fitness Tracker (Fravell, Nasser, & Cornum, 2011, this issue). This powerful platform creates an unprecedented, hypermassive database in which psychological variables, medical variables, and performance variables are merged. All of these activities continue as we write, in active collaboration with our peers from the Army.

Future Opportunities

We can only speculate about what the future may hold. The validation of the GAT, the effects of the fitness courses, the effects of resilience and positive psychology training, and the efficacy of the master resilience trainers will all be carefully measured by the Army over the months and years to come. We underscore the importance of delineating the four dimensions of psychological "fitness": emotional, social, family, and spiritual (Cornum, Matthews, & Seligman, 2011, this issue). These are the capacities that underpin human flourishing not only in the Army but in schools, corporations, and communities, and the building of these fitnesses may help define the role of the practicing psychologist of the future. The Army will rigorously ask whether building these fitnesses decreases rates of PTSD, depression, and anxiety; improves performance and morale; improves mental and physical well-being; and helps soldiers and their families in the successful transition back to civilian employment.

If the results are positive, we hope to see expanded collaboration between the military and psychology in creating an Army that is just as psychologically fit as it is physically fit. Among the future possibilities are the following:

- Training of all ranks of soldiers and of civilian employees of the Army in resilience and positive psychology
- Parallel training offered for all family members of soldiers
- Mobile training units for resilience training in far-flung outposts
- Comprehensive Military Fitness: the training of *all* the armed services and their employees in the techniques of resilience and positive psychology
- Expanded online and in-person courses for the military in emotional, social, family, and spiritual fitness

- One million soldiers taking the GAT is an unprecedented database for the prospective longitudinal study of the effects of psychological variables on physical health, mental health, and performance. The Soldier Fitness Tracker is the backbone of this longitudinal study, and we predict that this database will become a national treasure for psychological and medical research.

The use of resilience training and positive psychology in the Army is consciously intended as a model for civilian use. The bulk of health care costs in civilian medicine go not to building health but rather to treating illness. The Army's emphasis on building psychological fitness preventively is intended to be a model for the future of medicine generally. Imagine that building emotional, social, family, and spiritual fitness among young soldiers noticeably reduces morbidity, mortality, and mental illness, offers a betters prognosis when illness strikes, and cuts down on treatment costs. We should know whether this is the case in the next decade. If the CSF program turns out to work, it should—in any rational system—revolutionize the balance between treatment and prevention and radically reform how civilian health care is provided.

The implications for public education and for the corporation may be just as sweeping. Positive education claims that teaching young people the skills of emotional fitness along with teaching the traditional goals of education will enable youth to perform better at school and to perform better later in the workplace. And, more important, perhaps these young people will enjoy lives that have more positive emotion, engagement, and meaning and better relationships. All of these claims will be directly tested prospectively in the CSF program: The resilience training and the fitness courses offered are almost exact parallels of the courses we use in positive education (Seligman et al., 2009). If it turns out that soldiers given this training perform better in their jobs, are more engaged, have more meaning in their lives, enjoy better relationships, and have more fruitful employment when they return to civilian society, this will ground a new model for our public schools. Again we will know whether this is so within the next decade.

Objections

We are not unmindful of those segments of American society, including some psychologists, who look askance on working with the military in any way.

The task of the military is to provide the capability of defending the nation from threat. Revulsion toward war is understandable, but it is not the military that sets the nation's policies on war and peace. The military carries out the policies that emerge from our democratic form of government. Withholding professional and scientific support for the people who provide the nation's defense is, we believe, simply wrong. Psychologists are as diverse in their views as any other group of citizens, but the American Psychological Association has, for six decades, been solid in its support on behalf of the men and women who serve in our armed forces.

Here, in unvarnished form, are three of the objections that might be raised to working with the military, and our responses:

- Psychology should devote its scarce resources to helping those who are suffering, not those who are well.

Positive psychology seeks to broaden the scope of psychological science and practice. It seeks to build more positive emotion, engagement, and meaning and better relationships among all people, and it has developed new interventions to do just that. It is a supplement, not a replacement, for the science and practice of relieving suffering. We believe that soldiers with PTSD, depression, anxiety, and other disorders should continue to receive the best of treatments. We are also mindful, however, that the known treatments are of limited effectiveness (Seligman, 1993, 2006). The CSF program will not subtract from the treatment resources; rather it is a preventive program that will likely reduce the need for them by effectively preventing suffering.

- Psychology should do no harm: Aiding the military will make people who kill for a living feel better about killing and help them do a better job of it.

If we had discovered a way of preventing malaria—mosquito netting, draining swamps, quinine—and our soldiers were fighting in a malaria-infested theater, would these voices also counsel withholding our discoveries? We would not withhold our help: The balance of good done by building the physical and mental fitness of our soldiers far outweighs any harm that might be done. The alleged harm—making healthier killers or helping them to feel better—turns also on the final objection.

- Psychology should not aid the foreign policy of the United States.

Three ideologies have arisen in the past century that have sought to overthrow democracy by force: fascism, communism, and jihadist Islam. It should be noted that without a strong military and the will to use force responsibly in self-defense, our victories would not have happened, and defense against current and future threats would be impossible. Psychology materially aided in the defeat of the first two threats, and in doing so it carved out its identity. We are proud to aid our military in defending and protecting our nation right now, and we will be proud to help our soldiers and their families into the peace that will follow.

References

Capshew, J. H. (1999). *Psychologists on the march: Science, practice, and professional identity in America, 1929–1969.* Cambridge, England: Cambridge University Press. doi:10.1017/CBO9780511572944

Cornum, R., Matthews, M., & Seligman, M. (2011). Comprehensive Soldier Fitness: Building resilience in a challenging institutional context. *American Psychologist, 66,* 4–9. doi:10.1037/a0021420

Fravell, M., Nasser, K., & Cornum, R. (2011). The Soldier Fitness Tracker: Global delivery of Comprehensive Soldier Fitness. *American Psychologist, 66,* 73–76. doi:10.1037/a0021632

LeardMann, C. A., Smith, T. C., Smith, B., Wells, T. S., & Ryan, M. A. K. (2009). Baseline self reported functional health and vulnerability to post-traumatic stress disorder after combat deployment: Prospective US military cohort study. *British Medical Journal, 338,* 1–9. doi:10.1136/bmj.b1273

Napoli, D. S. (1981). *Architects of adjustment: The history of the psychological profession in the United States.* Port Washington, NY: Kennikat Press.

Seligman, M. E. P. (1993). *What you can change and what you can't.* New York, NY: Knopf.

Seligman, M. E. P. (2006). Afterword: Breaking the 65 percent barrier. In M. Csikszentmihalyi & I. Selega (Eds.), *A life worth living: Contributions to positive psychology* (pp. 230–236). New York, NY: Oxford University Press.

Seligman, M. E. P., Ernst, R. M., Gillham, J., Reivich, K., & Linkins, M. (2009). Positive education: Positive psychology and classroom interventions. *Oxford Review of Education, 35,* 293–311. doi:10.1080/03054980902934563

Smith, L. P. (1948). Foreword. In C. Bray (Ed.), *Psychology and military proficiency: A history of the Applied Psychology Panel of the National Defense Research Committee.* Princeton, NJ: Princeton University Press.

Yerkes, R. M. (1918). Psychology in relation to the war. *Psychological Review, 25,* 85–115. doi:10.1037/h0069904

Yerkes, R. M. (1941). Psychology and defense. *Proceedings of the American Philosophical Society, 84,* 527–542.

Critical Thinking

1. Historically, what role has psychology played in the armed services? How is this role changing today?

2. What is positive psychology and what role might it play in helping combat veterans readjust to life after war?

3. What are some of the objections that some psychologists may have in working with the military, and how do psychologists address these objections?

Create Central

www.mhhe.com/createcentral

Internet References

Ready Army: Comprehensive soldier fitness
www.acsim.army.mil/readyarmy/ra_csf.htm

Building the warrior within
www.stripes.com/building-the-warrior-within-comprehensive-soldier-fitness-program-aims-to-boost-soldiers-psychological-resiliency-1.119529

Article   Prepared by: Eric Landrum, *Boise State University*

Improving Health, Worldwide

Psychology is ramping up efforts to improve global health and well-being.

Kirsten Weir

Learning Outcomes

After reading this article, you will be able to:

- Describe the nature of the looming healthcare crisis regarding healthcare needs.

- Provide an example of how economics can specifically effect the delivery of effective healthcare.

A serious shortage of health-care providers threatens well-being around the world. With the planet's population soaring, the global health crisis stands to get even worse. According to the World Health Organization, 57 countries have fewer than 23 health workers for every 10,000 citizens, and 13 low- and middle-income countries have fewer than one hospital per million people.

Those proportions are expected to deteriorate by 2045, when the world's population is predicted to swell to 9 billion, from 7 billion today.

Clearly, there's work to be done to meet the world's burgeoning health-care needs, especially within the developing world. But more medicine and more doctors aren't the only answers. Most global health concerns—including HIV, obesity, malnutrition and sanitation—have a behavioral component, says Robert Balster, PhD, a psychologist at Virginia Commonwealth University and currently a Jefferson science fellow at the United States Agency for International Development (USAID). As a result, he says, "focusing on behavior change would have huge benefits."

"Regardless of the kind of health-care intervention, psychology needs to be at the table," adds Chris Stout, PsyD, who directs the Center for Global Initiatives and is a clinical professor at the College of Medicine, University of Illinois, Chicago. "Psychologists are probably better trained than any other health-care professional to have cultural awareness and sensitivity, and that queues us up to be really helpful when we deal with global health issues."

Psychologists are gradually becoming more tuned into global health, says Merry Bullock, PhD, senior director of APA's Office of International Affairs. The International Congress of Psychology, (/news/events/2012/international-congress-psychology.aspx),

scheduled to be held in Cape Town, South Africa, in July, features health as a central topic and will include a symposium on models of health care around the world, organized by APA's Senior Science Advisor Ellen Garrison, PhD, Bullock says. And APA President Suzanne Bennett Johnson, PhD, serves on a committee for the International Council of Science, which recently issued a global call for research on a systems approach to global health issues. Those collaborations, Bullock says, "make opportunities available for broader international exchange."

Psychological Perspective

Among the greatest threats to human life is infectious disease. In 2010, malaria alone killed 655,000 people—a tragedy made even more heartbreaking by the fact that the disease is both preventable and curable.

In the poverty-stricken regions where malaria is endemic, however, prevention and treatment are hard to come by. Most malaria-carrying mosquitoes bite at night, and insecticide-treated bed nets are one of the most effective and affordable defenses against the deadly disease. "[Bed nets] are a very cheap intervention and they're quite available," says Balster. "The trick is to get people to use them, and use them properly."

To do that, health workers have implemented a variety of behavior-change initiatives in countries throughout Africa, Balster says. USAID-supported behavior-change workers took steps to make it easy for people to obtain bed nets, encouraged local leaders to endorse their use and recruited community health workers to go door-to-door distributing nets and explaining how to use them. They distributed pamphlets, broadcast radio campaigns, held town hall meetings, and led community workshops. The efforts paid off. In nine countries where baseline data are available, bed net ownership more than doubled from 2004 to 2010, Balster says, with corresponding improvement in malaria rates. In Ethiopia, for instance, villages that received malaria prevention and treatment programs saw malaria cases fall by 73 percent between 2005 and 2010.

Educating communities about the importance of bed nets is one thing. Health workers face bigger hurdles when trying to convince people to change their sexual behavior. HIV/AIDS (/topics/hiv-aids/index.aspx) infects some 34 million people worldwide. Much of the effort to control AIDS focuses on bio-medical advances such as vaccines and anti-retroviral medications. Those are clearly important, says Balster. "[But] an equally important and effective use of resources is in prevention."

Among the psychologists applying their talents to AIDS prevention is Kathleen Sikkema, PhD, a professor of psychology and neuroscience at the Duke Global Health Institute. Sikkema, who studies HIV prevention and mental health in South Africa and other developing nations, argues that mental health treatment should be a key element in any HIV prevention program (*AIDS and Behavior,* 2010). After all, she says, researchers have compiled strong evidence of the link between HIV transmission risk and mental health. A person with a poor mental health status is more likely to engage in risky sexual behaviors and less likely to adhere to drug treatment protocols that could minimize the spread of the disease.

To address these issues, Sikkema and her colleagues are developing and testing a number of HIV interventions in South Africa and elsewhere. One project promotes adaptive coping among HIV-positive men and women with a history of childhood sexual abuse. Another teaches coping skills to young children of HIV-positive mothers, while a third aims to reduce risky behavior among women who drink alcohol in informal drinking establishments where gender-based violence is prevalent. With these projects, she and her colleagues hope to identify effective techniques to ultimately reduce the spread of HIV.

Of course, infectious diseases such as malaria and HIV make up just one subset of the global health agenda. Worldwide, rates of chronic, non-communicable diseases such as heart disease, lung disease, diabetes and cancer have been rising sharply alongside skyrocketing obesity (*The Lancet,* 2011). Many people think of obesity and related diseases as plights of prosperity, but in fact, nearly 80 percent of deaths from chronic, non-communicable diseases occurred in low- and middle-income countries in 2008, according to the WHO.

With primary risk factors such as poor diet, tobacco use and inactivity, those diseases have a clear behavioral component. And that's where psychologists like Gary Bennett, PhD, also at the Duke Global Health Institute, can help. Bennett has developed obesity interventions in the United States, and is now working to adapt some of those successful interventions for China. It's a good place to start. "There are more than 1.5 billion overweight people in the world, and at least a quarter of them are in China," he says.

He's testing an innovative project that provides tailored diet and exercise goals to participants via text message. In China, as in many other countries around the world, nutrition labeling on food is inconsistent. And as the country becomes more prosperous, eating out is becoming much more popular. As a result, he says, "counting calories is a real challenge." The text message program provides accessible, understandable goals that ultimately help people reduce their caloric intake and increase their activity levels—even if they aren't charting every calorie they swallow.

Bennett is still testing the intervention, but he's hopeful that it can be adapted to communities and cultures around the world.

Access to technology is growing at a rapid pace. "Cell phone towers are now found in most remote parts of the world," he says. Unfortunately, the same cannot be said for psychologists. "Obesity and other health behaviors present major opportunities for psychology," he says. "I think, frankly, we need many more psychologists focusing on these issues."

Another important area where psychologists are making a difference is at the intersection of early nutrition and behavior, says Maureen Black, PhD, a psychologist at the University of Maryland School of Medicine. Scientists have learned a lot about the relationship between psychology and nutrition over the last decade, Black says. Maternal depression, for instance, puts children at risk of nutritional deficiencies, poor growth and cognitive delays (*Bulletin of the World Health Organization,* 2011). On the flip side, maternal education and protective factors such as breastfeeding and early cognitive and socio-emotional opportunities can reduce a child's future health risks, as Susan Walker, PhD, at the University of the West Indies, with Black and other colleagues from the Global Child Development Group, reported last fall (*The Lancet,* 2011). Together with economists, psychologists have shown that ensuring early child development puts children on a positive trajectory to benefit from educational opportunities, become productive citizens and enhance the social capital of the society, Black says.

Such findings now form a basis for global policy recommendations, she says, and international agencies such as the WHO, the World Bank and UNICEF are incorporating a psychological angle into their strategies to promote early childhood development and nutrition.

Mental health experts can also help improve people's use of health-care services, says Balster. People in resource-poor regions may not take advantage of opportunities such as vaccination and prenatal care. As experts in behavior, psychologists can help identify and address the underlying reasons to help people make the most of health-care resources. "It's one thing to have medicines," Balster says, "but people have to take them properly."

Local Knowledge

When working in other countries, the best approaches aren't always the most intuitive. Sometimes it makes sense to adapt models from the United States to fit the needs of a developing country or community. In other instances it's better to create a program from scratch for a particular place and culture. "Understanding cultural context and adaptation to the local community are essential for interventions to be effective," Sikkema says.

As health workers implement behavior-change programs, they must also ensure their strategies are good for the long haul, Balster says. "Historically, there's been too much of Western nations coming in, dumping a lot of money on a problem and disappearing when the money runs out." Fortunately, that appears to be changing, he says.

Stout, who works with communities around the world through the Center for Global Initiatives, has also witnessed a growing emphasis on involving locals to create sustainable programs. Drawing on local experience just makes sense, he says.

"Natural healers in South Africa provide services that you and I would see as pretty close to counseling," he points out. "In Cambodia and Vietnam, midwives become the de facto medical responders." When global health workers collaborate with these local sources of knowledge, they stand to reach more people and continue to benefit communities well into the future, he says.

Nevertheless, the psychology angle still sometimes gets short shrift among global health initiatives. That's gradually changing, Stout says, as researchers continue to demonstrate the value of psychology to global health. Black adds that, in her view, most global health agencies and organizations are happy to include the psychological perspective—especially when that perspective includes a preventive point of view. "I think psychologists would be much better positioned to have a global impact if they took their theories, which are strong and effective in promoting positive behavioral changes, and put them in a public health perspective," she adds. "Don't wait until the problem has occurred. Think about prevention, or better yet, health promotion."

Ultimately, Balster adds, psychologists are poised to make an important contribution to global health. "There are associations of psychology in most every country of the world," he notes. "Psychology has the wherewithal to be an organized global presence."

Critical Thinking

1. How is the growing population on the planet impacting the provision of health care services? Is supply keeping up with demand?

2. Provide an example of a behavior change intervention that can have an impact on the spread of infectious disease. What psychological principles are in play here with regard to behavior change?

3. What, if anything, is the link between HIV transmission risk and mental health?

Create Central

www.mhhe.com/createcentral

Internet References

How science is crucial to improving health worldwide
www.huffingtonpost.com/susan-blumenthal/public-health-how-science_b_784726.html

Maternal and child health
www.globalhealth.gov/global-health-topics/maternal-and-child-health

KIRSTEN WEIR is a writer in Minneapolis.

Article   Prepared by: Eric Landrum, *Boise State University*

A Scientific Pioneer and a Reluctant Role Model

ERIN MILLAR

Learning Outcomes

After reading this article, you will be able to:

- Understand the challenges for women entering neuroscience fields.

- Comprehend some of the challenges in working in the neuroscience field.

In the early 1950s, Wilder Penfield, one of the world's leading neurosurgeons at the time, performed what should have been a straightforward elective surgery. The patient, an engineer who headed his department, had come to the Montreal Neurological Institute and Hospital, affiliated with McGill University, with epileptic seizures. The results of the surgery were catastrophic. "He couldn't remember anything that happened. He couldn't go out for dinner and follow a conversation," recalls the neuropsychologist Brenda Milner. "He had to be demoted to draftsman. But there was no loss of intelligence, no loss in reasoning."

Dr. Milner was then a 30-something PhD candidate, one of the few women employed by The Neuro (as those who work there call it). "Dr. Penfield was shocked. He didn't know what happened." She and the master surgeon wrote up the case, not knowing what would come of it. Soon after, she received an invitation from a neurosurgeon at Harvard. He had a similar case he hadn't thought significant; did she have any interest?

"I couldn't imagine why he would invite a young woman to study this case," remembers Dr. Milner, who at 94 continues her research full-time. The patient, identified for decades only as H.M., became the most important case study in the history of neuroscience, leading to many discoveries about how the brain creates memories. Although doctors had assumed H.M. was unable to form any new memories, Dr. Milner's groundbreaking research showed that he could develop new motor skills and spatial memories, proving for the first time that there are different types of memory. The Nobel Laureate Eric Kandel credited Dr. Milner with creating a whole new field called cognitive neuroscience.

On November 21, Dr. Milner became the ninth woman to be named to the Canadian Science and Engineering Hall of Fame, joining 53 other history-making researchers such as Alexander Graham Bell and J. Armand Bombardier. But she doesn't like to to be recognized as being one of the few women who have reached the highest ranks of science in Canada.

After her Hall of Fame acceptance speech, a group of young female scientists swarmed her eagerly to snap photos with her, showing how Dr. Milner, albeit somewhat unwillingly, has become an icon of what female scientists can accomplish in a male-dominated field.

"I have not set myself up to be a role model for women, but it does seem to be more of an issue than it used to be," Dr. Milner explains, recalling how she increasingly gets mobbed by women after public lectures in the past five years. "There is rarely a man in the group."

Although the landscape, particularly at medical schools, has changed significantly since Dr. Milner began her career, women continue to be underrepresented in many scientific fields. They make up only 39 per cent of students in physical sciences and 17 per cent in engineering and computer science. According to a recent study from the Council of Canadian Academies, only a third of faculty members in Canada are women, and that number shrinks to 15 per cent in the physical sciences, engineering and computer science.

Yet the toughest competition that Dr. Milner says she ever faced was against other women. When she was in high school she announced her intention to pursue mathematics against her headmistress's wishes she go into languages. The best science students in her native Britain went to Cambridge, yet the school's rigid college system only allowed for 400 female students to enroll. "It was tremendously difficult to get in," she says. "My competition was all women." Her all-girls school didn't have the calibre of teacher in math and physics to get her up to a competitive level, so they sent her elsewhere to a male lecturer.

For the rest of her career, however, Dr. Milner was determined to compete with the best scientists, male or female. "She never wanted to win prizes that were only for women, she wanted to win prizes open to both genders so she could beat the men," says Denise Klein, who has worked at The Neuro since starting a post-doc with Dr. Milner in 1992.

Early in her studies at Cambridge, Dr. Milner realized she would never be a great mathematician and switched to psychology, earning her degree in 1939. She met her husband Peter Milner while working for the military during the Second World War. They hastily married when he was asked to launch Canada's atomic energy program, and moved to Montreal.

After a teaching stint at the Université de Montréal, she realized that "in North America you were nobody if you didn't have a PhD." Dr. Milner wanted more than a teaching career. "I knew I had it in me to do something big," she says.

When she arrived at The Neuro in June, 1950, to begin her PhD, she was one of few women. "The institute was authoritarian," Dr. Milner recalls. "People who were junior would not speak out of turn. But it was not sexist." Dr. Klein goes a step further in describing it as a "chauvinistic environment."

Dr. Milner's response to the male-dominated atmosphere was to challenge stereotypes about psychology being a less rigorous approach to brain science than the work of the primarily male neurosurgeons. "She took what she did seriously enough that other people took her seriously and did not dismiss her work as soft science," says Dr. Klein. "She showed people that her field could be as scientific, as useful and as data-driven as other fields that are taken more seriously." During this period before brain imaging, when surgery was required to see what was happening in the brain, Dr. Milner's behaviour-based diagnostic work was eventually seen as crucial.

Dr. Milner insists she never encountered any barriers because of her gender. Her resistance to being recognized as an outstanding woman seems to stem from her desire to be a great scientist in general. "Brenda was good at showing people she was necessary," says Dr. Klein. "She showed people that the pieces of information she was providing from thinking about the brain and behaviour were important. She told me to make myself useful and I would have a job."

Far from being dismissed as a woman, Dr. Milner intimidated people. "Remember that she was a very strong woman," explains Gabriel Leonard, a clinical scientist at The Neuro. "There were very few people that had the courage and the necessary tenacity to fight her. She was a formidable person to debate, with a large vocabulary and a great knowledge of literature."

Three years ago, Dr. Milner received the prestigious international Balzan Prize, netting $1-million for her research. Now, she is in the midst of launching into a new research area looking at how the hemispheres of the brain interact. This year she is taking on two new post-docs and her colleagues reckon that she may be the oldest scientist in the world to do so.

Critical Thinking

1. Thinking about your own career trajectory, are there goals that you have that may be impacted by your gender? Explore and explain.

2. What role do you think one's involvement in a famous study may help or hinder advancement in one's particular chosen field?

Create Central

www.mhhe.com/createcentral

Internet References

The Finkbeiner test
   www.doublexscience.org/the-finkbeiner-test
Psychology's feminist voices
   www.feministvoices.com/Brenda-Milner

Article   Prepared by: R. Eric Landrum, *Boise State University*

That's So Random: Why We Persist in Seeing Streaks

CARL ZIMMER

Learning Outcomes

After reading this article, you will be able to:

- Better understand the nature of random events.

- Understand the instinctual nature of looking for patterns and trends in our world.

From time to time, athletes get on a streak. Suddenly, the basketball goes through the net every time, or a batter gets a hit in every game. This blissful condition is often known as the hot hand, and players have come to believe it is real—so much so that they have made it a part of their strategy for winning games.

"On offense, if someone else has a hot hand, I constantly lay the ball on him," wrote the N.B.A. legend Walt Frazier in his 1974 memoir, *Rockin' Steady: A Guide to Basketball & Cool.*

In the 1980s, Thomas Gilovich, a psychologist at Cornell University, and his colleagues did a study of the hot hand. They confirmed that the vast majority of basketball players believed in it. The audiences at basketball games were also convinced. But then Dr. Gilovich and his colleagues analyzed the hot hand statistically, and it fell apart.

The hot hand was, they concluded, an illusion caused "by a general misconception of chance."

Today, there still isn't much evidence for a hot hand in basketball or beyond. But our belief in it is unquestionably real. Roulette players will bet on more numbers after they win than after they lose, psychologists have found. A store that issues a winning lottery ticket will tend to sell more lottery tickets afterward, economists have observed. Investors often assume that a rising stock's price will keep rising.

Time and again, we don't want to believe that streaks can be the result of pure chance—probably because the bias appears to be deeply ingrained in our minds, researchers say. Indeed, a new study in *The Journal of Experimental Psychology: Animal Learning and Cognition* suggests that the hot hand phenomenon is so ancient that monkeys display it, too.

"What it suggests is that there's something going back at least 25 million years," said Benjamin Y. Hayden, a neuroscientist at the University of Rochester who wrote the study with his graduate student, Tommy C. Blanchard, and a psychologist at Clarkson University, Andreas Wilke.

The new study builds on earlier tests that Dr. Wilke and his colleagues carried out on people. In one such study, the scientists had volunteers play a computer game that showed a picture of either a pear or a bunch of cherries. The volunteers had to guess which fruit would appear next.

The order was random, and yet the volunteers tended to guess that the next fruit would be the same as the current one. In other words, they expected the fruit to arrive in streaks.

In another trial, Dr. Wilke and his colleagues let volunteers choose among different versions of the game so that they could increase their winnings. One version of the game was more likely to switch the fruit each time. As a result, the game had fewer streaks.

It should have been an easy game to win. All Dr. Wilke's volunteers needed to do was guess that the next fruit would be different each time. And yet the volunteers tended to avoid the alternating game in favor of the random game, "where they see a pattern that doesn't exist," said Dr. Wilke.

Dr. Wilke and his colleagues argue that this mental quirk is a side effect of how our brains have evolved.

"Our idea is that the driving force of the hot hand phenomenon was our history of foraging," said Dr. Wilke.

Our ancestors were constantly searching for food, either gathering plants or hunting animals. As they searched, they had to continually decide where to look next. The wrong choice could mean starvation.

Dr. Wilke argues that this threat led our ancestors to evolve some rules of thumb based on the fact that animals and plants aren't scattered randomly across a landscape. Instead, they can be found in clumps.

This meant that if our ancestors picked up a fruit from the ground, they were likely to find more by looking nearby, rather than going somewhere else. As a result, they became very sensitive to these streaks. They were an indication that good fortune would keep coming.

On the other hand, if our ancestors kept looking in a place for food and found nothing, they could predict that another look wouldn't yield anything to eat.

In the modern world, Dr. Wilke argues, we can't get rid of this instinct to think that streaks will continue, even when we're dealing with random patterns.

To vet this hypothesis, Dr. Wilke has collaborated with H. Clark Barrett of the University of California, Los Angeles, to give his hot hand tests to a group of people who live deep in the Amazon rain forest and depend in part on hunting and foraging for their food. They had the same bias found in American volunteers, suggesting that the hot hand phenomenon went beyond Western societies obsessed with basketball and slot machines.

Dr. Wilke's latest experiment sought to test whether the hot hand bias was even more universal.

"The strongest test to see if it's evolutionary is to find it in another species," said Dr. Hayden, who studies how monkeys make decisions.

So, he and Dr. Wilke developed a game for monkeys to play. In each round, the monkeys saw either a purple rectangle on the left side of a computer screen or a blue rectangle on the right. In order to get a reward, the monkeys had to guess which rectangle would appear next, directing their gaze to the left or right side of the screen.

The monkeys played thousands of rounds, developing a strategy to get the biggest reward they could. And their performance revealed that they have a hot hand bias in their decision-making, researchers said.

When streaks were common, the scientists found, the monkeys learned to get a high score. In other versions of the game, with fewer streaks, they did worse. They couldn't help guessing that a new rectangle would be the same as the previous one.

Dr. Barrett, who was not involved in the new study, cautioned that the results need to be replicated. Nevertheless, he agreed that it raised the possibility that foraging gave rise to the hot hand phenomenon millions of years ago.

"This may be a deep evolutionary history indeed, stretching back to before we were human," Dr. Barrett said.

Similarly, Laurie Santos, a psychologist at Yale, said, "They're on to something." But she questioned whether the new study actually showed that monkeys experienced the same feeling as a basketball player on a streak.

Just because the monkeys expected the rectangles to come in streaks didn't mean that they believed their own actions had anything to do with it. Some psychologists distinguish between these two effects, calling them "hot hands" and "hot outcomes."

Dr. Santos was confident that Dr. Hayden and his colleagues could devise another experiment to test the two alternatives. "That's harder, but Ben does all kinds of crazy things," said Dr. Santos. "I'm sure he could find a way to do it."

Dr. Wilke said that hot hands and hot outcomes both could have evolved from the same underlying rules of thumb for searching for food. By understanding their origins, we may be able to better understand the particular ways they influence our thinking today.

In the July issue of *Evolution and Human Behavior*, Dr. Wilke and his colleagues report that habitual gamblers have a stronger hot hand bias than non-gamblers. It might eventually be possible to predict who will be at risk of problem gambling by measuring hot hand bias in advance.

"That's a first step into some sort of application of this research," said Dr. Wilke.

Critical Thinking

1. If people believe so much in the hot hand yet the scientific evidence does not support that belief, what problems might that cause when individuals believe in something that isn't real?

2. To what extent does gambling, such as playing the lottery, capitalize on people's beliefs about hot hands and non-random events?

Internet References

Hot hands in basketball
   http://psych.cornell.edu/sites/default/files/Gilo.Vallone.Tversky.pdf

Monkeys also believe in winning streaks
   http://www.rochester.edu/newscenter/monkeys-also-believe-in-winning-streaks-study-shows

Article   Prepared by: R. Eric Landrum, *Boise State University*

Why Wait? The Science Behind Procrastination

After a long delay, psychological science is beginning to understand the complexities of procrastination.

ERIC JAFFE

Learning Outcomes

After reading this article, you will be able to:

- Understand the impact of procrastination.

- Appreciate the different viewpoints about procrastination being a self-regulation issue or personality characteristic.

- Articulate some of the potential interventions that might help individuals who are chronic procrastinators.

Believe it or not, the Internet did not give rise to procrastination. People have struggled with habitual hesitation going back to ancient civilizations. The Greek poet Hesiod, writing around 800 B.C., cautioned not to "put your work off till tomorrow and the day after." The Roman consul Cicero called procrastination "hateful" in the conduct of affairs. (He was looking at you, Marcus Antonius.) And those are just examples from recorded history. For all we know, the dinosaurs saw the meteorite coming and went back to their game of Angry Pterodactyls.

What's become quite clear since the days of Cicero is that procrastination isn't just hateful, it's downright harmful. In research settings, people who procrastinate have higher levels of stress and lower well-being. In the real world, undesired delay is often associated with inadequate retirement savings and missed medical visits. Considering the season, it would be remiss not to mention past surveys by H&R Block, which found that people cost themselves hundreds of dollars by rushing to prepare income taxes near the April 15 deadline.

In the past 20 years, the peculiar behavior of procrastination has received a burst of empirical interest. With apologies to Hesiod, psychological researchers now recognize that there's far more to it than simply putting something off until tomorrow. True procrastination is a complicated failure of self-regulation: experts define it as the voluntary delay of some important task that we intend to do, despite knowing that we'll suffer as a result. A poor concept of time may exacerbate the problem, but an inability to manage emotions seems to be its very foundation.

"What I've found is that while everybody may procrastinate, not everyone is a procrastinator," says APS Fellow Joseph Ferrari, a professor of psychology at DePaul University. He is a pioneer of modern research on the subject, and his work has found that as many as 20 percent of people may be chronic procrastinators.

"It really has nothing to do with time-management," he says. "As I tell people, to tell the chronic procrastinator to *just do it* would be like saying to a clinically depressed person, *cheer up.*"

Suffering More, Performing Worse

A major misperception about procrastination is that it's an innocuous habit at worst, and maybe even a helpful one at best. Sympathizers of procrastination often say it doesn't matter when a task gets done, so long as it's eventually finished. Some even believe they work best under pressure. Stanford philosopher John Perry, author of the book *The Art of Procrastination,* has argued that people can dawdle to their advantage by restructuring their to-do lists so that they're always accomplishing *something* of value. Psychological scientists have a serious problem with this view. They argue that it conflates beneficial, proactive behaviors like pondering (which attempts to solve a problem) or prioritizing (which organizes a series of problems) with the detrimental, self-defeating habit of genuine procrastination. If progress on a task can take many forms, procrastination is the absence of progress.

"If I have a dozen things to do, obviously #10, #11, and #12 have to wait," says Ferrari. "The real procrastinator has those 12 things, maybe does one or two of them, then rewrites the list, then shuffles it around, then makes an extra copy of it. That's procrastinating. That's different."

One of the first studies to document the pernicious nature of procrastination was published in *Psychological Science* back in 1997. APS Fellow Dianne Tice and APS William James Fellow Roy Baumeister, then at Case Western Reserve University, rated college students on an established scale of procrastination, then tracked their academic performance, stress, and general health throughout the semester. Initially there seemed to be a benefit to procrastination, as these students had lower levels of stress compared to others, presumably as a result of putting off their work to pursue more pleasurable activities. In the end, however, the costs of procrastination far outweighed the temporary benefits. Procrastinators earned lower grades than other students and reported higher cumulative amounts of stress and illness. True procrastinators didn't just finish their work later—the quality of it suffered, as did their own well-being.

"Thus, despite its apologists and its short-term benefits, procrastination cannot be regarded as either adaptive or innocuous," concluded Tice and Baumeister (now both at Florida State University). "Procrastinators end up suffering more and performing worse than other people."

A little later, Tice and Ferrari teamed up to do a study that put the ill effects of procrastination into context. They brought students into a lab and told them at the end of the session they'd be engaging in a math puzzle. Some were told the task was a meaningful test of their cognitive abilities, while others were told that it was designed to be meaningless and fun. Before doing the puzzle, the students had an interim period during which they could prepare for the task or mess around with games like Tetris. As it happened, chronic procrastinators only delayed practice on the puzzle when it was described as a cognitive evaluation. When it was described as fun, they behaved no differently from non-procrastinators. In an issue of the *Journal of Research in Personality* from 2000, Tice and Ferrari concluded that procrastination is really a self-defeating behavior—with procrastinators trying to undermine their own best efforts.

"The chronic procrastinator, the person who does this as a lifestyle, would rather have other people think that they lack effort than lacking ability," says Ferrari. "It's a maladaptive lifestyle."

A Gap Between Intention and Action

There's no single type of procrastinator, but several general impressions have emerged over years of research. Chronic procrastinators have perpetual problems finishing tasks, while situational ones delay based on the task itself. A perfect storm of procrastination occurs when an unpleasant task meets a person who's high in impulsivity and low in self-discipline. (The behavior is strongly linked with the Big Five personality trait of conscientiousness.) Most delayers betray a tendency for self-defeat, but they can arrive at this point from either a negative state (fear of failure, for instance, or perfectionism) or a positive one (the joy of temptation). All told, these qualities have led researchers to call procrastination the "quintessential" breakdown of self-control.

"I think the basic notion of procrastination as self-regulation failure is pretty clear," says Timothy Pychyl of Carleton University, in Canada. "You know what you ought to do and you're not able to bring yourself to do it. It's that gap between intention and action."

Social scientists debate whether the existence of this gap can be better explained by the inability to manage time or the inability to regulate moods and emotions. Generally speaking, economists tend to favor the former theory. Many espouse a formula for procrastination put forth in a paper published by the business scholar Piers Steel, a professor at the University of Calgary, in a 2007 issue of *Psychological Bulletin*. The idea is that procrastinators calculate the fluctuating utility of certain activities: pleasurable ones have more value early on, and tough tasks become more important as a deadline approaches.

Psychologists like Ferrari and Pychyl, on the other hand, see flaws in such a strictly temporal view of procrastination. For one thing, if delay were really as rational as this utility equation suggests, there would be no need to call the behavior *procrastination*—on the contrary, *time-management* would fit better. Beyond that, studies have found that procrastinators carry accompanying feelings of guilt, shame, or anxiety with their decision to delay. This emotional element suggests there's much more to the story than time-management alone. Pychyl noticed the role of mood and emotions on procrastination with his very first work on the subject, back in the mid-1990s, and solidified that concept with a study published in the *Journal of Social Behavior and Personality* in 2000. His research team gave 45 students a pager and tracked them for five days leading up to a school deadline. Eight times a day, when beeped, the test participants reported their level of procrastination as well as their emotional state. As the preparatory tasks became more difficult and stressful, the students put them off for more pleasant activities. When they did so, however, they reported high levels of guilt—a sign that beneath the veneer of relief there was a lingering dread about the work set aside. The result made Pychyl realize that procrastinators recognize the temporal harm in what they're doing, but can't overcome the emotional urge toward a diversion.

A subsequent study, led by Tice, reinforced the dominant role played by mood in procrastination. In a 2001 issue of the *Journal of Personality and Social Psychology,* Tice and colleagues reported that students didn't procrastinate before an intelligence test when primed to believe their mood was fixed. In contrast, when they thought their mood could change (and particularly when they were in a bad mood), they delayed practice until about the final minute. The findings suggested that self-control only succumbs to temptation when present emotions can be improved as a result.

"Emotional regulation, to me, is the real story around procrastination, because to the extent that I can deal with my emotions, I can stay on task," says Pychyl. "When you say *task-aversiveness,* that's another word for lack of enjoyment. Those are feeling states—those aren't states of which [task] has more utility."

Frustrating the Future Self

In general, people learn from their mistakes and reassess their approach to certain problems. For chronic procrastinators, that feedback loop seems continually out of service. The damage suffered as a result of delay doesn't teach them to start earlier the next time around. An explanation for this behavioral paradox seems to lie in the emotional component of procrastination. Ironically, the very quest to relieve stress in the moment might prevent procrastinators from figuring out how to relieve it in the long run.

"I think the mood regulation piece is a huge part of procrastination," says Fuschia Sirois of Bishop's University, in Canada. "If you're focused just on trying to get yourself to feel good now, there's a lot you can miss out on in terms of learning how to correct behavior and avoiding similar problems in the future."

A few years ago, Sirois recruited about 80 students and assessed them for procrastination. The participants then read descriptions of stressful events, with some of the anxiety caused by unnecessary delay. In one scenario, a person returned from a sunny vacation to notice a suspicious mole, but put off going to the doctor for a long time, creating a worrisome situation.

Afterward, Sirois asked the test participants what they thought about the scenario. She found that procrastinators tended to say things like, "At least I went to the doctor before it really got worse." This response, known as a *downward counterfactual,* reflects a desire to improve mood in the short term. At the same time, the procrastinators rarely made statements like, "If only I had gone to the doctor sooner." That type of response, known as an *upward counterfactual,* embraces the tension of the moment in an attempt to learn something for the

future. Simply put, procrastinators focused on how to make themselves feel better at the expense of drawing insight from what made them feel bad.

Recently, Sirois and Pychyl tried to unify the emotional side of procrastination with the temporal side that isn't so satisfying on its own. In the February issue of *Social and Personality Psychology Compass,* they propose a two-part theory on procrastination that braids short-term, mood-related improvements with long-term, time-related damage. The idea is that procrastinators comfort themselves in the present with the false belief that they'll be more emotionally equipped to handle a task in the future.

"The future self becomes the beast of burden for procrastination," says Sirois. "We're trying to regulate our current mood and thinking our future self will be in a better state. They'll be better able to handle feelings of insecurity or frustration with the task. That somehow we'll develop these miraculous coping skills to deal with these emotions that we just can't deal with right now."

The Neuropsychology of Procrastination

Recently the behavioral research into procrastination has ventured beyond cognition, emotion, and personality, into the realm of neuropsychology. The frontal systems of the brain are known to be involved in a number of processes that overlap with self-regulation. These behaviors—problem-solving, planning, self-control, and the like—fall under the domain of *executive functioning.* Oddly enough, no one had ever examined a connection between this part of the brain and procrastination, says Laura Rabin of Brooklyn College.

"Given the role of executive functioning in the initiation and completion of complex behaviors, it was surprising to me that previous research had not systematically examined the relationship between aspects of executive functioning and academic procrastination—a behavior I see regularly in students but have yet to fully understand, and by extension help remediate," says Rabin.

To address this gap in the literature, Rabin and colleagues gathered a sample of 212 students and assessed them first for procrastination, then on the nine clinical subscales of executive functioning: impulsivity, self-monitoring, planning and organization, activity shifting, task initiation, task monitoring, emotional control, working memory, and general orderliness. The researchers expected to find a link between procrastination and a few of the subscales (namely, the first four in the list above). As it happened, procrastinators showed significant associations with *all nine,* Rabin's team reported in a 2011 issue of the *Journal of Clinical and Experimental Neuropsychology.*

Rabin stresses the limitations of the work. For one thing, the findings were correlative, meaning it's not quite clear those elements of executive functioning caused procrastination directly. The assessments also relied on self-reports; in the future, functional imaging might be used to confirm or expand the brain's delay centers in real time. Still, says Rabin, the study suggests that procrastination might be an "expression of subtle executive dysfunction" in people who are otherwise neuropsychologically healthy.

"This has direct implications for how we understand the behavior and possibly intervene," she says.

Possible Interventions

As the basic understanding of procrastination advances, many researchers hope to see a payoff in better interventions. Rabin's work on executive functioning suggests a number of remedies for unwanted delay. Procrastinators might chop up tasks into smaller pieces so they can work through a more manageable series of assignments. Counseling might help them recognize that they're compromising long-term aims for quick bursts of pleasure. The idea of setting personal deadlines harmonizes with previous work done by behavioral researchers Dan Ariely and Klaus Wertenbroch on "precommitment." In a 2002 issue of *Psychological Science,* Ariely and Wertenbroch reported that procrastinators were willing to set meaningful deadlines for themselves, and that the deadlines did in fact improve their ability to complete a task. These self-imposed deadlines aren't as effective as external ones, but they're better than nothing.

The emotional aspects of procrastination pose a tougher problem. Direct strategies to counter temptation include blocking access to desirable distraction, but to a large extent that effort requires the type of self-regulation procrastinators lack in the first place. Sirois believes the best way to eliminate the need for short-term mood fixes is to find something positive or worthwhile about the task itself. "You've got to dig a little deeper and find some personal meaning in that task," she says. "That's what our data is suggesting."

Ferrari, who offers a number of interventions in his 2010 book *Still Procrastinating? The No Regrets Guide to Getting It Done,* would like to see a general cultural shift from punishing lateness to rewarding the early bird. He's proposed, among other things, that the federal government incentivize early tax filing by giving people a small break if they file by, say, February or March 15. He also suggests we stop enabling procrastination in our personal relationships.

"Let the dishes pile up, let the fridge go empty, let the car stall out," says Ferrari. "Don't bail them out." (Recent work suggests he's onto something. In a 2011 paper in *Psychological Science,* Gráinne Fitzsimons and Eli Finkel report that people who think their relationship partner will help them with a task are more likely to procrastinate on it.)

But while the tough love approach might work for couples, the best personal remedy for procrastination might actually be self-forgiveness. A couple years ago, Pychyl joined two Carleton University colleagues and surveyed 119 students on procrastination before their midterm exams. The research team, led by Michael Wohl, reported in a 2010 issue of *Personality and Individual Differences* that students who forgave themselves after procrastinating on the first exam were less likely to delay studying for the second one.

Pychyl says he likes to close talks and chapters with that hopeful prospect of forgiveness. He sees the study as a reminder that procrastination is really a self-inflicted wound that gradually chips away at the most valuable resource in the world: time.

"It's an existentially relevant problem, because it's not getting on with life itself," he says. "You only get a certain number of years. What are you doing?"

References and Further Reading:

Ariely, D., & Wertenbroch, K. (2002). Procrastination, deadlines, and performance: Self-control by precommitment. *Psychological Science, 13,* 219–224.

Ferrari, J. R. (2010). *Still Procrastinating? The No Regrets Guide to Getting It Done.* (Hoboken, N.J.: Wiley).

Perry, J. (2012). *The Art of Procrastination: A Guide to Effective Dawdling, Lollygagging and Postponing.* (New York, Workman).

Pychyl, T. A., Lee, J. M., Thibodeau, R., & Blunt, A. (2000). Five days of emotion: An experience sampling study of undergraduate student procrastination. *Journal of Social Behavior and Personality, 15,* 239–254.

Rabin, L. A., Fogel, J., & Nutter-Upham, K. E. (2011). Academic procrastination in college students: The role of self-reported executive function. *Journal of Clinical and Experimental Neuropsychology, 33,* 344–357.

Sirois, F. M. (2004). Procrastination and counterfactual thinking: Avoiding what might have been. *British Journal of Social Psychology, 43,* 269–286.

Sirois, F. M. & Pychyl, T. A. (2013). Procrastination and the Priority of Short-Term Mood Regulation: Consequences for Future Self. *Social and Personality Psychology Compass, 7,* 115–127.

Steel, P. (2007). The nature of procrastination: A meta-analytic and theoretical review of quintessential self-regulatory failure. *Psychological Bulletin, 133,* 65–94.

Tice, D. M., & Baumeister, R. F. (1997). Longitudinal study of procrastination, performance, stress, and health: The costs and benefits of dawdling. *Psychological Science, 8,* 454–458.

Tice, D. M., Bratslavsky, E., & Baumeister, R. F. (2001). Emotional distress regulation takes precedence over impulse control: If you feel bad, do it! *Journal of Personality and Social Psychology, 80,* 53–67.

Wohl, M. J. A., Pychyl, T. A., & Bennett, S. H. (2010). I forgive myself, now I can study: How self-forgiveness for procrastinating can reduce future procrastination. *Personality and Individual Differences, 48,* 803–808.

Critical Thinking

1. The authors made the distinction between the behavior of procrastinating and someone who is a procrastinator; thinking about yourself, which of those categories applies to you, and why?

2. In what situations might a delay in completing a task be considered a good outcome, rather than procrastination? How is procrastination related to time management?

3. If a friend came to you and told you that he or she had a severe procrastination problem, based on the available evidence and intervention strategies, what advice would you give him or her, and why?

Internet References

Brain freeze: The science of procrastination and our 'smart' brains
    http://thenextweb.com/lifehacks/2014/03/27/brain-freeze-science-procrastination-smart-brains/

Six reasons people procrastinate
    http://success.oregonstate.edu/six-reasons-people-procrastinate

To stop procrastinating, start by understanding the emotions involved
    http://www.wsj.com/articles/to-stop-procrastinating-start-by-understanding-whats-really-going-on-1441043167

Article   Prepared by: R. Eric Landrum, *Boise State University*

Ten Famous Psychological Experiments That Could Never Happen Today

MEREDITH DANKO

Learning Outcomes

After reading this article, you will be able to:

- Discuss some of the most famous experiments in the history of modern psychology.

- Appreciate the role that deception can sometimes play in conducting psychological research.

- Discern that temporary deception in research occurs in certain areas of psychology (i.e., social) compared to other areas.

Nowadays, the American Psychological Association has a **Code of Conduct** in place when it comes to ethics in psychological experiments. Experimenters must adhere to various rules pertaining to everything from confidentiality to consent to overall beneficence. Review boards are in place to enforce these ethics. But the standards were not always so strict, which is how some of the most famous studies in psychology came about.

1. The Little Albert Experiment

At Johns Hopkins University in 1920, John B. Watson conducted a study of classical conditioning, a phenomenon that pairs a conditioned stimulus with an unconditioned stimulus until they produce the same result. This type of conditioning can create a response in a person or animal towards an object or sound that was previously neutral. Classical conditioning is commonly associated with Ivan Pavlov, who rang a bell every time he fed his dog until the mere sound of the bell caused his dog to salivate.

Watson tested classical conditioning on a 9-month-old baby he called Albert B. The young boy started the experiment loving animals, particularly a white rat. Watson started pairing the presence of the rat with the loud sound of a hammer hitting metal. Albert began to develop a fear of the white rat as well as most animals and furry objects. The experiment is considered particularly unethical today because Albert was never desensitized to the phobias that Watson produced in him. (The child died of an unrelated illness at age 6, so doctors were unable to determine if his phobias would have lasted into adulthood.)

2. Asch Conformity Experiments

Solomon Asch tested conformity at Swarthmore College in 1951 by putting a participant in a group of people whose task was to match line lengths. Each individual was expected to announce which of three lines was the closest in length to a reference line. But the participant was placed in a group of actors, who were all told to give the correct answer twice then switch to each saying the same incorrect answer. Asch wanted to see whether the participant would conform and start to give the wrong answer as well, knowing that he would otherwise be a single outlier.

Thirty-seven of the 50 participants agreed with the incorrect group despite physical evidence to the contrary. Asch used deception in his experiment without getting informed consent from his participants, so his study could not be replicated today.

3. The Bystander Effect

Some psychological experiments that were designed to test the bystander effect are considered unethical by today's standards. In 1968, John Darley and Bibb Latané developed an interest in crime witnesses who did not take action. They were particularly intrigued by the **murder of Kitty Genovese,** a young woman whose murder was witnessed by many, but still not prevented.

The pair conducted a study at Columbia University in which they would give a participant a survey and leave him alone in a room to fill out the paper. Harmless smoke would start to seep into the room after a short amount of time. The study showed that the solo participant was much faster to report the smoke than participants who had the exact same experience, but were in a group.

The studies became progressively unethical by putting participants at risk of psychological harm. Darley and Latané played a recording of an actor pretending to have a seizure in the headphones of a person, who believed he or she was listening to an actual medical emergency that was taking place down the hall. Again, participants were much quicker to react when they thought they were the sole person who could hear the seizure.

4. The Milgram Experiment

Yale psychologist Stanley Milgram hoped to further understand how so many people came to participate in the cruel acts of the Holocaust. He theorized that people are generally inclined to obey authority figures, **posing the question,** "Could it be that Eichmann and his million accomplices in the Holocaust were just following orders? Could we call them all accomplices?" In 1961, he began to conduct experiments of obedience.

Participants were under the impression that they were part of a **study of memory.** Each trial had a pair divided into "teacher" and "learner," but one person was an actor, so only one was a true participant. The drawing was rigged so that the participant always took the role of "teacher." The two were moved into separate rooms and the "teacher" was given instructions. He or she pressed a button to shock the "learner" each time an incorrect answer was provided. These shocks would increase in voltage each time. Eventually, the actor would start to complain followed by more and more desperate screaming. Milgram learned that the **majority of participants** followed orders to continue delivering shocks despite the clear discomfort of the "learner."

Had the shocks existed and been at the voltage they were labeled, the majority would have actually killed the "learner" in the next room. Having this fact revealed to the participant after the study concluded would be a clear example of psychological harm.

5. Harlow's Monkey Experiments

In the 1950s, Harry Harlow of the University of Wisconsin tested infant dependency using rhesus monkeys in his experiments rather than human babies. The monkey was removed from its actual mother which was replaced with two "mothers,"

one made of cloth and one made of wire. The cloth "mother" served no purpose other than its comforting feel whereas the wire "mother" fed the monkey through a bottle. The monkey spent the majority of his day next to the cloth "mother" and only around one hour a day next to the wire "mother," despite the association between the wire model and food.

Harlow also used intimidation to prove that the monkey found the cloth "mother" to be superior. He would scare the infants and watch as the monkey ran towards the cloth model. Harlow also conducted experiments which isolated monkeys from other monkeys in order to show that those who did not learn to be part of the group at a young age were unable to assimilate and mate when they got older. Harlow's experiments ceased in 1985 due to APA **rules against the mistreatment of animals as well as humans.** However, Department of Psychiatry Chair Ned H. Kalin, MD. of the University of Wisconsin School of Medicine and Public Health has recently begun similar experiments that involve isolating infant monkeys and exposing them to frightening stimuli. He hopes to discover data on human anxiety, but is **meeting with resistance** from animal welfare organizations and the general public.

6. Learned Helplessness

The ethics of Martin Seligman's experiments on learned helplessness would also be called into question today due to his mistreatment of animals. In 1965, Seligman and his team used dogs as subjects to test how one might perceive control. The group would place a dog on one side of a box that was divided in half by a low barrier. Then they would administer a shock, which was avoidable if the dog jumped over the barrier to the other half. Dogs quickly learned how to prevent themselves from being shocked.

Seligman's group then harnessed a group of dogs and randomly administered shocks, which were completely unavoidable. The next day, these dogs were placed in the box with the barrier. Despite new circumstances that would have allowed them to escape the painful shocks, these dogs did not even try to jump over the barrier; they only cried and did not jump at all, demonstrating learned helplessness.

7. Robbers Cave Experiment

Muzafer Sherif conducted the Robbers Cave Experiment in the summer of 1954, testing group dynamics in the face of conflict. A group of preteen boys were brought to a summer camp, but they did not know that the counselors were actually psychological researchers. The boys were split into two groups, which were kept very separate. The groups only came into contact with each other when they were competing in sporting events or other activities.

The experimenters orchestrated increased tension between the two groups, particularly by keeping competitions close in points. Then, Sherif created problems, such as a water shortage, that would require both teams to unite and work together in order to achieve a goal. After a few of these, the groups became completely undivided and amicable.

Though the experiment seems simple and perhaps harmless, it would still be considered unethical today because Sherif used deception as the boys did not know they were participating in a psychological experiment. Sherif also did not have informed consent from participants.

8. The Monster Study

At the University of Iowa in 1939, Wendell Johnson and his team hoped to discover the cause of stuttering by attempting to turn orphans into stutterers. There were 22 young subjects, 12 of whom were non-stutterers. Half of the group experienced positive teaching whereas the other group dealt with negative reinforcement. The teachers continually told the latter group that they had stutters. No one in either group became stutterers at the end of the experiment, but those who received negative treatment did develop many of the self-esteem problems that stutterers often show. Perhaps Johnson's interest in this phenomenon had to do with **his own stutter as a child,** but this study would never pass with a contemporary review board.

Johnson's reputation as an unethical psychologist has not caused the University of Iowa to remove his name from its **Speech and Hearing Clinic.**

9. Blue Eyed Versus Brown Eyed Students

Jane Elliott was not a psychologist, but she developed one of the most famously controversial exercises in 1968 by dividing students into a blue-eyed group and a brown-eyed group. Elliott was an elementary school teacher in Iowa, who was trying to give her students hands-on experience with discrimination the day after Martin Luther King Jr. was shot, but this exercise still has significance to psychology today. The famous exercise even transformed Elliott's career into one centered around diversity training.

After dividing the class into groups, Elliott would cite phony scientific research claiming that one group was superior to the other. Throughout the day, the group would be treated as such. Elliott learned that it only took a day for the "superior" group to turn crueler and the "inferior" group to become more insecure. The blue eyed and brown eyed groups then switched so that all students endured the same prejudices.

Elliott's exercise (which she repeated in 1969 and 1970) received plenty of public backlash, which is probably why it would not be replicated in a psychological experiment or classroom today. The main ethical concerns would be with deception and consent, though some of the original participants **still regard the experiment as life-changing.**

10. The Stanford Prison Experiment

In 1971, Philip Zimbardo of Stanford University conducted his famous prison experiment, which aimed to examine group behavior and the importance of roles. Zimbardo and his team picked a group of 24 male college students who were considered "healthy," both physically and psychologically. The men had signed up to participate in a **"psychological study of prison life,"** which would pay them $15 per day. Half were randomly assigned to be prisoners and the other half were assigned to be prison guards. The experiment played out in the basement of the Stanford psychology department where Zimbardo's team had created a makeshift prison. The experimenters went to great lengths to create a realistic experience for the prisoners, including **fake arrests** at the participants' homes.

The prisoners were given a fairly standard introduction to prison life, which included being deloused and assigned an embarrassing uniform. The guards were given vague instructions that they should never be violent with the prisoners, but needed to stay in control. The first day passed without incident, but the prisoners rebelled on the second day by barricading themselves in their cells and ignoring the guards. This behavior shocked the guards and presumably led to the psychological abuse that followed. The guards started separating "good" and "bad" prisoners, and doled out punishments including push ups, solitary confinement, and public humiliation to rebellious prisoners.

Zimbardo **explained,** "In only a few days, our guards became sadistic and our prisoners became depressed and showed signs of extreme stress." Two prisoners dropped out of the experiment; one eventually **became a psychologist and a consultant for prisons.** The experiment was originally supposed to last for two weeks, but it ended early when Zimbardo's future wife, psychologist Christina Maslach, visited the experiment on the fifth day and **told him,** "I think it's terrible what you're doing to those boys."

Despite the unethical experiment, Zimbardo is still a working psychologist today. He was even honored by the American Psychological Association with a **Gold Medal Award for Life Achievement in the Science of Psychology in 2012.**

Critical Thinking

1. If you wanted to conduct an experiment about conformity similar to Asch, how might you achieve that goal without using any deception or misdirection at all?

2. Thinking about Harlow's experiment with monkeys, where do you draw the line between the benefits of understanding human behavior due to animal experimentation vs. preventing research with animals due to the potential harm of animal experimentation?

3. The Stanford Prison Experiment is one of the classic studies in all of modern psychology; even a movie was released in 2015 about the topic. Was this truly a research experiment or a research study, and why?

Internet References

25 mind blowing psychology experiments . . . you won't believe what's inside your head
http://list25.com/25-intriguing-psychology-experiments/

Classic studies in psychology
http://psychology.about.com/od/classicpsychologystudies/

Top 10 unethical psychological experiments
http://listverse.com/2008/09/07/top-10-unethical-psychological-experiments/

Danko, Meredith. "Ten Famous Psychological Experiments That Could Never Happen Today," *Mental Floss*, September 2013. Copyright © 2013 by Mental Floss. Used with permission.

Unit 2

UNIT

Prepared by: Eric Landrum, *Boise State University*

Biological Bases of Behavior

As a child, Angel vowed that she did not want to turn out like either of her parents. Angel's mother was passive and silent about her father's drinking. When her father was drunk, her mom always called his boss to report that he was "sick" and then acted as if there was nothing wrong at home. Angel's childhood was a nightmare. Her father's behavior was erratic and unpredictable. If he drank a little, he seemed to be happy. If he drank a lot (which was usually the case), he often became belligerent.

Despite vowing not to become like her father, as an adult Angel found herself as an in-patient in the alcohol rehabilitation unit of a large hospital. Angel's employer could no longer tolerate her on-the-job mistakes or her unexplained absences from work. Angel's supervisor referred her to the clinic for help. As Angel pondered her fate, she wondered whether her genes preordained her to follow in her father's drunken footsteps or whether the stress of her childhood had brought her to this point in her life. After all, being the adult child of an alcoholic is difficult.

Psychologists are concerned with discovering the causes (when possible) of human behavior. Once the cause is known, treatments for problematic behaviors can be developed. In fact, certain behaviors might even be prevented when the cause is identified early enough. But for Angel, prevention was too late. One of the paths to understanding human behavior is the task of understanding its biological underpinnings. Genes and chromosomes, the body's chemistry (as found in hormones, neurotransmitters, and enzymes), and the central and peripheral nervous systems are all implicated in human behavior.

Physiological psychologists, biopsychologists, and neuroscientists examine the role of biology in behavior. These experts often utilize one of a handful of techniques to understand the biology–behavior connection. Animal studies involving manipulation, stimulation, or destruction of certain parts of the brain offer one method of study, but these studies remain controversial with animal rights activists. There is an alternative technique that involves the study of individuals born with unusual or malfunctioning brains or those whose brains are damaged by accidents or disease—some case studies of these individuals are famous in psychology for the insights yielded. By studying an individual's behavior in comparison to both natural and adoptive parents, or by studying identical twins reared together or apart, we also can begin to understand the role of genetics and environment on human behavior.

Article   Prepared by: Eric Landrum, *Boise State University*

Reflections on Mirror Neurons

TEMMA EHRENFELD

Learning Outcome

After reading this article, you will be able to:

- Describe mirror neurons and explain their role in influencing observational behavior and communication.

In 1992, a team at the University of Parma, Italy discovered what have been termed "mirror neurons" in macaque monkeys: cells that fire both when the monkey took an action (like holding a banana) and saw it performed (when a man held a banana). Giacomo Rizzolati, the celebrated discoverer, will deliver the Keynote Address at the APS Convention in Washington DC, USA, on May 26, 2011, and report on his latest findings. To tide us over until then, here's a report on the state of mirror neuron science.

Like monkeys, humans have mirror neurons that fire when we both perceive and take an action. Locating the tiny cells means attaching electrodes deep inside the brain. As this has hardly been practical in humans, studies have had to rely on imaging, which shows which areas of the brain "light up" in different circumstances. By last year, a meta-analysis of 139 imaging studies confirmed mirroring activity in parts of the human brain where, in monkeys, mirror neurons are known to reside. Because the lit-up areas contain millions of neurons, for humans most researchers speak of a "mirror system," rather than mirror cells. Last year, single mirror neurons were recorded in humans for the first time, using in-depth electrodes, in 21 epileptic patients.

The cells showed up unexpectedly in an area known for memory, the medial temporal lobe, as well as in areas where they were expected. The discovery suggests that memory is embedded in our mirror system, says Marco Iacoboni (University of California, Los Angeles), a leading authority in the field and a co-author of the epilepsy study. Perhaps, he says, we form memory "traces" whenever we see or observe an action. "It's a lovely idea," says Rizzolati, though he adds that it's too early to say.

The mirroring system includes a mechanism that helps the brain record the difference between seeing and acting. In the epilepsy study, some neurons fired more during action and others fired more during observation. These same cells, Iacoboni proposes, help us distinguish between the self and others.

That's an important issue, to say the least. We often confuse our own actions with those of other people. In a study published recently in *Psychological Science,* Gerald Echterhoff, University of Muenster, Germany, and his co-authors reported that people who had watched a video of someone else doing a simple action—shaking a bottle or shuffling a deck of cards—often mistakenly recalled two weeks later that they had done so themselves. The mistake occurred even when participants were warned that they could mix up other people's actions with their own. Echterhoff and a co-author, Isabel Lindner, of the University of Cologne, Germany, plan to conduct imaging studies to test if the phenomenon is related to mirroring.

Mirror neurons are present in infant monkeys. Three years ago, the first abstract appeared reporting that surface electrodes had recorded mirroring in monkeys one- to seven-days old as they watched humans stick out their tongues and smack their lips. Says Pier Francesco Ferrari, of the University of Parma, and co-author of an upcoming study, "This is the first evidence that infants have a mirror mechanism at birth that responds to facial gestures. Without any experience of stimulation, they are able to focus their attention on the most relevant stimuli and respond." Sometimes the days-old monkeys even stuck out their tongues when they saw the human tongue, Ferrari says.

In monkeys, mirror neurons are present in the insula, an emotion center. Despite all the claims linking mirror neurons to empathy, Rizzolatti says he is only now reporting the discovery of a few mirror neurons in the insula in monkeys, "a reservoir for disgust and pain. Many other factors control how we react," he says, "but mirror neurons are how we recognize an emotion in others neurally."

Mimicry, linked to mirror neurons, makes monkeys bond. The idea that mimicry helps humans bond is well-accepted, but the first controlled experiment, with a monkey, came last year, Ferrari says. In that study, reported in *Science,* his team presented monkeys with a token and rewarded them with treats if they returned it. The monkeys had a choice of returning the token to either of two investigators, only one of whom was imitating the monkey. The monkeys consistently chose to return the token to the person who imitated them and spent more time near that investigator.

Mimicry in humans reflects social cues. The idea that we're primed in one part of our brain to like those who mimic us doesn't rule out other discriminations. Unconscious mimicry is deeply social and, as such, reflects prejudice, says Rick van Baaren of Radboud University in the Netherlands. In a 2009 overview of the science of mimicry published in the *Philosophical Transactions of The Royal Society,* he points out that people are more likely to mimic a member of the same ethnic group, less likely to mimic a stigmatized person who is obese or has a scar, and less likely to mimic members of a group we view with prejudice. In fact, humans tend to react badly when mimicked by someone from an "out group."

The mirror systems of two people can move in tandem. Many researchers had proposed that the brains of two people "resonate" with each other as they interact, with one person's mirror system reflecting changes in the other. Last spring, *the Proceedings of the National Academy of Sciences* reported on the brain activity of people playing the game of charades. The observer and gesturer performing the charade did move neurologically in tandem, says co-author Christian Keysers, of the University Medical Center in Groningen, The Netherlands. Keysers says the discovery backs up the idea that mirroring plays a key role in the evolution of language. We're exquisitely responsive to gestures, he says; "Nobody had ever shown that during gestural communication the observer's mirror system tracks the moment to moment state of the gesturer's motor system."

Mirror neurons respond to sound. In monkeys, mirror neurons fire at sounds associated with an action, such as breaking a peanut or tearing paper. Mirroring has been discovered in birds hearing bird song, and in humans. Recent work, led by Emiliano Ricciardi at the University of Pisa, Italy, found that blind people, using their hearing, interpret the actions of others by recruiting the same human mirror system brain areas as sighted people.

Mirror neurons code intentions. Whether mirror neurons register the goal of an action or other higher-level systems must chip in to judge other people's intentions has been the subject of much debate. The evidence is accumulating that mirror neurons "implement a fairly sophisticated and rather abstract coding of the actions of others," says Iacoboni. One clue is that while a third of all mirror neurons fire for exactly the same action, either executed or observed, the larger number—about two thirds—fire for actions that achieve the same goal or those that are logically related—for example, first grasping and then bringing an object to the mouth. And these neurons make fine distinctions: When a monkey observed an experimenter grasping an object and pantomiming the same action, the neurons fired when the experimenter grasped the object but not during the pantomime. "In academia, there is a lot of politics and we are continuously trying to figure out the 'real intentions' of other people," Iacoboni says. "The mirror system deals with relatively simple intentions: smiling at each other, or making eye contact with the other driver at an intersection."

Mirroring increases with experience. In the first studies, monkeys mirrored when they saw a person grasping food but not if the person used a tool. That made sense because monkeys don't use tools. In later research, monkeys did mirror humans using a tool; Iacoboni suggests that their brains had "learned," adjusting to seeing researchers with tools. In humans, more mirroring activity occurs when dancers see other dancers perform routines they know well. Mirroring in blind people is more active in response to more familiar action sounds.

Stimulating the mirror system helps stroke victims. If mirroring develops as we learn, perhaps triggering mirroring can teach. Two studies with stroke victims, for example, have found that stimulating the mirror system helped them recover particular motor actions, says Ferdinand Binkofski at the University of Luebeck, Germany. When stroke victims received "action observation therapy," in which they observed an action repeatedly, they regained more ability. Compared to a control group, the stroke victims also showed more mirroring in brain scans.

Children with autistic syndromes have mirroring defects. As early as 2001, researchers hypothesized that a deficit in the mirror neuron system could explain some of the problems of autistic patients. As of September, 2010 twenty published papers using brain imaging, magnetoencephalography, electroencephalography, and transcranial magnetic stimulation support this idea, and four failed to support it, according to Iacoboni.

The hope is that basic science in the mirror system could lead to a better understanding of emotional difficulties. As Ferrari points out, some infant monkeys separated from their mothers show "symptoms like those in autistic kids. You see them rocking and avoiding your gaze." Others develop normally. Ferrari and his colleagues plan to follow the infants they studied and measure whether strong mirror neuron activity in the first week of life indicates sociability later on. "We hope to create a picture of how brain activity interacts with the social environment to put some monkeys more at risk," he says. "The obvious direction is to translate this to humans."

Mirror neuron research continues to grow fast, across disciplines. Already the number of items produced by a PubMed search, for example, increased twenty-fold between 2000 and 2010, although that number only doubled for "Stroop and brain," another popular topic. The ongoing technical challenge remains: Mirror neurons are not the majority of cells in the brain areas where they are located, so it is still difficult to pinpoint their role when those areas show spiking activity. Iacoboni suggests that mathematical modeling will help make more of this data useful. Such modeling allowed Keysers, for example, to establish the existence of resonance in the charades study. So what can we expect next? Most likely, Iacoboni, says, more work with depth electrodes in neurological patients and studies like Ferrari's to test whether mirroring is a biomarker of sociality. A promising underexplored subject is the inhibitors that keep us from mimicking (but fail recovering addicts who relapse when they see others consume). Behind all this work will be a growing consensus that mirror neurons evolved in humans so we could learn from observation and communication.

References

Ertelt, D., Small, S., Solodkin, A., Dettmers, C., McNamara, A., Binkofski, F., & Buccino, G. (2007). Action observation has a positive impact on rehabilitation of motor deficits after stroke. *Neuroimage, 36*(Suppl 2), T164–T173.

Ferrari, P.F., Vanderwert, R., Herman, K., Paukner, A., Fox, N.A., & Suomi, S.J. (2008). Society for Neuroscience Abstract, *297,* 13.

Lindner, I., Echterhoff, G., Davidson, P.S., & Brand, M. (2010). Observation inflation: Your actions become mine. *Psychological Science, 21,* 1291–1299.

Mukamel, R., Ekstrom, A.D., Kaplan, J., Iacoboni, M., & Fried, I. (2010). Single-neuron responses in humans during execution and observation of actions. *Current Biology, 20,* 750–756.

Paukner, A., Suomi, S., Visalberghi, E., & Ferrari, P.F. (2009). Capuchin monkeys display affiliation toward humans who imitate them. *Science, 325,* 880.

Ricciardi, E., Bonino, D., Sani, L., Vecchi, T., Guazzelli, M., Haxby, J.V., Fadiga, L., Pietrini, P. (2009). Do we really need vision? How blind people "see" the actions of others. *Journal of Neuroscience, 29,* 9719-9724.

Schippers, M.B., Roebroeck, A., Renken, R., Nanetti, L., & Keysers, C. (2010). Mapping the information flow from one brain to another during gestural communication. *Proceedings of the National Academy of Sciences, USA, 107,* 9388–9393.

van Baaren, R., Janssen, L., Chartrand, T.L., & Dijksterhuis, A. (2009). Where is the love? The social aspects of mimicry. *Philosophical Transactions of the Royal Society of London, B: Biological Sciences, 364*(1528), 2381–2389.

Critical Thinking

1. What are mirror neurons and what role do they play in learning?
2. Generally speaking, what significance does understanding neural function hold for psychology?
3. How is the functioning of mirror neurons both similar and different when comparing their functions in monkeys and human infants?

Create Central

www.mhhe.com/createcentral

Internet References

The mind's mirror
www.apa.org/monitor/oct05/mirror.aspx
What's so special about mirror neurons?
http://blogs.scientificamerican.com/guest-blog/2012/11/06/whats-so-special-about-mirror-neurons

Article   Prepared by: Eric Landrum, *Boise State University*

Does Thinking Really Hard Burn More Calories?

Unlike physical exercise, mental workouts probably do not demand significantly more energy than usual.
Believing we have drained our brains, however, may be enough to induce weariness

FERRIS JABR

Learning Outcomes

After reading this article, you will be able to:

- Identify the relationship between mental effort and the consumption of glucose during brain functioning.

- Apply the concept of resting metabolic rate to better understanding how cognitive activities are linked to burning calories and consuming energy.

Between October and June they shuffle out of auditoriums, gymnasiums and classrooms, their eyes adjusting to the sunlight as their fingers fumble to awaken cell phones that have been silent for four consecutive hours. Some raise a hand to their foreheads, as though trying to rub away a headache. Others linger in front of the parking lot, unsure of what to do next. They are absolutely exhausted, but not because of any strenuous physical activity. Rather, these high school students have just taken the SAT. "I was fast asleep as soon as I got home," Ikra Ahmad told The Local, a *New York Times* blog, when she was interviewed for a story on "SAT hangover."

Temporary mental exhaustion is a genuine and common phenomenon, which, it is important to note, differs from chronic mental fatigue associated with regular sleep deprivation and some medical disorders. Everyday mental weariness makes sense, intuitively. Surely complex thought and intense concentration require more energy than routine mental processes. Just as vigorous exercise tires our bodies, intellectual exertion should drain the brain. What the latest science reveals, however, is that the popular notion of mental exhaustion is too simplistic. The brain continuously slurps up huge amounts of energy for an organ of its size, regardless of whether we are tackling integral calculus or clicking through the week's top 10 LOLcats. Although firing neurons summon extra blood, oxygen and glucose, any local increases in energy consumption are tiny compared with the brain's gluttonous baseline intake. So, in most cases, short periods of additional mental effort require a little more brainpower than usual, but not much more. Most laboratory experiments, however, have not subjected volunteers to several hours' worth of challenging mental acrobatics. And something must explain the *feeling* of mental exhaustion, even if its physiology differs from physical fatigue. Simply believing that our brains have expended a lot of effort might be enough to make us lethargic.

Brainpower

Although the average adult human brain weighs about 1.4 kilograms, only 2 percent of total body weight, it demands 20 percent of our resting metabolic rate (RMR)—the total amount of energy our bodies expend in one very lazy day of no activity. RMR varies from person to person depending on age, gender, size and health. If we assume an average resting metabolic rate of 1,300 calories, then the brain consumes 260 of those calories just to keep things in order. That's 10.8 calories every hour or 0.18 calories each minute. (For comparison's sake, see Harvard's table of calories burned during different activities.) With a little math, we can convert that number into a measure of power:

- Resting metabolic rate: 1300 kilocalories, or kcal, the kind used in nutrition
- 1,300 kcal over 24 hours = 54.16 kcal per hour = 15.04 gram calories per second
- 15.04 gram calories/sec = 62.93 joules/sec = about 63 watts
- 20 percent of 63 watts = 12.6 watts

So a typical adult human brain runs on around 12 watts—a fifth of the power required by a standard 60 watt lightbulb. Compared with most other organs, the brain is greedy; pitted against man-made electronics, it is astoundingly efficient. IBM's Watson, the supercomputer that defeated *Jeopardy!* champions, depends on ninety IBM Power 750 servers, each of which requires around one thousand watts.

Energy travels to the brain via blood vessels in the form of glucose, which is transported across the blood-brain barrier and used to produce adenosine triphosphate (ATP), the main currency of chemical energy within cells. Experiments with both animals and people have confirmed that when neurons in a particular brain region fire, local capillaries dilate to deliver more blood than usual, along with extra glucose and oxygen. This consistent response makes neuroimaging studies possible: functional magnetic resonance imaging (fMRI) depends on the unique magnetic properties of blood flowing to and from firing neurons. Research has also confirmed that once dilated blood vessels deliver extra glucose, brain cells lap it up.

Extending the logic of such findings, some scientists have proposed the following: if firing neurons require extra glucose, then especially challenging mental tasks should decrease glucose levels in the blood and, likewise, eating foods rich in sugars should improve performance on such tasks. Although quite a few studies have confirmed these predictions, the evidence as a whole is mixed and most of the changes in glucose levels range from the miniscule to the small. In a study at Northumbria University, for example, volunteers that completed a series of verbal and numerical tasks showed a larger drop in blood glucose than people who just pressed a key repeatedly. In the same study, a sugary drink improved performance on one of the tasks, but not the others. At Liverpool John Moores University volunteers performed two versions of the Stroop task, in which they had to identify the color of ink in which a word was printed, rather than reading the word itself: In one version, the words and colors matched—BLUE appeared in blue ink; in the tricky version, the word BLUE appeared in green or red ink. Volunteers who performed the more challenging task showed bigger dips in blood glucose, which the researchers interpreted as a direct cause of greater mental effort. Some studies have found that when people are not very good at a particular task, they exert more mental effort and use more glucose and that, likewise, the more skilled you are, the more efficient your brain is and the less glucose you need. Complicating matters, at least one study suggests the opposite—that more skillful brains recruit more energy.

Not So Simple Sugars

Unsatisfying and contradictory findings from glucose studies underscore that energy consumption in the brain is not a simple matter of greater mental effort sapping more of the body's available energy. Claude Messier of the University of Ottawa has reviewed many such studies. He remains unconvinced that any one cognitive task measurably changes glucose levels in the brain or blood. "In theory, yes, a more difficult mental task requires more energy because there is more neural activity," he says, "but when people do one mental task you won't see a large increase of glucose consumption as a significant percentage of the overall rate. The base level is quite a lot of energy—even in slow-wave sleep with very little activity there is still a high baseline consumption of glucose." Most organs do not require so much energy for basic housekeeping. But the brain must actively maintain appropriate concentrations of charged particles across the membranes of billions of neurons, even when those cells are not firing. Because of this expensive

and continuous maintenance, the brain usually has the energy it needs for a little extra work.

Authors of other review papers have reached similar conclusions. Robert Kurzban of the University of Pennsylvania points to studies showing that moderate exercise improves people's ability to focus. In one study, for example, children who walked for 20 minutes on a treadmill performed better on an academic achievement test than children who read quietly before the exam. If mental effort and ability were a simple matter of available glucose, then the children who exercised—and burnt up more energy—should have performed worse than their quiescent peers.

The influence of a mental task's difficulty on energy consumption "appears to be subtle and probably depends on individual variation in effort required, engagement and resources available, which might be related to variables such as age, personality and gluco-regulation," wrote Leigh Gibson of Roehampton University in a review on carbohydrates and mental function.

Both Gibson and Messier conclude that when someone has trouble regulating glucose properly—or has fasted for a long time—a sugary drink or food can improve their subsequent performance on certain kinds of memory tasks. But for most people, the body easily supplies what little extra glucose the brain needs for additional mental effort.

Body and Mind

If challenging cognitive tasks consume only a little more fuel than usual, what explains the feeling of mental exhaustion following the SAT or a similarly grueling mental marathon? One answer is that maintaining unbroken focus or navigating demanding intellectual territory for several hours really does burn enough energy to leave one feeling drained, but that researchers have not confirmed this because they have simply not been tough enough on their volunteers. In most experiments, participants perform a single task of moderate difficulty, rarely for more than an hour or two. "Maybe if we push them harder, and get people to do things they are not good at, we would see clearer results," Messier suggests.

Equally important to the duration of mental exertion is one's attitude toward it. Watching a thrilling biopic with a complex narrative excites many different brain regions for a good two hours, yet people typically do not shamble out of the theater complaining of mental fatigue. Some people regularly curl up with densely written novels that others might throw across the room in frustration. Completing a complex crossword or sudoku puzzle on a Sunday morning does not usually ruin one's ability to focus for the rest of the day—in fact, some claim it sharpens their mental state. In short, people routinely enjoy intellectually invigorating activities without suffering mental exhaustion.

Such fatigue seems much more likely to follow sustained mental effort that we do not seek for pleasure—such as the obligatory SAT—especially when we *expect* that the ordeal will drain our brains. If we think an exam or puzzle will be difficult, it often will be. Studies have shown that something similar happens when people exercise and play sports: a large component of physical exhaustion is in our heads. In related research, volunteers that cycled on an exercise bike following a 90-minute computerized test of sustained attention quit pedaling from exhaustion sooner than participants that watched emotionally neutral documentaries before exercising. Even if the attention test did not consume significantly more energy than watching movies, the volunteers reported feeling less energetic. That feeling was powerful enough to limit their physical performance.

In the specific case of the SAT, something beyond pure mental effort likely contributes to post-exam stupor: stress. After all, the brain does not function in a vacuum. Other organs burn up energy, too. Taking an exam that partially determines where one will spend the next four years is nerve-racking enough to send stress hormones swimming through the blood stream, induce sweating, quicken heart rates and encourage fidgeting and contorted body postures. The SAT and similar trials are not just mentally taxing—they are physically exhausting, too.

A small but revealing study suggests that even mildly stressful intellectual challenges change our emotional states and behaviors, even if they do not profoundly alter brain metabolism. Fourteen female Canadian college students either sat around, summarized a passage of text or completed a series of computerized attention and memory tests for 45 minutes before feasting on a buffet lunch. Students who exercised their brains helped themselves to around 200 more calories than students who relaxed. Their blood glucose levels also fluctuated more than those of students who just sat there, but not in any consistent way. Levels of the stress hormone cortisol, however, were significantly higher in students whose brains were busy, as were their heart rates, blood pressure and self-reported anxiety. In all likelihood, these students did not eat more because their haggard brains desperately needed more fuel; rather, they were stress eating.

Messier has related explanation for everyday mental weariness: "My general hypothesis is that the brain is a lazy bum," he says. "The brain has a hard time staying focused on just one thing for too long. It's possible that sustained concentration creates some changes in the brain that promote avoidance of that state. It could be like a timer that says, 'Okay you're done now.' Maybe the brain just doesn't like to work so hard for so long."

Critical Thinking

1. How does the rate of energy consumption of the brain relate, proportionally speaking, to the size of the brain compared to the size of the rest of the body?

2. What is the resting metabolic rate, and why does it matter?

3. What role does glucose play in supporting the energy consumption needs of the brain?

Create Central

www.mhhe.com/createcentral

Internet References

Do you burn more calories when you think hard?
www.straightdope.com/columns/read/3083/do-you-burn-more-calories-when-you-think-hard

Does extra mental effort burn more calories?
www.nytimes.com/2008/09/02/science/02qna.html?_r=0

Article   Prepared by: Eric Landrum, *Boise State University*

A Single Brain Structure May Give Winners That Extra Physical Edge

An extraordinary insula helps elite athletes better anticipate their body's upcoming feelings, improving their physical reactions

SANDRA UPSON

Learning Outcomes

After reading this article, you will be able to:

- Describe the role of the insular cortex and its relationship to athletic performance.
- Understand the process of interoception.

All elite athletes train hard, possess great skills and stay mentally sharp during competition. But what separates a gold medalist from an equally dedicated athlete who comes in 10th place? A small structure deep in the brain may give winners an extra edge.

Recent studies indicate that the brain's insular cortex may help a sprinter drive his body forward just a little more efficiently than his competitors. This region may prepare a boxer to better fend off a punch his opponent is beginning to throw as well as assist a diver as she calculates her spinning body's position so she hits the water with barely a splash. The insula, as it is commonly called, may help a marksman retain a sharp focus on the bull's-eye as his finger pulls back on the trigger and help a basketball player at the free-throw line block out the distracting screams and arm-waving of fans seated behind the backboard.

The insula does all this by anticipating an athlete's future feelings, according to a new theory. Researchers at the OptiBrain Center, a consortium based at the University of California, San Diego, and the Naval Health Research Center, suggest that an athlete possesses a hyper-attuned insula that can generate strikingly accurate predictions of how the body will feel in the next moment. That model of the body's future condition instructs other brain areas to initiate actions that are more tailored to coming demands than those of also-rans and couch potatoes.

This heightened awareness could allow Olympians to activate their muscles more resourcefully to swim faster, run farther and leap higher than mere mortals. In experiments published in 2012, brain scans of elite athletes appeared to differ most dramatically from ordinary subjects in the functioning of their insulas.

Emerging evidence now also suggests that this brain area can be trained using a meditation technique called mindfulness—good news for Olympians and weekend warriors alike.

Peak Performance

Stripped of the cheering fans, the play-by-play commentary and all the trappings of wealth and fame, professional sports reduced to a simple concept: The athletes who enthrall us are experts at meeting specific physical goals. They execute corporeal feats smoothly, without wasting a single drop of sweat.

Such performance is a full-brain phenomenon. The motor cortex and memory systems, for example, encode years of practice. Nerve fibers become ensconced in extra layers of a protective sheath that speeds up communication between neurons, producing lightning-fast reflexes. Understanding the brain at its athletic best is the goal of psychiatrist Martin Paulus and his colleagues at the OptiBrain Center. They propose that the insula may serve as the critical hub that merges high-level cognition with a measure of the body's state, to insure proper functioning of the muscles and bones that throw javelins and land twirling dismounts from the high bar. "The key idea we're after is how somebody responds when they get a cue that predicts something bad will happen," Paulus says. "The folks that are performing more optimally are the ones who are able to use that anticipatory cue to adjust themselves and return to equilibrium."

Slightly larger than a kumquat, the insula is part of the cerebral cortex, the thick folds of gray tissue that form the brain's outer layer. The densely rippled structure sits on the inside of the cortical mantle, resembling a tiny Japanese fan tucked neatly into the brain's interior. It is commonly thought of as the seat of interoception, or the sense of your body's internal state.

The insula generates this sense by maintaining a map of all your far-flung organs and tissues. Certain neurons in the insula respond to rumblings in the intestines, for example, whereas others fire to reflect a toothache. To manage the influx of messages bombarding it from throughout the body, the insula collaborates closely with the anterior cingulate cortex, an area crucial for decision-making, to evaluate and prioritize those stimuli. This raw representation of bodily signals has been hypothesized for more than a century to be the origin of emotions.

At first glance, pegging the insula as critical to anything can seem almost meaningless. It has been implicated in functions as diverse as decision-making, anticipation, timekeeping, singing, addiction, speech, even consciousness. The insula and the anterior cingulate cortex are the most commonly activated regions in brain-imaging experiments, according to a 2011 study, making it all the more difficult to discern their core functions.

Nevertheless, the case for the insula as the hub of athleticism has been building slowly for more than a decade. In the late 1990s neuroanatomist A. D. Craig at Barrow Neurological Institute was mapping the pathways that deliver pain and temperature sensations to the brain through the spinal cord. Upon discovering that these conduits led to the insula, he posited that one of the brain's core functions is to help the body maintain homeostasis, or equilibrium. For example, the body's internal temperature usually stays within a narrow range, and perturbations, registered by the insula, motivate us to restore it to that comfortable zone—perhaps by drinking cool water, seeking a shady patch or ceasing movement. Indeed, when scientists damaged the insula in rats, their ability to regulate their bodies was impaired.

When we exercise, we agitate our internal state. "Everything we do requires a calculation of how much energy it costs us, and this is what the insula seems to be performing," Craig says. By predicting how certain exertions will affect the body, the brain can initiate actions to temper those perturbations before they happen.

A compelling study from 2004 showed clear anatomical differences that matched variation in interoceptive ability. Hugo Critchley, now at the University of Sussex in England, asked participants to estimate the rate at which their hearts were beating without taking their own pulses. The people who guessed their heart rates most accurately had greater activity in the insula and more gray matter in this region. That last point is crucial, because it suggests that the physical size of the insula is directly related to differences in ability. This neural imprinting is similar to what is seen in professional violinists, whose motor cortex devotes greater real estate to the representations of fingers than is seen in an amateur's brain.

The OptiBrain researchers hypothesized that athletes need to be intensely aware of sensations such as heartbeat—and capable of recognizing the important ones and dismissing the red herrings. "The vast majority of NBA players are amazing athletes. But some of them stand out. It's not that Kobe Bryant or Derrick Rose has more energy, it's how they choose to expend that energy in critical moments that will decide their success," clinical psychologist Alan Simmons at the Veterans Affairs San Diego Healthcare System says.

Thinking Ahead

To test the idea that extremely fit individuals have superior interoception—and to investigate what this superiority looks like in action—Paulus and Simmons recently recruited a group of elite athletes to lie in a scanner and perform cognitive tests while an apparatus restricted their breathing. The feeling of shortness of breath is an unpleasant sensation that is known to rev up the insula.

Paulus and Simmons tested 10 of the world's most accomplished adventure racers—men and women who perform wilderness challenges that can include climbing, swimming, running and paddling. They asked the racers and 11 healthy control subjects to lie in a scanner and breathe through a tube while wearing a nose clip. While in the magnetic resonance imaging (MRI) machine, the subjects were instructed to view arrows pointing either left or right on a screen and press a button to note the direction. Sporadically, the researchers adjusted the airflow so that breathing became significantly more difficult. A change in the screen's color alerted the participants that breathing was about to become labored. The color change did not always accurately predict breathing restriction, however.

In all phases of the experiment, the insula was active, but to varying degrees. The healthy volunteers performed equally well on the arrow tests throughout the study—with no interference, when the screen's color changed and when struggling to inhale. But the adventure racers got more answers correct when either anticipating or undergoing the breathing load. Perturbing these individuals' interoceptive experience actually *improved* their performances. The racers also showed more brain activation when anticipating the breathing restriction but not while experiencing the restriction itself. It was as if the racers' brains made better use of cues to prepare themselves, thus gaining a cognitive edge. When the challenging moment arrived—when their breathing became labored—their insulas were comparatively placid.

Another study from Paulus's group, also published in 2012, adds nuance to this finding. The group sought to investigate elite athletes' cognitive flexibility. Considered a landmark of intelligence, this skill involves switching easily between opposing demands. Mental agility can plummet in a trying situation, however. Experiments on Navy SEALs and Army Rangers revealed that exposure to combatlike conditions impaired their reaction times, vigilance, learning, memory and reasoning. For Olympic-level athletes, too, grace under fire is a major objective.

To observe cognitive flexibility in action, Simmons asked 10 Navy SEALs and 11 healthy male civilians to perform a simple task in a brain scanner. Navy SEALs are extremely athletic individuals who are trained to cope with great demands on their physical, mental and emotional faculties. The exercise involved observing either a green or red shape followed by an emotionally laden photograph on a screen. Participants were to press one button when they saw a circle and another when they viewed a square. A green shape signaled that a positive image (such as a child playing) would follow; a red shape indicated that a negative picture (for example, a combat scene) would appear next. The subjects were then judged on their speed and accuracy in identifying the shapes.

Compared with healthy participants, the elite warriors sent more blood coursing through their insulas and a few other regions when the shapes' colors differed in consecutive trials. In short, they were more aware of the impending switch from positive to negative or vice versa and engaged brain systems involved in modulating emotional and interoceptive responses. They were quicker to prepare for a looming shift in their internal states, buying their brains time to tamp down their reactions.

Taken together, the studies indicate that men and women who have extreme physical abilities show greater insula activation when anticipating a change to their internal feelings, whether emotional or physical.

"To me that's really huge if you have a region of the brain that's anticipating a response and preparing the body for it," physiologist Jon Williamson at the University of Texas Southwestern Medical Center says. "If an athlete is approaching a hill and can anticipate the delivery of blood to muscles, he or she may perform better on that hill."

The studies so far have been small, however—it's not easy to corral top-tier athletes into brain-imaging labs—so larger experiments are still needed to firm up the observations. Even so, the results echo earlier findings on the insula's involvement in imagining the future, whether anticipating physical pain from, say, a boxer's punch or contemplating the purchase of an overpriced item.

To Simmons, the evidence suggests that the insula does not live in the present, but the future. "We're responding to information incorporated from physiology, cognition, our surroundings," Simmons says. "By the time we've integrated all that, it's part of the past." The ability to forecast can also backfire, producing disorders such as anorexia nervosa, which combines lapses in bodily awareness with a concern for how food consumption now will alter body image in the future. "It's the anticipation that's getting in your way," Simmons says. Indeed, brain scans of individuals with eating disorders and post-traumatic stress disorder show that insula activity diverges from that seen in healthy subjects, suggesting impairments in this area.

Train Your Interoception

For aspiring athletes or individuals who suffer insular dysfunction, there are reasons to hope interoception is trainable. A meditation technique called mindfulness encourages people to tune into their present thoughts, emotions and bodily sensations. Derived from Buddhist teachings, this training seeks to heighten awareness of feelings but also to temper our reactions to them. The OptiBrain researchers have collected preliminary data, not yet published, suggesting that healthy subjects and military personnel who received mindfulness training improved in cognitive performance during a stressful situation—as measured with a breathing-restriction task—and

reacted to challenges with less emotion, with the insular activation changes to match.

Small-scale studies on athletes, too, show benefit. This awareness of the feeling of the moment has been shown, for example, to improve the success of basketball players on the free-throw line. Sports psychologist Claudio Robazza at the University of Chieti in Italy has seen firsthand how mindfulness and similar techniques can single out successful athletes. He has worked for six years with Italy's Olympic shooting team, a mentally demanding sport that favors individuals who can still nail their targets when the pressure is highest. "Emotional states can reflect bodily changes, an increase in heart rate, muscular tension and breathing—all those things cause changes in the performance and the final outcome," Robazza says. "Certainly athletes need to be aware of their responses."

With tens of thousands of people gazing down from stadium seats, and millions more tuned in to television broadcasts, an Olympic athlete runs a high risk of choking. The stress of the moment can trigger many physical changes that interfere in the execution of even the most deeply ingrained maneuvers. A heightened awareness of the body's condition, facilitated by the insula, can alert a champion to tensed muscles or shallow breaths before these responses have a chance to undermine performance. The insula—where the body meets the brain—serves as the springboard from which athletic brilliance can soar.

Critical Thinking

1. What is the insular cortex, and how might it be related to athletic performance?

2. How does the protective sheath surrounding nerve fibers influence the speed of processing between neurons?

3. If damage were to occur to one's insular cortex, what would be the likely result to be observed?

Create Central

www.mhhe.com/createcentral

Internet References

Does the insula help elite athletes better anticipate their body's upcoming feelings, improving their physical reactions?
http://subrealism.blogspot.com/2012/07/does-insula-help-elite-athletes-better.html

Marines expanding use of meditation training
www.washingtontimes.com/news/2012/dec/5/marines-expanding-use-of-meditation-training/?page=all

Article   Prepared by: R. Eric Landrum, *Boise State University*

The New Science of Mind

ERIC R. KANDEL

Learning Outcomes

After reading this article, you will be able to:

- Understand that there is a biological basis to depression.

- Appreciate that research can be conducted with therapeutic approaches and those with depression.

These days it is easy to get irritated with the exaggerated interpretations of brain imaging—for example, that a single fMRI scan can reveal our innermost feelings—and with inflated claims about our understanding of the biological basis of our higher mental processes.

Such irritation has led a number of thoughtful people to declare that we can never achieve a truly sophisticated understanding of the biological foundation of complex mental activity.

In fact, recent newspaper articles have argued that psychiatry is a "semi-science" whose practitioners cannot base their treatment of mental disorders on the same empirical evidence as physicians who treat disorders of the body can. The problem for many people is that we cannot point to the underlying biological bases of most psychiatric disorders. In fact, we are nowhere near understanding them as well as we understand disorders of the liver or the heart.

But this is starting to change.

Consider the biology of depression. We are beginning to discern the outlines of a complex neural circuit that becomes disordered in depressive illnesses. Helen Mayberg, at Emory University, and other scientists used brain-scanning techniques to identify several components of this circuit, two of which are particularly important.

One is Area 25 (the subcallosal cingulate region), which mediates our unconscious and motor responses to emotional stress; the other is the right anterior insula, a region where self-awareness and interpersonal experience come together.

These two regions connect to the hypothalamus, which plays a role in basic functions like sleep, appetite, and libido, and to three other important regions of the brain: the amygdala, which evaluates emotional salience; the hippocampus, which is concerned with memory; and the prefrontal cortex, which is the seat of executive function and self-esteem. All of these regions can be disturbed in depressive illnesses.

In a recent study of people with depression, Professor Mayberg gave each person one of two types of treatment: cognitive behavioral therapy, a form of psychotherapy that trains people to view their feelings in more positive terms, or an antidepressant medication. She found that people who started with below-average baseline activity in the right anterior insula responded well to cognitive behavioral therapy but not to the antidepressant. People with above-average activity responded to the antidepressant but not to cognitive behavioral therapy. Thus, Professor Mayberg found that she could predict a depressed person's response to specific treatments from the baseline activity in the right anterior insula.

These results show us four very important things about the biology of mental disorders. First, the neural circuits disturbed by psychiatric disorders are likely to be very complex.

Second, we can identify specific, measurable markers of a mental disorder, and those biomarkers can predict the outcome of two different treatments: psychotherapy and medication.

Third, psychotherapy is a biological treatment, a brain therapy. It produces lasting, detectable physical changes in our brain, much as learning does.

And fourth, the effects of psychotherapy can be studied empirically. Aaron Beck, who pioneered the use of cognitive behavioral therapy, long insisted that psychotherapy has an empirical basis, that it is a science. Other forms of psychotherapy have been slower to move in this direction, in part because a number of psychotherapists believed that human behavior is too difficult to study in scientific terms.

ANY discussion of the biological basis of psychiatric disorders must include genetics. And, indeed, we are beginning to fit new pieces into the puzzle of how genetic mutations influence brain development.

Most mutations produce small differences in our genes, but scientists have recently discovered that some mutations give rise to structural differences in our chromosomes. Such differences are known as copy number variations.

People with copy number variations may be missing a small piece of DNA from a chromosome, or they may have an extra piece of that DNA.

Matthew State, at the University of California, San Francisco, has discovered a remarkable copy number variation involving chromosome 7. An extra copy of a particular segment of this chromosome greatly increases the risk of autism, which is characterized by social isolation. Yet the loss of that same segment results in Williams syndrome, a disorder characterized by intense sociability.

This single segment of chromosome 7 contains about 25 of the 21,000 or so genes in our genome, yet an extra copy or a missing copy has profound, and radically different, effects on social behavior.

The second finding is de novo point mutations, which arise spontaneously in the sperm of adult men. Sperm divide every 15 days. This continuous division and copying of DNA leads to errors, and the rate of error increases significantly with age: a 20-year-old will have an average of 25 de novo point mutations in his sperm, whereas a 40-year-old will have 65. These mutations are one reason that older fathers are more likely to have children with autism and schizophrenia.

Our understanding of the biology of mental disorders has been slow in coming, but recent advances like these have shown us that mental disorders are biological in nature, that people are not responsible for having schizophrenia or depression, and that individual biology and genetics make significant contributions.

The result of such work is a new, unified science of mind that uses the combined power of cognitive psychology and neuroscience to examine the great remaining mysteries of mind: how we think, feel, and experience ourselves as conscious human beings.

This new science of mind is based on the principle that our mind and our brain are inseparable. The brain is a complex biological organ possessing immense computational capability: it constructs our sensory experience, regulates our thoughts and emotions, and controls our actions. It is responsible not only for relatively simple motor behaviors like running and eating but also for complex acts that we consider quintessentially human, like thinking, speaking, and creating works of art. Looked at from this perspective, our mind is a set of operations carried out by our brain. The same principle of unity applies to mental disorders.

In years to come, this increased understanding of the physical workings of our brain will provide us with important insight into brain disorders, whether psychiatric or neurological. But if we persevere, it will do even more: it will give us new insights into who we are as human beings.

Critical Thinking

1. What is the benefit of understanding behavioral disorders at the chromosomal level? Explain.

2. What are some of the powerful benefits that may be realized from the combination of cognitive psychology and neuroscience?

Internet References

How to become a cognitive neuroscientist
http://careersinpsychology.org/becoming-a-cognitive-neuroscientist
These are revolutionary times for the biology of psychology
http://www.psychologytoday.com/blog/the-athletes-way/201309/these-are-revolutionary-times-the-biology-psychology

---

ERIC R. KANDEL, a professor at the Mortimer B. Zuckerman Mind Brain Behavior Institute at Columbia, a senior investigator at the Howard Hughes Medical Institute and a recipient of the 2000 Nobel Prize in Physiology or Medicine, is the author of *The Age of Insight: The Quest to Understand the Unconscious in Art, Mind and Brain, From Vienna 1900 to the Present.*

Article   Prepared by: R. Eric Landrum, *Boise State University*

How to Spot a Murderer's Brain

Do your genes, rather than upbringing, determine whether you will become a criminal? Adrian Raine believed so—and breaking that taboo put him on collision course with the world of science.

TIM ADAMS

Learning Outcomes

After reading this article, you will be able to:

- Understand how brain scan results may sometimes be related to patterns in human behaviour.

- Appreciate the role that epigenetics may play in influencing a child's development.

- Describe the complexities of linking biological markers to behaviours and personality traits.

In 1987, Adrian Raine, who describes himself as a neuro-criminologist, moved from Britain to the United States. His emigration was prompted by two things. The first was a sense of banging his head against a wall. Raine, who grew up in Darlington and is now a professor at the University of Pennsylvania, was a researcher of the biological basis for criminal behaviour, which, with its echoes of Nazi eugenics, was perhaps the most taboo of all academic disciplines.

In Britain, the causes of crime were allowed to be exclusively social and environmental, the result of disturbed or impoverished nurture, rather than fated and genetic nature. To suggest otherwise, as Raine felt compelled to, having studied under Richard Dawkins and been persuaded of the "all-embracing influence of evolution on behaviour", was to doom yourself to an absence of funding. In America, there seemed more open-mindedness on the question and, as a result, more money to explore it. There was also another good reason why Raine headed initially to California: there were more murderers to study than there were at home.

When Raine started doing brain scans of murderers in American prisons, he was among the first researchers to apply the evolving science of brain imaging to violent criminality. His most comprehensive study, in 1994, was still, necessarily, a small sample. He conducted PET (positron emission tomography) scans of 41 convicted killers and paired them with a "normal" control group of 41 people of similar age and profile. However limited the control, the colour images, which showed metabolic activity in different parts of the brain, appeared striking in comparison. In particular, the murderers' brains showed what appeared to be a significant reduction in the development of the prefrontal cortex, "the executive function" of the brain, compared with the control group.

The advancing understanding of neuroscience suggested that such a deficiency would result in an increased likelihood of a number of behaviours: less control over the limbic system that generates primal emotions such as anger and rage; a greater addiction to risk; a reduction in self-control; and poor problem-solving skills, all traits that might predispose a person to violence.

Even two decades ago, these were difficult findings to publish, however. When Raine presented a far less controversial paper in 1994 to a peer group, one that showed a combination of birth complications and early maternal rejection in babies had significant correlation with individuals becoming violent offenders 18 years later, it was denounced as "racist and ideologically motivated" and, according to *Nature* magazine, was simply further strong evidence that "the uproar surrounding attempts to find biological causes for social problems will continue". Similarly, when, 15 years ago, at the urging of his friend Jonathan Kellerman, the child psychologist and crime writer,

Raine put together a proposal for a book on some of his scientific findings, no publisher would touch it. That book, *The Anatomy of Violence,* a clear-headed, evidence-based and carefully provocative account of Raine's 35 years of study, has only now appeared.

The reason for this delay seems mired in ideological enmities. For all Raine's rigour, his discipline of "neurocriminology" still remains tarnished, for some, by association with 19th-century phrenology, the belief that criminal behaviour stemmed from defective brain organisation as evidenced in the shape of the skull. The idea was first proposed by the infamous Franz Joseph Gall, who claimed to have identified over- or underdeveloped brain "organs" that gave rise to specific character: the organ of destructiveness, of covetousness and so on, which were recognisable to the phrenologist by bumps on the head. Phrenology was widely influential in criminal law in both the United States and Europe in the middle of the 1800s, and often used to support crude racial and class-based stereotypes of criminal behaviour.

The divisive thinking was developed further in 1876 by Cesare Lombroso, an Italian surgeon, after he conducted a postmortem on a serial murderer and rapist. Lombroso discovered a hollow part of the killer's brain, where the cerebellum would be, from which he proposed that violent criminals were throwbacks to less evolved human types, again identifiable by ape-like physical characteristics. The political manipulation of such hypotheses in the eugenics movement eventually saw them wholly outlawed and discredited.

As one result, after the second world war, crime became attributable to economic and political factors, or psychological disturbances, but not to biology. Prompted by advances in genetics and neuroscience, however, that consensus is increasingly fragile, and the implications of those scientific advances for law—and for concepts such as culpability and responsibility— are only now being tested. He draws on a number of studies that show the links between brain development, in particular— and brain injury and impairment by extension—and criminal violence. Already legal defence teams, particularly in the United States, are using brain scans and neuroscience as mitigating evidence in the trials of violent criminals and sex offenders. In this sense, Raine believes a proper public debate on the implications of his science is long overdue.

Raine was in part drawn to his discipline by his own background. In the course of scanning his murderers, Raine also examined his own PET profile and found, somewhat to his alarm, that the structure of his brain seemed to share more characteristics with the psychopathic murderers than with the control group.

He laughs quickly when I ask how that discovery felt. "When you have a brain scan that looks like a serial killer's it does give you pause," he says. And there were other factors: he has always had a markedly low heart rate (which his research has shown to be a truer indicator of a capacity for violence than, say, smoking is as a cause of lung cancer). He was plagued by cracked lips as a child, evidence of riboflavin deficiency (another marker); he was born at home; he was a blue baby, all factors in the kind of developmental difficulties that might set his own researcher's alarm bells ringing.

"So," he says, "I was on the spectrum. And in fact I did have some issues. I was taken to hospital aged five to have my stomach pumped because I had drunk a lot of alcohol. From age 9 to 11 I was pretty antisocial, in a gang, smoking, letting car tyres down, setting fire to mailboxes and fighting a lot, even though I was quite small. But at that age I burnt out of that somehow. At 11, I changed schools, got more interested in studying and really became a different sort of kid. Still, when I was graduating and thinking 'what shall I research?', I looked back on the essays I'd written and one of the best was on the biology of psychopaths; I was fascinated by that, partly, I think, because I had always wondered about that early behaviour in myself."

As Raine began to explore the subject more, he began to look at the reasons he became a researcher of violent criminality, rather than a violent criminal. (Recent studies suggest his biology might equally have propelled him towards other careers— bomb disposal expert, corporate executive or journalist—that tend to attract individuals with those "psychopathic" traits.) Despite his unusual brain structure, he didn't have the low IQ that is often apparent in killers, or any cognitive dysfunction. Still, as he worked for four years interviewing people in prison, a lot of the time he was thinking: what stopped me being on their side of the bars?

Raine's biography, then, was a good corrective to the seductive idea that our biology is our fate and that a brain scan can tell us who we are. Even as he piles up evidence to show that people are not the free-thinking, rational agents they like to imagine themselves to be—entirely liberated from the limitations set by our inherited genes and our particular neuroanatomy—he never forgets that lesson. The question remains, however, that if these "biomarkers" do exist and exert an influence—and you begin to see the evidence as incontrovertible—then what should we do about them?

Perhaps we should do nothing, simply ignore them, assume, when it comes to crime, that every individual has much the same brain, the same capacity to make moral choices, as we tend to do now. As Raine suggests: "The sociologist would say if we concentrate on these biological things, or even acknowledge them, we are immediately taking our eyes off other causes of criminal behaviour—poverty, bad neighbourhoods, poor nutrition, lack of education and so on. All things that need to change. And that concern is correct. It is why social scientists have fought this science for so long."

The implication of neurocriminology, though—where it differs from the crude labelling of phrenology, say—is that the choice it presents is not an either/or between nurture and nature, but a more complex understanding of how our biology reacts with its environment. Reading Raine's account of the most recent research into these reactions, it still seems to me quite new and surprising that environmental factors change the physical structure of the brain. We tend to talk about a child's development in terms of more esoteric ideas of mind rather than material brain structures, but the more you look at the data the clearer the evidence that abuse or neglect or poor nutrition or prenatal smoking and drinking have a real effect on whether or not those healthy neural connections—which lead to behaviour associated with maturity, self-control and empathy—are made. The science of this is called epigenetics, the way our environment regulates the expression of our innate genetic code.

One result of epigenetics might be, Raine suggests, that "social scientists can actually win from this. I mean, if a child experiences a murder in his or her neighbourhood, we have found that their test scores on a range of measures go down. There is something happening in the brain as a result of that experience of violence to affect cognition. So social scientists can have their cake and eat it. They can say look, we can prove that these environmental social factors are causing brain impairment, which leads to some real, measurable problems."

One difficulty of embracing this "epigenetical" idea of crime is the degree to which such factors should be taken into account in courts of law. There have been several landmark cases in recent years in which particular neurological disorders caused by blows to the skull or undetected tumours have resulted in arguable changes in character and behaviour—and the violent or sexual crime is blamed on the disorder, not the individual. In most of these cases, it has been argued by the prosecution that brain imaging is prejudicial, that the brightly coloured pictures are too compelling to a jury and more emotional than scientific. But if neural scanning becomes more routine, and neuroscience more precise, will there not come a point where most violent behaviour—that of the Boston bombers, say, or the Newtown killer—is argued away in court as an illness, rather than a crime?

Raine believes that there might well be. He even likens such a shift to our change in perception of cancer, until fairly recently often deemed the "fault" of the sufferer because of some repressive character trait. "If we buy into the argument that for some people factors beyond their control, factors in their biology, greatly raise the risk of them becoming offenders, can we justly turn a blind eye to that?" Raine asks. "Is it really the fault of the innocent baby whose mother smoked heavily in pregnancy that he went on to commit crimes? Or if he was battered from pillar to post, or even if he was born with an abnormally low resting heart rate, how harshly should we punish him? How much should we say he is responsible? There is, and increasingly will be, an argument that he is not fully responsible and therefore, when we come to think of punishment, should we be thinking of more benign institutions than prison?"

But then there is a further thought, that if you start to see criminality as a biological illness, where does a sense of retributive justice stand?

Raine himself was forced to face this dilemma when he became a victim of violent crime. As he recounts in his book, while on holiday in Turkey several years ago, a burglar entered his bedroom and in the struggle that followed tried to cut Raine's throat with a knife. He fought the attacker off, but when the following morning he was presented with two possible suspects by police, he admits to not only choosing the one who looked most like a thug [the man later admitted the crime, under duress], but also to wanting to visit on him the terror he had felt himself.

"I wasn't proud to discover I was a bit Jekyll and Hyde—perhaps we all are in that situation," Raine says when I ask him about his response. "The rational Dr Jekyll knew that if I took this man's brain scan and found he had prefrontal dysfunction, low resting heart rate, a background of neglect, then of course I should cut him some slack. With understanding comes mercy. But the Mr Hyde, the emotional voice in my head, was saying nothing of the sort: he was saying, he cut my throat, I want to cut his. That event changed me from someone dead set against the death penalty to someone who wouldn't be ruled out of a jury on a capital case in America. I think now my mind will always go backwards and forwards on this, the scientific understanding of the causes of crime versus being a human in society with all these gut reactions to people who commit awful crimes."

If the neuroscience raises as many questions as it answers about culpability after a crime has been committed, what about its role in crime prevention? Here, the questions seem no less fraught.

One of them was posed a couple of years ago by the arch-inquisitor Jeremy Paxman of Shami Chakrabarti, director of Liberty, on *Newsnight*. "If science could predict with 100% certainty who was going to commit a violent crime, would it be legitimate to act before they commit that crime?"

Chakrabarti was in no doubt: "I would have to say that in a liberal society of human beings, and not animals, my answer to your question would be 'no'."

But if such intervention could prevent Newtown, you wonder, or Dunblane, would any of us be quite so certain? The fact is that the reality will always be a much greyer area because even the most nuanced neuroscience will never produce a perfect prediction of human behaviour. But is there a point at which the science—in identifying the possibility of repeat offending, for example—will be accurate enough to warrant routine scanning of those on the sexual offenders' register?

"The fact is," Raine says, "parole boards are making exactly these kind of predictive decisions every day about which prisoner or young offender we are going to release early, often with crummy evidence. At the moment, the predictors are social and behavioural factors, marital status, your past record. What is not used are biological measures. But I believe that if we added those things even now into the equation, we could only improve the prediction."

Raine cites two very recent brain-imaging studies to back this up. One is a study in New Mexico in which prisoners are scanned on release. "What they are discovering is that if the functioning of the anterior cingulate, part of the limbic system, is lower than normal before release, they are twice as likely to be reconvicted in the next three years. And that marker is more accurate a guide than all other social factors," Raine says. A second study apparently shows if a released prisoner has a significantly smaller volume in the amygdala, the almond-shaped part of the brain crucial for processing memory and emotion, he or she is three times more likely to reoffend. "Now, this is only two studies, but what they are beginning to show is proof of concept, that if we added neurological factors into the equation we could do a better job at predicting future behaviour."

At the end of his book, Raine suggests various possible Orwellian futures of such science, an ethical "slippery slope" of interventions that ultimately imagines a society that assesses the biological risk of all individuals—a wide-scale version of *We Need to Talk About Kevin*—and pre-emptively locks up those at the extreme end of the curve (a sort of evidence-based Guantánamo). He by no means advocates any of it, though when I ask if he would have his own children, two boys of 11, scanned, he suggests he probably would.

"If there was the opportunity for screening at school or through a GP programme, would I do it? Well, if my kids had problems, as a parent I would want to know about them and I would want to know how I might deal with them. If you brought in such things as emotion regulation and impulse control, which we know are risk factors for behaviour, then to me, as a parent, I would sort of want to know what could be done to help with those."

It is perhaps not too wildly far-fetched to imagine that such scans will one day be as routine as immunisation programmes; the bigger question then will be how we begin to react to the results. Raine rather likes the idea of public health programmes as crime prevention: "The teenage brain is still very malleable. There is good evidence from randomised control testing that omega-3 [fish oil] has a positive effect on young offenders, and even mindfulness seems to improve behaviour and brain structures."

You can't help thinking: if only it were as simple as that.

Critical Thinking

1. What was phrenology, and how are the ideas of phrenology related to the ideas of neurocriminology today?

2. The idea of being able to predict a crime with 100% accuracy before it happens is a notion offered in the movie and TV show *Minority Report*. If the prediction were indeed 100% accurate, would it be fair and just to arrest someone before the crime was committed? Why or why not?

3. Is it that more criminal behaviour influences brain chemistry and function to change, or is it that changes in brain chemistry and function influence increases in criminal behaviour? Explain your viewpoint.

Internet References

Born to kill? Psychopaths have different brains than normal people—and current "therapies" for killers may be useless
http://www.dailymail.co.uk/sciencetech/article-2141160/Born-bad-Rapists-psychopathic-murderers-physically-different-brains-normal-people.html

Inside the mind of a killer
http://abcnews.go.com/WNT/story?id=130048&page=1

What would we find wrong in the brain of a serial killer?
https://www.psychologytoday.com/blog/blame-the-amygdala/201304/what-would-we-find-wrong-in-the-brain-serial-killer

Unit 3

UNIT

Prepared by: Eric Landrum, *Boise State University*

Perceptual Processes

Marina and her roommate Claire have been friends since their first year of college. Because they share so much in common, they decided to become roommates in their sophomore year. They both want to travel abroad one day. They both enjoy the same restaurants and share the same preference for red wine. Both have significant others from the same hometown, both are education majors, and both want to work with young children someday. Today they are at the local art museum. As they walk around the galleries, Marina is astonished at Claire's taste in art. Whatever Claire likes, Marina finds hideous. The paintings and sculptures that Marina admires are the very ones to which her roommate turns up her nose. "How can our tastes in art be so different when we share so much in common?" Marina wonders. What Marina and Claire experience is a difference in perception—the interpretation of the sensory stimulation. Perception and sensation are closely connected topics in psychology, as well as the topic of this unit.

As you will learn in your study of psychology, the study of sensation and perception dates back to psychology's earliest beginnings, and even prior to psychology's formal start. Understanding how the physical energy of sound waves is translated to the language we hear and how waves of light are translated into the images we see are processes occurring in the nervous system and have long fascinated psychologists. Although the laboratory study of sensation and perception is well over 100 years old, psychologists are still seeking to further their understanding of these phenomena.

For many years, it was popular for psychologists to consider sensation and perception as two distinct processes. Sensation was defined in passive terms as the simple event of some stimulus energy (e.g., a sound wave) impinging on a specific sensory organ (e.g., the ear) that then reflexively transmitted the appropriate information to the central nervous system and brain. Perception, on the other hand, was defined as the interpretive process that the higher centers of the brain supposedly accomplish based on sensory information and available memories of similar events. Interesting abberations can occur, however, such as when individuals who suffer from the amputation of a limb still report pain from that missing limb (called phantom pain).

The dichotomy of sensation and perception is no longer widely accepted by today's psychologists. The revolution came in the mid-1960s, when a psychologist published a then-radical treatise in which he reasoned that perceptual processes included all sensory events that he believed were directed by an actively searching central nervous system. This viewpoint provided that certain perceptual patterns, such as recognition of a piece of art work, may be species specific. Thus, all humans, independent of learning history, should share some of the same perceptual repertoires. Optical illusions are intriguing because the sensations collected by the visual system, once the brain attempts to translate sensations into perceptions, cause humans to deduce that what was "seen" cannot be true. This is probably one of the reasons that magic tricks are so entertaining to so many people—and sometimes we are blind to events that occur right before our eyes. This unit on perceptual processes is designed to expand your understanding of these incredibly interesting processes.

As you will find, understanding perception is a complex process that made even more difficult by the fact that perception is fluid, continual, and often takes place below everyday levels of consciousness.

Article

Prepared by: Eric Landrum, *Boise State University*

Corporeal Awareness and Proprioceptive Sense of the Phantom

Melita J. Giummarra et al.

Learning Outcomes

After reading this article, you will be able to:

• Understand some of the hypothesized theories as to why phantom limb pain occurs.

• Comprehend how survey methodology can be used to advance our knowledge of phantom limb pain.

Amputees invariably continue to perceive a ghost of their amputated limb as a phantom. The phantom limb is often plagued by unpleasant, annoying, or distressing phantom pain, but may also retain other features that suggest it is still highly represented in proprioceptive body maps. We report a large scale investigation of phantom limb experiences that systematically explored somatic and proprioceptive aspects of phantom phenomena. These include (a) the perception of bodily aspects of phantom limbs including the size (e.g., compared to the intact limb, thinner, or thicker/swollen), shape, posture, and telescoping (or shortening) of the phantom; (b) exteroceptive and proprioceptive sensations (e.g., touch, pressure, temperature, itching, vibration, pins, and needles, 'electric'/shooting; see also Hunter, Katz, & Davis, 2003); and (c) prosthesis embodiment. Embodiment involves the perception that one's sense of self is localized within one's bodily borders (Arzy, Thut, Mohr, Michel, & Blanke, 2006), but may extend to a habitually used tool or prosthesis that effectively extends the body's area of influence (Giummarra, Gibson, Georgiou-Karistianis, & Bradshaw, 2008). We do not presently report detailed data on phantom limb movement, even though they are principally relevant to phantom limb proprioception, as these observations have been reported elsewhere (Giummarra *et al.*,). The somatic and proprioceptive aspects of phantom phenomena offer a fascinating insight to corporeal bodily awareness.

Current accounts of somatic phantom limb awareness are typically based on anecdotal or incomplete descriptions (e.g., only exploring isolated features of the phantom, such as

telescoping, position, shape, or size), based on small sample sizes or simply clinical observations of more extraordinary cases (e.g., limbs that can be moved through anatomically impossible ranges; Price, 1976). While various studies report the perception of somatic, non-painful phantom sensations (Aglioti, Smania, Atzei, & Berlucchi, 1997; Halligan, Marshal, Wade, Davey, & Morrison, 1993; Knecht *et al.*, 1995), few have systematically explored these aspects of phantom phenomena. Jensen, Krebs, Nielsen, and Rasmussen (1983) documented kinaesthetic sensations, present in 85% of amputees, over the first 6 months post-amputation. In particular, the phantom was perceived to be (a) normal length for 55% (43% at 6 months), longer for 7% (0 at 6 months), or shorter/telescoped for 7% (30% at 6 months); (b) normal volume for 48% (33% at 6 months), increased volume for 3% (4% at 6 months), or decreased volume for 9% (12% at 6 months). More recently, Fraser (2002) reported somatic qualities in the phantom limb in upper limb amputees. They found that a massive 64 of 66 upper limb amputees with phantom sensations experienced a phantom limb that resembled the limb prior to amputation in *shape and form;* however, for 28% the phantom was shortened/telescoped (but in some cases ultimately retained the pre-amputation shape and form), and for others the phantom was larger/magnified (8%). We intend to significantly extend these prior findings in both sample characteristics (with a much larger sample of both upper and lower limb amputees), and the types of sensations perceived to characterize the phantom.

The distal portion of the phantom is typically perceived either where it would be if the entire limb was present, or to be closer or attached to the stump (i.e., telescoped) in 28–67% of cases (Carlen, Wall, Nadvorna, & Steinbach, 1978; Fraser, 2002; Richardson, Glenn, Horgan, & Nurmikko, 2007), with approximately 30% reporting some telescoping within the first 6 months of amputation (Jensen *et al.*, 1983). Telescoping usually begins within weeks or months of amputation and the phantom limb may then disappear (Hunter *et al.*, 2003; Shukla, Sahu, Tripathi, & Gupta, 1982) or remain 'dangling' from the stump (Ramachandran & Hirstein, 1998). The telescoped phantom may resemble an ontogenetic form of the amputated limb, sometimes resembling the form of pho-comelic limbs (e.g., from thalidomide) with portions of the limb shrunken, deformed, or absent. Phantom limbs apparently do not telescope in patients with pre-existing peripheral nerve injury, spinal cord transection, or brachial plexus avulsion, perhaps due to 'learned paralysis' and reinforcement of the 'extended' representation of the deafferented limb (Katz, 1992; Ramachandran & Hirstein, 1998). In amputees with telescoped phantoms, motor imagery of the phantom hand shows a medial shift in primary somatosensory cortex, activating cortical areas remote from the amputated limb (Flor, Nikolajsen, & Jensen, 2006), which suggests an association between changes in the perceived size or length of the phantom (i.e., telescoping) and perceptual remapping of primary somatosensory neurons subserving the amputated limb.

Phantom limbs are known to typically adopt a 'habitual' position and posture, resting at the side of the body, or in a posture that resembles that of the limb prior to amputation (Ramachandran & Hirstein, 1998). Often the phantom is stuck in a frozen or fixed position (Devor, 1997), particularly when moving other body parts (Fraser, 2002). The phantom may also assume an abnormal posture, such as the fingers twisted out of shape or grossly intertwined, or the thumb pushing through the palm (Bailey & Moersch, 1941; Henderson & Smyth, 1948). Kooijman, Dijkstra, Geertzen, Elzinga, and van der Schans (2000) report that abnormal shape and posture are perceived by 9 and 22% of upper limb amputees, respectively; however, the characteristics of abnormal phantom posture, and associations with aspects of amputation or other phantom limb phenomena, are not presently known. We would expect that pre-amputation history may affect the posture in the phantom; for example, functional impairment or immobilization prior to amputation may correspond to abnormal or fixed posture in the phantom.

Phantom limbs may be characterized by various exteroceptive or proprioceptive sensations, such as touch, pressure, temperature, itch, and vibration, tingling or buzzing (Hunter *et al.,* 2003; Jensen *et al.,* 1983; Weinstein, 1998). While these perceptions are frequently described they have rarely been examined with respect to aspects of amputation or other phantom limb phenomena. Jensen *et al.* (1983) indicated that 15% of their sample experienced exteroceptive sensations, including itching, tingling, cold, heat, and paraesthesia; however, they did not quantify the respective sensations. Richardson *et al.* (2007) found that 50% of amputees perceived pins and needles, 43% perceived itching, and 15% had 'super-added' sensations (primarily characterized by the perception of clothing on the phantom) in the phantom at 6 months. In a small study of 11 upper limb amputees, Hunter, Katz, and Davis (2008) reported a significant increase in the number of subjects experiencing additional exteroceptive sensations in the phantom over time (e.g., tickling, tingling, and 'pins and needles').

Evidently, while various studies have reported aspects of somatic and proprioceptive qualities that characterize phantom limbs, we aimed to systematically explored these phenomena in a large cohort of amputees.

Method
Participants
Two hundred and eighty-three amputees participated, aged 22–96 (mean = 59; SD = 15), and had been amputees for between 9 days and 70 years (median = 12.1 years, mean = 19 years; SD = 17.7 years).

Materials
Questionnaires assessed participants' neurological (e.g., stroke, peripheral neuropathy, or movement disorders), psychological, and surgical histories. The *Changes in Body Sensation Following Limb Loss* questionnaire (CIBS-questionnaire; see supplementary material for the full questionnaire) was developed for the present study, following appraisal of the literature on phantom limb phenomena, to explore aspects of phantom limb experience (e.g., perception of the size, shape, and posture of the phantom) that had not previously been quantified in a large sample of amputees. The CIBS-questionnaire is long, time consuming, and ultimately most useful when implemented in the manner for which it was designed: as an exploration of the perception of somatic and other qualities in the phantom limb following amputation, not as a clinical or diagnostic tool. While the questionnaire did not include 'control' questions, or measures of suggestibility, we did contact nearly all participants for a follow-up telephone interview to verify their answers.

The CIBS-questionnaire was implemented alongside existing pain [e.g., McGill Pain Questionnaire (Melzack, 1975) and the Brief Pain Inventory (Cleeland, 1989)], coping [e.g., Coping Strategies Questionnaire (Rosentstiel & Keefe, 1983)], mood [e.g., Hospital Anxiety and Depression Scale (Zigmond & Snaith, 1983)], and amputation scales [e.g., Trinity Amputation and Prosthetics Experiences Scales (Gallagher & MacLachlan, 2000)]. We report only a small portion of the results from the larger questionnaire study, findings from which are described elsewhere (Giummarra *et al.,*). The following questions from the CIBS-questionnaire were used in analyses for the present paper:

(a) *Information about limb loss* including: dates of amputation(s); side and level of each amputation; cause of limb loss, and duration and nature of functional impairment prior to amputation.

(b) *Information about prosthesis use,* including: prosthesis type, years/months of prosthesis use, frequency of use (all of the time, most of the time, some of the time, not often, never), and interaction between the phantom and prosthesis.

(c) *Information about phantom sensations and pain,* including: phantom limb perception; frequency of phantom limb perception now and in the past (always, a few times an hour, day, week, month, year, or very infrequently); duration of phantom limb perception now and in the past (seconds, minutes, hours, days, constantly); perception of the parts, size, shape, and posture of the phantom limb; static and dynamic changes in size or shape of the phantom limb (telescoping);

exteroceptive sensations in the phantom limb (including perception of itching, touching, pressure, vibration, electric sensations, or temperature in the phantom); referred sensations to the phantom limb; movement of the phantom (in particular, whether the phantom moves spontaneously, reflexively, or voluntarily); perception of pain in the phantom, stump, or residual limb now or in the past; Visual Analogue Scale (VAS) for current, and usual (during a typical episode of pain), intensity of phantom pain; VAS for current, and usual (during a typical episode of pain), intensity of stump pain. VASs comprised a line 10 cm long, with the left-most side labelled 'no pain' and the right-most side labelled 'worst possible pain'.

Procedure

Participants gave informed consent prior to inclusion in the study, which was approved by local university and hospital ethics boards, and met the ethical standards laid down in the 1964 Declaration of Helsinki. Participants were primarily recruited from the Caulfield General Medical Centre Amputee Unit, Australia. One thousand amputees were invited, 249 of whom responded, and 199 returned valid questionnaires (20% response rate). The true reason for the low response rate cannot be known; however, invitees who *no longer* perceived phantom sensations may not have volunteered as they assumed that they were not the target of the study (which was advertised as examining phantom limb perception). Furthermore, the letter of invitation requested volunteers with no personal history of mental illness or neurological condition, which would have further reduced the size of the eligible sample. Finally, the overall questionnaire was large and time consuming. The sample was heterogeneous—although likely comprising a larger proportion of upper limb and traumatic amputees than in the general amputee population—and is likely to be representative of the larger population of amputees perceiving phantom limb sensations.

The study was also reported in various Australian media (including mainstream television news programmes, and mainstream and regional newspapers) and resulted in another 108 amputees volunteering, of whom 84 returned valid questionnaires. Questionnaires were mailed to participants to be returned to the researchers in a reply paid envelope. The researchers then contacted each participant to clarify any ambiguities and verify their responses. Participants who did not return their questionnaires were sent a reminder letter, and a follow-up phone call requesting the return of the questionnaire.

Statistical Analyses

Univariate chi-square and Fisher exact tests (FET) were used to analyse the associations between dichotomous variables. Non-parametric (Mann–Whitney) analyses were performed to examine interval data that was not normally distributed (i.e., time since amputation and phantom limb posture). Factors potentially associated with somatic aspects of phantom limb phenomena (parts, size, telescoping, posture, and exteroceptive sensations) of the phantom limb perceived were examined. These included: cause of limb loss (trauma, vascular, diabetes),

functional impairment before amputation, time since amputation, level of limb loss (upper vs. lower limb; as well as level of loss in the respective limb), complications of amputation (e.g., gangrene or infection), and phantom pain. Ultimately, analyses were theory driven; for example, exploring the association between bent/fixed posture of the phantom and functional impairment or limb immobilization; and exploring the relationship between prosthesis embodiment and phantom limb sensations/pain, telescoping, and referred sensations.

Results

We separately report findings relating to parts of the phantom limb perceived, size of the phantom limb, telescoping, posture of the limb, exteroceptive and proprioceptive sensations, prosthesis use and embodiment.

Frequency of phantom sensations was not correlated with time since amputation; Spearman's $r = .11$, $p = .05$. This may be due to a recruitment bias in that amputees were more likely to participate if they were still experiencing phantom sensations or pain, particularly with the participants who volunteered following media exposure of the study who were more likely to experience phantom pain (82% media generated participants compared with 65% for invited participants); FET $\chi^2(1) = 8.14$, $p < .01$.

Parts of the Phantom Limb Perceived

The majority of amputees perceived the parts of their phantom limb to be similar to the limb before amputation. We have found, for the first time, that 11 (4.3%) primarily perceived proximal parts of the limb. Such amputees described that 'it is like an extension to the stump (but not foot), about 3 cm below the stump,' that they were 'just aware of the shin,' or that they just felt sensation 'below the stump.' Vascular amputees were more likely to perceive only the proximal portion of their phantom limb compared to other amputees (8.6% cf. 2.0%), and were less likely to report that their phantom resembled the shape (whole and/or deformed) of the limb as it was prior to amputation ($N = 21$, 36.21% cf. $N = 100$, 50.50%); $\chi^2(3) = 8.53$, $p < .05$. Some amputees ($N = 17$, 6.64%) perceived a 'whole' phantom limb, that was of an abnormal shape *unlike* the shape of the limb prior to amputation, and 19 (7.4%) did not perceive the parts/shape of their phantom limb.

Differences emerged in the parts of the phantom perceived according to the level of limb loss, $\chi^2(5) = 16.51$, $p < .01$. Upper limb amputees primarily perceived the phantom limb in its entirety as it was prior to amputation ($N = 27$, 72.97%) with 18.91% ($N = 7$) perceiving only the distal portion of the limb, whereas lower limb amputees generally perceived their phantom to be either whole as it was prior to amputation ($N = 88$, 41.71%) or to consist only of the distal portion of the limb ($N = 98$, 46.45%).

Size of the Phantom Limb

The majority ($N = 213$, 75.3%) of participant's phantom limbs were of a normal size, while some individuals could not perceive the size of their limb ($N = 34$, 13.3%), and others reported that their limb was smaller/thinner ($N = 4$, 1.4%; e.g., foot feels smaller than the remaining foot; phantom limb feels thinner), or bigger ($N = 4$, 1.4%; e.g., phantom feels swollen; leg has become shorter [telescoped] and fatter) than it should be. The size of the phantom limb did not differ according to level of amputation or limb amputated. A higher proportion of participants with phantom pain ($N = 173$, 89.2%) perceived the size of their phantom limb compared with those without phantom pain ($N = 48$, 78.7%); FET $\chi^2(1) = 4.42$, $p < .05$.

Telescoping

Fifty-five (21.6%) participants reported that their phantom limb was telescoped, including 4 of 11 (36.4%) amputees with a brachial plexus avulsion. All participants with brachial plexus avulsion retained their limb for between 1 and 4 years following injury ($m = 2.28$ years, $SD = 1.11$). Upper limb amputees (35.1%) were more likely to experience a telescoped phantom than lower limb amputees (20.1%); FET $\chi^2(1) = 4.10$, $p < .05$. Furthermore, across upper and lower limb amputees, the higher level of amputation (excluding finger/toe amputations) the more likely participants were to report telescoping; $\chi^2(4) = 13.42$, $p < .01$. Evidently, the finding that 35% of upper limb amputees experience a telescoped phantom limb, and 72% experience their limb as if it was whole could be seen to be contradictory. However, the seven amputees for whom this was the case described the distal portion of their phantom as being closer to the stump, or that the phantom was shortened, but still comprising the key joints and parts of the limb. An overlap between telescoping and perceiving the phantom as a 'whole' was also reported in 22 lower limb amputees. Similar observations (i.e., overlap between the phantom resembling the shape and form of the phantom, and being telescoped or shortened) have previously been reported by Fraser (2002).

Telescoping was less common among amputees with (a) vascular amputation ($N = 4$, 6.9%), which was nearly four times less likely to be associated with telescoping compared with other causes of limb loss ($N = 51$, 25.9%); FET $\chi^2(1) = 9.55$, $p < .01$; or (b) diabetic amputation ($N = 1$, 4%) compared with other causes of limb loss ($N = 54$, 23.5%); FET $\chi^2(1) = 5.06$, $p = .01$; and (c) functional impairment prior to limb loss ($N = 22$, 15%) compared with those without functional impairment ($N = 33$, 31%); FET $\chi^2(1) = 9.81$, $p < .01$. Telescoping was more common following (a) traumatic amputation [N(trauma) $= 38$, 29.7% compared with N(other) $= 17$, 13.4%; FET $\chi^2(1) = 10.01$, $p < .01$] and (b) cancer-related amputation [N(cancer) $= 11$, 44% compared with N(other) $= 44$, 19.1%; FET $\chi^2(1) = 8.24$, $p < .01$].

An aspect of telescoping not previously understood is that of *active* telescoping. Seven (2.5%) amputees reported that their phantom actively telescoped. For example, 'the phantom moves into the stump when in bed at night, not wearing the prosthesis', 'phantom withdraws towards the stump when taking the prosthesis off', or 'sometimes I wake up and it feels like whole leg is there, then I move it and it disappears back up towards the stump'.

Posture of the Limb

Most participants ($N = 203$, 79.3%) with phantom sensations perceived that their phantom occupied a normal or habitual position, and 30 (11.7%) reported that their limb occupied an abnormal position (see Figure 2 for participant illustrations of normal and abnormal postures). Abnormal and anatomically impossible postures consisted of the phantom (a) fingers or toes curled or clenched ($N = 5$); (b) in a fixed bent posture at the knee or elbow ($N = 10$); (c) limb twisted or pointing inwards/outwards ($N = 13$); (d) digits switched/crossed/confused or 'all over the place' ($N = 3$) and other ($N = 3$); data partially overlapping. Participants reporting anatomically impossible postures (c and d) were more likely to be traumatic amputees, FET $\chi^2(1) = 6.44$, $p = .01$.

Perception of normal posture was more common in those *with* functional impairment prior to limb loss, vascular and diabetic amputation, phantom pain, and lower limb amputation. Cancer-related amputation was less likely to result in perception of a normal posture. Among both upper and lower limb amputees, those with higher levels of amputation perceived more varied postures, such that those with higher levels of amputation were equally likely to perceive a normal posture, a telescoped (shortened) phantom in a normal posture (e.g., the phantom takes a habitual posture but is shorter, or that it switches between an extended and telescoped phantom in a normal/habitual posture), or an abnormal posture in the phantom, compared with those with lower levels of amputation who were more likely to perceive a normal posture; $\chi^2(3) = 68.87$, $p = .006$.

Ten amputees perceived their phantom to be in a fixed position where the limb was bent at the knee or elbow. This fixed position did not vary during prosthesis use when the phantom would typically dissociate from the prosthesis when walking, but merge when sitting. Amputees who perceived their phantom limb to be fixed in a bent position at the knee/elbow were more likely to have had their amputation for a longer time (median $= 32.8$ years; range: 22 months–61.7 years) than those who did not perceive their phantom limb in a fixed bent position (median $= 10$ years; range: 9 days–65 years); Mann–Whitney $U = 633.0$, $N_1 = 203$, $N_2 = 10$, $p < .05$, two-tailed. However, perception of a bent, fixed phantom knee/elbow did not differ according to functional impairment or immobilization prior to amputation, age at amputation, or present age. Furthermore, there was no apparent relationship with occupation (i.e., amputees with a fixed bent phantom knee/elbow did not perform sedentary jobs, but included an apprentice motor mechanic, architect, butcher, company director, computer programmer, disability support worker, electrical instrument maker, geologist, lecturer in mathematics, and television technician).

Nineteen (7.6%) amputees reported that the distal portion or the entire length of their phantom seemed to float at a distance from the stump, or that they could not perceive parts of the limb between the distal portion (e.g., the hand or foot) and the stump, but that the distal portion was at a distance from the stump. For example, one person explained that 'the phantom becomes dissociated from the limb when walking'. A further

17 reported that there was a space between their phantom and their stump, but that the phantom was not 'floating' *per se*.

Exteroceptive and Proprioceptive Sensations

At least half of all amputees with phantom sensations perceived one or more exteroceptive/proprioceptive 'super-added' (Richardson *et al.,* 2007) sensation. In particular, participants perceived itching ($N = 129$, 50%), pressure ($N = 92$, 36.7%), touch ($N = 41$, 16%), temperature [hot ($N = 43$, 16.6%), cold ($N = 40$, 15.6%), hot and cold ($N = 12$, 4.7%), and warm ($N = 14$, 17.6%)], electric sensations ($N = 120$, 43%; e.g., 'electrical nerve impulses', shooting/lightning bolt type pains, or electric shocks/jolts), vibration ($N = 32$, 11.5%), and pins and needles ($N = 49$, 17.6%). There were no differences in perception of any of these exteroceptive sensations according to cause of limb loss, functional impairment prior to amputation, infection or gangrene prior to amputation, or posture of the phantom limb. The only difference was found between upper and lower limb amputees, such that the former were more likely to report perceiving temperature in their phantom limb than the latter (52.78% cf. 41.04%); $\chi^2(5) = 12.582$, $p < .05$. While some medications used for relieving phantom pain can cause itching as a side effect, medication use was not significantly related to the perception of itching in the phantom.

Prosthesis Use and Embodiment

Nearly, all lower limb amputees used a prosthesis ($N = 202$, 88%) whereas only 59% ($N = 24$) upper limb amputees used a prosthesis; FET $\chi^2(1) = 22.45$, $p < .001$. Among lower limb amputees, those with higher levels of amputation used their prosthesis less often than those with below knee or lower amputations; $\chi^2(24) = 71.69$, $p < .001$. For example, no hindquarter amputees and 66.7% ($N = 40$) above knee amputees used their prosthesis all of the time compared with 78.1% ($N = 100$) of below knee amputees.

Of those who wore a prosthesis, 23 (11.6%) reported that their phantom limb 'becomes the prosthesis' or vice versa, and 34 (17.2%) reported that the phantom disappears, which may equally suggest that the prosthesis is embodied (i.e., the perception that one's sense of bodily self is localized within a 'tool' or prosthesis that extend the body's area of influence; Giummarra *et al.,* 2008) and the amputee therefore feels normal and whole. Experiences of embodiment included reporting that: 'the prosthesis fits like a glove/shoe'; 'it all feels like one . . . like it's in a shoe when I put the prosthesis on'; 'the artificial leg is my leg, if I have it off it is very strange'; and 'the phantom limb and prosthesis become one and the same'.

Among those who used a prosthesis 'most of the time' or 'all of the time' (i.e., excluding those who only wear their prosthesis 'some of the time' or 'never'), we combined participants who explicitly affirmed prosthesis embodiment and those who indicated that their phantom disappeared during prosthesis use as the 'prosthesis embodiment' group ($N = 57$), and compared these participants against others ($N = 170$) for differences in perception of phantom pain, frequency of phantom limb

perception, and telescoping. Prosthesis embodiment was more frequent in amputees with an extended phantom ($N = 15/47$, 32%) compared to a telescoped phantom ($N = 18/118$, 15%); FET $\chi^2(1) = 5.83$, $p < .05$. Furthermore, prosthesis embodiment was more common in amputees who reported perceiving referred sensations from the amputated limb to the phantom ($N = 23/47$, 49%) than those without such referred sensations ($N = 40/120$, 33%); FET $\chi^2(1) = 3.50$, $p < .05$; although the accuracy of sensory maps in the amputated limb could not be verified using the present questionnaire-based method.

Prosthesis embodiment did not differ according to: perception of phantom pain or phantom pain intensity, level of amputation, limb amputated (upper vs. lower), whether the amputated limb was the dominant limb, frequency of phantom limb perception, or type of prosthesis used (functional vs. cosmetic; however, only 13 amputees used a cosmetic prosthesis most or all of the time).

Ten (3.5%) amputees indicated that the phantom did not embody their prosthesis, including all five with a phantom in a fixed bent posture who still used a prosthesis. Others described that their 'phantom sensations are completely independent of the prosthesis as it doesn't fit into the prosthesis', or that 'the phantom feels smothered because the prosthesis isn't long enough for the phantom limb'. Those who indicated that their phantom explicitly did not embody the prosthesis described a distinct perception of a mismatch between the phantom limb and the prosthesis. Those who reported 'no change', on the other hand, were more likely to explain that they had never noticed whether the phantom did or did not embody the prosthesis, or that they primarily perceived phantom pain rather than a phantom 'limb' *per se,* and could not relate to the concept of a phantom embodying the prosthesis.

Discussion

The present study examined the somatic and corporeal aspects of phantom phenomena. The properties that were found to define phantom limbs—including the size, shape, posture, and exteroceptive/proprioceptive qualities—parallel the sensations perceived in the intact body. Most amputees perceived a phantom that was of a normal size, and assumed a normal posture (whether extended or shortened/telescoped). Some perceived abnormal qualities in the phantom: the frequency (12%) of amputees with phantom limbs that occupied abnormal or anatomically impossible postures (e.g., the limb being twisted or pointing in the wrong direction, or digits on the phantom hand being switched, or crossed over) is quite high. Abnormal posture was more common following traumatic limb loss, and may be a consequence of the observation and perception of the affected limb occupying 'unnatural' positions during accidental injury (Anderson-Barnes, McAuliffe, Swanberg, & Tsao, 2009). Furthermore, upper limb amputees were more likely to perceive abnormal postures, which may relate to the higher degrees of freedom of movement of the joints of intact upper limbs compared to lower limbs. Upper limb amputees were also more likely to perceive temperature in their phantom, perhaps because temperature fluctuations are typically perceived more often in the upper limbs, which are often exposed and unprotected, compared with the lower limbs, which are typically enclosed in clothing and footwear.

The rare perception of the phantom being smaller/thinner or larger/swollen compared to the intact limb appears analogous to the perception of magnified or shrinking body parts in *Alice in Wonderland* illusions, which might result from reduced blood supply to the somatotopic representation of affected body parts (Kew, Wright, & Halligan, 1998). We have found for the first time that approximately 4% of amputees experienced the *proximal* portion of the phantom only. The finding that these patients were more likely to be vascular amputees may be because the distal portion of the limb contains finer vessels than proximal portions, and is more likely to have suffered prolonged sensory impairment leading to gradual reduction of somatosensory representation of the distal portion of the limb.

Telescoping was less frequent in the present sample than many previous studies (i.e., 21% compared with prior reports of 28–67%; Carlen *et al.,* 1978; Fraser, 2002; Richardson *et al.,* 2007), and was more common following proximal amputation. This is likely because the distal portion of the phantom can be apparently displaced (i.e., telescoped) a greater distance with more proximal amputation. Furthermore, cancer and traumatic amputees were more likely to experience telescoping, suggesting an association between telescoping and rapid limb loss compared with diabetic or vascular limb loss, which is characterized by more gradual sensory, neuropathic, and ischaemic changes prior to amputation. Contrary to prior reports (Katz, 1992; Ramachandran & Hirstein, 1998), over a third of patients with brachial plexus avulsion experienced a telescoped phantom, even though the physical limb was retained following injury for an average of 2 years and 4 months before amputation. Visual experience of a 'paralysed' limb does not, therefore, guarantee that the limb will be constrained by 'learned paralysis' and retain its extended form following amputation.

Consciously focusing on the phantom limb, as participants inevitably did in the present study, recruits the perceptual, conceptual, and emotional qualities (Gallagher & Cole, 1995) of the missing limb's body image (i.e., higher order, top-down bodily and perceptual representations; Gallagher, 2005; Kammers, van der Ham, & Dijkerman, 2006). Ordinarily, however, most amputees try not to allow their phantom limb to enter into conscious awareness because it is usually annoying or painful. Phantom limb awareness therefore likely results from much more complex mechanisms than mere conscious experience of the sensations of that limb. Most sensations typically occur spontaneously, and many properties that persist following amputation do so against one's wishes (e.g., itch, pressure, touch).

The present study was part of a larger study on phantom limb phenomena and phantom pain, and we have not presently examined phantom limb movement as these observations—and related literature—have been reported and discussed in depth elsewhere (Giummarra *et al.,*). However, we will briefly note these findings in order to satisfactorily account for the phantom limb's proprioceptive qualities—that is, the perception of feedback about limb position based on the combination of efferent information about limb movement and afferent information from somatosensory receptors (Tsakiris, Haggard, Franck, Mainy, & Sirigu, 2005). Key observations from our related substudy included the significant association between the *ability to move* the phantom and the perception of phantom pain, pain of a greater intensity, and an experience of phantom pain characterized by deep tissue-mediated qualities (e.g., cramping). Similarly, *spontaneous* phantom limb movements were associated with perception of heightened phantom and stump pain, and pain characterized by cramping, as well as electric-shooting pain, suggesting peripheral dysfunction. Furthermore, those who were able to wilfully move their phantom were more likely to perceive the size, shape, and posture of their phantom, suggesting that the body image of the limb was better preserved in those with voluntary phantom limb movement. Others have also described the perception of painful spontaneous phantom limb movements (Shukla *et al.,* 1982), and an association between voluntary phantom limb movement and phantom pain (Richardson *et al.,* 2007). Amputees suffering from phantom pain also exhibit decreased phantom limb motor control, taking longer to perform phantom limb movements (Gagne *et al.,* 2009). Increased phantom pain associated with phantom movement likely corresponds to an incongruence between sensory feedback and efference copy (Harris, 1999), consistent with forward prediction models (Blakemore, Wolpert, & Frith, 2002); that is, that we are unaware of the results of the comparison between predicted and intended outcome and sensory feedback from motor commands as long as the desired state is successfully achieved. In amputees, efferent and afferent information is in conflict. The associated phantom pain may be reduced with illusory phantom movement via mirrors, virtual reality, and prosthesis use, or mental imagery supplemented with observing others perform the imagined movement, thus involving mirror neuron systems (Giummarra *et al.,*).

Ultimately, rather than resulting from a mental image of the limb alone, perception of the corporeal phantom probably also stems from proprioceptive adjustments and minute, involuntary movements that occur during attempts to locate the limb in space. The phantom limb percept enters into awareness, or is even strengthened (Hunter *et al.,* 2003), during both non-conscious and intentional execution of motor schemata, including performance of automatic movements stored as limb-specific proprioceptive memories (Anderson-Barnes *et al.,* 2009). Various properties of the phantom may enter into conscious awareness as a result of non-conscious recruitment of body schemata (i.e., automatic, bottom-up sensory, and organizational processes that encode spatial and action capabilities of body parts; Gallagher, 2005; Giummarra *et al.,* 2008; Higuchi, Imanaka, & Patla, 2006) for the missing limb during proprioception, and maintenance of the (body) image of the limb (Gallagher, 1986; Gallagher & Cole, 1995; Paillard, 1991). This is somewhat analogous to the finding that the ability to see the visual illusion of apparent motion in *Enigma*, a display of closely spaced concentric rings and radiating black and white lines, relies upon the eyes making microsaccades (Troncoso, Macknik, Otero-Milian, & Martinez-Conde, 2008). The speed of illusory motion is related to the rate of microsaccades, and if microsaccades cease or the eyes are immobilized (e.g., stabilized retinal image) then illusory motion ceases, or elements of the stimulus display disappear from vision, and one experiences a *ganzfeld* (Inhoff & Topolski, 1994). Likewise, when amputees are engaged in tasks that would not ordinarily require the use of the amputated limb or demand postural corrections (e.g., a lower limb amputee typing rapidly at the computer), or when occupied in a task that produces profound mental arousal (e.g., while working or engaged in socially stimulating activities), the proprioceptive sense of the phantom typically fades from awareness (Giummarra & Bradshaw, 2010).

The body image undoubtedly plays a large role in successful prosthesis use, as conscious awareness of the newly configured body is essential for this ambulatory transition. Not all amputees can use their prosthesis as a 'natural limb'—particularly those with proximal amputations for whom prosthesis use is more physically and mentally fatiguing (Smith, 2009)—and most continue to self-monitor, and consciously initiate movements using the body image and visual feedback. Prosthesis embodiment—which was reported by one third of prosthesis users—suggests successful merging of the phantom with the prosthesis in both body image and body schema. In some cases, the phantom did not 'fit' or embody the prosthesis (e.g., amputees with a permanently bent phantom). Prosthesis embodiment was more common in amputees with an extended phantom (i.e., not telescoped), which may suggest the importance of correspondence between the perceived proprioceptive and somatic qualities of the phantom and the physical and/or visual properties of the prosthesis. However, rubber limb embodiment seems not to depend upon correspondence between the visual properties of the rubber limb and visual and/or perceived somatic qualities in an amputee's limb/phantom (Giummarra, Georgiou-Karistianis, Gibson, Nicholls, & Bradshaw, 2010). The fundamental factor that appears to improve rubber limb embodiment in upper limb amputees is the presence of a 'sensory map' of sensations referred from the stump to the phantom (Ehrsson *et al.*, 2008). Likewise, we found that amputees reporting referred sensations from the stump and/or amputated limb were more likely to experience prosthesis embodiment; however, it was not possible to verify whether such referred sensations related to 'sensory maps' of the phantom on the stump or to more general referral or exacerbation of pain from the stump to the phantom.

Prosthesis use likely enables adaptive feed-forward mechanisms, reducing conflict between intended and actual movements of the amputated limb and its associated phantom, and provides for a 'surrogate' extension of kinaesthetic feedback. Functional prosthesis use, compared to cosmetic prosthesis use, among upper limb amputees has been found to correspond to maintenance of a more vivid phantom limb percept over time (Hunter *et al.*, 2008). Extensive prosthesis use, especially of a myoelectric prosthesis, is typically associated with decreased cortical reorganization, reduced phantom pain and likely preserved motor schemata for the phantom limb in upper limb amputees (Lotze *et al.*, 1999; Weiss, Miltner, Adler, Bruckner, & Taub, 1999); however, some studies have not replicated these findings (Hunter *et al.*, 2008; Kooijman *et al.*, 2000). We did not find any differences in prosthesis embodiment according to prosthesis type; however, only 13 amputees used a cosmetic prosthesis at least most or all of the time. Ultimately, the corporeal characteristics of non-painful phantom phenomena may affect the success of pain management strategies; e.g., the likely effectiveness of prosthesis training, mirror box therapy (Chan *et al.*, 2007; Ramachandran & Rogers-Ramachandran, 1996), or motor imagery (Moseley & Brugger, 2009) in alleviating phantom pain.

In summary, the phantom limb is, on the whole, characterized by properties that parallel the properties in the intact body—with respect to size, shape, and posture—with a small percentage experiencing anatomically impossible properties in the limb. While an amputee can deliberately focus on aspects of his or her phantom limb using the body image, this is unlikely to underlie ongoing and spontaneous phantom limb perception considering most phantom sensations are annoying. We therefore propose that phantom limb perception results in part from generation and maintenance of a conscious, long-term mental image of the missing limb (e.g., see O'Shaughnessy, 1995). Further studies should now compare and contrast the role of voluntary and involuntary proprioceptive adjustments (i.e., execution of *motor schemata* for the missing limb) in the maintenance of phantom limb phenomena.

References

Aglioti, S., Smania, N., Atzei, A., & Berlucchi, G. (1997). Spatiotemporal properties of the pattern of evoked phantom sensations in a left index amputee patient. *Behavioral Neuroscience, 111*(5), 867–872. doi:10.1037/0735-7044.111.5.867

Anderson-Barnes, V. C., McAuliffe, C., Swanberg, K. M., & Tsao, J. W. (2009). Phantom limb pain – a phenomenon of proprioceptive memory? *Medical Hypotheses, 73,* 555–558. doi:10.1016/j.mehy.2009.05.038

Arzy, S., Thut, G., Mohr, C., Michel, C. M., & Blanke, O. (2006). Neural basis of embodiment: Distinct contributions of temporoparietal junction and extrastriate body area. *Journal of Neuroscience, 26*(31), 8074–8081. doi:10.1523/JNEUROSCI.0745-06.2006

Bailey, A. A., & Moersch, F. P. (1941). Phantom limb. *Canadian Medical Association Journal, 45*(1), 37–42.

Blakemore, S.-J., Wolpert, D. M., & Frith, C. (2002). Abnormalities in the awareness of action. *Trends in Cognitive Sciences, 6*(6), 237–242. doi:10.1016/S1364-6613(02)01907-1

Carlen, P. L., Wall, P. D., Nadvorna, H., & Steinbach, T. (1978). Phantom limbs and related phenomena in recent traumatic amputations. *Neurology, 28,* 211–217.

Chan, B. L., Witt, R., Charrow, A. P., Magee, A., Howard, R., Pasquina, P. F., . . . Tsao, J. W. (2007). Mirror therapy for phantom limb pain. *New England Journal of Medicine, 357,* 2206–2207.

Cleeland, C. S. (1989). Measurement of pain by subjective report. In C. R. Chapman & J. D. Loeser (Eds.), *Advances in pain research and therapy: Issues in pain measurement* (Vol. 12, pp. 391–403). New York: Raven Press.

Devor, M. (1997). Phantom limb phenomena and their neural mechanism. In M. S. Myslobodsky (Ed.), *The mythomanias: The nature of deception and self-deception* (pp. 237–361). Hove, UK: Psychology Press.

Ehrsson, H. H., Rosen, B., Stockselius, A., Ragno, C., Kohler, P., & Lundborg, G. (2008). Upper limb amputees can be induced to experience a rubber hand as their own. *Brain, 131,* 3443–3452. doi:10.1093/brain/awn297

Flor, H., Nikolajsen, L., & Jensen, T. S. (2006). Phantom limb pain: A case of maladaptive CNS plasticity. *Nature Reviews Neuroscience, 7*(11), 873–881. doi:10.1038/nrn1991

Fraser, C. (2002). Fact and fiction: A clarification of phantom limb phenomena. *British Journal of Occupational Therapy, 65*(6), 256–260.

Gagne, M., Reilly, K. T., Hetu, S., & Mercier, C. (2009). Motor control over the phantom limb in above-elbow amputees and its relationship with phantom limb pain. *Neuroscience, 162*(1), 78–86.

Gallagher, P., & MacLachlan, M. (2000). Development and psychometric evaluation of the Trinity Amputation and Prosthesis Experience Scales (TAPES). *Rehabilitation Psychology, 45,* 130–154. doi:10.1037/0090-5550.45.2.130

Gallagher, S. (1986). Body image and body schema: A conceptual clarification. *Journal of Mind and Behavior, 7,* 541–554.

Gallagher, S. (2005). *How the body shapes the mind.* New York: Oxford University Press.

Gallagher, S., & Cole, J. (1995). Body image and body schema in a deafferented subject. *Journal of Mind and Behaviour, 16,* 369–390.

Giummarra, M. J., & Bradshaw, J. (2010). The phantom of the night: Restless legs syndrome in amputees. *Medical Hypotheses, 74,* 968–972. doi:10.1016/j.mehy.2009.12.009

Giummarra, M. J., Georgiou-Karistianis, N., Gibson, S. J., Nicholls, M. E. R., & Bradshaw, J. L. (2010). The phantom in the mirror: A modified rubber hand illusion in amputees and normals. *Perception, 39*(1), 103–118. doi:10.1068/p6519

Giummarra, M. J., Gibson, S. J., Georgiou-Karistianis, N., & Bradshaw, J. L. (2008). Mechanisms underlying embodiment, disembodiment and loss of embodiment. *Neuroscience and Biobehavioral Reviews, 32,* 143–160. doi:10.1016/j.neubiorev.2007.07.001

Giummarra, M. J., Gibson, S. J., Georgiou-Karistianis, N., Nicholls, M. E. R., Chou, M., & Bradshaw, J. L. Maladaptive plasticity in amputees: Imprinting of enduring, intense or 'core-trauma' experiences on phantom limb schemata.

Giummarra, M. J., Gibson, S. J., Georgiou-Karistianis, N., Nicholls, M. E. R., Chou, M., & Bradshaw, J. L. Maladaptive plasticity, phantom pain and movement.

Giummarra, M. J., Gibson, S. J., Georgiou-Karistianis, N., Nicholls, M. E. R., Chou, M., & Bradshaw, J. L. The menacing phantom: What pulls the trigger?

Halligan, P. W., Marshal, J. C., Wade, D. T., Davey, J., & Morrison, D. (1993). Thumb in cheek? Sensory reorganization and perceptual plasticity after limb amputation. *Neuroreport, 4*(3), 233–236. doi:10.1097/00001756-199303000-00001

Harris, A. J. (1999). Cortical origin of pathological pain. *Lancet, 354,* 1464–1466. doi:10.1016/S0140-6736(99)05003-5

Henderson, W. R., & Smyth, G. E. (1948). Phantom limbs. *Journal of Neurology, Neurosurgery and Psychiatry, 11,* 88–112. doi:10.1136/jnnp.11.2.88

Higuchi, T., Imanaka, K., & Patla, A. E. (2006). Action-oriented representation of peripersonal and extrapersonal space: Insights from manual and locomotor actions. *Japanese Psychological Research, 48*(3), 126–140. doi:10.1111/j.1468-5884.2006.00314.x

Hunter, J. P., Katz, J., & Davis, K. D. (2003). The effect of tactile and visual sensory inputs on phantom limb awareness. *Brain, 126*(3), 579–589. doi:10.1093/brain/awg054

Hunter, J. P., Katz, J., & Davis, K. D. (2008). Stability of phantom limb phenomena after upper limb amputation: A longitudinal study. *Neuroscience, 156*(4), 939–949. doi:10.1016/j.neuroscience.2008.07.053

Inhoff, A. W., & Topolski, R. (1994). Seeing morphemes: Loss of visibility during the retinal stabilization of compound and pseudocompound words. *Journal of Experimental Psychology: Human perception and Performance, 20*(4), 840–853. doi:10.1037/0096-1523.20.4.840

Jensen, T. S., Krebs, B., Nielsen, J., & Rasmussen, P. (1983). Phantom limb, phantom pain and stump pain in amputees during the first 6 months following limb amputation. *Pain, 17,* 243–256. doi:10.1016/0304-3959(83)90097-0

Kammers, M. P., van der Ham, I. J., & Dijkerman, H. C. (2006). Dissociating body representations in healthy individuals: Differential effects of a kinaesthetic illusion on perception and action. *Neuropsychologia, 44*(12), 2430-2436. doi:10.1016/j.neuropsychologia.2006.04.009

Katz, J. (1992). Psychophysiological contributions to phantom limbs. *Canadian Journal of Psychiatry, 37,* 282–298.

Kew, J., Wright, A., & Halligan, P. W. (1998). Somesthetic aura: The experience of 'Alice in Wonderland'. *Lancet, 351,* 1934. doi:10.1016/S0140-6736(05)78619-0

Knecht, S., Henningsen, H., Elbert, T., Flor, H., Höhling, C., Pantev, C., . . . Taub, E. (1995). Cortical reorganization in human amputees and mislocalization of painful stimuli to the phantom limb. *Neuroscience Letters, 201,* 262–264. doi:10.1016/0304-3940(95)12186-2

Kooijman, C. M., Dijkstra, P. U., Geertzen, J. H. B., Elzinga, A., & van der Schans, C. P. (2000). Phantom pain and phantom sensations in upper limb amputees: An epidemiological study. *Pain, 87,* 33–41. doi:10.1016/S0304-3959(00)00264-5

Lotze, M., Grodd, W., Birbaumer, N., Erb, M., Huse, E., & Flor, H. (1999). Does use of a myoelectric prosthesis prevent cortical reorganization and phantom limb pain? *Nature Neuroscience, 2*(6), 501–502. doi:10.1038/9145

Melzack, R. (1975). The McGill Pain Questionnaire: Major properties and scoring methods. *Pain, 1*(3), 277–299. doi:10.1016/0304-3959(75)90044-5

Moseley, G. L., & Brugger, P. (2009). Interdependence of movement and anatomy persists when amputees learn a physiologically impossible movement of their phantom arm. *Proceedings of the National Academy of Sciences of the United States of America, 106*(44), 18798–18802. doi:10.1073/pnas.0907151106

O'Shaughnessy, B. (1995). Proprioception and the body image. In J. L. Bermúdez, A. Marcel, & N. Eilan (Eds.), *The body and the self* (pp. 175–203). Cambridge, MA: MIT Press.

Paillard, J. (1991). Motor and representational framing of space. In J. Paillard (Ed.), *Brain and space* (pp. 163–182). New York: Oxford University Press.

Price, D. B. (1976). Phantom limb phenomena in patients with leprosy. *Journal of Nervous and Mental Disease, 163,* 108–116.

Ramachandran, V. S., & Hirstein, W. (1998). The perception of phantom limbs: The D.O. Hebb lecture. *Brain, 121,* 1603–1630. doi:10.1093/brain/121.9.1603

Ramachandran, V. S., & Rogers-Ramachandran, D. (1996). Synaesthesia in phantom limbs induced with mirrors.

Corporeal Awareness and Proprioceptive Sense of the Phantom by et. al. Melita Giummarra

63

Proceedings of the Royal Society of London B: Biological Science, 263, 377–386. doi:10.1098/rspb.1996.0058

Richardson, C., Glenn, S., Horgan, M., & Nurmikko, T. (2007). A prospective study of factors associated with the presence of phantom limb pain six months after major lower limb amputation in patients with peripheral vascular disease. *Journal of Pain, 8*(10), 793–801. doi:10.1016/j.jpain.2007.05.007

Rosentstiel, A. K., & Keefe, F. J. (1983). The use of coping strategies in chronic low back pain patients: Relationship to patient characteristics and current adjustment. *Pain, 17*(1), 33–44. doi:10.1016/0304-3959(83)90125-2

Shukla, G. D., Sahu, S. C., Tripathi, R. P., & Gupta, D. K. (1982). Phantom limb: A phenomenological study. *British Journal of Psychiatry, 141*, 54–58. doi:10.1192/bjp.141.1.54

Smith, J. (2009). We have the technology. *New Scientist*, 36–39. doi:10.1016/S0262-4079(09)60307-9

Troncoso, X. G., Macknik, S. L., Otero-Milian, J., & Martinez-Conde, S. (2008). Microsaccades drive illusory motion in the Enigma illusion. *Proceedings of the National Academy of Sciences of the United States of America, 105*(41), 16033–16038. doi:10.1073/pnas.0709389105

Tsakiris, M., Haggard, P., Franck, N., Mainy, N., & Sirigu, A. (2005). A specific role for efferent information in self-recognition. *Cognition, 96*, 215–231. doi:10.1016/j.cognition.2004.08.002

Weinstein, S. M. (1998). Phantom limb pain and related disorders. *Neurologic Clinics, 16*(4), 919–935. doi:10.1016/S0733-8619(05)70105-5

Weiss, T., Miltner, W. H. R., Adler, T., Bruckner, L., & Taub, E. (1999). Decrease in phantom limb pain associated with prosthesis-induced increased use of an amputation stump in humans. *Neuroscience Letters, 272*(2), 131–134. doi:10.1016/S0304-3940(99)00595-9

Zigmond, A. S., & Snaith, R. P. (1983). The Hospital Anxiety and Depression Scale. *Acta Psychiatrica Scandinavica, 67*, 361–370. doi:10.1111/j.1600-0447.1983.tb09716.x

Critical Thinking

1. Try to imagine that you no longer have the use of your right arm, and it has been amputated just above the elbow. Think about and brainstorm about all the different aspects of life that would be impacted by this event. See how many you can list. What do you think would be the most difficult behavioral change to adjust to, and why?

2. What is an "Alice in Wonderland" illusion, and how does it apply to the loss of a limb?

Create Central

www.mhhe.com/createcentral

Internet References

How to improve proprioception
www.bettermovement.org/2008/proprioception-the-3-d-map-of-the-body

Current treatments for phantom limb pain
www.practicalpainmanagement.com/pain/neuropathic/phantom-limb-syndrome/current-treatments-phantom-limb-pain

Article   Prepared by: Eric Landrum, *Boise State University*

You Do Not Talk about Fight Club if You Do Not Notice Fight Club: Inattentional Blindness for a Simulated Real-World Assault

CHRISTOPHER F. CHABRIS ET AL.

Learning Outcomes

After reading this article, you will be able to:

- Understand the concept of inattentional blindness.
- Identify some of the key variables that influence the ooccurrence and intensity of inattentional blindness.

At 2:00 in the morning on 25 January 1995, Boston police officer Kenny Conley was chasing a shooting suspect who climbed over a chain-link fence. An undercover officer named Michael Cox had arrived on the scene moments earlier, but other officers had mistaken him for a suspect, assaulted him from behind, and brutally beat him. Conley chased the suspect over the fence and apprehended him some time later. In later testimony, Conley said that he ran right past the place where Cox was under attack, but he claimed not to have seen the incident. The investigators, prosecutors, and jurors in the case all assumed that because Conley could have seen the beating, Conley must have seen the beating, and therefore must have been lying to protect his comrades. Conley was convicted of perjury and obstruction of justice and was sentenced to thirty-four months in jail (Lehr 2009).

We have used the term 'illusion of attention' to denote the common but mistaken belief that people pay attention to, and notice, more of their visual world than they actually do (Chabris and Simons 2010; Levin and Angelone 2008). None of the principals in this case seem to have realized that Conley could have been telling the truth (Chabris and Simons 2010). He could have failed to notice the beating of Cox because of inattentional blindness (Mack and Rock 1998; Neisser 1979; Simons and Chabris 1999; Simons 2010): While his attention was focused on the suspect he was chasing, he may have been essentially blind to unexpected events that he otherwise would have seen easily.

This explanation is plausible, but generalization from studies using videos or computerized displays (eg, Most et al 2000) to real-world events is not necessarily valid. In laboratory studies participants are seated in front of a screen, under artificial light, indoors, tracking one or more objects within a confined display space at close range. Conley was running outdoors at night chasing a moving target at some distance.

Although some studies have examined inattentional blindness in relatively complex displays (eg, Haines 1991; Neisser 1979; Simons and Chabris 1999), and anecdotal evidence suggests that it plays a role in many real-world contexts (eg, the prevalence of 'looked but failed to see' driving accidents), to our knowledge, only one study has systematically documented a failure to notice an unexpected real-world event. Hyman and colleagues (2010) asked pedestrians whether they had noticed a clown that was riding a unicycle near where they were walking; many missed it, especially if they were talking on a mobile phone at the time. Here we ask whether inattentional blindness can occur under realistic conditions similar to those in the Conley-Cox scenario. In contrast to the clown study, our subjects knew they were participating in research, and they were assigned a task requiring focused attention.

In study 1 we asked 20 subjects (college students, tested individually, participating for money or course credit) to pursue a male confederate while he jogged a 400-meter route at night in an area lit with streetlamps. The confederate and subject ran at a speed of approximately 2.4 meters per second, for a total running time of about 2 minutes and 45 seconds. At the end of the run, the confederate's heart rate was approximately 148 beats per minute.

Subjects were told to maintain a distance of 30 feet (9.1 meters) while counting the number of times the runner touched his head. At approximately 125 meters into the route, in a driveway 8 meters off the path, three other male confederates staged a fight in which two of them pretended to beat up the third. These confederates shouted, grunted, and coughed during the fight, which was visible to subjects for at least 15 seconds before they passed by it. The runner touched his head three times with his left hand and six times with his right hand, following the same sequence on every trial. The touches always started 30 meters into the run and occurred at approximately 40-meter intervals.

At the end of the route, we first asked the subjects how many head-touches they had counted. Then we asked whether the subjects had seen anything unusual along the route, and then whether they had seen anyone fighting. Only 7 out of 20 subjects (35%) reported seeing the fight in response to at least one of these questions. All seven noticers were able to describe some details of the fight, such as the number of participants and the location. We asked about two additional events that we did not stage (someone dribbling a basketball and someone juggling), and no subjects falsely reported seeing either. These results demonstrate that under real-world visual conditions approximating those experienced by Kenny Conley, people can fail to notice a nearby fight.

In study 2 we asked whether the low rates of noticing resulted only from poor viewing conditions due to darkness. We repeated the procedure, on the same route, during the daytime. Now the fight first became visible to the subjects about 20 seconds into their run, and it remained visible for at least 30 seconds. Even so, only 9 out of 16 subjects (56%) noticed the fight, consistent with the inattentional blindness hypothesis.

One hallmark of inattentional blindness is that increasing the effort required by the primary task decreases noticing of unexpected events (eg, Jensen and Simons 2009; Simons and Chabris 1999). If the failure to notice the fight results from inattentional blindness, then manipulating the demands of the counting task should affect noticing rates. Study 3 used the same daytime protocol as study 2, but each of the 58 subjects was randomly assigned (by coin flip) to either keep separate counts of head touches by the runner's left and right hands (high load condition) or to follow the runner without counting (low load).

Under a high-attentional load 14 of 33 subjects noticed the fight (42%), but under a low load 18 of 25 noticed (72%). This difference was significant, $\chi 2(1) = 5.03$, $p = 0.02$, supporting the hypothesis that subjects who missed the unexpected event displayed inattentional blindness. Moreover, participants in the dual-counting condition who did notice the fight counted less accurately (off by $M = 1.1$ touches) than those who missed it (off by $M = 0.2$ touches), $t(31) = 2.65$, $p = 0.01$, $d = 0.86$, suggesting that engaging in the counting task had a direct impact on noticing. (In studies 1 and 2 there were no significant differences in accuracy between noticers and missers, $p > 0.30$ in both cases.) It is possible that the amount of physical exertion during the run, which varied among subjects, would also predict inattentional blindness in this task; future research should examine this.

In three studies with 94 total participants, a substantial number of subjects failed to notice a three-person fight as they ran past it. This real-world inattentional blindness happened both at night and during the day and was modulated by attentional load. Our results represent the first experimental induction of inattentional blindness outside the laboratory.

Kenny Conley eventually won an appeal, and the government decided not to retry him. The inattentional blindness explanation did not contribute to either of these decisions (Chabris and Simons 2010; Lehr 2009). Although no scientific study can prove or disprove a particular cause of a specific historical event, our results show that Conley's claim that he did not see the beating of Michael Cox, the claim that led to his indictment and conviction, might well have been truthful.

References

Chabris C, Simons D, 2010 *The Invisible Gorilla, and Other Ways Our Intuitions Deceive Us* (New York, NY: Crown)

Haines R F, 1991 "A breakdown in simultaneous information processing" in *Presbyopia Research* Eds G Obrecht, L W Stark (New York, NY: Plenum Press)

Hyman Jr I E, Boss S M, Wise B M, McKenzie K E, Caggiano J M, 2010 "Did you see the unicycling clown? Inattentional blindness while walking and talking on a cell phone" *Applied Cognitive Psychology* **24** 597–607 doi:10.1002/acp.1638

Jensen M, Simons D J, 2009 "The effects of individual differences and task difficulty on inattentional blindness" *Psychonomic Bulletin & Review* **16** 398–403 doi:10.3758/PBR.16.2.398

Lehr D, 2009 *The Fence: A Police Cover-up Along Boston's Racial Divide* (New York, NY: Harper-Collins)

Levin D T, Angelone B L, 2008 "The visual metacognition questionnaire: A measure of intuitions about vision" *The American Journal of Psychology* **121** 451–472 doi:10.2307/20445476

Mack A, Rock I, 1998 *Inattentional Blindness* (Cambridge, MA: MIT Press)

Most S B, Simons D J, Scholl B J, Jimenez R, Clifford E, Chabris C F, 2000 "How not to be seen: The contribution of similarity and selective ignoring to sustained inattentional blindness" *Psychological Science* **12** 9–17 doi:10.1111/1467-9280.00303

Neisser U, 1979 "The control of information pickup in selective looking" in *Perception and its Development: A Tribute to Eleanor J Gibson* Ed. A D Pick pp 201–219 (Hillsdale, NJ: Lawrence Erlbaum Associates)

Simons D J, 2010 "Monkeying around with the gorillas in our midst: Familiarity with an inattentional-blindness task does not improve the detection of unexpected events" *i-Perception* **1** 3–6 doi:10.1068/i0386

Simons D J, Chabris C F, 1999 "Gorillas in our midst: Sustained inattentional blindness for dynamic events" *Perception* **28** 1059–1074 doi:10.1068/p2952

Critical Thinking

1. If inattentional blindness commonly occurs, what does that say about the accuracy of eyewitness testimony? What is the consequence of not seeing what is before us?

2. Thinking about the concept of attentional load, how might that influence a student's ability to effectively study? How would a person know if he or she was in the midst of a high or low attentional load?

Create Central

www.mhhe.com/createcentral

Internet References

Dan Simons

www.dansimons.com/research.html

Inattentional blindness and conspicuity

www.visualexpert.com/Resources/inattentionalblindness.html

Acknowledgements—These studies were approved by the Union College Human Subjects Research Committee. Michael Corti, Joseph Dammann, Elon Gaffin-Cahn, Alexander Katz, Andrew McKeegan, Corey Milan, Timothy Riddell, and Jacob Schneider, all students at Union College who played the roles of the runner and the fighters, and otherwise assisted in the execution of these studies. Diana Goodman, Allie Litt, Lisa McManus, Robyn Schneiderman, and Rachel Scott provided suggestions for the design of these studies during a seminar course at Union College. Dick Lehr's brilliant journalism made us aware of the Boston case of Michael Cox and Kenny Conley and the possibility that inattentional blindness was involved in it. CFC designed and conducted the research, analyzed the data, and drafted the manuscript. AW helped to design and conduct the research. MF helped to conduct the research. DJS contributed to the research design and edited the manuscript.

Article   Prepared by: R. Eric Landrum, *Boise State University*

Rethinking Motion Sickness

Peter Andrey Smith

Learning Outcomes

After reading this article, you will be able to:

- Better understand the reasons for motion sickness.

- Explain the role of the vestibular system as a possible explanation for motion sickness.

In a cavernous basement laboratory at the University of Minnesota, Thomas Stoffregen thrusts another unwitting study subject—well, me—into the "moving room." The chamber has a concrete floor and three walls covered in faux marble. As I stand in the middle, on a pressure-sensitive sensor about the size of a bathroom scale, the walls lurch inward by about a foot, a motion so disturbing that I throw up my arms and stumble backward. Indeed, the demonstration usually throws adults completely off balance.

I'm getting off lightly. Dr. Stoffregen, a professor of kinesiology, uses the apparatus to study motion sickness, and often subjects must stand and endure subtle computer-driven oscillations in the walls until they are dizzy and swaying. Dr. Stoffregen's research has also taken him on cruises—cruise ships are to motion sickness what hospitals are to pneumonia.

"No one's ever vomited in our lab," he said. "But our cruises are a different story."

For decades now, Dr. Stoffregen, 56, director of the university's Affordance Perception-Action Laboratory, has been amassing evidence in support of a surprising theory about the causes of motion sickness. The problem does not arise in the inner ear, he believes, but rather in a disturbance in the body's system for maintaining posture. The idea, once largely ignored, is beginning to gain grudging recognition.

"Most theories say when you get motion sick, you lose your equilibrium," said Robert Kennedy, a psychology professor at the University of Central Florida. "Stoffregen says because you lose your equilibrium, you get motion sick."

Motion sickness is probably a problem as old as passive transportation. The word "nausea" derives from the Greek for "boat," but the well-known symptoms arise from a variety of stimuli: lurching on the back of a camel, say, or riding the Tilt-a-Whirl at a fair. "Pandemonium," the perpetually seasick Charles Darwin called it.

No definitive explanation for it exists. In 1977, Dr. Michel Treisman, a psychologist at the University of Oxford, proposed that motion sickness may have evolved as a way to cope with food poisoning. If taste or the gut's chemosensory system fail to detect a toxin in a meal, he said, then perhaps the dizziness, loss of coordination, and vomiting exist as a fallback system.

Whatever its origins, Dr. Stoffregen said motion sickness may worsen with the proliferation of digital devices and displays. We travel turbulent skies; we bury our noses in smartphones, play video games on moving buses. Anecdotal reports suggest that Google Glass and Apple's latest software update, iOS7, can induce motion sickness. Dr. Stoffregen has published research on young adults who get queasy, or not, in front of an Xbox or PlayStation.

Despite its prevalence, Charles M. Oman, the director of the Man Vehicle Lab at M.I.T., said, "There has been relatively little research on nausea, vomiting and motion sickness in the modern era. Most of the research is 30 or 50 years old."

Dr. Oman believes that neuroscience may confirm the traditional explanation, known as the sensory conflict theory, which holds that motion sickness arises because of a conflict in the inner ear when the perception of movement in the brain doesn't match stored patterns.

It's generally accepted that a functioning vestibular system is a prerequisite for motion sickness: An unlikely study published in 1968, for example, found that deaf participants did not experience seasickness on a narrow, wooden boat in 40-foot swells off the shore of Nova Scotia.

Dr. Stoffregen rejects the theory, which, he says, fails to explain why women are more prone to motion sickness than men or why it's harder to stomach being a passenger than a driver. He argues that humans become nauseated in situations where they have not yet learned strategies effective in maintaining a stable posture.

The body has a subtle, natural wobble, or "postural sway." In one study, he found that the more a video game player's head swayed, the more likely he was afterward to experience symptoms of motion sickness. In another small study, pregnant women who experienced morning sickness also exhibited more swaying.

A boxer's postural sway before a bout can predict whether he will feel sick after a few punches to the head, Dr. Stoffregen has reported. Similarly, undergrads prone to seasickness showed more body sway on dry land before embarking on a semester at sea. Widening one's stance reduced the swaying and the risk of motion sickness.

Simply put, Dr. Stoffregen believes that new movement patterns must be learned, and until they are, the body's posture-maintenance system rebels—along with the stomach. Some people adapt more quickly.

Still, like the common cold, there may be no single explanation for motion sickness. Neither he nor anyone else has explained why there should be any subjective consequences to getting in a car, or why we maintain a lifelong talent for riding a bicycle while even experienced sailors struggle at sea after months on land.

Current treatments for motion sickness do little more than induce drowsiness, Dr. Stoffregen said. On a recent cruise, the crew spent two days wondering where he'd disappeared to.

He was in his room, another scientist laid low by the very thing he studies. He refuses to take Dramamine or any of the countless alternative treatments.

"I know they don't work for me. Not even as a placebo."

Critical Thinking

1. What might be some of the beneficial effects of motion sickness?

2. To what extent do you think motion sickness might impact the cruise industry? Explain.

Internet References

Dizziness and motion sickness
http://www.entnet.org/content/dizziness-and-motion-sickness

Motion sickness: Causes
http://www.nhs.uk/Conditions/Motion-sickness/Pages/Causes.aspx

Unit 4

UNIT

Learning

Prepared by: Eric Landrum, *Boise State University*

Do you remember your first week of college classes? There were so many new buildings and so many people's names to remember. You needed to remember accurately where all your classes were as well as your professors' names. Just remembering your class schedule was problematic enough. If you lived in a residence hall, you had to remember where your building was, recall the names of individuals living on your floor, and learn how to navigate from your room to other places on campus. Did you ever think you would survive college tests? The material, in terms of difficulty level and amount, was perhaps more than you thought you could manage, especially compared to high school. Or, it may be that it has been many years since you took tests in high school. What a stressful time you experienced when you first came to campus! Much of what created the stress was the strain on your learning and memory systems. Indeed, most students survive just fine—and with memories, learning strategies, and mental health intact.

Today, with their sophisticated experimental techniques, psychologists have identified several types of memory processes and have discovered what makes learning more efficient so that subsequent recall and recognition are more accurate. We also have discovered that humans aren't the only organisms capable of these processes. Nearly all types of animals can learn, even if the organism is as simple as an earthworm or amoeba.

You may be surprised to learn, though, that in addition to researching memory processes and the types of learning you most often experience in school, psychologists have spent a considerable amount of time and effort studying other types of learning, particularly classical conditioning, operant conditioning, and social learning. Classical conditioning is a form of learning that governs much of our involuntary responses to stimuli, such as environmental events and our emotions. Operant conditioning centers on how the consequences of our behavior shape and otherwise influence the frequency with which those behaviors subsequently occur and the circumstances under which they take place. Most of the time, these associations are beneficial to us, but sometimes individuals develop phobias, and operant conditioning can be used to help people "unlearn" the associations that result in irrational fears. Social learning happens when we learn from watching what other people do and how others' actions change the environment—that is, we sometimes learn vicariously from others.

Historically, psychologists used nonhuman laboratory animals as well as human participants to study learning processes. Such research has led to many widely accepted principles of learning that appear to be universal across many species. Although nonhuman laboratory research is still a popular area of psychological inquiry, many psychologists today test and extend the application of these principles to humans under a wide array of laboratory and non-laboratory settings. We explore these principles and their applications in the articles in this unit.

Article

Prepared by: Eric Landrum, *Boise State University*

Will Behave for Money

Contingency management—sometimes in the form of simply paying people to quit drugs or exercise more—is making the jump from small-scale studies to populationwide programs.

SADIE F. DINGFELDER

Learning Outcomes

After reading this article, you will be able to:

- Describe what is meant by a contingency management intervention.
- Explain the challenge of having positive behaviors continue after the termination of successful contingency management programs.

It was a chilly February day in Concord, N.H., and the audience of a hundred judges, prosecutors and probation officers facing psychologist Douglas Marlowe, JD, PhD, was perhaps even chillier. They'd invited him to speak because newly enacted legislation made it tough to incarcerate nonviolent addicted and mentally ill offenders. Instead, the criminal justice system would provide alternative programs, including drug courts that reward good behavior and punish missteps—a system that many of Marlowe's audience members viewed skeptically.

"I know what a lot of you are thinking right now: 'You want me to take these high-risk antisocial, addicted individuals and give them,'"—Marlowe switches to a mocking voice—*"positive reinforcement."* You're thinking, 'Why should I give them rewards for doing what the rest of us are legally, ethically and morally required to do anyway? Who rewards me for not breaking the law? Who rewards me for not doing drugs?' "But you have to remember there was a time in all your lives when people *did* reward you for doing simple, basic things. People applauded when you went poopie in the potty. . . . Your families did an extraordinarily good job of socializing you, and that is why you are all judges and lawyers and corrections officers today."

It's a talk Marlowe has given many times as chief of science, policy and law for the National Association of Drug Court Professionals. And it works, he says. If you remind people of their own learning histories, they become more receptive to the idea that even hardened criminals can change. Then, he tells them how to use psychology's fundamental laws of reinforcement to help drug-addicted offenders quit—the technique psychologists call contingency management.

For example, some judges send offenders to jail the first time they fail a urine test. But research shows that it's more effective to have gradually escalating penalties. Positive reinforcement—in the form of token gifts and pep-talks from judges—also improves abstinence and recidivism rates. But perhaps the most important quality of a good drug court is regular drug testing and swift consequences, Marlowe says.

"The courtroom is the perfect place to deliver a contingency management intervention," says Marlowe. "I think Skinner himself would have loved a courtroom where punishment and reward were delivered systematically."

The courtroom, however, is just one of many venues where psychologists are applying contingency management on a larger scale than ever before. After spending the better part of a century germinating in psychology labs, psychologist-designed programs are finally taking root in the wider world, especially in drug treatment programs and company wellness initiatives. The results, so far, are nothing short of staggering: Homeless people with HIV are remembering to take their medications, cocaine addicts are showing up to work on time and drug-free, and already healthy workers are becoming even healthier, by increasing their gym attendance and refilling prescriptions on time. As for drug courts, those that faithfully apply principles pioneered by B.F. Skinner are reducing recidivism by upward of 35 percent, according to a research review by Marlowe (in the *Chapman Journal of Criminal Justice*). That success has spurred a huge uptick in drug court participation nationwide, to the point that every state now offers drug courts, says Marlowe.

In essence, Skinner is scaling up.

"We're on the cusp of a new generation of contingency management," says Joshua Klapow, PhD, a public health professor and contingency management researcher at the University of Alabama at Birmingham. "We're taking mom-and-pop projects, designed for a few hundred people at most, and learning how to apply them to whole populations."

Pay to Play

Contingency management programs are often deceptively simple. Most reinforce good behavior by giving people cash or vouchers. For example, a program developed by James

Sorensen, PhD, a University of California, San Francisco, psychology professor, paid HIV-positive methadone patients for taking their antiretroviral medication. By giving 66 participants vouchers worth an average of $5 per day, Sorensen and his colleagues increased pill taking from 56 percent to 78 percent, according to a study published in *Drug and Alcohol Dependence* (Vol. 88, No. 1).

Getting people to take lifesaving medications may not seem like a major accomplishment, but many of the study's participants were homeless, which makes keeping track of medications—not to mention refrigerating them—difficult, Sorensen says. Previous attempts to increase medication compliance by getting people into housing and providing counseling were popular with patients, but didn't improve their medication taking.

"HIV is not the highest thing on your priority list when you are hungry and living without shelter," Sorensen says.

It may seem obvious that paying people will encourage them to do what you want—that is, after all, how all jobs work—but the details are critically important, Sorensen says. For instance, you can't just ask people if they took their medications; you have to objectively verify it and provide reinforcement as quickly as possible. To do that, Sorensen uses MEMS caps, medication bottles that record the time and date of every opening. Also, you don't just want to pay a flat rate—escalating payments for consecutive instances of good behavior are far more effective, according to more than a decade of research by Stephen Higgins, PhD, a psychology professor at the University of Vermont.

"You want people to be more invested as time goes on," Higgins says. That technique worked well in a 2010 study published in *Addiction*. In the study, 166 pregnant smokers provided a urine sample twice a week. If that sample showed no evidence of smoking, the woman earned a shopping voucher worth $6.25, a sum that grew by $1.25 for each consecutive clean sample. If a participant slipped, that reset the payments to $6.25, though participants could get back to their highest-previous payout for returning two more consecutive clean samples.

This payment system may seem complicated, but it helped 34 percent of the women quit smoking, compared with 7.4 percent in the control condition. It also resulted in healthier babies, with women in the incentive program having low-birth-weight infants only 6 percent of the time, compared with 19 percent in the control condition.

So, if contingency management is so effective, even with people who have otherwise intractable problems, what's the catch? They can be more expensive than treatment-as-usual, and many people worry about the ethics of paying some people to do what everyone else does for free. However, such qualms are lessening in the face of the growing health-care crisis, Higgins says.

"There is some resistance or discomfort with the concept of economic incentives, but people are beginning to see that we all pay for unhealthy behaviors anyway," he says. "If somebody is engaging in cigarette smoking, or not managing any chronic illness, or engaging in a sedentary lifestyle, we all end up paying for it through insurance pools, Medicaid or Medicare."

Secrets of Sustainability

Another criticism of contingency management programs is that, like most interventions, effects tend to fade after the program ends. For example, HIV-positive participants in Sorenson's study returned to taking their medications only half the time as soon as the study ended. One solution is to continue the program indefinitely—a tack which, while expensive, would save the health-care system money by reducing the spread of AIDS, Sorenson says.

Another solution is to have contingency management programs pay for themselves. That's the tack Kenneth Silverman, PhD, a psychology professor at Johns Hopkins School of Medicine, is taking. In his lab, drug-free urine samples are the price of admission to a data-entry workplace that pays an average of $10 an hour. The company, Johns Hopkins Data Services, provides its employees—all of whom have drug problems—with a higher base pay rate for workers for each consecutive clean urine sample and gives bonuses for good job performance.

Corporate and university clients defray the cost of the program, but it still requires grant money to run. As a result, people can only work at Johns Hopkins Data Services for the duration of a study—a few years, at most. However, three Maryland employers have expressed a willingness to hire program graduates, who would continue to take random drug tests as a condition of employment, says Anthony DeFulio, PhD, associate director of the program.

"We are harnessing the power of wages to maintain drug abstinence," DeFulio says.

Another way to fund contingency management programs is to have people pay for them themselves. That's the business model of the website www.stickK.com, where you set a goal for yourself and put a price on that goal—say, to lose a pound a week for $5 a week. If you meet your goal, you keep the money. If you don't, that $5 goes to what stickK.com founder Jordan Goldberg calls an "anti-charity," a group that you have identified that you strongly disagree with.

"If you're for gun control, you'll be extra-motivated to keep us from sending your money to the National Rifle Association," says Goldberg, adding that you can choose other consequences, such as betting against friends or sending money to causes you support. (The company makes money through advertising and corporate partnerships.)

These kinds of automated systems are driving the movement of contingency management from small-scale studies to major population-level applications, says Joe Schumacher, PhD, a professor of medicine and contingency management researcher at the University of Alabama at Birmingham.

"Incentive systems are going high-tech," he says.

Schumacher is best known for his work using contingency management to get homeless people with crack addictions to quit, but he's now extending that work to larger populations through a Birmingham-based company called ChipRewards.

ChipRewards recently collaborated with Chattanooga, Tenn., to create a program for 3,200 of the city's workers. They adapted software originally created for business loyalty programs to monitor how often employees, for example, go to the gym, refill prescriptions or attend preventative health screenings. The program automatically issues employees good-behavior points, which can be exchanged online for a variety of products.

That means the same computer program that encourages you to eat nine burritos to get one free may soon help you lose the weight you gained eating all those burritos.

ChipRewards has been hired by several large companies and is being used by more than 100,000 employees, says Klapow, ChipRewards' chief behavioral scientist. In the future, programs like his could create large-scale medication adherence programs for pharmacetical companies, since they stand to earn money if people remember to refill their prescriptions. Adherence also helps people better manage chronic illness and reduces the nation's health-care costs, Klapow says.

Of course, not everyone is enthusiastic about the idea of having companies electronically monitor and reward healthy behaviors. It's one thing to use contingency management to help people with drug addictions, but it's quite another to apply these programs to the wider population, says George Loewenstein, PhD, a behavioral economics professor at Carnegie Mellon University.

A case in point, he says, is weight loss. We can pay people to eat more healthfully—in fact, he did just that in a randomized controlled trial in the June *Journal of General Internal Medicine.* In the study, participants in the contingency management condition lost an average of eight more pounds than people in the control condition. But to address widespread obesity, it's better to lower the cost of fresh fruits and vegetables and raise the cost of processed food, he says.

"Contingency management tackles the problem at the individual level, but we risk losing sight of the real underlying causes of the problem and possibly even blaming the victim," he says.

Then, there's the larger issue of free will. As contingency management systems spread, will we begin to see ourselves as nothing more than rats in Skinner boxes?

"There's the potential of going overboard," Loewenstein says. "Ending up in a 'Walden Two'-type society doesn't seem like such a great outcome to me."

Critical Thinking

1. What is positive reinforcement, and what is the ultimate intended effect of positive reinforcement on a particular behavior of interest?

2. How are drug courts using the principles of contingency management to change the behavior of drug offenders?

3. To what extent are the roots of behavioral problems explored within contingency management scenarios?

Create Central

www.mhhe.com/createcentral

Internet References

Game-based contingency management for smoking cessation
www.c4tbh.org/the-center/what-we-re-up-to/active-projects/game-based-contingency-management-for-smoking-cessation.html

Reward programs help smokers quit, research shows
www.rti.org/newsroom/news.cfm?obj=F63D3E6B-5056-B100-0C72F10915811617

Article   Prepared by: Eric Landrum, *Boise State University*

Phobias: The Rationale behind Irrational Fears

DEAN BURNETT

Learning Outcomes

After reading this article, you will be able to:

- Identify some of the basic types of phobias and their formal names.
- Consider the difficulty in diagnosing phobias.

Recently, this section featured an article about the tarantula *Typhochlaena costae*. While the piece was very interesting, this was likely lost on some readers, as it's difficult to focus on details while distracted by the sound of your own screaming.

Arachnophobia is one of the more well-known phobias and can be very potent. Searching the science section for some lunchtime reading is not the sort of activity that typically includes spiders, so to be suddenly confronted, apropos of nothing, by an image of a humungous tarantula probably caught many unawares. How many tablets/phones/laptops were ruined due to being hurled across the room in a panic?

Most would consider this an overreaction. Granted, there are many dangerous species of spider (I'd link to examples but can't find any without pictures, and I'm not a hypocrite) but the odds of encountering one are, in the UK at least, vanishingly small. And even then, the biggest spider is physically no match for a person; a rolled up newspaper is not considered a lethal weapon among humans. Arachnophobes substantially outnumber people who have been genuinely injured by spiders, and yet the irrational fear of spiders is commonplace.

What scares people often makes little logical sense. As I do stand-up comedy on occasion, I'm regularly told I'm "incredibly brave," yet all I'm doing is saying words in front of people. The people who tell me I'm brave think nothing of driving, an often fatal practice. But when you do genuinely fear something for no rational reason, then you may have a phobia.

Phobias are psychologically interesting. There are three possible types: specific phobias, social phobias and agoraphobia. Agoraphobia isn't just a fear of open spaces; it describes a fear of any situation where escape would be difficult and/or help wouldn't be forthcoming. The fact that most such situations occur outside the sufferer's home results in them not going out much, which is probably where the "open spaces" confusion comes from.

Specific phobias are probably the most recognised. Specific phobias are an irrational fear of a specific thing or situation. Specific phobias can be further subdivided into situational (eg claustrophobia), natural environment (eg acrophobia), animal (eg the aforementioned arachnophobia) or blood-injection-injury types (eg … blood and injections, I guess). You could still have a phobia which doesn't fit any of these descriptors though. Maybe you've got an irrational fear of being categorised? If so, sorry.

Social phobias are where you have an irrational fear of how people will react to you in a situation. The fear of rejection or judgement from others is a powerful force for humans; much of how we think and behave is calibrated around the views and behaviours of others. There's a whole discipline about it. People value the views of others differently of course. One way to reduce the value you place on the opinions of strangers is to read the comments on the internet. Any comments, anywhere.

How do we even develop a fear that is by definition irrational? One explanation is classical conditioning; you experience something bad involving a thing, you associate the bad experience with that thing, then you become afraid of that thing. But clever humans can also learn by observation; you see your mother panicking frantically in response to a wasp when you're a child, you'll likely be afraid of wasps too.

If we are given enough (possibly inaccurate) information, we may just "figure out" things are scary via instructional fear acquisition. Certain horror films are particularly good at this, presenting everyday things like birds as things to be feared, associations which stay with people for a long time. The Final Destination series is particularly cruel in that it tries to make people terrified of "not dying". We may even have evolved to acquire some phobias. Research has shown that primates tend to learn to fear snakes very quickly when compared to other stimuli. If you're evolving in an environment where snakes are a genuine but subtle threat, this tendency would help no doubt. It might explain the spider thing too.

Not so sure about aerophobia though, we probably didn't need to worry about that on the African Savannah.

What can you do about this? It's not like those with phobias aren't aware of them. One of the criteria in the DSM-IV for diagnosing phobias is that the sufferer is aware of the irrational nature of their fear. There are a lot of brain regions involved, like the insular cortex and amygdala. And you can't simply make someone encounter the thing they're afraid of to show them it's harmless. As far as the brain is concerned, the fear response IS a negative physical consequence, so on a subconscious level the phobia is self-fulfilling.

There are methods of treating phobias if they're genuinely debilitating. Systematic desensitisation is one approach (where the source of the phobia is introduced in easily-managed stages), cognitive behavioural therapy, even antidepressants if all else fails.

It's different if you're talking about things like homophobia or Islamophobia, as often these are more likely to be misleadingly named prejudices than genuine phobias. There are fewer options for treating these though; science has tackled many psychological conditions, but there's still no known cure for being a dick.

Critical Thinking

1. How do you think psychologists distinguish between a rational fear and an irrational fear? Think about snakes—could there be both rational fears and irrational fears? Explain.

2. How do different social phobias impact how a person acts around others? Are there sometimes hidden benefits to phobias? Explain.

Create Central

www.mhhe.com/createcentral

Internet References

The rationale behind the irrational
www.smh.com.au/lifestyle/life/the-rationale-behind-the-irrational-20130730-2qw5h.html

Why do people have phobias?
http://io9.com/5881188/why-do-people-have-phobias

Article   Prepared by: R. Eric Landrum, *Boise State University*

Incentives for Drivers Who Avoid Traffic Jams

John Markoff

Learning Outcomes

After reading this article, you will be able to:

- Understand how behaviorism principles can be used to relieve traffic jams and parking congestion.
- Appreciate the social networking approach to changing the behavior of large numbers of individuals.

London, Singapore, Stockholm, and a few other cities around the world battle heavy traffic with a "congestion charge," a stiff fee for driving in crowded areas at peak hours. But drivers generally hate the idea, and efforts to impose it in this country have failed.

Balaji Prabhakar, a professor of computer science at Stanford University, thinks he has a better way.

A few years ago, trapped in an unending traffic jam in Bangalore, India, he reflected that there was more than one way to get drivers to change their behavior. Congestion charges are sticks; why not try a carrot?

So this spring, with a $3 million research grant from the federal Department of Transportation, Stanford deployed a new system designed by Dr. Prabhakar's group. Called Capri, for Congestion and Parking Relief Incentives, it allows people driving to the notoriously traffic-clogged campus to enter a daily lottery, with a chance to win up to an extra $50 in their paycheck, just by shifting their commute to off-peak times.

The program has proved so popular that it is to be expanded soon to also cover parking.

Amaya Odiaga, the director of business operations for Stanford's physical education department, now drives to campus a few minutes earlier and says she has won just $15. But a co-worker got $50—creating a competitive atmosphere that makes the program fun, Ms. Odiaga said.

Better yet, Ms. Odiaga's commute now takes as little as 7 minutes, down from 25 minutes at peak hours.

Dr. Prabhakar is a specialist in designing computer networks and has conducted a variety of experiments in using incentives to get people to change their behavior in driving, taking public transit, parking, and even adopting a more active lifestyle. Unlike congestion pricing, which is mandatory for everyone and usually requires legislation, "incentives can be started incrementally and are voluntary," he said.

Moreover, systems based on incentives can offer a huge advantage in simplicity. Until recently, the Stanford system required sensors around campus to detect signals from radio-frequency identification tags that participants carried in their cars. But the need for such an infrastructure has vanished now that so many drivers carry smartphones with GPS chips or other locaters.

Administrators can use the network to set up a centralized web-based service to manage any number of incentive campaigns.

"Through smartphones we're getting more at ease about fine-grained information about space and time," said Frank Kelly, a mathematician at the University of Cambridge in England who specializes in traffic networks. "This is possible because information and communications systems are becoming cheaper and cheaper."

Samuel I. Schwartz, a transportation consultant and former New York City traffic commissioner, says a smartphone-based system is inevitable, though he predicts that it will be used for congestion pricing as well as incentives.

"Ultimately we will be charged, or money will be added to our accounts, by using the cloud infrastructure," he said.

"It's so precise that you will be able to charge people for how much of Fifth Avenue they use and for how long a period. In Christmas season, you may decide to charge them $10 to use Fifth Avenue for each block."

In New York City, Mayor Michael R. Bloomberg's plan for congestion pricing died in 2008 for lack of support from the state Legislature. Pravin Varaiya, an expert on transportation systems at the University of California, Berkeley, said enforcement costs would have been "huge," adding that "carrots, as opposed to sticks, frequently work very well."

Still, Charles Komanoff, a transportation expert who has designed a computer model of New York traffic, said he had reservations about such a system as an alternative to congestion pricing.

"The incentives will be far too small," he wrote in an e-mail, adding: "You really do need big disincentives (big sticks). Little carrots won't do the job of changing drivers' decisions" in New York or in San Francisco.

Dr. Prabhakar said congestion pricing and his incentive system need not be mutually exclusive, and he noted that highway congestion was an example of "nonlinear" behavior, in which even a small reduction in vehicles at a given time—10 percent or less—can have a big effect on traffic flow.

And conversely, added Dr. Kelly, the mathematician, "when the system is close to critical levels, very small increases in traffic can create time delays for everyone."

Dr. Prabhakar's experiments have offered different kinds of incentives, from airline-style reward points to lottery cash prizes. Now his system is poised to reach a much larger audience.

Singapore is considering a system he and his students designed that offers lottery participation or a fare discount to public transit riders who travel at off-peak times. A trial run begun in January lowered rush-hour ridership by more than 10 percent. (Given a choice between discounts and lottery, riders overwhelmingly chose the lottery.)

Bill Reinert, an advanced technology manager at Toyota, says incentives are no panacea. "Incentives the government gives you" to buy hybrid vehicles "are a good way not to establish markets," he said. But he added: "Do incentives work? Yes. I fly 300,000 miles a year on United."

The Stanford experiment adds a social network component to the lottery, in effect making it a game where friends can observe one another's "good" behavior. The researchers say this tends to reinforce changes in behavior and individual commitment. Next fall, the university plans to expand the system to encourage people to park farther from the busiest parking structures.

The idea of using incentives to change social and personal behavior has grown increasingly popular. In their 2008 book *Nudge: Improving Decisions About Health, Wealth and Happiness*, the economist Richard H. Thaler and the legal scholar Cass R. Sunstein argued that organizational structures could be created that guide people toward better behavior.

Dr. Thaler noted that variable tolls, like those used on the Hudson River crossings in New York at different times of day, "are clearly an attempt to shift people's incentives." Of traffic systems like Stanford's, he said, "this is just as efficient."

Dr. Prabhakar's first experiment was in Bangalore in 2008, when he created a system to encourage employees at the software company Infosys to choose different travel times to its suburban campus. The system significantly lowered congestion.

More recently, he worked with Accenture, a business services company, to set up a system that used pedometers to measure the number of footsteps more than 3,000 employees took each day, encouraging them to walk more for better health. The campaign, called "Steptacular," included a social network component and a web-based game to add a random element to the incentives; it handed out $238,000 in rewards.

Dr. Prabhakar said the power of his method was that only a small change could have a drastic effect.

"This is one of the nicer problems," he said. "You don't have to change everyone's behavior; in fact, it's better if you don't."

Critical Thinking

1. Compare the carrot vs. the stick approaches to relieving parking congesting. What are the pros and cons of each approach?

2. How might gamification principles combined with health-related goals (such as increased exercise) be used to achieve health improvements?

Internet References

How to unjam traffic
http://www.slate.com/articles/health_and_science/transportation/2013/08/traffic_stopping_technologies_waze_smart_traffic_lights_road_trains_and.html

Incentives for drivers who avoid traffic jams
http://www.nytimes.com/2012/06/12/science/experimental-campaigns-pay-drivers-to-avoid-rush-hour-traffic.html?pagewanted=all&_r=0

Article Prepared by: R. Eric Landrum, *Boise State University*

You Have No Idea What Happened

Maria Konnikova

Learning Outcomes

After reading this article, you will be able to:

- Know the definition of "flashbulb memory."
- Understand the role of the hippocampus in the consolidation of memories.
- Appreciate the connection between memory accuracy and the role that eyewitness testimony plays in the legal system.

R. T. first heard about the *Challenger* explosion as she and her roommate sat watching television in their Emory University dorm room. A news flash came across the screen, shocking them both. R. T., visibly upset, raced upstairs to tell another friend the news. Then she called her parents. Two and a half years after the event, she remembered it as if it were yesterday: the TV, the terrible news, the call home. She could say with absolute certainty that that's precisely how it happened. Except, it turns out, none of what she remembered was accurate.

R. T. was a student in a class taught by Ulric Neisser, a cognitive psychologist who had begun studying memory in the seventies. Early in his career, Neisser became fascinated by the concept of flashbulb memories—the times when a shocking, emotional event seems to leave a particularly vivid imprint on the mind. William James had described such impressions, in 1890, as "so exciting emotionally as almost to leave a *scar* upon the cerebral tissues."

The day following the explosion of the *Challenger,* in January, 1986, Neisser, then a professor of cognitive psychology at Emory, and his assistant, Nicole Harsch, handed out a questionnaire about the event to the hundred and six students in their ten o'clock psychology 101 class, "Personality Development." Where were the students when they heard the news? Whom were they with? What were they doing? The professor and his assistant carefully filed the responses away.

In the fall of 1988, two and a half years later, the questionnaire was given a second time to the same students. It was then that R. T. recalled, with absolute confidence, her dorm-room experience. But when Neisser and Harsch compared the two sets of answers, they found barely any similarities. According to R. T.'s first recounting, she'd been in her religion class when she heard some students begin to talk about an explosion. She didn't know any details of what had happened, "except that it had exploded and the schoolteacher's students had all been watching, which I thought was sad." After class, she went to her room, where she watched the news on TV, by herself, and learned more about the tragedy.

R. T. was far from alone in her misplaced confidence. When the psychologists rated the accuracy of the students' recollections for things like where they were and what they were doing, the average student scored less than three on a scale of seven. A quarter scored zero. But when the students were asked about their confidence levels, with five being the highest, they averaged 4.17. Their memories were vivid, clear—and wrong. There was no relationship at all between confidence and accuracy.

At the time of the *Challenger* explosion, Elizabeth Phelps was a graduate student at Princeton University. After learning about the *Challenger* study, and other work on emotional memories, she decided to focus her career on examining the questions raised by Neisser's findings. Over the past several decades, Phelps has combined Neisser's experiential approach with the neuroscience of emotional memory to explore how such memories work, and why they work the way they do. She has been, for instance, one of the lead collaborators of an ongoing longitudinal study of memories from the attacks of 9/11, where confidence and accuracy judgments have, over the years, been complemented by a neuroscientific study of the subjects' brains as they make their memory determinations. Her hope is to understand how, exactly, emotional memories behave at all stages of the remembering process: how we encode them, how we consolidate and store them, how we retrieve them. When we met recently in her New York University lab to discuss her latest study, she told me that she has concluded that memories of emotional events do indeed differ substantially from regular memories. When it comes to the central details of the event, like that the *Challenger* exploded, they are clearer and more accurate. But when it comes to peripheral details, they are worse. And our confidence in them, while almost always strong, is often misplaced.

Within the brain, memories are formed and consolidated largely due to the help of a small seahorse-like structure called the hippocampus; damage the hippocampus, and you damage the ability to form lasting recollections. The hippocampus is located next to a small almond-shaped structure that is central to the encoding of emotion, the amygdala. Damage that, and basic responses such as fear, arousal, and excitement disappear or become muted.

A key element of emotional-memory formation is the direct line of communication between the amygdala and the visual cortex. That close connection, Phelps has shown, helps the amygdala, in a sense, tell our eyes to pay closer attention at moments of heightened emotion. So we look carefully, we study, and we stare—giving the hippocampus a richer set of inputs to work with. At these moments of arousal, the amygdala may also signal to the hippocampus that it needs to pay special attention to encoding this particular moment. These three parts of the brain work together to insure that we firmly encode memories at times of heightened arousal, which is why emotional memories are stronger and more precise than other, less striking ones. We don't really remember an uneventful day the way that we remember a fight or a first kiss. In one study, Phelps tested this notion in her lab, showing people a series of images, some provoking negative emotions, and some neutral. An hour later, she and her colleagues tested their recall for each scene. Memory for the emotional scenes was significantly higher, and the vividness of the recollection was significantly greater.

When we met, Phelps had just published her latest work, an investigation into how we retrieve emotional memories, which involved collaboration with fellow N.Y.U. neuroscientist Lila Davachi and post-doctoral student Joseph Dunsmoor. In the experiment, the results of which appeared in *Nature* in late January, a group of students was shown a series of sixty images that they had to classify as either animals or tools. All of the images—ladders, kangaroos, saws, horses—were simple and unlikely to arouse any emotion. After a short break, the students were shown a different sequence of animals and tools. This time, however, some of the pictures were paired with an electric shock to the wrist: two out of every three times you saw a tool, for instance, you would be shocked. Next, each student saw a third set of animals and tools, this time without any shocks. Finally, each student received a surprise memory

test. Some got the test immediately after the third set of images, some, six hours later, and some, a day later.

What Dunsmoor, Phelps, and Davachi found came as a surprise: it wasn't just the memory of the "emotional" images (those paired with shocks) that received a boost. It was also the memory of all similar images—even those that had been presented in the beginning. That is, if you were shocked when you saw animals, your memory of the *earlier* animals was also enhanced. And, more important, the effect only emerged after six or twenty-four hours: the memory needed time to consolidate. "It turns out that emotion retroactively enhances memory," Davachi said. "Your mind selectively reaches back in time for other, similar things." That would mean, for instance, that after the *Challenger* explosion people would have had better memory for all space-related news in the prior weeks.

The finding was surprising, but also understandable. Davachi gave me an example from everyday life. A new guy starts working at your company. A week goes by, and you have a few uninteresting interactions. He seems nice enough, but you're busy and not paying particularly close attention. On Friday, in the elevator, he asks you out. Suddenly, the details of all of your prior encounters resurface and consolidate in your memory. They have retroactively gone from unremarkable to important, and your brain has adjusted accordingly. Or, in a more negative guise, if you're bitten by a dog in a new neighborhood, your memory of all the dogs that you had seen since moving there might improve.

So, if memory for events is strengthened at emotional times, why does everyone forget what they were doing when the *Challenger* exploded? While the memory of the event itself is enhanced, Phelps explains, the vividness of the memory of the central event tends to come at the expense of the details. We experience a sort of tunnel vision, discarding all the details that seem incidental to the central event.

In the same 2011 study in which Phelps showed people either emotionally negative or neutral images, she also included a second element: each scene was presented within a frame, and, from scene to scene, the color of the frames would change. When it came to the emotional images, memory of color ended up being significantly worse than memory of neutral scenes. Absent the pull of a central, important event, the students took in more peripheral details. When aroused, they blocked the minor details out.

The strength of the central memory seems to make us confident of all of the details when we should only be confident of a few. Because the shock or other negative emotion helps us to remember the animal (or the explosion), we think we also remember the color (or the call to our parents). "You just feel you know it better," Phelps says. "And even when we tell them they're mistaken people still don't buy it."

Our misplaced confidence in recalling dramatic events is troubling when we need to rely on a memory for something important—evidence in court, for instance. For now, juries tend to trust the confident witness: she knows what she saw. But that may be changing. Phelps was recently asked to sit on a committee for the National Academy of Sciences to make recommendations about eyewitness testimony in trials. After reviewing the evidence, the committee made several concrete suggestions to changes in current procedures, including "blinded" eyewitness identification (that is, the person showing potential suspects to the witness shouldn't know which suspect the witness is looking at at any given moment, to avoid giving subconscious cues), standardized instructions to witnesses, along with extensive police training in vision and memory research as it relates to eyewitness testimony, videotaped identification, expert testimony early on in trials about the issues surrounding eyewitness reliability, and early and clear jury instruction on any prior identifications (when and how prior suspects were identified, how confident the witness was at first, and the like). If the committee's conclusions are taken up, the way memory is treated may, over time, change from something unshakeable to something much less valuable to a case. "Something that is incredibly adaptive normally may not be adaptive somewhere like the courtroom," Davachi says. "The goal of memory isn't to keep the details. It's to be able to generalize from what you know so that you are more confident in acting on it." You run away from the dog that looks like the one that bit you, rather than standing around questioning how accurate your recall is.

"The implications for trusting our memories, and getting others to trust them, are huge," Phelps says. "The more we learn about emotional memory, the more we realize that we can never say what someone will or won't remember given a particular set of circumstances." The best we can do, she says, is to err on the side of caution: unless we are talking about the most central part of the recollection, assume that our confidence is misplaced. More often than not, it is.

Critical Thinking

1. With flashbulb memories, the accuracy of the memory can be quite low, but the confidence can be high. Can you think of other situations in which a college student might have over-confidence, and what might be the effect of that over-confidence?

2. After an emotional image is presented to a participant in a research session, not only are memories heightened for that image, but that event enhances memories for images presented before the key emotional image. How does that work?

3. Based on the information presented in this article, if you wanted to remember a key fact for a long time, what would be the best way to ensure your memory for that fact? Explain.

Internet References

Do you really remember where you were on 9/11?
http://www.livescience.com/15914-flashbulb-memory-september-11.html

Flashbulb memory in psychology: Definition and examples
http://study.com/academy/lesson/flashbulb-memory-in-psychology-definition-examples.html

The consistency of flashbulb memories
https://www.psychologytoday.com/blog/ulterior-motives/201506/the-consistency-flashbulb-memories

Article   Prepared by: R. Eric Landrum, *Boise State University*

A 'Learning' Attitude Helps Boost Job Search Success

SCOTT SLEEK, ALEXANDRA MICHEL, AND ANNA MIKULAK

Learning Outcomes

After reading this article, you will be able to:

- Appreciate that in some situations, stress can be helpful.

- Understand that how a person perceives the stress can be related to how the stress affects the person.

- Comprehend the benefit effect of learning from failure when continuing to persevere toward an ultimate goal.

For most jobseekers, the job hunt is no picnic— disappointment, rejection, and desperation seem to have become hallmarks of the typical job search. It's common to hear stories of job hunters who have submitted hundreds of applications before getting a single interview.

No one will argue that looking for a new job isn't stressful, but new research finds that the way people manage and channel this stress could have a big impact on their ultimate success.

Psychological scientists Serge da Motta Veiga from Lehigh University and Daniel Turban of the University of Missouri found that people who viewed their job hunt as an opportunity to learn may increase their odds of successfully landing a job.

The researchers spent 3 months tracking a group of 120 college seniors just getting ready to hit the job market for the first time. While on the search for full-time employment, students completed surveys every other week assessing their levels of stress, mood, and job search activities.

While we may tend to think of stress as [a] bad thing, that's not always the case. Given the right circumstances, a moderate amount of stress can actually help motivate people to accomplish their goals. The researchers hypothesized that an attitude focused on learning—known as a learning goal orientation (LGO)—would help jobseekers deal with rejection and stress in ways that actually helped them accomplish their goals.

While the students high in LGO were dealing with the same kind of stress as students low in LGO, they showed big differences in how they responded to stress and rejection. As expected, regardless of whether their job search was stressful and frustrating or going well, students high in LGO tended to maintain a productive job search strategy.

People lower in LGO may see a lack of progress as a sign of personal failure, tempting them to give up trying altogether. In contrast, da Motta Veiga and Turban found that people high in LGO are more likely to react to disappointment by working harder and finding new ways to tackle problems, ultimately helping them maintain the motivation necessary to succeed.

"Because individuals with higher learning goal orientation see ability as something that can be developed, they are likely to respond to adverse events with increased effort following perceived failure," da Motta Veiga and Turban write in the journal *Organizational Behavior and Human Decision Processes*.

If they felt like the job search was going well, students low in LGO tended to slack off and decrease their job search efforts. Those with a high learning focus, on the other hand, maintained or even increased the intensity of their job search when they felt like things were going well.

This study did not track the students' ultimate success in getting hired. However, previous research has demonstrated that the perseverance shown by individuals high in LGO can result in real-world payoffs in the job market.

Another study looking at 245 unemployed adult job seekers led by Gera Noordzij of Erasmus University Rotterdam found that not only did high learning orientation help people land a job, it was also something that could be effectively taught.

One group of unemployed adults received training in developing a learning-goal orientation, while another group received a standard employment training.

Rather than viewing rejection as an insurmountable problem, LGO training helped jobseekers see it as something that they could successfully learn from. This, in turn, led them to better manage stress and resulted in higher rates of reemployment compared to the comparison group.

"Job seekers, who think they can learn from failure and who are more aware of different strategies, were found to be more likely to plan job-search activities, resulting in higher probabilities to find a job," they conclude in the journal *Personnel Psychology.*

References

da Motta Veiga, S. P., & Turban, D. B. (2014). Are affect and perceived stress detrimental or beneficial to job seekers? The role of learning goal orientation in job search self-regulation. *Organizational Behavior and Human Decision Processes,* 125(2), 193–203. doi:10.1016/j.obhdp.2014.09.007

Noordzij, G., Hooft, E. A., Mierlo, H., Dam, A., & Born, M. P. (2013). The Effects of a Learning-Goal Orientation Training on Self-Regulation: A Field Experiment Among Unemployed Job Seekers. *Personnel Psychology,* 66(3), 723–755. doi: 10.1111/peps.12011

Critical Thinking

1. Under what other conditions might stress have a positive outcome? [Note that this is sometimes referred to as eustress.]

2. What are the strategies that job seekers follow when they are classified as having a high learning goal orientation (LGO)? Explain.

3. The authors claim that a learning goal orientation with regards to job searchers could be taught. What types of techniques do you think would be used in that kind of teaching-learning scenario? Why?

Internet References

A job search structured = excellent learning experience
http://www.job-hunt.org/job-search-for-new-grads/job-search-learning-experience.shtml

How to overcome job-search misery
http://money.usnews.com/money/careers/articles/2015/08/24/how-to-overcome-job-search-misery

Six steps to job search success
https://netimpact.org/careers/six-steps-to-job-search-success

Article   Prepared by: R. Eric Landrum, *Boise State University*

B.F. Skinner at Harvard

GREGORY A. BRIKER

Learning Outcomes

After reading this article, you will be able to:

- Appreciate the historical significance of B.F. Skinner's significant time spent at Harvard University.

- Understand the fundamental, foundational principle of behaviorism.

- Relate the occurrence of superstitious behavior to some of Skinner's operant conditioning principles.

Long before there were grab and go lunches and weekly pub trivia nights, slot machines, and pianos filled the basement of Memorial Hall. The lucky gamblers and musicians were not students or faculty, but pigeons.

Established in 1948, the Harvard Pigeon Lab was one of the many Psychological Laboratories occupying the space below Sanders Theater. It was led by a newly tenured professor who had spent the last few years trying to create a pigeon-guided missile program for the U.S. military to use during World War II. Burrhus Frederic Skinner, known to the academic world as B.F. Skinner, would continue to experiment on pigeons, but his years at Harvard proved to be as dynamic and eclectic as his contributions to the fields of psychology and education.

Skinner's connection to Harvard began in 1928 when he enrolled in the graduate program in psychology within what was then the Department of Philosophy and Psychology. He split most of his time between Emerson Hall, where the department was located, and his house three blocks from the Yard on Harvard Street.

The path that brought Skinner to psychology was an unusual one. Jerome Kagan, Professor Emeritus of Psychology, recalled a lunch date with Skinner, in which the eminent psychologist noted, "when he was an undergraduate, he decided to be a writer because his main goal was to change the world. He had very high ambitions. He wanted to have an effect on the world and decided that writing was the best way to do it."

Everything changed for Skinner in his second half of college when, according to Kagan, "he read [John] Watson, who is the original behaviorist, and that persuaded him that if you want to change the world, becoming a psychologist was probably more effective."

Graduate school at Harvard for Skinner was an experience almost completely confined to academics. He would later write in his autobiography, "The Shaping of a Behaviorist," that "Harvard University takes little or no interest in the private lives of its graduate students," explaining that all matters of social and residential life were not of concern to the University. He would also reflect on the fact that graduate school pushed him harder than anything before, consuming nearly all of his daytime hours.

"At Harvard I entered upon the first strict regimen of my life," he wrote. "I would rise at six, study until breakfast, go to classes, laboratories, and libraries with no more than fifteen minutes unscheduled during the day, study until exactly nine o'clock at night, and go to bed. I saw no movies or plays, seldom went to concerts. I had scarcely any dates, and read only psychology and physiology."

Skinner soon became interested in behaviorism, a school of psychology more concerned with behaviors themselves than the unseen mental processes behind them. Kagan explained that behaviorism is rooted in the belief that in order to teach some behavior to an organism, "all we have to do is control the rewards, the desirable things that the animal or human wants, and punish the behaviors that we don't want. There's no mind, there are no thoughts, everything is behavior." Steven Pinker, Professor of Psychology, described behaviorism as "not a theory of psychology," but instead, "really a meta-theory or a philosophy of psychology."

While still a graduate student, Skinner invented the operant conditioning chamber, in which animals are taught certain behaviors by rewarding or punishing the animal's actions. Later known as the Skinner Box, the apparatus was instrumental in pursuing the study of operant conditioning, an alternative to the more widely studied classical conditioning à la Pavlov's dog.

Operant conditioning opened the door to a world of new theories and possibilities regarding control and learning. "What Skinner did was say, 'Well, if we really want to control behavior, we've got to control habits that are not innately biological,'" notes Kagan. "If you want to control what people do—control their aggression, control their work habits, control their study habits—that's all operant conditioning."

Skinner's years as a graduate student were spent surrounded by the giants of a field emerging as its own distinct science. He studied under professors like Henry Murray—the developer of a personality psychology called personology—and took classes alongside students like Fred Keller, who would become a renowned champion of scientific education reform. But despite contact with pioneering members of the field, Skinner largely took his own approach.

After passing his preliminary exams, Skinner all but ignored by-the-book psychology. He noted in his autobiography that upon reading through a copy of the *American Journal of Psychology,* he concluded "there must be a better way to find out what was going on in the field."

"I never learned how to read the 'literature' in psychology, and the literature remained largely unread by me," he went on to write. Even in his research ventures, he recalled working "entirely without supervision" and that "some kind of flimsy report" would usually suffice.

Nevertheless, Skinner would later reflect that in his late graduate years, "that [he] was doing exactly as [he] pleased." He received his PhD. in 1931 and remained at Harvard to do research until 1936. After over a decade of teaching at colleges in the Midwest, he came back to Cambridge in 1948 when Harvard offered him a tenured professorship. He became the Edgar Pierce Professor of Psychology in 1958, a position he maintained until his retirement in 1974.

In his faculty position at Harvard, Skinner was able to continue his research into animal behavior as well as expand to other fields, both in and out of psychology. The Pigeon Lab, set up in Skinner's first year as a professor, used birds to study behavioral principles that could be applied to humans. A *Crimson* article from 1949 observed Skinner in his element. "Skinner places his pigeons in a small closed box with a button in one wall," the article reports. "The birds must peck at this button at least once every five minutes to be paid off with food. The eager but ignorant pigeon, however, not knowing he will get the same reward with less exertion, will hammer away rapidly for great lengths of time to get his dinner." Skinner saw the experiment as providing valuable insight to the work habits and monetary incentives of human beings.

Working out of his office at the south end of Memorial Hall's basement, Skinner put forth theories on topics ranging from the superstitious tendencies of rodents to the synthesis of internal emotions and external behaviors—a field of his own that became known as radical behaviorism.

Memorial Hall was a beloved site for experimentation. Skinner and his colleagues had significant freedom in modifying the space because administrators had little concern for the building's underground level. When William James Hall was built as a new home for the Department of Psychology, Pinker said that Skinner and others "had to be dragged kicking and screaming out of the basement of Memorial Hall." Scientists, Pinker notes, "love space that you can modify yourself indefinitely."

Nonetheless, the Department managed to adapt to the move. "The 7th Floor of William James Hall was [Skinner's] empire," said Pinker. "When the elevator doors opened there were two bumper stickers that you could see. One of them said 'Think Behavior,' and the other one said 'God is a VI,' which is a very nerdy in-joke, VI being a variable interval schedule of reinforcement."

By the time Skinner retired, behaviorism began to see a decline in popularity. A shift toward cognitive elements of psychology was already underway. Kagan describes the move toward study of the brain as occurring because of both technical advances that made it easier to do cognitive imaging and the desire of psychologists to examine people's inner emotions.

"Humans think. Humans feel. Humans feel guilty if they have a bigoted thought. Operant conditioning can't explain that," he says.

Skinner also explored non-psychological fields, contributing to linguistics and philosophy through books like "Verbal Behavior" and "Beyond Freedom and Dignity". One of the fields outside of psychology that was influenced by Skinner's work is educational theory. He predicted that technology would play an increasingly greater role in the classroom, theorizing that "audio-visual aids" would come to supplement, and maybe even replace, lectures and textbooks. He developed pedagogical methods based on his conditioning theories.

Skinner's legacy at Harvard and more broadly in his discipline remains ambiguous. Many of his theories have suffered extensive criticism and even been eclipsed by modern methods. His thoughts on education and philosophy were unique but often controversial. In any case, he was arguably one of the most famous psychologists of his time, with an unmatched drive to leave a mark in some way.

"There are two kinds of scientists," says Kagan. "I call one kind hunters. Hunters win prizes. Hunters want a victory, they want to establish a fact that's reliable, unambiguous, replicable . . . They don't particularly care what the problem is." He goes on, "then there are the birdwatchers. I'm a birdwatcher. Birdwatchers fall in love with a particular domain."

This dichotomy represents, according to Kagan, "the difference between a passion about a domain and a passion to make an important discovery about anything."

"Skinner," he concludes, "was a hunter."

Critical Thinking

1. One has to be careful when thinking about the control of behavior, because in the wrong context, controlling others' behavior could be seen as more evil than good. What type of behavioral control was Skinner interested in, and why?

2. Regarding scientists, it was said that there are hunters and there are birdwatchers. Is it possible for a scientist to be both at the same time? Why or why not?

3. In his own reflections, B.F. Skinner wrote about the regimens that he would follow each day that he believed were related to his success. What are your regimens or routines for each day, and do you think those patterns are related to your successes (or failures)? Why or why not?

Internet References

B.F. Skinner: The man who taught pigeons to play ping-pong and rats to pull levers

http://www.smithsonianmag.com/science-nature/bf-skinner-the-man-who-taught-pigeons-to-play-ping-pong-and-rats-to-pull-levers-5363946/

B.F. Skinner Foundation

http://www.bfskinner.org/archives/biographical-information/

Computing in the classroom

http://harvardmagazine.com/2015/03/computing-in-the-classroom

Unit 5

UNIT

Prepared by: Eric Landrum, *Boise State University*

Cognitive Processes

As Reggie watches his 4-month-old child, he is convinced that his baby possesses some degree of understanding of the world around her. In fact, Reggie is sure he has one of the smartest babies in the neighborhood. Although he is a proud father, he keeps his thoughts to himself so as not to alienate the parents of less capable babies.

George lives in the same neighborhood as Reggie. George doesn't have any children, but he does own two golden retrievers. Despite George's most concerted efforts, the dogs never come to him when he calls them. In fact, they have been known to run in the opposite direction on occasion. Instead of being furious, George accepts his dogs' disobedience because he is sure the dogs are just not all that bright.

Both of these scenarios illustrate important and interesting ideas about cognition or thought processes. In the first vignette, Reggie ascribes cognitive abilities and high intelligence to his child; in fact, Reggie perhaps ascribes too much cognitive ability to his 4-month-old. On the other hand, George assumes that his dogs are not intelligent—more specifically, that the dogs are incapable of premeditated disobedience—and therefore forgives the dogs.

As you read about Reggie and his child and George and his dogs, you used many well-researched cognitive resources. You deciphered the marks on the page that we call letters and words and made sense of them. As you go through this process of comprehension, you are forming thoughts—effortlessly and automatically—about the meaning of what you are reading. You may think to yourself, "Reggie is really biased about his baby's

intellectual abilities" or that "It's not George's dogs who lack intelligence, it is George". As you are processing this information, you are also drawing on your memories of any experiences you may have had with babies or with golden retrievers or both—although before you started reading this scenario, you probably were not thinking about babies or golden retrievers. The story tapped your long-term memory story, and your previous experiences were brought to mind.

What you are experiencing firsthand is cognition, which psychologists like to define as the mental abilities involved in the acquisition, maintenance, and use of knowledge. Cognition is critical to our survival as adults. Of course, people think differently from one another, and psychologists report on interesting differences in cognitive development and in adult cognition.

Psychologists have also studied, and continue to study, nonhuman (animal) cognition and how it helps these creatures adapt to their unique environmental demands. New research presented in this unit even points to the influence of one's environment—such as how clean or messy a room can be—as influencing our attitudes and behaviors. These and other related phenomena form the heart and soul of cognitive science, which is showcased in this unit.

You may be doing many other tasks while reading this unit, such as listening to music in the background, checking your cell phone for text messages, and chatting with your roommate. While it may feel like you are being productive, dividing your attention to complete many tasks at one time may not be as efficient as you think!

Article

Prepared by: Eric Landrum, *Boise State University*

The Secret Life of Pronouns by James Pennebaker: What Do "I" and "We" Reveal about Us?

Are There Hidden Messages in Pronouns?
James Pennebaker says computers reveal secret patterns.

JULIET LAPIDOS

Learning Outcomes

After reading this article, you will be able to:

- Explain how the use of function words could be valuable in a situation where lie detection was the goal.

- Describe how frequent users of I-words may be different from others on additional psychological variables.

Some 110 years after the publication of the *Psychopathology of Everyday Life*, in which Sigmund Freud analyzed seemingly trivial slips of the tongue, it's become common knowledge that we disclose more about ourselves in conversation—about our true feelings, or our unconscious feelings—than we strictly intend. Freud focused on errors, but correct sentences can betray us, too. We all have our signature tics. We may describe boring people as "nice" or those we dislike as "weird." We may use archaisms if we're trying to seem smart, or slang if we'd prefer to seem cool. Every time we open our mouths we send out coded, supplementary messages about our frame of mind.

Although much of this information is easy to decode ("nice" for "boring" won't fool anyone), linguistic psychologist James Pennebaker suggests in *The Secret Life of Pronouns* that lots of data remain hidden from even the most astute human observers. "Nice" and "weird" are both content words; he's concerned with function words such as pronouns (I, you, they), articles (a, an, the), prepositions (to, for, of), and auxiliary verbs (is, am, have). We hardly notice these bolts of speech because we encounter them so frequently.

With the help of computer programs to count and scrutinize them, however, patterns emerge.

Sounds enticing; sounds, in fact, rather like a publisher's fantasy pitch, combining the strangely long-lasting craze for language books laced with pop psychology, and the added hook, the modern touch, of a computer that observes and catalogs beyond measly human capacity: a Watson for the psychiatric establishment. To Pennebaker's credit, his claims are fairly modest, especially when compared with those of Deborah Tannen and other practitioners of the word-sleuth genre. (He doesn't promise that if we change our pronoun usage we'll see tangible improvements in our social lives.) The problem is that much of what he turns up is even more modest than he seems to notice. Counting function words as they're used in ordinary life often yields the opposite of what Freud detected in confessions from the couch: confirmation of the obvious.

The most ingenious application Pennebaker proposes for function-word analysis is lie-detection, something of a dark art. Several years ago, Pennebaker and a couple of colleagues recruited 200 students and asked them to write two essays about abortion, one espousing a true belief, the other a falsehood. They asked another group to state their true and false takes in front of a video camera. When judges were called in to figure out which was which, they were accurate 52 percent of the time. (50 percent is chance.) A computer, programmed to look for specific "markers of honesty" gleaned from previous studies, performed much better, with a 67 percent accuracy rate. Truth-tellers, Pennebaker explains, tend to use more words, bigger words, more complex sentences, more exclusive words (except, but, without, as in the sentence "I think this but not that"), and more I-words (I, me, my, etc.). Liars, apparently, trade in simple, straightforward statements lacking in specificity because—Pennebaker posits—it's actually pretty difficult to make stuff up. They avoid self-reference because they don't feel ownership of their expressed views.

When Pennebaker dips into the more general field of "emotion detection" (he calls it that), his word-counting feels a bit Rube Goldberg-ish. After Sept. 11, 2001, Pennebaker and a colleague saved the LiveJournal.com postings of over a thousand amateur bloggers. They found that "bloggers immediately dropped in their use of I-words" following the attacks, and that their use of we-words almost doubled. Pennebaker takes these fluctuations to mean that "shared traumas bring people together," "shared traumas deflect attention away from the self," and that "shared traumas, in many ways, are positive experiences" (because people feel more socially connected). The brute fact that Sept. 11 influenced pronoun usage may interest readers, but Pennebaker's analysis merely reiterates long-held psychological dogma. (Try Googling "shared traumas bring people together.") I can't help but wonder if Pennebaker—albeit unconsciously—interpreted his results to match the conventional wisdom.

Perhaps that's harsh: Certainly there's nothing wrong with devising yet another way to elucidate common human responses, and Pennebaker's experiments are always imaginative. Yet it's often the case that his conclusions, especially the ones he draws from I-word usage, are heavily dependent on context and prior knowledge.

In one chapter, Pennebaker notes that Rudolph Giuliani demonstrated a dramatic increase in I-words during the late spring of 2000, when he was still mayor of New York. Pennebaker fills us in that "Giuliani's life [was] turned upside down . . . . He was diagnosed with prostate cancer, withdrew from the senate race against Hillary Clinton, separated from his wife on national television . . . and, a few days later, acknowledged his 'special friendship' with Judith Nathan." Pennebaker adds that "by early June, friends, acquaintances, old enemies, and members of the press all noticed that Giuliani seemed more genuine, humble, and warm." So it's reasonable to conclude that Giuliani's ascending I-word usage reflected a "personality switch from cold and distanced to someone who [due to a few significant setbacks] was more warm and immediate."

But we already knew that. If we didn't, where would Pennebaker's method leave us? He argues, at various points, that the following groups use I-words at higher rates:

1. Women
2. Followers (not leaders)
3. Truth-tellers (not liars)
4. Young
5. Poor

6. Depressed
7. Afraid (but not angry)
8. Sick

The common thread unifying these seemingly random clusters is, roughly, an enhanced focus on personal experience. Sick and depressed people dwell on their conditions and are thus more likely than their healthy counterparts to talk about themselves. Followers, in conversation with leaders, might be after something: "I was wondering if I could have a raise." That's pretty close to a tautology, though, and does nothing to solve the problem that, without insider information, it's impossible to know which condition or attribute I-usage reflects. A word-count-wannabe presented with Giuliani's speeches might deduce, erroneously, that the mayor had become more truthful, or less leaderly, or had lost money.

For obvious reasons, I'm unusually attuned to my pronoun usage at the moment, and I've noticed a thing or two. I start off this essay with lots of we-words (16 in the introduction), and sprinkle them throughout. With the exception of the section you're currently reading, I drop only one self-referencing I (in the fifth paragraph). I don't deny that this imbalance might mean something. Perhaps it indicates that, like politicians who drone on about what "we" expect from the president, or how "we" want a return to old-fashioned American values, I'm trying to imply audience agreement when, in truth, I have no clue what the audience thinks. But you don't need to count pronouns to figure that out. You only need to know that you're reading a book review.

Critical Thinking

1. What is the difference between content words and function words?
2. What is the pattern of word use differences between truth-tellers and liars?
3. What does the research indicate when one person uses a high frequency of I-words compared to someone else who uses I-words infrequently?

Create Central

www.mhhe.com/createcentral

Internet References

The secret language code
www.scientificamerican.com/article.cfm?id=the-secret-language-code

It's all about "me": What pronouns reveal about us
www.pri.org/stories/arts-entertainment/books/how-you-use-pronouns-lie-detectors-personality-projectors5676.html

Article   Prepared by: Eric Landrum, *Boise State University*

The Epidemic of Media Multitasking While Learning

ANNIE MURPHY PAUL

Learning Outcomes

After reading this article, you will be able to:

- Define multitasking, including what actually happens when students think they are multitasking.

- Understand mental fatigue and the impact it has on student performance.

Living rooms, dens, kitchens, even bedrooms: Investigators followed students into the spaces where homework gets done. Pens poised over their "study observation forms," the observers watched intently as the students—in middle school, high school, and college, 263 in all—opened their books and turned on their computers.

For a quarter of an hour, the investigators from the lab of Larry Rosen, a psychology professor at California State University-Dominguez Hills, marked down once a minute what the students were doing as they studied. A checklist on the form included: reading a book, writing on paper, typing on the computer—and also using email, looking at Facebook, engaging in instant messaging, texting, talking on the phone, watching television, listening to music, surfing the web. Sitting unobtrusively at the back of the room, the observers counted the number of windows open on the students' screens and noted whether the students were wearing ear-buds.

Although the students had been told at the outset that they should "study something important, including homework, an upcoming examination or project, or reading a book for a course," it wasn't long before their attention drifted: Students' "on-task behavior" started declining around the two-minute mark as they began responding to arriving texts or checking their Facebook feeds. By the time the 15 minutes were up, they had spent only about 65 percent of the observation period actually doing their schoolwork.

"We were amazed at how frequently they multitasked, even though they knew someone was watching," Rosen says. "It really seems that they could not go for 15 minutes without engaging their devices," adding, "It was kind of scary, actually."

Concern about young people's use of technology is nothing new, of course. But Rosen's study, published in the May issue of *Computers in Human Behavior,* is part of a growing body of research focused on a very particular use of technology: media multitasking while learning. Attending to multiple streams of information and entertainment while studying, doing homework, or even sitting in class has become common behavior among young people—so common that many of them rarely write a paper or complete a problem set any other way.

But evidence from psychology, cognitive science, and neuroscience suggests that when students multitask while doing schoolwork, their learning is far spottier and shallower than if the work had their full attention. They understand and remember less, and they have greater difficulty transferring their learning to new contexts. So detrimental is this practice that some researchers are proposing that a new prerequisite for academic and even professional success—the new marshmallow test of self-discipline—is the ability to resist a blinking inbox or a buzzing phone.

The media multitasking habit starts early. In "Generation M2: Media in the Lives of 8- to 18-Year-Olds," a survey conducted by the Kaiser Family Foundation and published in 2010, almost a third of those surveyed said that when they were doing homework, "most of the time" they were also watching TV, texting, listening to music, or using some other medium. The lead author of the study was Victoria Rideout, then a vice president at Kaiser and now an independent research and policy consultant. Although the study looked at all aspects of kids' media use, Rideout told me she was particularly troubled by its findings regarding media multitasking while doing schoolwork.

"This is a concern we should have distinct from worrying about how much kids are online or how much kids are media multitasking overall. It's multitasking while learning that has the biggest potential downside," she says. "I don't care if a kid wants to tweet while she's watching American Idol, or have music on while he plays a video game. But when students are doing serious work with their minds, they have to have focus."

For older students, the media multitasking habit extends into the classroom. While most middle and high school students don't have the opportunity to text, email, and surf the

Internet during class, studies show the practice is nearly universal among students in college and professional school. One large survey found that 80 percent of college students admit to texting during class; 15 percent say they send 11 or more texts in a single class period.

During the first meeting of his courses, Rosen makes a practice of calling on a student who is busy with his phone. "I ask him, 'What was on the slide I just showed to the class?' The student always pulls a blank," Rosen reports. "Young people have a wildly inflated idea of how many things they can attend to at once, and this demonstration helps drive the point home: If you're paying attention to your phone, you're not paying attention to what's going on in class." Other professors have taken a more surreptitious approach, installing electronic spyware or planting human observers to record whether students are taking notes on their laptops or using them for other, unauthorized purposes.

Such steps may seem excessive, even paranoid: After all, isn't technology increasingly becoming an intentional part of classroom activities and homework assignments? Educators are using social media sites like Facebook and Twitter as well as social sites created just for schools, such as Edmodo, to communicate with students, take class polls, assign homework, and have students collaborate on projects. But researchers are concerned about the use of laptops, tablets, cellphones, and other technology for purposes quite apart from schoolwork. Now that these devices have been admitted into classrooms and study spaces, it has proven difficult to police the line between their approved and illicit uses by students.

In the study involving spyware, for example, two professors of business administration at the University of Vermont found that "students engage in substantial multitasking behavior with their laptops and have non-course-related software applications open and active about 42 percent of the time." The professors, James Kraushaar and David Novak, obtained students' permission before installing the monitoring software on their computers—so, as in Rosen's study, the students were engaging in flagrant multitasking even though they knew their actions were being recorded.

Another study, carried out at St. John's University in New York, used human observers stationed at the back of the classroom to record the technological activities of law students. The spies reported that 58 percent of second- and third-year law students who had laptops in class were using them for "nonclass purposes" more than half the time. (First-year students were far more likely to use their computers for taking notes, although an observer did note one first-year student texting just 17 minutes into her very first class—the beginning of her law school career.)

Texting, emailing, and posting on Facebook and other social media sites are by far the most common digital activities students undertake while learning, according to Rosen. That's a problem, because these operations are actually quite mentally complex, and they draw on the same mental resources—using language, parsing meaning—demanded by schoolwork.

David Meyer, a psychology professor at the University of Michigan who's studied the effects of divided attention on learning, takes a firm line on the brain's ability to multitask: "Under most conditions, the brain simply cannot do two complex tasks at the same time. It can happen only when the two tasks are both very simple and when they don't compete with each other for the same mental resources. An example would be folding laundry and listening to the weather report on the radio. That's fine. But listening to a lecture while texting, or doing homework and being on Facebook—each of these tasks is very demanding, and each of them uses the same area of the brain, the prefrontal cortex."

Young people think they can perform two challenging tasks at once, Meyer acknowledges, but "they are deluded," he declares. It's difficult for anyone to properly evaluate how well his or her own mental processes are operating, he points out, because most of these processes are unconscious. And, Meyer adds, "there's nothing magical about the brains of so-called 'digital natives' that keeps them from suffering the inefficiencies of multitasking. They may like to do it, they may even be addicted to it, but there's no getting around the fact that it's far better to focus on one task from start to finish."

Researchers have documented a cascade of negative outcomes that occurs when students multitask while doing schoolwork. First, the assignment takes longer to complete, because of the time spent on distracting activities and because, upon returning to the assignment, the student has to refamiliarize himself with the material.

Second, the mental fatigue caused by repeatedly dropping and picking up a mental thread leads to more mistakes. The cognitive cost of such task-switching is especially high when students alternate between tasks that call for different sets of expressive "rules"—the formal, precise language required for an English essay, for example, and the casual, friendly tone of an email to a friend.

Third, students' subsequent memory of what they're working on will be impaired if their attention is divided. Although we often assume that our memories fail at the moment we can't recall a fact or concept, the failure may actually have occurred earlier, at the time we originally saved, or encoded, the memory. The moment of encoding is what matters most for retention, and dozens of laboratory studies have demonstrated that when our attention is divided during encoding, we remember that piece of information less well—or not at all. As the unlucky student spotlighted by Rosen can attest, we can't remember something that never really entered our consciousness in the first place. And a study last month showed that students who multitask on laptops in class distract not just themselves but also their peers who see what they're doing.

Fourth, some research has suggested that when we're distracted, our brains actually process and store information in different, less useful ways. In a 2006 study in the *Proceedings of the National Academy of Sciences,* Russell Poldrack of the University of Texas–Austin and two colleagues asked participants to engage in a learning activity on a computer while also carrying out a second task, counting musical tones that sounded while they worked. Study subjects who did both tasks at once appeared to learn just as well as subjects who did the first task by itself. But upon further probing, the former group proved much less adept at extending and extrapolating their new knowledge to novel contexts—a key capacity that psychologists call transfer.

Brain scans taken during Poldrack's experiment revealed that different regions of the brain were active under the two conditions, indicating that the brain engages in a different form of memory when forced to pay attention to two streams of information at once. The results suggest, the scientists wrote, that "even if distraction does not decrease the overall level of learning, it can result in the acquisition of knowledge that can be applied less flexibly in new situations."

Finally, researchers are beginning to demonstrate that media multitasking while learning is negatively associated with students' grades. In Rosen's study, students who used Facebook during the 15-minute observation period had lower grade-point averages than those who didn't go on the site. And two recent studies by Reynol Junco, a faculty associate at Harvard's Berkman Center for Internet & Society, found that texting and using Facebook—in class and while doing homework—were negatively correlated with college students' GPAs. "Engaging in Facebook use or texting while trying to complete schoolwork may tax students' capacity for cognitive processing and preclude deeper learning," write Junco and a co-author. (Of course, it's also plausible that the texting and Facebooking students are those with less willpower or motivation, and thus likely to have lower GPAs even aside from their use of technology.)

Meyer, of the University of Michigan, worries that the problem goes beyond poor grades. "There's a definite possibility that we are raising a generation that is learning more shallowly than young people in the past," he says. "The depth of their processing of information is considerably less, because of all the distractions available to them as they learn."

Given that these distractions aren't going away, academic and even professional achievement may depend on the ability to ignore digital temptations while learning—a feat akin to the famous marshmallow test. In a series of experiments conducted more than 40 years ago, psychologist Walter Mischel tempted young children with a marshmallow, telling them they could have two of the treats if they put off eating one right away. Follow-up studies performed years later found that the kids who were better able to delay gratification not only achieved higher grades and test scores but were also more likely to succeed in school and their careers.

Two years ago, Rosen and his colleagues conducted an information-age version of the marshmallow test. College students who participated in the study were asked to watch a 30-minute videotaped lecture, during which some were sent eight text messages while others were sent four or zero text messages. Those who were interrupted more often scored worse on a test of the lecture's content; more interestingly, those who responded to the experimenters' texts right away scored significantly worse than those participants who waited to reply until the lecture was over.

This ability to resist the lure of technology can be consciously cultivated, Rosen maintains. He advises students to take "tech breaks" to satisfy their cravings for electronic communication: After they've labored on their schoolwork uninterrupted for 15 minutes, they can allow themselves two minutes to text, check websites, and post to their hearts' content. Then the devices get turned off for another 15 minutes of academics.

Over time, Rosen says, students are able extend their working time to 20, 30, even 45 minutes, as long as they know that an opportunity to get online awaits. "Young people's technology use is really about quelling anxiety," he contends. "They don't want to miss out. They don't want to be the last person to hear some news, or the ninth person to 'like' someone's post." Device-checking is a compulsive behavior that must be managed, he says, if young people are to learn and perform at their best.

Rideout, director of the Kaiser study on kids and media use, sees an upside for parents in the new focus on multitasking while learning. "The good thing about this phenomenon is that it's a relatively discrete behavior that parents actually can do something about," she says. "It would be hard to enforce a total ban on media multitasking, but parents can draw a line when it comes to homework and studying—telling their kids, 'This is a time when you will concentrate on just one thing.' "

Parents shouldn't feel like ogres when they do so, she adds. "It's important to remember that while a lot of kids do media multitask while doing homework, a lot of them don't. One out of five kids in our study said they 'never' engage in other media while doing homework, and another one in five said they do so only 'a little bit.' This is not some universal norm that students and parents can't buck. This is not an unreasonable thing to ask of your kid."

So here's the takeaway for parents of Generation M: Stop fretting about how much they're on Facebook. Don't harass them about how much they play video games. The digital native boosters are right that this is the social and emotional world in which young people live. Just make sure when they're doing schoolwork, the cellphones are silent, the video screens are dark, and that every last window is closed but one.

Critical Thinking

1. What is the impact of multitasking on grades? If a student wanted to improve his or her grades, what would be the optimum strategy regarding schoolwork and study?

2. Think about the modern day version of the marshmallow test. If a student has to check for text messages 8 times in 30 minutes, what do you think this means for his or her ability to deeply process and learn?

Create Central

www.mhhe.com/createcentral

Internet References

Media multitasking: The new marshmallow test
http://blogs.edweek.org/teachers/teaching_now/2013/05/media_multitasking_the_new_marshmallow_test.html

Expert advice: Kids and multitasking
www.commonsensemedia.org/educators/blog/expert-article-kids-and-multitasking

Murphy Paul, Annie. From The *Brilliant Blog*, May 3, 2013, Online. Copyright © 2013 by Annie Murphy Paul. Reprinted by permission of the author.

Article   Prepared by: Eric Landrum, *Boise State University*

Pigeons, Like Humans, Can Behave Irrationally

SANDRA UPSON

Learning Outcomes

After reading this article, you will be able to:

- Understand the types of behaviors that pigeons participate in.
- Appreciate some of the parallels between human and animal behavior.

Gambling may seem like a uniquely human activity. Twinkling slot machines and croupiers in starched white shirts may be about as far from the natural world as we can get. Yet one team of researchers, led by psychologist Thomas Zentall at the University of Kentucky, has taken a particular interest in how animals gamble. The group reasons that if we can identify irrational behaviors in animals, such as gambling, we might discover common brain mechanisms related to such seemingly complex behaviors.

According to behavioral ecologists, Zentall recounts, animals should never gamble because evolution has honed them over many thousands of years into optimal foragers. That is, animals should expend the least amount of energy and time to consume the greatest number of calories. Yet this is not always the case.

In a recent series of experiments Zentall and his colleagues have found that pigeons make some of the same common reasoning mistakes as humans do. For example, they exhibit a strong tendency to select a riskier option over a smaller, safer reward. In one avian version of a casino, pigeons had to choose between a low-probability payoff of 10 food pellets (versus zero) and a high-probability payoff of three pellets. (The expected value is two pieces of kibble in the first case and three in the second.) Although at first the birds chose the more profitable three-pellet option, over time they switched strategies and went for the suboptimal 10-pellet gamble again and again. Research on human gamblers reveals a complementary trend. Compulsive gamblers pay little attention to their losses, tending to remember when they won but not the frequency of winning.

Other studies have shown that pigeons fall prey to the sunk cost fallacy, just as humans do. We might sit through a disappointing movie on the off chance it improves and thus redeems our ticket purchase, or we might stick with a failing business because we hope that our fortunes will change. Similarly, pigeons will continue working on a challenging task to earn a snack rather than switching mid-task to a much easier activity with the same reward. "There's something fundamental about this tendency," Zentall says. "It's not just something cultural for us, such as a belief that we should finish what we've started."

At the annual meeting of the *American Psychological Association* this past weekend, Zentall presented new research on the pigeon version of yet another cognitive bias, the "less is more" heuristic. When making rapid judgments between two things, we tend to give greater weight to the average quality of our options rather than the overall quantity. For example, in one famous experiment done by behavioral scientist Christopher Hsee, participants were asked to rate two collections of dinnerware. One set consisted of 24 pristine plates. The other set contained 31 perfect pieces plus nine broken ones. The participants tended to place a higher value on the smaller set—even though the second option contained more flawless dishes.

Rhesus macaques display similar behavior. They like but do not love to eat a slice of cucumber as a snack. Yet if you let a monkey choose between a grape plus a cucumber or just a grape, the monkey will choose just the grape. Like humans, these monkeys appear to judge their choices by the average quality of the offer, rather than the quantity, suggesting that this cognitive shortcut has deep evolutionary roots.

Now for the pigeons. Instead of grapes or plates, the pigeons were presented with peas, which they find delicious. They consider milo seeds, also known as sorghum, less appealing but still palatable. When given the option of either a sole pea or a pea and a milo seed, however, the birds chose the pea and the milo seed. They appeared to behave more rationally than either humans or monkeys.

To look more closely at this surprising behavior, the team divided the pigeons into two groups to see if the birds' level of hunger might play a role. When the pigeons were hungrier, they made the optimal choice, going for the pea and the milo seed. When the pigeons were only somewhat hungry, they suddenly behaved like humans and chose just the pea. "If it's really important to them they go for quantity," Zentall explains. "If they're not so hungry they go for quality."

Zentall suggests that across species, quality may be easier—that is, faster—to judge than quantity. In the wild pigeons typically face competition from their fellow birds, so the bird that reacts the fastest to the sight of food is most likely to snag the morsel. Our ancestors likely faced similar pressures.

As for why pigeons seem to outperform us some of the time? Zentall suggests that motivation may be the answer. Our biases are not inviolable rules of behavior—they are tendencies we reveal when making quick decisions. When humans are tested in the lab, the stakes are typically very low. Given sufficient motivation, we, too, become more likely to think through a scenario and make the better choice.

Critical Thinking

1. What is the sunk cost fallacy, and how does that phenomenon influence how humans make decisions over time?

2. Decision-making biases tend to emerge more when humans are in a hurry to make a decision rather than when deliberation is possible. Why do you think this is so? Explain.

Create Central

www.mhhe.com/createcentral

Internet References

Are animals as irrational as humans?
www.plosbiology.org/article/info%3Adoi%2F10.1371%2Fjournal.pbio.0020434

Are we rational animals?
http://psychcentral.com/blog/archives/2011/01/31/are-we-rational-animal

16. Steinfield C, Ellison NB, Lampe C. Social capital, self-esteem, and use of online social network sites: A longitudinal analysis. Journal of Applied Developmental Psychology 2008; 29:434–45.

17. Park N, Kee KF, Valenzuela S. Being immersed in social networking environment: Facebook groups, uses and gratifications, and social outcomes. CyberPsychology & Behavior 2009; 12:729–33.

18. Mazer JP, Murphy RE, Simonds CJ. I'll see you on Facebook: The effects of computer-mediated teacher self-disclosure on student motivation, affective learning, and classroom climate. Communication Education 2007; 56:1–17.

19. Valkenburg PM, Peter J, Schouten AP. Friend networking sites and their relationship to adolescents' well-being and social self-esteem. CyberPsychology & Behavior 2006; 9:584–90.

20. Muise A, Christofides E, Desmarais S. More information than you ever wanted: Does Facebook bring out the green-eyed monster of jealousy? CyberPsychology & Behavior 2009; 12:441–4.

21. Acar A. Antecedents and consequences of online social networking behavior: The case of Facebook. Journal of Website Promotion 2008; 3:62–83.

22. Tong ST, Van Der Heide B, Langwell L. Too much of a good thing? The relationship between number of friends and interpersonal impressions on Facebook. Journal of Computer-Mediated Communication 2008; 13:531–49.

23. Hill RA, Dunbar RIM. Social network size in humans. Human Nature 2003; 14:53–72.

24. Lea M, Spears R. (1995) Love at first byte? Building personal relationships over computer networks. In Wood JT, Duke S, eds. *Understudied relationships: Off the beaten track.* Thousand Oaks, CA: Sage, pp. 197–233.

25. Spears R, Lea M. Panacea or panopticon? The hidden power in computer-mediated communication. Communication Research 1994; 21:427–59.

26. Wallace P. (1999) *The psychology of the Internet.* New York: Cambridge University Press.

27. MacLeod C, Campbell L. Memory accessibility and probability judgments: An experimental evaluation of the availability heuristic. Journal of Personality & Social Psychology 1992; 63:890–902.

28. Tversky A, Kahneman D. Availability: A heuristic for judging frequency and probability. Cognitive Psychology 1973; 5:207–32.

29. Jones EE. The rocky road from acts to dispositions. American Psychologist 1979; 34:107–17.

30. Jones EE. (1990) *Interpersonal perception.* New York: Macmillan.

31. Jones EE, Harris VA. The attribution of attitudes. Journal of Experimental Social Psychology 1967; 3:1–24.

32. Snyder M, Jones EE. Attitude attribution when behavior is constrained. Journal of Experimental & Social Psychology 1974; 10:585–600.

33. Alicke MD. Global self-evaluation as determined by the desirability and controllability of trait adjectives. Journal of Personality & Social Psychology 1985; 3:1621–30.

34. Brown JD. Evaluations of self and others: Self-enhancement biases in social judgments. Social Cognition 1986; 4:353–76.

Critical Thinking

1. Describe how multiple regression coefficients are interpreted by these researchers and briefly discuss the possible dangers (or overgeneralizations) that can be made using such an approach.

2. What is the relationship between the number of "friends" reported on Facebook and the other outcome variables in this research? Explain.

Internet References

An investigation of status posts and happiness of Facebook users
http://www.kon.org/urc/v13/galioto.html

Got loads of friends? Then you're probably unhappy: People who appear popular may actually be withdrawn and sad, claims study
http://www.dailymail.co.uk/sciencetech/article-2562070/How-having-friends-makes-LESS-sociable-Study-finds-people-appear-popular-actually-withdrawn-sad.html

Appendix

Appendix Table A1   Operationalization of variables, mean, and standard deviation

	Survey items and coding	Minimum	Maximum	Mean	S.D.
1. Others are having a better life	How much would you agree with this statement? "Many of my friends have a better life than me" (1: strongly disagree; 10: strongly agree)	1	10	3.86	2.32
2. Others are happier	How much would you agree with this statement? "Many of my friends are happier than me" (1: strongly disagree; 10: strongly agree)	1	10	3.89	2.32
3. Life is fair	How much would you agree with this statement? "I believe that life is fair" (1: strongly disagree; 10: strongly agree)	1	10	5.93	2.78
4. Years of using Facebook	How many years have you been using Facebook?	0	8	2.55	1.36
5. Number of hours spent on Facebook each week	How many hours do you spend on Facebook each week?	0	80	4.83	7.77
6. Number of people listed as Facebook friends	Questions about your Facebook friends: "How many people do you currently have on your Facebook?"	3	1400	317.67	239.77
7. Number of Facebook friends not personally known	Questions about your Facebook friends: "How many people you do not personally know?"	0	700	46.53	105.87
8. Number of hours going out with friends each week	How many hours do you usually go out with friends each week? 1: Never; 2: 1–3 hours; 3: 4–6 hours; 4: 7 hours or more	1	4	2.62	1.01
9. Religiosity	How much do you agree with this statement? "I am a very religious person" (1: strongly disagree; 10: strongly agree)	1	10	7.02	3.13
10. Gender (male)	Your gender is: 1: male; 0: female	0	1	0.43	0.50
11. Single without a steady dating partner	Your current marital status is: 1: single without a steady dating partner; 0: other	0	1	0.35	0.48
12. Single with a steady dating partner	Your current marital status is: 1: single with a steady dating partner; 0: other	0	1	0.20	0.40
13. Married	Your current marital status is: 1: married; 0: other	0	1	0.39	0.49

Article   Prepared by: R. Eric Landrum, *Boise State University*

Cognitive Shields

Investigating Protections Against Dementia

Andrew Merluzzi

Learning Outcomes

After reading this article, you will be able to:

- Comprehend the scope of dementia disorders and the impact they will have culturally in the next 15 years.

- Explain the concept of cognitive reserve and how it may be able to help delay the onset of dementia.

- Understand the impact of movement for adults later in life.

Novelist Terry Pratchett once noted that because aging baby boomers will spend more years as senior citizens than any previous generation, they will "run right into the dementia firing range."

Indeed, dementia afflicts an estimated 35.6 million people across the globe, according to the World Health Organization, and that number is projected to double in the next 15 years. Pratchett himself suffers from an atypical form of Alzheimer's disease.

Unfortunately, cures for various types of dementia remain elusive, making rising life expectancies look like a curse as much as a blessing.

But psychological researchers and other scientists are closely investigating some apparent cognitive shields against age-related impairment. In doing so, they have discovered that several protective factors appear to operate even in brains that have all the molecular signs of dementia. A 2006 study from Rush University, for instance, found that about a third of post-mortem brains with telltale features of dementia—protein tangles or miniature strokes—came from people who never exhibited symptoms during life. How is it that the cellular pathologies so seemingly intertwined with Alzheimer's and other forms of dementia don't always produce illness?

According to psychological scientist Barbara B. Bendlin, Alzheimer's investigator at the University of Wisconsin–Madison, certain individuals may build buffers over their lifetimes, a phenomenon called *cognitive reserve.*

"What's interesting is that there are several protective factors against developing dementia, including higher education, and higher physical and possibly mental fitness," Bendlin explains. "Some individuals remain cognitively healthy even in the face of increasing burdens of brain pathology."

If that's true—if cognitive reserve can help protect against the onset of dementia—the next question is obvious: How do we develop more of it?

Energizing the Mind

Over the last couple of decades, researchers have found evidence that various behavioral therapies can strengthen mental buffers and help people maintain memory later in life, often at a fraction of the cost required for large-scale drug development. These therapies—cognitive training, exercise, and a healthy diet, for instance—are the same factors that ward off other chronic diseases, and psychological scientists are investigating them in earnest as a means to offset a dementia epidemic.

To date, most studies examining lifestyle factors and dementia have been retrospective and correlational, with researchers relying on participants to report how frequently they engaged in certain activities and when their symptoms began to emerge. That kind of research is valuable for tracking trends, but only a few studies have actually examined lifestyle factors in an experimental context, directly pitting one set of activities against another to see which produces the greatest cognitive benefits.

One study published in *Psychological Science* did just that, examining how actively engaging the brain can actually boost older adults' recall power.

In this experiment, Past APS Board Member Denise C. Park and colleagues at the University of Texas at Dallas randomly assigned more than 200 older adults (ages 60–90) to engage in a particular type of activity for 15 hours a week over the course of 3 months. Some participants learned skills that required significant cognitive investment, like digital photography or quilting. Other participants were asked to take part in more leisurely activities—say, listening to classical music or completing word puzzles. Park wanted these activities to mirror the types of activities people might engage in anyway, rather than using obscure memory-training tasks.

"I think it's very important to understand the types of everyday tasks or hobbies that maintain or improve cognitive health," she explains. At the end of 3 months, Park and her colleagues tested the participants' overall cognitive abilities.

As it turned out, the participants who engaged in digital photography or quilting showed a significant improvement in memory compared with those who took part in the leisure activities. Importantly, the researchers accounted for participants' overall social contact throughout the 3-month period, which allowed them to conclude that it was the psychological challenge, and not social interaction, that was critical for bolstering participants' cognitive performance.

Another recent study from the University of California, San Francisco, revealed similarly encouraging results. In this experiment, led by psychological scientists Adam Gazzaley and Joaquin A. Anguera, 16 older adults were recruited to play a videogame called "Neuroracer." In the game, participants attempted to drive a car down a virtual road, keeping constant speed and lane position. While doing so, they also had to pay attention to sporadically appearing shapes, pressing a button whenever they observed a green circle. As participants improved, the game became increasingly more challenging, ensuring that it was always difficult enough to be mentally engaging.

For comparison, another 15 participants played an easier version of the game, requiring that they drive *or* pay attention to the shapes, but not both. Fifteen more participants didn't play Neuroracer at all. After 1 month, the researchers brought all the participants back to complete several cognitive tests.

The results indicated that those who played the difficult version of Neuroracer were much better at multitasking *within* the game, and they also scored better on unrelated cognitive tests. This kind of transfer—with improvement on one task leading to a more general boost in cognitive functioning—has been notoriously elusive in studies of so-called "brain games," making the Neuroracer results particularly intriguing. Brain imaging with EEG revealed noticeable differences at the neural level: Participants who played the difficult version of the game showed more coherent activation patterns in cognitive control networks, including the prefrontal cortex.

And the benefits seemed to last: Adults who played the difficult game maintained the cognitive gains 6 months later.

Although these results are promising, it's not clear how these particular cognitive improvements would actually play out in the daily lives of older adults, much less whether they might aid in curbing full-blown dementia; larger, longitudinal experiments will be required to answer these questions. As Park points out, such studies might address a crucial gap between animal and human dementia research.

"The animal literature suggests that without continued engagement in a stimulating activity, gains for engaging in cognitive challenges are quickly lost," she says. Just like booster shots, periodically revisiting the challenging activities may be necessary to buffer against later dementia.

Still, these experiments reveal that it's never too late to challenge the mind, and that even short stints of training can produce tangible benefits.

Moving to Protect the Brain

Continuing to exercise the mind in the later years of life is important, but research suggests that physical exercise is equally critical. According to Art Kramer, APS Fellow and director of the Beckman Institute for Advanced Science and Technology at the University of Illinois at Urbana–Champaign, both the mind and brain thrive when the body is in motion.

Kramer and colleagues have designed numerous randomized experimental studies to identify the types of exercise that are most effective at boosting cognition later in life.

In one study, Kramer randomly assigned 120 older adults to either an aerobic fitness routine—about 40 minutes of brisk walking 3 days a week—or a less intense stretching routine for the same amount of time. Both groups stuck to their respective routines for about a year, and Kramer used MRI to assess any change in the structure and size of participants' brains over time.

In doing so, he and his colleagues hoped to determine whether demonstrated changes in memory map onto specific changes in the brain. That is, is there evidence for "brain reserve" that can be linked to cognitive reserve?

Their findings suggest so. Participants in the stretching group—who didn't undergo aerobic exercise over that year—showed a typical age-related decrease in volume of the hippocampus, a brain region crucially involved in memory. Participants in the aerobic group, on the other hand, exhibited *increases* in hippocampal volume, effectively offsetting 1–2 years' worth of volume loss.

Together, the findings suggest that aerobic fitness produced increased hippocampal volume, which in turn was directly related to improvements on memory tests in the walking (aerobic training) group. Because of these potential neuroprotective effects, Kramer and his coauthors stress the importance of squeezing in an exercise routine at any stage in life and especially as we age.

Other studies support these findings. Stephen Rao, professor at the Schey Center for Cognitive Neuroimaging at the Cleveland Clinic, was interested in whether exercise can grant neuroprotective effects in people who are at genetic risk for Alzheimer's. Alzheimer's is considered a heritable disease, and a variation in one particular gene, apolipoprotein E (APOE), confers an elevated risk. For this investigation, Rao and his colleagues studied about 100 older adults, many of whom carried the APOE gene. The participants explained their normal exercise habits and had their brains scanned twice over a period of 18 months.

By comparing the first and second brain scans, Rao and his colleagues found evidence suggesting that exercise was critically important for the at-risk group: People with the APOE gene who didn't routinely exercise exhibited about a 3 percent decrease in hippocampal volume over time. By contrast, those carrying the gene who did incorporate exercise into their lives—more than 15 minutes of moderate exercise at least 3 days a week—didn't show any decreases in hippocampal volume. People without the risk gene did not show a decrease in hippocampal volume, whether they were sedentary or exercised regularly. This finding suggests that the neuroprotective effects of exercise may be specific to persons at risk for Alzheimer's.

Although the study doesn't point to a specific mechanism linking exercise and brain volume, Rao and colleagues have some hypotheses: for example, staying active might reduce inflammation in the brain and promote neuronal growth in the hippocampus, effectively building up cognitive reserve *and* brain reserve in people at risk for developing Alzheimer's.

The Language Buffer

Although studies have identified the hippocampus as one area of the brain linked with cognitive reserve and brain reserve, other studies suggest an important role for networks involved in executive control. Investigations of bilingual people have shown that the networks we use for language—and the executive control required for learning new languages—are the same networks that seem to deteriorate with dementia.

The first hints that bilingualism might promote cognitive reserve came from epidemiological research. Two investigations led by APS Fellow Ellen Bialystok and APS William James Fellow Fergus I. M. Craik, psychological scientists from the Rotman Research Institute at Baycrest, Canada, indicated that older adults who regularly used at least two languages for most of their lives were, on average, diagnosed with dementia 4 years later than their monolingual counterparts. And that held true even when the researchers accounted for potentially related factors like education, cognitive skills, occupation history, and immigration status.

Bialystok and Craik believe that because using two languages requires the recruitment of many higher order cognitive abilities, bilingualism may delay dementia in the same ways as other cognitive challenges. The ability to learn diverse grammatical rules, suppress one language in favor of another, and quickly switch sentence styles is difficult, and difficult tasks have the potential to strengthen cognitive reserve.

Several dementia-research studies have provided neural evidence in support of the protective effects of bilingualism. In one investigation, Tom Schweizer from the University of Toronto, Canada, used CT scans to measure brain atrophy in 40 older adults with probable Alzheimer's disease, some of whom were bilingual and some of whom were monolingual. Crucially, the researchers ensured that both groups exhibited the same level of dementia symptoms; that way, any differences in the brain could not be accounted for by dementia severity.

Compared to monolingual individuals, patients who spoke two languages exhibited more atrophy in regions most associated with Alzheimer's disease decline.

These findings may seem paradoxical at first blush, but they are actually directly predicted by the cognitive reserve hypothesis.

As Schweizer and colleagues hypothesized, a lifetime of speaking two languages may build stronger shields *against* the effects of brain atrophy—which may explain why bilinguals' symptoms of dementia weren't worse than their monolingual counterparts, despite the greater degree of atrophy. In effect, it's as if the bilingual individuals were cognitively "younger" than one would predict by simply looking at the deterioration in their brains.

In another recent study, Gigi Luk of Harvard University, along with Craik, Bialystok, and Cheryl Grady of the University of Toronto, discovered that bilingual older adults had more robust white matter tracts than did monolingual participants. This suggests that the myelin on axons in these nerve bundles is more intact (less degraded), which would help to maintain efficient transmission of nerve signals. Ultimately, preservation of white matter among bilinguals may help to buffer against age-related changes in the size and structure of critical areas of the brain.

Mark Antoniou, a psychological scientist from the Chinese University of Hong Kong, is especially convinced by these findings and has suggested that language training later in life might be a useful method for reducing rates of dementia.

"The end result of foreign language learning may be that language function is promoted, the integrity of brain structures involved is maintained, and a greater number of potential neural circuits could be available that allow for compensation of age-related cognitive declines," write Antoniou and his colleagues.

Just as with physical exercise and other cognitive training techniques, however, moving from principle to practice is not so straightforward.

"Motivation also plays a larger role in determining language-learning success in older adults," Antoniou suggests. "Therefore, it is crucial to identify the optimal learning method for older learners, namely by ensuring that older learners are motivated, that the material has immediate practical value, and is personally rewarding."

From Cortex to Community

The results of these studies are exciting, but translating the science of cognitive reserve into healthier people is another problem entirely.

Research has shown, for example, that although people may have a vague understanding that they can shield themselves against age-related memory decline, they're fuzzy on the details. Funded by the US Centers for Disease Control, a collaborative research effort among nine universities found that most people recognize the link between exercise and cognitive health, but they're unsure about how much exercise they should be getting and what types of exercise are most effective. That is, they have difficulty translating what they *should* do into actual healthy actions.

Kristen Felten, a social worker and dementia specialist in the Wisconsin Department of Health Services, believes fixing this problem is of paramount importance.

"You can have a good quality of life, you can mitigate the symptoms of the disease, you can affect the trajectory of its progression with lifestyle changes," Felten explains. "Often, people don't realize they can take control."

As the research suggests, it's crucial that early symptoms be taken seriously. Some symptoms simply reflect the quotidian annoyances of an aging brain, but, in other cases, they may be early signs of dementia.

And this issue underlies perhaps the most critical policy measure societies can take: early dementia screening. Studies have shown that detecting signs of cognitive impairment early and targeting intervention programs appropriately can provide significant government savings in the long run. Furthermore, it can reduce the time patients spend in severe stages of the illness, leading to reduced emotional stress for families.

To address these dementia challenges, state and local authorities are beginning to develop strategic plans using the most recent scientific evidence. In her home state of Wisconsin, Felten has worked tirelessly to construct a systematic response to what is most certainly a large-scale problem, including building public awareness campaigns, disseminating evidence-based educational materials, and conducting outreach with rural and minority populations.

Perhaps most importantly, Felten and others are developing "dementia-capable" communities.

"We work with local businesses, grocery stores, pharmacies, banks, and restaurants—anywhere someone with dementia might go as part of their daily life," she says. "It's important that older individuals stay socially active and engaged, and communities need to be ready and willing to have that happen."

These opportunities for community engagement, she adds, may promote cognitive reserve.

Helping people make lifestyle changes that boost cognitive reserve is an important component of addressing the dementia epidemic, but there is no magic bullet. Invariably, there will be people who exercise, stay mentally fit, and keep an eye out for the early symptoms, but still develop dementia. These cases reinforce the notion that the onset of cognitive impairment is governed by a complex mix of biological and environmental risks, and there is much about the ailment that scientists don't yet know. Detaching dementia from aging will be an important part of ensuring that well-being increases alongside human longevity.

References and Further Reading

Anguera, J. A., Boccanfuso, J., Rintoul, J. L., Al-Hashimi, O., Faraji, F., Janowich, J., . . . Gazzaley, A. (2013). Video game training enhances cognitive control in older adults. *Nature, 501,* 97–101. doi: 10.1038/nature12486

Antoniou, M., Gunasekera, G. M., & Wong, P. (2013). Foreign language training as cognitive therapy for age-related cognitive decline: A hypothesis for future research. *Neuroscience & Biobehavioral Reviews, 37,* 2689–2698. doi: 10.1016/j.neubiorev.2013.09.004

Barnett, J. H., Lewis, L., Blackwell, A. D., & Taylor, M. (2014). Early intervention in Alzheimer's disease: A health economic study of the effects of diagnostic timing. *BMC Neurology, 14,* 101. doi: 10.1186/1471-2377-14-101

Bennett, D. A., Schneider, J. A., Arvanitakis, Z., Kelly, J. F., Aggarwal, N. T., Shah, R. C., & Wilson, R. S. (2006). Neuropathology of older persons without cognitive impairment from two community-based studies. *Neurology, 66,* 1837–1844. doi: 10.1212/01.wnl.0000219668.47116.e6

Bialystok, E., Craik, F. I. M., & Freedman, M. (2007). Bilingualism as a protection against the onset of symptoms of dementia. *Neuropsychologia, 45,* 459–464. doi: 10.1016/j.neuropsychologia.2006.10.009

Centers for Disease Control and Prevention. (2009). *What is a healthy brain? New research explores perceptions of cognitive health among diverse older adults.* Retrieved January 6, 2015 from http://www.cdc.gov/aging/pdf/perceptions_of_cog_hlth_factsheet.pdf

Craik, F. I. M., Bialystok, E., & Freedman, M. (2010). Delaying the onset of Alzheimer's disease: Bilingualism as a form of cognitive reserve. *Neurology, 75*, 1726–1729. doi: 10.1212/WNL.0b013e3181fc2a1c

Erickson, K. I., Voss, M. W., Prakash, R. S., Basek, C., Szabo, A., Chaddock, L. . . . Kramer, A. F. (2011). Exercise training increases size of hippocampus and improves memory. *Proceedings of the National Academy of Sciences, USA, 108*, 3017–3022. doi: 10.1073/pnas.1015950108

Luk, G., Bialystok, E., Craik, F. I., & Grady, C. L. (2011). Lifelong bilingualism maintains white matter integrity in older adults. *Journal of Neuroscience, 31*, 16808–16813. doi: 10.1523/JNEUROSCI.4563-11.2011

Park, D. C., Lodi-Smith, J., Drew, L., Haber, S., Hebrank, A., Bischof, G. N., & Aamodt, W. (2013). The impact of sustained engagement on cognitive function in older adults. *Psychological Science, 25*, 103–112. doi: 10.1177/0956797613499592

Schweizer, T. A., Ware, J., Fischer, C., Craik, F. I. M., & Bialystok, E. (2012). Bilingualism as a contributor to cognitive reserve: Evidence from brain atrophy in Alzheimer's disease. *Cortex, 48*, 991–996. doi: 10.1016/j.cortex.2011.04.009

Smith, J. C., Nielson, K. A., Woodard, J. L., Seidenberg, M., Durgerian, S., Hazlett, K. E., . . . Rao, S. M. (2014). Physical activity reduces hippocampal atrophy in elders at genetic risk for Alzheimer's disease. *Frontiers in Aging Neuroscience, 6.* doi: 10.3389/fnagi.2014.00061

Critical Thinking

1. Was cognitive performance improved more by psychological challenge or social interaction; and what is the explanation for the pattern of results that emerged?

2. Translate this sentence so that a five-year-old would understand the concepts: "Without continued engagement in a stimulating activity, gains for engaging in cognitive challenges are quickly lost."

3. It seems that exercise is critical for older adults, especially those at risk for different types of dementia. Using psychological principles, how might you design an exercise program for older adults that encourages consistent aerobic exercise?

Internet References

A life-course study of cognitive reserve in dementia—from childhood to old age
http://www.sciencedirect.com/science/article/pii/S1064748115000822

Cognitive reserve and Alzheimer's disease
http://www.crisisprevention.com/Blog/August-2010/Cognitive-Reserve-and-Alzheimer-s-Disease

Cognitive reserve: The first line of defense against dementia
https://www.agingcare.com/Articles/cognitive-reserve-avoid-dementia-symptoms-150033.htm

Merluzzi, Andrew. "Cognitive Shields: Investigating Protections against Dementia," *APS Observer*, February 2015. Copyright © 2015 by American Psychological Society. Permission conveyed through Copyright Clearance Center, Inc.

Article   Prepared by: R. Eric Landrum, *Boise State University*

We Aren't the World

Joe Henrich and his colleagues are shaking the foundations of psychology and economics—and hoping to change the way social scientists think about human behavior and culture.

ETHAN WATTERS

Learning Outcomes

After reading this article, you will be able to:

- Understand that there are cultural differences with respect to ideas about fairness.

- Appreciate the difficulty of only conducting studies on Westerners when trying to draw conclusions about people in general.

- Comprehend the impact the environment may have in a child's ability to make judgments about optical illusions such as the Muller-Lyer illusion.

In the Summer of 1995, a young graduate student in anthropology at UCLA named Joe Henrich traveled to Peru to carry out some fieldwork among the Machiguenga, an indigenous people who live north of Machu Picchu in the Amazon basin. The Machiguenga had traditionally been horticulturalists who lived in single-family, thatch-roofed houses in small hamlets composed of clusters of extended families. For sustenance, they relied on local game and produce from small-scale farming. They shared with their kin but rarely traded with outside groups.

While the setting was fairly typical for an anthropologist, Henrich's research was not. Rather than practice traditional ethnography, he decided to run a behavioral experiment that had been developed by economists. Henrich used a "game"—along the lines of the famous prisoner's dilemma—to see whether isolated cultures shared with the West the same basic instinct for fairness. In doing so, Henrich expected to confirm one of the foundational assumptions underlying such experiments, and indeed underpinning the entire fields of economics and psychology: that humans all share the same cognitive machinery—the same evolved rational and psychological hardwiring.

The test that Henrich introduced to the Machiguenga was called the ultimatum game. The rules are simple: in each game there are two players who remain anonymous to each other. The first player is given an amount of money, say $100, and told that he has to offer some of the cash, in an amount of his choosing, to the other subject. The second player can accept or refuse the split. But there's a hitch: players know that if the recipient refuses the offer, both leave empty-handed. North Americans, who are the most common subjects for such experiments, usually offer a 50-50 split when on the giving end. When on the receiving end, they show an eagerness to punish the other player for uneven splits at their own expense. In short, Americans show the tendency to be equitable with strangers—and to punish those who are not.

Among the Machiguenga, word quickly spread of the young, square-jawed visitor from America giving away money. The stakes Henrich used in the game with the Machiguenga were not insubstantial—roughly equivalent to the few days' wages they sometimes earned from episodic work with logging or oil companies. So Henrich had no problem finding volunteers. What he had great difficulty with, however, was explaining the rules, as the game struck the Machiguenga as deeply odd.

When he began to run the game it became immediately clear that Machiguengan behavior was dramatically different from that of the average North American. To begin with, the offers from the first player were much lower. In addition, when on the receiving end of the game, the Machiguenga rarely refused even the lowest possible amount. "It just seemed ridiculous to the Machiguenga that you would reject an offer of free money," says Henrich. "They just didn't understand why anyone would sacrifice money to punish someone who had the good luck of getting to play the other role in the game."

Joe Henrich and research assistant administer the Third Party Punishment Game in the village of Teci on Fiji's Yasawa Island.

The potential implications of the unexpected results were quickly apparent to Henrich. He knew that a vast amount of scholarly literature in the social sciences—particularly in economics and psychology—relied on the ultimatum game and similar experiments. At the heart of most of that research was the implicit assumption that the results revealed evolved psychological traits common to all humans, never mind that the test subjects were nearly always from the industrialized West. Henrich realized that if the Machiguenga results stood up, and if similar differences could be measured across other populations, this assumption of universality would have to be challenged.

Henrich had thought he would be adding a small branch to an established tree of knowledge. It turned out he was sawing at the very trunk. He began to wonder: What other certainties about "human nature" in social science research would need to be reconsidered when tested across diverse populations?

Henrich soon landed a grant from the MacArthur Foundation to take his fairness games on the road. With the help of a dozen other colleagues he led a study of 14 other small-scale societies, in locales from Tanzania to Indonesia. Differences abounded in the behavior of both players in the ultimatum game. In no society did he find people who were purely selfish (that is, who always offered the lowest amount, and never refused a split), but average offers from place to place varied widely and, in some societies—ones where gift-giving is heavily used to curry favor or gain allegiance—the first player would often make overly generous offers in excess of 60 percent, and the second player would often reject them, behaviors almost never observed among Americans.

The research established Henrich as an up-and-coming scholar. In 2004, he was given the U.S. Presidential Early Career Award for young scientists at the White House. But his work also made him a controversial figure. When he presented his research to the anthropology department at the University of British Columbia during a job interview a year later, he recalls a hostile reception. Anthropology is the social science most interested in cultural differences, but the young scholar's methods of using games and statistics to test and compare cultures with the West seemed heavy-handed and invasive to some. "Professors from the anthropology department suggested it was a bad thing that I was doing," Henrich remembers. "The word 'unethical' came up."

So instead of toeing the line, he switched teams. A few well-placed people at the University of British Columbia saw great promise in Henrich's work and created a position for him, split between the economics department and the psychology department. It was in the psychology department that he found two kindred spirits in Steven Heine and Ara Norenzayan. Together

the three set about writing a paper that they hoped would fundamentally challenge the way social scientists thought about human behavior, cognition, and culture.

A modern liberal arts education gives lots of lip service to the idea of cultural diversity. It's generally agreed that all of us see the world in ways that are sometimes socially and culturally constructed, that pluralism is good, and that ethnocentrism is bad. But beyond that the ideas get muddy. That we should welcome and celebrate people of all backgrounds seems obvious, but the implied corollary—that people from different ethnocultural origins have particular attributes that add spice to the body politic—becomes more problematic. To avoid stereotyping, it is rarely stated bluntly just exactly what those culturally derived qualities might be. Challenge liberal arts graduates on their appreciation of cultural diversity and you'll often find them retreating to the anodyne notion that under the skin everyone is really alike.

If you take a broad look at the social science curriculum of the last few decades, it becomes a little more clear why modern graduates are so unmoored. The last generation or two of undergraduates have largely been taught by a cohort of social scientists busily doing penance for the racism and Eurocentrism of their predecessors, albeit in different ways. Many anthropologists took to the navel gazing of postmodernism and swore off attempts at rationality and science, which were disparaged as weapons of cultural imperialism.

Economists and psychologists, for their part, did an end run around the issue with the convenient assumption that their job was to study the human mind stripped of culture. The human brain is genetically comparable around the globe, it was agreed, so human hardwiring for much behavior, perception, and cognition should be similarly universal. No need, in that case, to look beyond the convenient population of undergraduates for test subjects. A 2008 survey of the top six psychology journals dramatically shows how common that assumption was: more than 96 percent of the subjects tested in psychological studies from 2003 to 2007 were Westerners—with nearly 70 percent from the United States alone. Put another way: 96 percent of human subjects in these studies came from countries that represent only 12 percent of the world's population.

Henrich's work with the ultimatum game was an example of a small but growing countertrend in the social sciences, one in which researchers look straight at the question of how deeply culture shapes human cognition. His new colleagues in the psychology department, Heine and Norenzayan, were also part of this trend. Heine focused on the different ways people in Western and Eastern cultures perceived the world, reasoned, and understood themselves in relationship to others. Norenzayan's research focused on the ways religious belief influenced bonding and behavior. The three began to compile examples of cross-cultural research that, like Henrich's work with the

Machiguenga, challenged long-held assumptions of human psychological universality.

Some of that research went back a generation. It was in the 1960s, for instance, that researchers discovered that aspects of visual perception were different from place to place. One of the classics of the literature, the Müller-Lyer illusion, showed that where you grew up would determine to what degree you would fall prey to the illusion that these two lines are different in length:

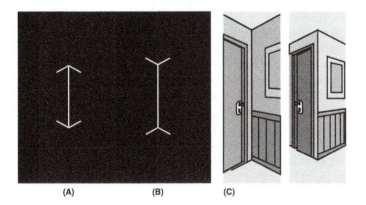

(A)   (B)   (C)

Researchers found that Americans perceive the line with the ends feathered outward (B) as being longer than the line with the arrow tips (A). San foragers of the Kalahari, on the other hand, were more likely to see the lines as they are: equal in length. Subjects from more than a dozen cultures were tested, and Americans were at the far end of the distribution—seeing the illusion more dramatically than all others.

More recently psychologists had challenged the universality of research done in the 1950s by pioneering social psychologist Solomon Asch. Asch had discovered that test subjects were often willing to make incorrect judgments on simple perception tests to conform with group pressure. When the test was performed across 17 societies, however, it turned out that group pressure had a range of influence. Americans were again at the far end of the scale, in this case showing the least tendency to conform to group belief.

As Heine, Norenzayan, and Henrich furthered their search, they began to find research suggesting wide cultural differences almost everywhere they looked: in spatial reasoning, the way we infer the motivations of others, categorization, moral reasoning, the boundaries between the self and others, and other arenas. These differences, they believed, were not genetic. The distinct ways Americans and Machiguengans played the ultimatum game, for instance, wasn't because they had differently evolved brains. Rather, Americans, without fully realizing it, were manifesting a psychological tendency shared with people in other industrialized countries that had been refined and handed down

through thousands of generations in ever more complex market economies. When people are constantly doing business with strangers, it helps when they have the desire to go out of their way (with a lawsuit, a call to the Better Business Bureau, or a bad Yelp review) when they feel cheated. Because Machiguengan culture had a different history, their gut feeling about what was fair was distinctly their own. In the small-scale societies with a strong culture of gift-giving, yet another conception of fairness prevailed. There, generous financial offers were turned down because people's minds had been shaped by a cultural norm that taught them that the acceptance of generous gifts brought burdensome obligations. Our economies hadn't been shaped by our sense of fairness; it was the other way around.

The growing body of cross-cultural research that the three researchers were compiling suggested that the mind's capacity to mold itself to cultural and environmental settings was far greater than had been assumed. The most interesting thing about cultures may not be in the observable things they do—the rituals, eating preferences, codes of behavior, and the like—but in the way they mold our most fundamental conscious and unconscious thinking and perception.

For instance, the different ways people perceive the Müller-Lyer illusion likely reflects lifetimes spent in different physical environments. American children, for the most part, grow up in box-shaped rooms of varying dimensions. Surrounded by carpentered corners, visual perception adapts to this strange new environment (strange and new in terms of human history, that is) by learning to perceive converging lines in three dimensions.

When unconsciously translated in three dimensions, the line with the outward-feathered ends (C) appears farther away and the brain therefore judges it to be longer. The more time one spends in natural environments, where there are no carpentered corners, the less one sees the illusion.

As the three continued their work, they noticed something else that was remarkable: again and again one group of people appeared to be particularly unusual when compared to other populations—with perceptions, behaviors, and motivations that were almost always sliding down one end of the human bell curve.

In the end they titled their paper "The Weirdest People in the World?" By "weird" they meant both unusual and Western, Educated, Industrialized, Rich, and Democratic. It is not just our Western habits and cultural preferences that are different from the rest of the world, it appears. The very way we think about ourselves and others—and even the way we perceive reality—makes us distinct from other humans on the planet, not to mention from the vast majority of our ancestors. Among Westerners, the data showed that Americans were often the most unusual, leading the researchers to conclude that "American participants are exceptional even within the unusual population of Westerners—outliers among outliers."

Given the data, they concluded that social scientists could not possibly have picked a worse population from which to draw broad generalizations. Researchers had been doing the equivalent of studying penguins while believing that they were learning insights applicable to all birds.

Not long ago I met Henrich, Heine, and Norenzayan for dinner at a small French restaurant in Vancouver, British Columbia, to hear about the reception of their weird paper, which was published in the prestigious journal *Behavioral and Brain Sciences* in 2010. The trio of researchers are young—as professors go—good-humored family men. They recalled that they were nervous as the publication time approached. The paper basically suggested that much of what social scientists thought they knew about fundamental aspects of human cognition was likely only true of one small slice of humanity. They were making such a broadside challenge to whole libraries of research that they steeled themselves to the possibility of becoming outcasts in their own fields.

"We were scared," admitted Henrich. "We were warned that a lot of people were going to be upset."

"We were told we were going to get spit on," interjected Norenzayan.

"Yes," Henrich said. "That we'd go to conferences and no one was going to sit next to us at lunchtime."

Interestingly, they seemed much less concerned that they had used the pejorative acronym WEIRD to describe a significant slice of humanity, although they did admit that they could only have done so to describe their own group. "Really," said Henrich, "the only people we could have called weird are represented right here at this table."

Still, I had to wonder whether describing the Western mind, and the American mind in particular, as weird suggested that our cognition is not just different but somehow malformed or twisted. In their paper the trio pointed out cross-cultural studies that suggest that the "weird" Western mind is the most self-aggrandizing and egotistical on the planet: we are more likely to promote ourselves as individuals versus advancing as a group. WEIRD minds are also more analytic, possessing the tendency to telescope in on an object of interest rather than understanding that object in the context of what is around it.

The WEIRD mind also appears to be unique in terms of how it comes to understand and interact with the natural world. Studies show that Western urban children grow up so closed off in man-made environments that their brains never form a deep or complex connection to the natural world. While studying children from the U.S., researchers have suggested a developmental timeline for what is called "folkbiological reasoning." These studies posit that it is not until children are around 7 years old that they stop projecting human qualities onto animals and begin to understand that humans are one animal among many. Compared to Yucatec Maya communities in Mexico, however, Western urban children appear to be developmentally delayed

in this regard. Children who grow up constantly interacting with the natural world are much less likely to anthropomorphize other living things into late childhood.

Given that people living in WEIRD societies don't routinely encounter or interact with animals other than humans or pets, it's not surprising that they end up with a rather cartoonish understanding of the natural world. "Indeed," the report concluded, "studying the cognitive development of folkbiology in urban children would seem the equivalent of studying 'normal' physical growth in malnourished children."

During our dinner, I admitted to Heine, Henrich, and Norenzayan that the idea that I can only perceive reality through a distorted cultural lens was unnerving. For me the notion raised all sorts of metaphysical questions: Is my thinking so strange that I have little hope of understanding people from other cultures? Can I mold my own psyche or the psyches of my children to be less WEIRD and more able to think like the rest of the world? If I did, would I be happier?

Henrich reacted with mild concern that I was taking this research so personally. He had not intended, he told me, for his work to be read as postmodern self-help advice. "I think we're really interested in these questions for the questions' sake," he said.

The three insisted that their goal was not to say that one culturally shaped psychology was better or worse than another—only that we'll never truly understand human behavior and cognition until we expand the sample pool beyond its current small slice of humanity. Despite these assurances, however, I found it hard not to read a message between the lines of their research. When they write, for example, that weird children develop their understanding of the natural world in a "culturally and experientially impoverished environment" and that they are in this way the equivalent of "malnourished children," it's difficult to see this as a good thing.

The turn that Henrich, Heine, and Norenzayan are asking social scientists to make is not an easy one: accounting for the influence of culture on cognition will be a herculean task. Cultures are not monolithic; they can be endlessly parsed. Ethnic backgrounds, religious beliefs, economic status, parenting styles, rural upbringing versus urban or suburban—there are hundreds of cultural differences that individually and in endless combinations influence our conceptions of fairness, how we categorize things, our method of judging and decision making, and our deeply held beliefs about the nature of the self, among other aspects of our psychological makeup.

We are just at the beginning of learning how these fine-grained cultural differences affect our thinking. Recent research has shown that people in "tight" cultures, those with strong norms and low tolerance for deviant behavior (think India, Malaysia, and Pakistan), develop higher impulse control and more self-monitoring abilities than those from other places. Men raised in the honor culture of the American South have been shown to experience much larger surges of testosterone after insults than do Northerners. Research published late last year suggested psychological differences at the city level too. Compared to San Franciscans, Bostonians' internal sense of self-worth is more dependent on community status and financial and educational achievement. "A cultural difference doesn't have to be big to be important," Norenzayan said. "We're not just talking about comparing New York yuppies to the Dani tribesmen of Papua New Guinea."

As Norenzayan sees it, the last few generations of psychologists have suffered from "physics envy," and they need to get over it. The job, experimental psychologists often assumed, was to push past the content of people's thoughts and see the underlying universal hardware at work. "This is a deeply flawed way of studying human nature," Norenzayan told me, "because the content of our thoughts and their process are intertwined." In other words, if human cognition is shaped by cultural ideas and behavior, it can't be studied without taking into account what those ideas and behaviors are and how they are different from place to place.

This new approach suggests the possibility of reverse-engineering psychological research: look at cultural content first; cognition and behavior second. Norenzayan's recent work on religious belief is perhaps the best example of the intellectual landscape that is now open for study. When Norenzayan became a student of psychology in 1994, four years after his family had moved from Lebanon to America, he was excited to study the effect of religion on human psychology. "I remember opening textbook after textbook and turning to the index and looking for the word 'religion,'" he told me, "Again and again the very word wouldn't be listed. This was shocking. How could psychology be the science of human behavior and have nothing to say about religion? Where I grew up you'd have to be in a coma not to notice the importance of religion on how people perceive themselves and the world around them."

Norenzayan became interested in how certain religious beliefs, handed down through generations, may have shaped human psychology to make possible the creation of large-scale societies. He has suggested that there may be a connection between the growth of religions that believe in "morally concerned deities"—that is, a god or gods who care if people are good or bad—and the evolution of large cities and nations. To be cooperative in large groups of relative strangers, in other words, might have required the shared belief that an all-powerful being was forever watching over your shoulder.

If religion was necessary in the development of large-scale societies, can large-scale societies survive without religion? Norenzayan points to parts of Scandinavia with atheist majorities that seem to be doing just fine. They may have climbed the ladder of religion and effectively kicked it away. Or perhaps, after a thousand years of religious belief, the idea of an unseen entity always watching your behavior remains in our culturally shaped thinking even after the belief in God dissipates or disappears.

Why, I asked Norenzayan, if religion might have been so central to human psychology, have researchers not delved into the topic? "Experimental psychologists are the weirdest of the weird," said Norenzayan. "They are almost the least religious academics, next to biologists. And because academics mostly talk amongst themselves, they could look around and say, 'No one who is important to me is religious, so this must not be very important.'" Indeed, almost every major theorist on human behavior in the last 100 years predicted that it was just a matter of time before religion was a vestige of the past. But the world persists in being a very religious place.

Henrich, Heine, and Norenzayan's fear of being ostracized after the publication of the WEIRD paper turned out to be misplaced. Response to the paper, both published and otherwise, has been nearly universally positive, with more than a few of their colleagues suggesting that the work will spark fundamental changes. "I have no doubt that this paper is going to change the social sciences," said Richard Nisbett, an eminent psychologist at the University of Michigan. "It just puts it all in one place and makes such a bold statement."

More remarkable still, after reading the paper, academics from other disciplines began to come forward with their own mea culpas. Commenting on the paper, two brain researchers from Northwestern University argued that the nascent field of neuro-imaging had made the same mistake as psychologists, noting that 90 percent of neuroimaging studies were performed in Western countries. Researchers in motor development similarly suggested that their discipline's body of research ignored how different child-rearing practices around the world can dramatically influence states of development. Two psycholinguistics professors suggested that their colleagues had also made the same mistake: blithely assuming human homogeneity while focusing their research primarily on one rather small slice of humanity.

At its heart, the challenge of the WEIRD paper is not simply to the field of experimental human research (do more cross-cultural studies!); it is a challenge to our Western conception of human nature. For some time now, the most widely accepted answer to the question of why humans, among all animals, have so successfully adapted to environments across the globe is that we have big brains with the ability to learn, improvise, and problem-solve.

Henrich has challenged this "cognitive niche" hypothesis with the "cultural niche" hypothesis. He notes that the amount of knowledge in any culture is far greater than the capacity of individuals to learn or figure it all out on their own. He suggests that individuals tap that cultural storehouse of knowledge simply by mimicking (often unconsciously) the behavior and ways of thinking of those around them. We shape a tool in a certain manner, adhere to a food taboo, or think about fairness in a particular way, not because we individually have figured out that behavior's adaptive value, but because we instinctively trust our culture to show us the way. When Henrich asked Fijian women why they avoided certain potentially toxic fish during pregnancy and breastfeeding, he found that many didn't know or had fanciful reasons. Regardless of their personal understanding, by mimicking this culturally adaptive behavior they were protecting their offspring. The unique trick of human psychology, these researchers suggest, might be this: our big brains are evolved to let local culture lead us in life's dance.

The applications of this new way of looking at the human mind are still in the offing. Henrich suggests that his research about fairness might first be applied to anyone working in international relations or development. People are not "plug and play," as he puts it, and you cannot expect to drop a Western court system or form of government into another culture and expect it to work as it does back home. Those trying to use economic incentives to encourage sustainable land use will similarly need to understand local notions of fairness to have any chance of influencing behavior in predictable ways.

Because of our peculiarly Western way of thinking of ourselves as independent of others, this idea of the culturally shaped mind doesn't go down very easily. Perhaps the richest and most established vein of cultural psychology—that which compares Western and Eastern concepts of the self—goes to the heart of this problem. Heine has spent much of his career following the lead of a seminal paper published in 1991 by Hazel Rose Markus, of Stanford University, and Shinobu Kitayama, who is now at the University of Michigan. Markus and Kitayama suggested that different cultures foster strikingly different views of the self, particularly along one axis: some cultures regard the self as independent from others; others see the self as interdependent. The interdependent self—which is more the norm in East Asian countries, including Japan and China—connects itself with others in a social group and favors social harmony over self-expression. The independent self—which is most prominent in America—focuses on individual attributes and preferences and thinks of the self as existing apart from the group.

The classic "rod and frame" task: Is the line in the center vertical?

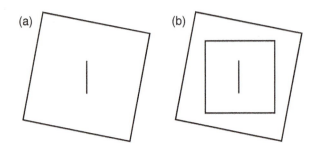

That we in the West develop brains that are wired to see ourselves as separate from others may also be connected to differences in how we reason, Heine argues. Unlike the vast majority of the world, Westerners (and Americans in particular) tend to reason analytically as opposed to holistically. That is, the American mind strives to figure out the world by taking it apart and examining its pieces. Show a Japanese and an American the same cartoon of an aquarium, and the American will remember details mostly about the moving fish while the Japanese observer will likely later be able to describe the seaweed, the bubbles, and other objects in the background. Shown another way, in a different test analytic Americans will do better on something called the "rod and frame" task, where one has to judge whether a line is vertical even though the frame around it is skewed. Americans see the line as apart from the frame, just as they see themselves as apart from the group.

Heine and others suggest that such differences may be the echoes of cultural activities and trends going back thousands of years. Whether you think of yourself as interdependent or independent may depend on whether your distant ancestors farmed rice (which required a great deal of shared labor and group cooperation) or herded animals (which rewarded individualism and aggression). Heine points to Nisbett at Michigan, who has argued that the analytic/holistic dichotomy in reasoning styles can be clearly seen, respectively, in Greek and Chinese philosophical writing dating back 2,500 years. These psychological trends and tendencies may echo down generations, hundreds of years after the activity or situation that brought them into existence has disappeared or fundamentally changed.

And here is the rub: the culturally shaped analytic/individualistic mind-sets may partly explain why Western researchers have so dramatically failed to take into account the interplay between culture and cognition. In the end, the goal of boiling down human psychology to hardwiring is not surprising given the type of mind that has been designing the studies. Taking an object (in this case the human mind) out of its context is, after all, what distinguishes the analytic reasoning style prevalent in the West. Similarly, we may have underestimated the impact of culture because the very ideas of being subject to the will of larger historical currents and of unconsciously mimicking the cognition of those around us challenges our Western conception of the self as independent and self-determined. The historical missteps of Western researchers, in other words, have been the predictable consequences of the WEIRD mind doing the thinking.

Critical Thinking

1. What, if anything, is a certainty about human behavior, and how would psychologists (and others interested in human behavior) go about establishing which behaviors are certainties and which behaviors are not certainties?

2. What are the challenges of truly embracing cultural diversity? Explain.

3. Societies with a strong tradition of gift-giving performed differently on the ultimatum task compared to other societies? If Americans were to become more gift-giving-centered, what effect do you think this would have on their performance in the ultimatum game?

Internet References

How understanding the prisoner's dilemma can help bridge liberal and conservative differences

http://theconversation.com/how-understanding-the-prisoners-dilemma-can-help-bridge-liberal-and-conservative-differences-46166

Introduction to social dilemmas

http://www.socialdilemma.com/content/introduction-social-dilemmas

The 'prisoner's dilemma' tests women in and out of jail

http://www.npr.org/sections/13.7/2013/07/29/206513599/the-prisoner-s-dilemma-goes-to-jail-and-some-science-reporting-should-follow

Unit 6

UNIT

Prepared by: Eric Landrum, *Boise State University*

Emotion and Motivation

Jasmine's sister was a working mother who always reminded Jasmine about how exciting life on the road was as a sales representative. Jasmine stayed home because she wanted to take care of her children, 2-year-old Jessica, 4-year-old Kristen, and newborn Jade. One day, Jasmine was having a difficult time with the children. The baby, Jade, had been crying all day from colic. The other two children had been bickering over their toys. Jasmine, realizing that it was already 5:15 pm and her husband would be home any minute, frantically started preparing dinner. She wanted to fix a nice dinner so that she and her husband could eat after the children went to bed, then relax together.

This particular evening, however, did not turn out as expected. Jasmine sat waiting for her no-show husband. When he finally walked in the door at 10:15 pm, Jasmine was furious. His excuse, that his boss had invited the whole office for dinner, didn't help Jasmine feel better. Jasmine reasoned that her husband could have called to say that he wouldn't be home for dinner; he could have taken 5 minutes to do that. He said he did but the phone was busy. Her face was red with rage. She screamed at her husband. Suddenly, bursting into tears, she ran into the living room. Her husband retreated to the safety of their bedroom. Exhausted and disappointed, Jasmine sat alone and pondered why she was so angry with her husband. Was she just tired? Was she frustrated by dealing with young children all day and simply wanted to be around another adult? Was she secretly worried and jealous that

her husband was seeing another woman and he had lied about his whereabouts? Was she combative because her husband's and her sister's lives seemed so much more rewarding than her own? Jasmine was unsure of how she felt and why she exploded in such rage at her husband, whom she loved dearly.

This story, although sad and gender stereotypical, is not necessarily unrealistic when it comes to emotions. There are times when we are moved by strong emotions. On other occasions, when we expect to cry, we find that our eyes are dry. What are these strange feelings we call emotions? What motivates us to become angry at someone we love? How is it sometimes when we need certain motivations (such as completing an assignment before a deadline), the motivation to do the work is absent until right before the deadline? How can we become more efficient (both at home and in the workplace) in understanding how our emotions influence our behavioral choices?

These questions and others have inspired psychologists to study motivation and emotion. Jasmine's story, besides introducing these topics to you, also illustrates why these two topics are usually interrelated in psychology. Some emotions are pleasant, so pleasant that we are motivated to keep experiencing them. Pleasant emotions are exemplified by love, pride, and joy. Other emotions are terribly draining and oppressive—so negative that we hope they will be over as soon as possible. Negative emotions are exemplified by anger, grief, and jealousy. Motivation, emotion, and their relationship to one another are the focus of this unit.

Women at the Top: Powerful Leaders Define Success as Work + Family in a Culture of Gender by Fanny M. Cheung and Diane F. Halpern

117

Article

Prepared by: Eric Landrum, *Boise State University*

Women at the Top
Powerful Leaders Define Success as Work + Family in a Culture of Gender

How do women rise to the top of their professions when they also have significant family care responsibilities? This critical question has not been addressed by existing models of leadership. In a review of recent research, we explore an alternative model to the usual notion of a Western male as the prototypical leader. The model includes (a) relationship-oriented leadership traits, (b) the importance of teamwork and consensus building, and (c) an effective work–family interface that women with family care responsibilities create and use to break through the glass ceiling. We adopted a cross-cultural perspective to highlight the importance of relational orientation and work–family integration in collectivistic cultures, which supplements models of leadership based on Western men. Our expanded model of leadership operates in the context of a "culture of gender" that defines expectations for women and men as leaders. This complex model includes women in diverse global contexts and enriches our understanding of the interplay among personal attributes, processes, and environments in leadership.

FANNY M. CHEUNG AND DIANE F. HALPERN

Learning Outcomes

After reading this article, you will be able to:

- Understand and explain the factors that contribute to how women with families achieve success as leaders.

- Describe the role of the "culture of gender" in how women in different cultures achieve success as leaders.

There are two very different stories about women's leadership around the world, and depending on which one you choose to tell, and your attitudes toward women in leadership positions, the news is either very good or very bad. Despite the endless blogging and newspaper headlines to the contrary, women are not "opting out" of the workforce to stay home with their babies. The workforce participation of mothers did drop by 2% since its peak in 2000, but as economist Boushey (2005) demonstrated, there was a similar drop in employment for women without children and for all men, which was caused by a general recession from 2001 to 2004. For the first time in U.S. history, women are close to surpassing men in their employment rate, largely because most of the jobs lost in the recent recession have occurred in manufacturing, construction, and finance, where the jobs are largely held by men. The most recently available data show that women now hold 49.1% of jobs in the United States (Rampell, 2009). On the other side of the globe is China,

where economic development and culture differ from those in the Western industrialized world but the figure for women's employment is quite similar (45%; "Women Take 45%," 2007). Women are better educated than ever before; they comprise the majority of undergraduate college enrollments in industrialized countries and are catching up in the developing countries (57% in the United States: Peter & Horn, 2005; 44% in China: Department of Population, Social, Science and Technology Statistics, National Bureau of Statistics, 2004). As might be expected from the growing trend of women's higher educational achievement, there are more women than men in mid-level management positions, which has created an overflowing "pipeline" of managers ready for advancement to top-level executive positions in the United States.

Now for the bad news: Despite women's success in education and mid-level management, few women make it to the "O" level—CEO, CFO (chief financial officer), CIO (chief information officer), or CTO (chief technology officer)—in the corporate world or to comparable top levels in noncorporate settings, such as the highest levels of political office or the top rungs of the academic ladder. In the United States, women hold approximately 50% of all management and professional positions, outnumbering "men in such occupations as financial managers; human resource managers; education administrators; medical and health services managers; accountants and auditors; budget analysts; property, real estate, and social and community service managers" (U.S. Department of Labor, Women's Bureau, 2006, para. 12). Despite their middle-management success, only 2% of the Fortune 500 CEOs and 2% of the Fortune 1000 CEOs are women ("Fortune 500 2006: Women CEOs," 2006). Comparable data from the FTSE (Financial Times Stock Exchange) 250 (Singh & Vinnicombe, 2006) show that 2.8% of CEOs for the top 250 companies listed on the London Stock Exchange are women.

A half century after the women's movement, women have only moved to the halfway mark in the corporate world and other organizations in the industrialized Western societies; most are stuck in middle management. Women in other parts of the world are still far from that halfway mark. For example, in China, women make up 16.8% of the heads of government departments and the Communist Party, social organizations, enterprises, and institutions (Department of Population, Social, Science and Technology Statistics, National Bureau of Statistics, 2004). Even in Hong Kong, which continues to be a more westernized and economically affluent special administrative region after its reunification with China in 1997, women constitute 29.1% of persons employed as managers and administrators (Census and Statistics Department, Government of the Hong Kong Special Administrative Region, 2007). A bevy of commentators have suggested that women are better suited for the "New Economy," with its emphasis on communication and interpersonal skills and the rapid loss of jobs in manufacturing, agriculture, and other job sectors in which physical strength is an asset. Although this may seem like a logical conclusion, there are very few women who have made it to the top leadership positions.

Why are there so few women at the top of the leading organizations given the large numbers that are stalled at middle management? An important clue can be found by taking a closer look at the women who have made it into the rarified atmosphere of life at the top. Almost half of these top executives have no children, and almost half of all women in the United States with salaries greater than $100,000 have no children (Dye, 2005; Hewlett, 2002). Similar data have been found for women who achieve at the highest ranks at research universities, where there have been extensive and eye-opening analyses of the success of women with children. Only one third of all women who began their jobs at research universities without children ever become mothers, and among those who attain tenure, women are twice as likely as their male counterparts to be single 12 years after obtaining their doctorates (Mason & Goulden, 2004). The double standard is alive and well in the workplace. The presence of children signals stability and responsibility for men, who are assumed to be better workers because of their roles as breadwinners. The identical situation for women has the opposite effect.

Recent studies have confirmed the *motherhood wage penalty*, a term that describes the consistent finding that mothers earn less than comparable women without children and less than men in general. By contrast, married men enjoy a *marriage premium,* which refers to one of the most reliable findings in the labor economics literature—the economic advantage that fathers enjoy in the workplace (Hersch & Stratton, 2000). In an experimental investigation of this phenomenon, Correll, Benard, and Paik (2007) responded to a variety of employment advertisements with applications from women that varied

according to whether the women had children or were childless. The applications were carefully matched on work-relevant dimensions. Only 3.1% of the mothers were invited for an interview, compared with 6.6% of the identically qualified women who had no children. Discriminatory practices against women were further documented by these researchers when paid undergraduates rated fictitious applicants for employment. Mothers were rated as less competent and were offered a lower starting salary than comparable women without children. The choice for highly successful women has been clear: Choose either a baby or a briefcase.

But what about those women who refused to make such a choice and succeeded at the top of their professions with children and other family care responsibilities? What can we learn from these women who are leading dually successful lives with (by their own description) happy, thriving families and occupational success at the highest levels? While there have been many studies on work–family conflicts for women workers or managers in general, there are few such studies on women leaders in the literature and none that specifically compared women with and without family care responsibilities.

Given the small number of women at the top, most studies on women leaders have relied on in-depth and qualitative interviews. Studies of these exceptional women are not representative of the norm, but they highlight gaps in our understanding of leadership from a gender-sensitive perspective. These studies do not have representative samples, as the population is small, but generally rely on personal networks and snowball techniques in reaching these exceptional targets. For example, Cantor and Bernay (1992) interviewed 25 American women politicians holding high federal, state, and local elected offices; they used structured questions to investigate how these women developed the leadership qualities that enable them to succeed in politics. Cantor and Bernay identified three critical elements in the leadership equation for these women politicians: competent self, creative aggression, and woman-power. Instead of attempting to behave like men in a male environment, these women leaders embraced and integrated typically female qualities, such as tenderness and caring, with assertiveness and achievement orientation. White, Cox, and Cooper (1992) interviewed 48 women executives, entrepreneurs, politicians, and senior professionals in the United Kingdom on their childhoods, education, and work and family histories to examine their career trajectories. Walton's (1997) study of 11 women heads of colleges in the United Kingdom also adopted an interview method to cover a range of themes, including the women's academic career paths, family influences, self-worth, and job satisfaction.

Qualitative studies of women leaders from other ethnic backgrounds have also been conducted in recent years. Gomez and her colleagues (2001) conducted semi-structured, in-depth interviews to investigate the career development of 20 notable Latinas in the United States whose contributions on the local, national, or international level were recognized in their communities. Their study included contextual and cultural variables in addition to personal variables and the family–work interface. The contextual and cultural factors included social movements, economic trends, public policies, and discrimination at the macro level. At the more personal or interpersonal level, the individual's socioeconomic and educational background, social support, availability of mentors, and role models were important factors.

Richie and her colleagues (1997) also used semistructured, in-depth interviews to compare nine high-achieving African women and nine European American women across eight occupational fields in the United States. The interviews covered the participants' work behaviors and attitudes, their sociocultural and personal backgrounds, and the current contextual conditions that led to particular career actions and consequences. The stories told by their participants showed that they achieved career success on their own terms. Their leadership styles were characterized by interconnectedness. Social support provided an important means for them to balance their personal and professional lives. The authors concluded that women's career development differed from men's, and they confirmed "the inappropriateness of applying career theories written by and based on White men to White women and people of color" (Richie et al., 1997, p. 145).

Kawahara, Esnil, and Hsu (2007) interviewed 12 Asian American women leaders who were considered to be high achievers. The themes that were covered in the interviews included the women's personal attributes, leadership styles, support systems, self-worth, and cultural competence. The comments collected from the interviews demonstrated the emphasis on relating to others and creating a harmonious environment, both of which are reflective of collectivistic values. Family and partner support were recognized as playing an important role in these women's achievement.

Studies with women leaders from different ethnic backgrounds highlight the additional context of culture in which women navigate through the *labyrinth,* a term preferred by Eagly and Carli (2007) to the *glass ceiling* metaphor. Culture defines the expectations for women's and men's roles in society and sets the norms and values in social behavior. Cross-cultural studies of top women leaders could provide a richer understanding of the convergent and divergent contextual factors that characterize women's leadership.

Using semi-structured open-ended interviews, we studied 62 women at the top of their professions who either were or had been married and who had significant family care responsibilities (usually children, but we also included care for other family members such as a disabled sibling or parent). Top-level positions included legislators, government ministers, business executives, college presidents, chiefs of police, and other senior-level professionals from China, Hong Kong, and the United States (Halpern & Cheung, 2008). These three societies provide a comparison in terms of cultural context and socioeconomic milieu. Hong Kong is more similar to China in cultural background but at the same time is more similar to the United States in terms of socioeconomic environment, whereas China and the United States are more distinct from one another in both culture and socioeconomic milieu (Watkins, 2006). In addition to describing their career development and leadership styles, these top women leaders in American and Chinese societies described how they created and negotiated a work–family

interface. These highly successful women shared their strategies for leading dually successful lives. This study provides a cross-cultural perspective on the key issues for studying women's leadership. We use the lessons we learned from our study to structure the framework of the following review of the research literature on women leaders.

Integrating Work and Family

Previous research on women in employment has highlighted work–family balance as a major concern (Allen, Herst, Bruck, & Sutton, 2000; Byron, 2005). Working mothers everywhere are known to be short on time, always working a "second shift" after they finish a day at their hectic jobs (Hochschild, 1989). Many countries across the world have conducted time use surveys (United Nations Statistics Division, n.d.). The common finding is that women in paid employment generally spend more hours per day on household duties than do their male counterparts (e.g. Galinsky, 2005). Early studies of work–family balance adopted a scarcity perspective (Greenhaus & Beutell, 1985). It was assumed that the demands of family and work were competing for a finite amount of time, resulting in conflict and stress.

By studying women leaders who managed to maintain their family lives while they advanced in their careers, we identified personal characteristics and strategies that women used to overcome these barriers. As workers in "extreme jobs" that require "24/7" commitment (Hewlett & Luce, 2006), the dually successful top women leaders we interviewed employed many strategies to "make more time." As revealed in our study and other studies of women leaders, these women considered themselves to be experts in multitasking. Because they each lived one life rather than two separate lives at work and at home, they created links between family and work, although they kept their role identities distinct. For example, children went to work with them and often accompanied them on business trips, not only because it allowed the women to spend more time with their children but also because it helped the children understand where their mommies went when they left the house. The women worked from home at least part of the time, often setting rules for switching activities, such as working on Sunday night rather than during the day when they spent the weekend with family, or always being at home for dinner and then working after the children went to bed.

Beyond Work–Family Balance

Recent research on the work–family interface has taken a more balanced view and considered more complex interactions between the work and family domains, which include both negative and positive spillovers in the work–family interface (Rapoport, Bailyn, Fletcher, & Pruitt, 2002). From their meta-analysis reviewing 178 studies on the work–family interface, Ford, Heinen, and Langkamer (2007) found that support from family and work domains was positively related to cross-domain satisfaction. Friedman and Greenhaus (2000) found that when work and family were integrated, the two roles could enhance each other. In integrating these two roles, managing role boundaries was more important than just reducing time at work. Particularly for women, the work–family boundary is more permeable. Thus, we propose that the metaphor of work–family balance be replaced with a metaphor that recognizes the gains that can be achieved by combining or integrating work and family roles (Halpern & Murphy, 2005).

Baltes and Heydens-Gahir (2003) extended a general model of life management strategy to study work–family conflict. They classified the repertoire of adaptive behavior strategies as SOC: selection, optimization, and compensation. The primary focus of *selection* is on the articulation and setting of goals, which give direction to behavior. In our study (Halpern & Cheung, 2008), the top women leaders were very clear about their goals and their priorities. Family and work were both important, and day-to-day decisions were based on family and work needs. They also excelled in the *optimization* strategies through scheduling of time and multitasking. They were flexible in adopting the *compensation* strategy by using alternative means such as outsourcing when time and material resources were limited.

In order to accept the alternative means of fulfilling the demands of a role, many women leaders redefine the structural and personal roles that the workplace and the society have imposed on women (Frone, 2003). In the studies reviewed, most of the women leaders who are married and have families embrace both their family and work roles. However, instead of being superwomen who hold themselves to the highest standards for all of the role-related tasks of being wives and mothers, they adopt different internal and external strategies to redefine their roles. They learn to let go and outsource household tasks just as they would outsource work in a busy office. They recognize that they do not have to do it all by themselves. They alter their internal conceptions of the demands of their work and family roles and define these roles in ways that are meaningful and helpful to them.

Research on work–family balance in Chinese societies suggests a different cultural perspective in understanding the definition of work and family roles. These studies show that work and family are viewed as interdependent domains, unlike the distinct segregation of these two domains in Western concepts of work and family. In individualistic societies, overwork would be considered as taking time away from the family and sacrificing the family for the advancement of one's own career. In collectivistic societies, overwork is likely to be seen as sacrificing oneself for the family, since commitment to work is viewed as a means to ensuring financial security for the family (Yang, Chen, Choi, & Zou, 2000). The needs of the self are subsumed under the needs of the collective. As such, the work–family boundary is more permeable in Chinese societies (Francesco & Shaffer, 2009).

A cross-national comparative study (Spector et al., 2004) involving 15 samples of managers across three culturally distinct regions—Anglo-majority countries (Australia, Canada, England, New Zealand, and the United States), China (Hong Kong, mainland China, and Taiwan), and seven Latin American countries—showed that for the Anglo culture, working long hours was related to work–family stress. For the Chinese and Latin cultures, this was not the case. For the Chinese managers, being married and having children were associated with higher job satisfaction and psychological well-being. A series of studies conducted by Aryee and his colleagues on the work–family interface in Hong Kong (Aryee, Field, & Luk, 1999; Aryee, Luk, Leung, & Lo, 1999) also showed that work and family involvement per se did not lead to work–family conflict. Time conflict did not necessarily lead to strain.

A recent study of working adults in the United States found that women and men with an egalitarian outlook on life, which means they were committed to both their work and their families, reported feeling less guilty when family life interfered with their work than traditional women and men whose commitment was to only one of these spheres of life (Livingston & Judge, 2008). It is interesting to note that these researchers did not find much guilt when work interfered with family life, although one possible explanation for this asymmetry is that few of their participants had partners (36%) or young children (25%). The successful combination of family and work will depend on the obligations people have in both of these spheres.

Past studies of work–life balance rarely included leaders at the top with substantial family care responsibilities and have not considered their responses as a distinct group. Partly it is because this is not an issue that is considered important to men as leaders; partly it is because there are very few top women leaders to be studied. In studies of women leaders, however, we found that the dually successful Western women leaders tended to integrate their work and family roles in the collective unit of the family. Many also regarded family as their priority, and the motivation to succeed at work was to contribute to the well-being of their families and children. In reframing their work as an ally instead of an enemy of the family (Friedman & Greenhaus, 2000), the women leaders in many of the qualitative studies we reviewed reported satisfaction in both domains.

Redefining Roles

In order to integrate their family roles and work roles, the women leaders in the studies we reviewed redefined their own norms for being a good mother and being a leader, making these roles more compatible than they were under the norms prescribed by the larger society. According to their own definitions, a good mother is highly involved in her children's lives and activities, but she does not need to spend all of her time with them. Typically, the women leaders in these studies described their devotion to their children and their families. But because they considered family their highest priority, they dedicated themselves to finding solutions to make it work. These solutions included self-enforced standards to ensure that they always had dinner with their families, took the children on any business trip that lasted more than three days, never missed an important event such as a school play or soccer game, and helped with homework every night. For example, in our study (Halpern & Cheung, 2008), one Hong Kong woman executive made a long-distance telephone call to her children every night when she was posted overseas (before Internet communication was widely accessible) and had them fax their homework to her hotel room, which she then faxed back to them after she reviewed it. Several Chinese women leaders talked about going home to eat dinner with their families before leaving for a business dinner or an evening meeting in order to maintain family togetherness. U.S. women leaders talked with pride about never or rarely missing an important event in their children's lives, which they achieved by arranging their work around these events.

These highly successful women also redefined their roles as successful leaders, which included work + family. They worked long hours, but they also managed to leave work for family time. They counted performance and outcome rather than the actual hours at work. Earlier in their careers, some of the women "flew below the radar" and just left work without announcing why to be at after-school events, completing their work later in the evening. Their employers learned that it was their performance that counted. Once they were in positions of leadership, the women leaders had more control over their work schedules, which allowed them to handle dual demands more openly.

Women's dual roles may be viewed as two circles, one representing family and one work. When the demands of a two-circle life are too much for anyone to manage, the total area for both circles needs to be reduced. One way to reduce the total area is to overlap the circles when possible, symbolically blending work and family (see Figure 1). The portion of the family circle that extends beyond the overlap can be reduced with practical strategies such as hiring help to clean the house, prepare meals, and even shop for presents—by outsourcing anything that does not directly contribute to spending time with one's family. In addition, the portion of the circle representing work that is not overlapping with family can also be reduced. Employees can be empowered to do their work without the direct involvement of the women leaders. Many of these high-powered mothers created work-related expectations that also reduced the size of the "work" circle, such as always leaving work at 7:00 or whatever time they routinely set for themselves and scheduling luncheon meetings instead of evening dinners with clients so as to eat dinner with their families.

Family and Spousal Support

Inevitably, the women leaders interviewed in the various studies all cited the importance of their family support in making it to the top. Having collective identities that emphasized family loyalty, they also fell back on their families to provide support. They relied on some combination of supportive husbands, extended families, and hired help in societies where domestic help was accessible.

The extended family provided much needed help with household chores and child care. Particularly for women from collectivistic societies, proximity to the extended family facilitated their support networks. Part-time and live-in home help supplemented this network. Even in the United States, home help is not as economically inaccessible to professional women as many people believe. The difficulty lies more in getting reliable and stable home help, as well as in women's personal belief that they have to do everything themselves. In interviews with women leaders, they would talk about child-care arrangements,

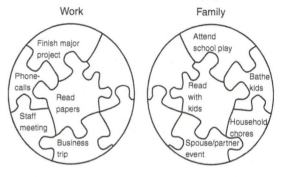

Distinct Work and Family Domains in a Segregated Model

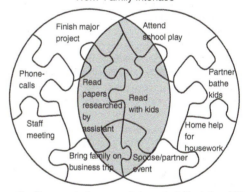

Overlapping Work–Family Domains in an Integrated Model
Work–Family Interface

Figure 1   Segregated versus Integrated Models of Work–Family Interface

supervision of domestic helpers, and maintaining emotional labor with the extended family. In studies of male leadership, these arrangements are assumed to be taken care of by someone and are rarely explicitly discussed.

Another distinctive concern for women leaders is their spousal relationships. Studies of marital relationships show that one of the biggest problems for working women is their husbands' lack of support for their careers (Gilbert, 1988; Vannoy-Hiller & Philliber, 1991). In Western studies of mate selection, men prefer to marry down, which usually includes marrying women who are shorter, weigh less, have less education, and earn less than they do (Schoen & Weinick, 1993). So the superior social status of women leaders may pose a threat to their marriages if their husbands are uncomfortable breaking with traditional sex role norms.

The married women leaders in the various studies converged in their appreciation of their husbands' support. Otherwise, their marriages might not have lasted. The supportive husbands were reported to take on a substantial share in housework. More important, they provided emotional support and encouragement. In our study (Halpern & Cheung, 2008), we specifically addressed the women leaders' relationships with their husbands. Under the strong patriarchal norms in Chinese families, the success of women leaders might have posed a stronger threat to their husbands. However, in this selective sample of women leaders who had stayed married, many described their husbands as their biggest fans, cheerleaders, coaches, and mentors. These husbands were self-assured and confident of themselves. They endorsed egalitarian values toward women. They did not endorse the hierarchical patriarchal norms of marriage and did not feel threatened by the reversed normative roles that put their wives in the limelight and gave them "superior" status.

It is particularly difficult when a family moves for the advancement of the wife's career and the husband takes up the role of the trailing spouse, often with uncertain career prospects at the new location and the loss of a good job at the old location. However, the couples who moved repeatedly to accommodate the wife's promotions considered the sacrifices made by the trailing spouse to be worthwhile. For these couples, the wife's accomplishments and the resources she brought to the marriage were redefined as collective assets to the family instead of threats in a power struggle.

The women leaders who stayed happily married emphasized that they and their husbands grew together in the marriage. They exhibited what marital counselors would call healthy couple behaviors—responsibility, alignment of goals, mutual encouragement and acceptance, commitment to equality in the relationship, empathic listening and open communication, willingness to discuss their relationship, and willingness to engage in joint conflict resolution (Blume, 2006). There was a great deal of give and take, discussion, and negotiation in these marriages. Amidst their busy schedules, our interviewees created the time and space to share their lives with their marital partners. Many of the women mentioned how they designated evenings or weekends for the family or for special dates with their husbands.

Women's Style of Leadership

Do women lead differently from men? Eagly and Carli (2007) observed that while leadership roles promote similarities in male and female leaders, women generally have a more democratic, participative, and collaborative style of leading. Stern (2008) reviewed studies of high-achieving women and concurred that these women tend to adopt a relational leadership style. They also demonstrate a strong sense of conviction and self-worth. Femininity and leadership are no longer considered incompatible. Virtually all of the women we interviewed believed that their style of leadership as women was better suited for the contemporary workplace. They did not reject femininity or shy away from including family roles as metaphors for their leadership roles. Some of the Chinese women talked about leading like grandmothers or mothers, which included being firm when necessary but always supportive, similar to what Cantor and Bernay (1992) described as "maternal strengths" in the American women politicians. These women were not advocating for a "mushy" or feel-good notion of what a "feminine" approach to leadership might be. Instead, the usual definition they provided included being serious about their work, maintaining the highest personal standards, promoting communication, and being considerate and respectful of their staffs. They

also strongly emphasized the notion of a leader as a person of moral character and a role model, which together with a relational orientation have been found to be defining characteristics of leadership in Chinese culture (Smith & Wang, 1996). In Stern's (2008) review of women leaders, making a social contribution and being of service to others were also featured in the women's narratives about their leadership. In Cantor and Bernay's (1992) description of the "womanpower" of women politicians, advancing an agenda of helping others was one of the key motives for their entering politics. Women leaders are particularly conscious of their role in promoting gender equality in their organizations.

In the narratives of women leaders, competition and power are rarely featured. Few of the women leaders in the studies we reviewed mentioned their own power in their narratives about their leadership style or goals. Instead, they emphasized empowering others and creating consensus. They demonstrated what Chin (2007) described as the collaborative process in feminist leadership. Almost all of the women talked about creating flatter organizations and sharing information widely throughout the organization. What emerged is a definition of what is known in the leadership literature as a *transformational* leadership style. Burns (1978) defined transformational leaders as those who "*engage* with others in such a way that leaders and followers raise one another to higher levels of motivation and morality" (p. 20). Over the past 30 years, the concept of transformational leadership has evolved to include leaders who are inspiring, optimistic, moral, and equitable. Judge and Piccolo (2004) built on earlier work in their study of transformational leadership and extended the concept to include charismatic individuals who provide others with inspirational motivation, intellectual stimulation, individual consideration, and a higher purpose in life. This style of leadership is most often contrasted with the more traditional and hierarchically organized transactional style. Transformational leaders transform others by pushing them to assume new points of view and to question their prior assumptions (Goethals, 2005). The perception that women tend to use transformational styles of leadership to a greater extent than do men was confirmed in a meta-analytic review by Eagly, Johannesen-Schmidt, and van Engen (2003) of 45 separate studies. These researchers also found that women leaders tended to engage in more reward-contingency behaviors than men leaders. In other words, the women leaders linked employee rewards to their behaviors in appropriate ways that allowed employees to see the link between their efforts and outcomes at work and the rewards they received. Although the size of the effect that differentiated women from men leaders was small, the meta-analysis showed consistent findings that favored women leaders.

The definition of transformational leadership is more congruent with the interpersonal characteristics associated with women leaders than with the aggressive and hierarchical characteristics associated with male leaders. Women leaders across different studies converge in stressing the importance of communication and team building. In a meta-analytic review of the literature, Lowe, Kroeck, and Sivasubramaniam (1996) found that transformational leadership has a greater association with effective outcomes than does transactional leadership. Logically, then, it might be expected that women, in general, would be more effective leaders because they are more likely to use the style that is associated with better outcomes. The few studies that have examined the effect of having women in top corporate positions confirm this prediction. In one study, researchers sampled over 700 businesses listed in a *Fortune* magazine list of 1,000 businesses (Krishnan & Park, 2005). They found that women constituted 6.7% of the "top management teams" and 2.8% of the line positions on these teams. (Line positions are those directly related to the profitability of the corporation, as opposed to positions in human resources or communications, which are more likely to be filled by women.) The main finding was a significant positive relationship between the number of women in top management and the financial performance of the company. This is a powerful and important finding. In explaining their results, these researchers noted that differences between female and male leadership styles were crucial, especially women's greater willingness to share information, which can drive better performance throughout the company. It is good for business to keep everyone in the know so they can act with fuller knowledge about the entire company.

Climbing One Rung at a Time

As Cantor and Bernay (1992) pointed out, most women leaders did not have sandbox dreams of greatness in their childhoods. The women leaders in our study (Halpern & Cheung, 2008) created successful lives for themselves by working hard and working smart. As in Gomez et al.'s (2001) study of Latina leaders, mothers and mentors figured prominently in the women's tales of how they got where they are today. Their mothers played an important role in inspiring them to try their best and in building their self-confidence early in life, and mentors provided an insider's guide to what they needed to know and provided networking opportunities. We note here that although the idea of mentoring is not as well recognized in Asian cultures as it is in the West, the Asian women often acknowledged informal mentoring relationships, without using this particular label.

An important path toward success for most of the contemporary women leaders was through education. The women achieved a high educational level, which built their self-efficacy and provided them upward mobility. Notwithstanding the sociocultural barriers to women's higher education during their lifetimes, the women in the various studies were either encouraged by their families to pursue education as a key to a better life or strived on their own at a later stage in life to get the preparation they needed for advancement. As Fassinger (2005) suggested, high self-efficacy is a key to women's career success.

In Madsen's (2007) study of 10 American women who served as college or university presidents, a pattern of ongoing personal and professional development was identified. These women leaders demonstrated a continuous process of self-monitoring and self-empowerment in taking on challenging responsibilities while inspiring and supporting the people around them.

In Gomez et al.'s (2001) study of 20 Latina leaders, the career–life path of the participants was characterized as an implementation of the self within an immediate context, influenced by their family background, sociopolitical conditions, and cultural environment. Equipped with an ardent sense of self, the participants used social support networks and cognitive reframing to maintain a balanced perspective or to open new doors when confronting challenges.

As in Gomez et al.'s (2001) study, the women we interviewed concurred in acknowledging a pattern of unintended leadership development. In the early stages of their careers, none of the women planned on making it to the top of their professions or, to use Eagly and Carli's (2007) metaphor, making career moves within a labyrinth. They did not strategically plan their routes or attempt to identify the blind alleys at that stage. As many of the women leaders told us, they never thought it would be possible. They found meaningful work that they loved and climbed one rung at a time as they rose to meet new challenges. Few of the women took career breaks or used any family-friendly policies such as part-time employment or flexible scheduling as they moved through the ranks, in part because these options were not generally available at the time. Their stories reflect that they used a blend of "whatever works."

It would be misleading to label circuitous and unplanned routes to the top as serendipity because the opportunities opened for women who were prepared for the uphill climb. The choices the women leaders made earlier in their careers were considered assets rather than losses. Take the example of Sarah Weddington, the former presidential advisor who did not get a job at a high powered law firm when she got out of law school because she was a woman. She ended up with the opportunity to argue the landmark *Roe v. Wade* case in the U.S. Supreme Court and then went on to find jobs in the higher rungs of politics and government. She called it the "step-by-step method of leadership" (Halpern & Cheung, 2008, p. 219). This is similar to the description by Cantor and Bernay (1992) of how women politicians turned what others perceived to be obstacles into possibilities for themselves.

Our sample included two women who became a chief of police and a chief of one of the largest sheriff's departments in the United States, positions that epitomize male leadership. The police chief told us that as she was being promoted within the department, she realized that she would need to have a college degree and a master's degree to make it anywhere near the top, and she had neither. What she did have at the time was a full-time-plus job as a detective with irregular work hours (homicides do not happen within a 9 to 5 day) and young children. She took her time and waited until her children were in high school and then went to college at night, earning both of the necessary degrees and, ultimately, promotion to the top of the force. A number of the women entrepreneurs from China served previously in the People's Liberation Army, a choice that becomes more understandable when one considers that the only alternative they might have had at the time was to be educated by peasants in the countryside, an educational experience that was in accord with the ideology of the Cultural Revolution. Their military training prepared them well for taking the risks they had to take in starting their own businesses later during the new economic reforms in China.

Now that they are in positions of leadership, the successful women leaders are making it easier for the mothers (and others) who are behind them to handle the often competing demands of running a corporation and going home to change diapers and read bedtime stories. As leaders and policymakers, they are competent professionals who overtly demonstrate their care for their employees and clients in their official policies and everyday interactions, thus creating a model of leadership that takes the best parts of both of the traditional roles of leader and mother.

Cultural Differences and Convergence

The field of cross-cultural leadership has underscored the importance of examining contextual factors when defining leadership (Avolio, 2007). Studies of ethnic women leaders have also highlighted how sociocultural context and cultural identity shape the interpretive lens with which women view the career–life paths they steer (Gomez et al., 2001; Richie et al., 1997).

In cross-cultural psychology, national cultures have been compared in terms of different dimensions of societal norms (Hofstede, 1980). Anglo cultures, like that of the United States, are considered to be individualistic. In these cultures, identity is based in the individual, and emphasis is placed on autonomy and independence. Individuals are supposed to take care of themselves and their immediate families, which consist of the nuclear unit of a couple and their children. In contrast, Asian cultures, like that of the Chinese, are considered to be collectivistic in orientation. Identity is embedded in the social system, an organization, or a group to which the individual belongs. People are born into extended families that take care of them in exchange for their loyalty. Interdependence and harmony among group members are emphasized. As in other societies that emphasize family orientation, the Chinese and the African American women leaders in our study as well as the Latina leaders in Gomez et al.'s (2001) study were more likely to receive social support from their extended families than were the Anglo women leaders.

Culture also defines the social expectations for women's and men's roles. In traditional Chinese culture, women's roles are defined by their different family roles throughout the life stages: daughter, wife, and mother, who should obey, respectively, their father, husband, and son. However, cultural ideologies change with historical events, although there is some lag time before normative attitudes and behaviors change. Socioeconomic and political developments in contemporary China have expanded women's roles. The Communist Party ideology has emphasized liberating Chinese women from their feudalistic oppression as one of the goals of class struggle, and the late Chairman Mao's motto that "women can hold up half the sky" during the 1960s encouraged women to participate in all walks of life. Global campaigns of the women's movement have raised consciousness on gender equality and women's empowerment. There are now legal instruments in China, Hong Kong, and the United States to protect women's rights in employment. However, the structure of the patriarchal family role ascribed to women has moved relatively little despite large changes in the everyday lives of women and men.

Despite great differences in the sociopolitical context during their childhoods, there were striking similarities among the women from China, Hong Kong, and the United States. Many of the mainland Chinese women experienced hardship as they grew up during the Japanese incursion, the Second World War in the 1940s, and the establishment of the People's Republic of China, which was followed by the horrific conditions during the Cultural Revolution, a time when education was denigrated and families were torn apart. The women leaders from Hong Kong had a "foot in two cultures," living first under British rule and, since 1997, under a special administrative region of China which continued to flourish as an international financial center. The leaders from the United States grew up just as opportunities for women opened up as a result of affirmative action and increased legal protection against overt discrimination, although the Equal Rights Amendment failed to gain sufficient support to become national law. Despite the vast sociopolitical differences among these three societies, the culture of gender, with its prescription of appropriate gender roles, exerted a stronger impact on women.

The narratives of the women leaders whom we interviewed (Halpern & Cheung, 2008) highlighted themes that reflected their cultural ideologies. Although all of the women leaders featured their family roles prominently in describing their personal identities, what they considered to be the essential tasks of these roles differed. The American women leaders prided themselves on never missing their children's school plays or soccer games; mothers in Hong Kong put more emphasis on helping their children with their schoolwork. A dominant feature in the Chinese mother's role is overseeing their children's education, with heavy emphasis on supervision of homework and preparation for examinations. Food is another cultural theme that is prominent in the Chinese family. The Chinese mothers from mainland China, Hong Kong, and the United States alike emphasized family dinners as a symbol of family togetherness, describing how they ate with their children before they went out to their own business dinners or went back to work at the office at night. When the hierarchical norms of husband and wife were reversed, the Chinese women leaders were sensitive to how their husbands might lose "face" and took measures to protect against such situations.

Although culture prescribes the expectations for gender roles and behaviors, there are differences within the culture in the way in which individuals play out these roles. We recognize that there are also ethnic, regional, and class differences within the larger cultural group. For example, some of the American women leaders relied on live-in helpers, with fewer of them relying on their extended families for help with child care than the women in mainland China and Hong Kong. The physical distance for the U.S. women from their extended families may have been a barrier that made using this resource a rare occurrence.

The Culture of Gender

When we began our study, we thought there would be many differences between the Chinese and American women leaders in how they managed the combination of top-level work and a successful family life. We expected that the American women leaders would segregate their work and family roles more distinctly, as suggested by Western theories and research on work–family conflict. However, the cultural differences we found relate more to the contents rather than the structure of the role ideology. There was more convergence in the way that these women leaders interwove work and family roles on their paths to the top. Even though they subscribed to gender roles, the Chinese and the American women leaders alike defied the constraints of sexism, which is pervasive across culture. They embraced the multifaceted roles involved in being women. With their growing confidence in their own identities, they did not need to conform to the roles and behaviors of men in order to become leaders. Unlike Western men, they did not segregate their work roles and family roles into distinct domains that could result in conflict. Instead, they integrated their work and family roles in ways that enabled them to harmonize both. Their successful strategies can inform our understanding of the work–family interface. A recent study of working adults in the Netherlands also found that women were more likely to use strategies that facilitated the combination of work and family than were men (van Steenbergen, Ellemers, & Mooijaart, 2007). Instead of viewing the combination of these two spheres of life as necessarily negative, the women found ways to benefit from combining their dual roles, which was a consistent theme among our sample of women leaders and other studies of women leaders with families.

In hindsight, one reason for the cross-cultural similarities is that all of the women share what we are calling "the culture of gender." Notwithstanding the cultural differences found according to the usual understanding of culture, there are pancultural gender role norms that create opportunities and constraints for all women leaders (Inglehart & Norris, 2003). In every society, gender norms prescribe the roles and behaviors that differentiate the experiences of women and men. There are restrictions inherent in the roles of women that make it difficult for them to achieve at high levels in demanding careers. Across national boundaries, women leaders are exposed to similar stereotypes that form sexist prejudice in organizations and to the same media that scutinize their physical appearance, clothing, and family responsibilities with a magnifying glass while portraying their male counterparts as dealing with substantive issues. Reviewing the culture of gender helps us to expand our understanding of leadership, which includes not only individual traits and behaviors but also the process of integrating work and family as two major domains in a leader's life.

An Alternative Model of Leadership

Leadership studies have moved beyond the "trait" and "situation" approaches to more integrated theories of leadership that include the contributions of relationships, contexts, and culture (Avolio, 2007). We note here that in all the qualitative studies of women leaders, researchers relied on the women's tales of their success and how they perceived the interplay among their life roles. The use of semi-structured interviews led the participants to respond to particular aspects of their careers in ways they chose to recall. Families, employers, and employees may have perceived the lives of these women very differently, but we were more concerned with how the women explained their own choices and actions. They were (mostly) pleased with their success at work and at home, which led us to label them as dually successful.

The success stories of the women leaders in various studies show us not only a fuller picture of how women can attain leadership but also how gender can inform leadership research. The study of women's leadership styles and their integration of work and family roles have enriched our understanding of the interplay of personal attributes, processes, and environment in a complex model of leadership that includes women in diverse global contexts. Their exceptional experiences guide us to consider an alternative model to the usual notion of a Western male as the prototypical leader in an organizational setting. This alternative model encompasses a fuller picture of leaders as human beings who steer their lives successfully (Figure 2). It includes the multiple roles of leaders in a complex world. It shows the developmental steps taken by the leaders navigating through their life courses, which are shaped by sociopolitical conditions and current contexts. These contexts may facilitate greater access to education and mentoring for women, which in turn build up their self-efficacy. Flexible working conditions and social support make it possible for women to combine work and family. These steps are not meant to be rigid sequences but are intended to illustrate the incremental and interactional nature of leadership development. The model strengthens the consideration of the interpersonal and relational dimensions of leadership. The transformational leadership style creates a flatter organization in a global work context. This model also recognizes the importance of the integration of different domains of a leader's life. The interplay of these domains varies during different developmental stages of the leader's life course. We suggest that filling family roles such as those of mothers and caregivers, becoming leaders at work, and making these roles compatible have helped women to cultivate the transformational style of leadership.

We base our suggestions on the lessons we learned from the successful women leaders who have families, which is an unusual group. We do not intend to paint an overly rosy picture of these women's lives. They had their share of hardship and strain at work and at home. But they have managed to steer through the labyrinth despite the barriers. We did not speak to their family members and get their perspectives. That will be a direction for future studies. We also recognize that women leaders without families may face convergent and divergent issues, and so do men leaders with and without families. What we are suggesting is that a more comprehensive and inclusive model takes into account the gaps in existing models. Future research could compare how women at different stages of the career

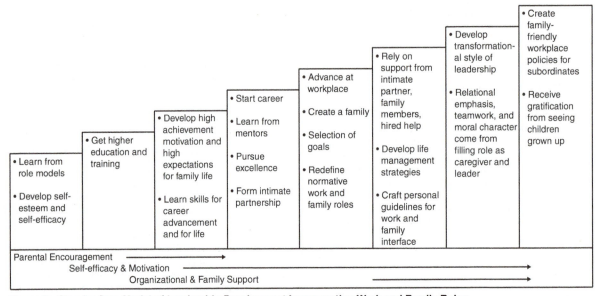

Figure 2   Step-by-Step Model of Leadership Development Incorporating Work and Family Roles

development and family life cycles construe their life purposes in incremental steps, and how powerful men and women define their success as work + family in a model of transformational leadership.

References

Allen, T. D., Herst, D. E. L., Bruck, C. S., & Sutton, M. (2000). Consequences associated with work-to-family conflict: A review and agenda for future research. *Journal of Occupational Health Psychology, 5,* 278–308, doi:101037/1076-8998.5.2.278

Aryee, S., Field, D., & Luk, V. (1999). A cross-cultural test of a model of work–family interface. *Journal of Management, 25,* 491–511. doi: 10.1177/014920639902500402

Aryee, S., Luk, V., Leung, A., & Lo, S. (1999). Role stressors, interrole conflict, and well-being: The moderating effect of spousal support and coping behaviors among employed parents in Hong Kong. *Journal of Vocational Behavior, 54,* 259–278. doi:10.1006/jvbe. 1998.1667

Avolio, B. J. (2007). Promoting more integrative strategies for leadership theory-building. *American Psychologist, 62,* 25–33. doi:10.1037/0003-066X.62.1.25

Baltes, B. B., & Heydens-Gahir, H. A. (2003). Reduction of work–family conflict through the use of selection, optimization, and compensation behaviors. *Journal of Applied Psychology, 88,* 1005–1018. doi:10.1037/0021-9010.88.6.1005

Blume, R. (2006). *Becoming a family counselor: A bridge to family therapy theory and practice.* Hoboken, NJ: Wiley.

Boushey, H. (2005, November). *Are women opting out? Debunking the myth* [Briefing paper]. Retrieved from the Center for Economic and Policy Research website: www.cepr.net/documents/publications/opt_out_2005_11_2.pdf

Burns, J. M. (1978). *Leadership.* New York, NY: Harper & Row.

Byron, K. (2005). A meta-analytic review of work–family conflict and its antecedents. *Journal of Vocational Behavior, 67,* 169–198. doi:10.1016/j.jvb.2004.08.009

Cantor, D. W., & Bernay, T. (1992). *Women in power: The secrets of leadership.* Boston, MA: Houghton Mifflin.

Census and Statistics Department, Government of the Hong Kong Special Administrative Region. (2007). *Women and men in Hong Kong: Key statistics.* Hong Kong, China: Author. Retrieved from www.censtatd.gov.hk/products_and_services/products/publications/statistical_report/social_2007_data/index_cd_B1130303_dt_back_yr_2007.jsp

Chin, J. L. (2007). Overview: Women and leadership: Transforming visions and diverse voices. In J. L. Chin, B. Lott, J. K. Rice, & J. Sanchez-Hucles (Eds.), *Women and leadership: Transforming visions and diverse voices* (pp. 1–17). Oxford, England: Blackwell.

Correll, S. J., Benard, S., & Paik, I. (2007). Getting a job: Is there a motherhood penalty? *American Journal of Sociology, 112,* 1297–1338. doi:10.1086/511799

Department of Population, Social, Science and Technology Statistics, National Bureau of Statistics. (2004). *Women and men in China: Facts and figures 2004.* Beijing, China: Author. Retrieved from www.stats.gov.cn/english/statisticaldata/otherdata/men&women_en.pdf

Dye, J. L. (2005, December). *Fertility of American women: June 2004* (Current Population Reports, P20–555). Retrieved from U.S. Census Bureau website: www.census.gov/prod/2005pubs/p20–555.pdf

Eagly, A. H., & Carli, L. L. (2007). *Through the labyrinth: The truth about how women become leaders.* Boston, MA: Harvard Business School Press.

Eagly, A. H., Johannesen-Schmidt, M. C., & van Engen, M. (2003). Transformational, transactional, and laissez-faire leadership styles: A meta-analysis comparing women and men. *Psychological Bulletin, 95,* 569–591. doi:10.1037/0033-2909.129.4.569

Fassinger, R. (2005). Theoretical issues in the study of women's career development: Building bridges in a brave new world. In W. B. Walsh & M. L. Savickas (Eds.), *Handbook of vocational psychology: Theory, research, and practice* (3rd ed., pp. 85–126). Mahwah, NJ: Erlbaum.

Ford, M. T., Heinen, B. A., & Langkamer, K. L. (2007). Work and family satisfaction and conflict: A meta-analysis of cross-domain relations. *Journal of Applied Psychology, 92,* 57–80. doi:10.1037/0021-9010.92.1.57

Fortune 500 2006: Women CEOs for Fortune 500 companies. (2006, April 17). *Fortune, 153*(7). Retrieved from http://money.cnn .com/magazines/fortune/fortune500/womenceos/

Francesco, A. M., & Shaffer, M. A. (2009). Working women in Hong Kong: *Neuih keuhng yahn* or oppressed class? In F. M. Cheung & E. Holroyd (Eds.), *Mainstreaming gender in Hong Kong society* (pp. 311–334). Hong Kong, China: Chinese University Press.

Friedman, S. D., & Greenhaus, J. H. (2000). *Work and family—Allies or enemies? What happens when business professionals confront life choices.* New York, NY: Oxford University Press.

Frone, M. R. (2003). Work–family balance. In J. C. Quick & L. E. Tetrick (Eds.), *Handbook of occupational health psychology* (pp. 143–162). Washington DC: American Psychological Association.

Galinsky, E. (2005). *Overwork in America: When the way we work becomes too much.* New York, NY: Families and Work Institute.

Gilbert, L. A. (1988). *Sharing it all: The rewards and struggles of two-career families.* New York, NY: Plenum Press.

Goethals, G. R. (2005). Presidential leadership. *Annual Review of Psychology, 56,* 545–570. doi:10.1146/annurev .psych.55.090902.141918

Gomez, M. J., Fassinger, R. E., Prosser, J., Cooke, K., Mejia, B., & Luna, J. (2001). Voces abriendo caminos (Voices forging paths): A qualitative study of the career development of notable Latinas. *Journal of Counseling Psychology, 48,* 286–300. doi:10.1037/0022-0167.48.3.286

Greenhaus, J. H., & Beutell, N. J. (1985). Sources of conflict between work and family roles. *Academy of Management Review, 10,* 76–88.

Halpern, D. F., & Cheung, F. M. (2008). *Women at the top: Powerful leaders tell us how to combine work and family.* New York, NY: Wiley/Blackwell.

Halpern, D. F., & Murphy, S. E. (Eds.). (2005). *From work–family balance to work–family interaction: Changing the metaphor.* Mahwah, NJ: Erlbaum.

Hersch, J., & Stratton, L. S. (2000). Household specialization and the male marriage wage premium. *Industrial and Labor Relations Review, 54,* 78–94. doi:10.2139/ssrn.241067

Hewlett, S. A. (2002). Executive women and the myth of having it all. *Harvard Business Review, 80,* 66–73.

Hewlett, S. A., & Luce, C. B. (2006). Extreme jobs: The dangerous allure of the 70-hour work week. *Harvard Business Review, 84,* 49–59.

Hochschild, A. R. (1989). *The second shift.* London, England: Penguin.

Hofstede, G. (1980). *Culture's consequences: International differences in work-related values.* Beverly Hill, CA: Sage.

Inglehart, R., & Norris, P. (2003). *Rising tide: Gender equality and cultural change around the world.* New York, NY: Cambridge University Press.

Judge, T. A., & Piccolo, R. F. (2004). Transformational and transactional leadership: A meta-analytic test of their relative validity. *Journal of Applied Psychology, 89,* 901–910. doi:10.1037/0021-9010.89.5.755

Kawahara, D. M., Esnil, E. M., & Hsu, J. (2007). Asian American women leaders: The intersection of race, gender, and leadership. In J. L. Chin, B. Lott, J. K. Rice, & J. Sanchez-Hucles (Eds.), *Women and leadership: Transforming visions and diverse voices* (pp. 297–313). Malden, MA: Blackwell.

Krishnan, H. A., & Park, D. (2005). A few good women—on top management teams. *Journal of Business Research, 58,* 1712–1720. doi:10.1016/j.jbusres.2004.09.003

Livingston, B. A., & Judge, T. A. (2008). Emotional responses to work–family conflict: An examination of gender role orientation among working men and women. *Journal of Applied Psychology, 93,* 207–211. doi:10.1037/0021-9010.93.1.207

Lowe, K. B., Kroeck, K. G., & Sivasubramaniam, N. (1996). Effectiveness correlates of transformational and transactional leadership: A meta-analytic review of the MLQ literature. *The Leadership Quarterly, 7,* 385–425. doi:10.1016/ S1048-9843(96)90027-2

Madsen, S. R. (2007). Women university presidents: Career paths and educational backgrounds. *Academic Leadership, 5,* 11–16.

Mason, M. A., & Goulden, M. (2004, November–December). Do babies matter (Part II)?: Closing the baby gap. *Academe, 90*(6) 10–15. Retrieved from http://ucfamilyedge.berkeley.edu/ babies%20matterII.pdf

Peter, K., & Horn, L. (2005). *Gender differences in participation and completion of undergraduate education and how they changed over time* (NCES 2005–169). Retrieved from National Center for Education Statistics website: http://nces.ed.gov/ pubs2005/2005169.pdf

Rampell, C. (2009, February 5). As layoffs surge, women may pass men in job force. *New York Times.* Retrieved from www.nytimes .com/2009/02/06/business/06women.html

Rapoport, R., Bailyn, L., Fletcher, J. K., & Pruitt, B. H. (2002). *Beyond work–family balance: Advancing gender equity and workplace performance.* San Francisco, CA: Jossey-Bass.

Richie, B. S., Fassinger, R. E., Linn, S. G., Johnson, J., Prosser, J., & Robinson, S. (1997). Persistence, connection, and passion: A qualitative study of the career development of highly achieving African American–Black and White women. *Journal of Counseling Psychology, 44,* 133–148. doi:10.1037/0022-0167.44.2.133

Schoen, R., & Weinick, R. M. (1993). Partner choice in marriage and cohabitations. *Journal of Marriage and the Family, 55,* 408–414. doi:10.2307/352811

Singh, V., & Vinnicombe, S. (2006). *The Female FTSE Report 2006: Identifying the new generation of women directors.* Retrieved from www.som.cranfield.ac.uk/som/dinamic-content/research/ documents/ftse2006full.pdf

Smith, P. B., & Wang, Z. M. (1996). Chinese leadership and organizational structures. In M. B. Bond (Ed.), *The handbook of Chinese psychology* (pp. 322–337). Hong Kong, China: Oxford University Press.

Spector, P. E., Cooper, C. L., Poelmans, S., Allen, T. D., O'Driscoll, M., Sanchez, J. I., . . . Lu. L. (2004). A cross-national comparative study of work–family stressors, working hours, and well-being: China and Latin America versus the Anglo world. *Personnel Psychology, 57,* 119–142. doi:10.1111/j.1744-6570.2004.tb02486.x

Stern, T. (2008). Self-esteem and high-achieving women. In M. A. Paludi (Ed.), *The psychology of women at work: Challenges and solutions for our female workforce. Vol. 3. Self, family and social affects* (pp. 25–53). Westport, CT: Praeger.

United Nations Statistics Division. (n.d.). Allocation of time and time use. Retrieved from http://unstats.un.org/unsd/demographic/ sconcerns/tuse/

U.S. Department of Labor, Women's Bureau. (2006). *Quick facts on women in the labor force in 2006.* Retrieved from www.dol.gov/ wb/factsheets/Qf-laborforce-06.htm

Vannoy-Hiller, D., & Philliber, W. W. (1991). *Equal partners: Successful women in marriage.* Newbury Park, CA: Sage.

van Steenbergen, E. F., Ellemers, N., & Mooijaart, A. (2007). How work and family can facilitate each other: Distinct types of work–family facilitation and outcomes for women and men. *Journal of Occupational Health Psychology, 12,* 279–300. doi:10.1037/1076-8998.12.3.279

Walton, K. D. (1997). UK women at the very top: An American assessment. In H. Eggins (Ed.), *Women as leaders and managers in higher education* (pp. 70–90). Bristol, PA: Open University Press.

Watkins, K. (2006). *Human development report 2006. Beyond scarcity: Power, poverty and the global water crisis.* New York, NY: United Nations Development Programme. Retrieved from http://hdr.undp.org/en/media/HDR06-complete.pdf

White, B., Cox, C., & Cooper, C. (1992). *Women's career development: A study of high flyers.* Cambridge, MA: Blackwell.

Women take 45% workforce in China. (2007, May 18). *People's Daily Online.* Retrieved from http://english.people.com.cn/200705/18/eng20070518_375703.html

Yang, N., Chen, C. C., Choi, J., & Zou, Y. (2000). Sources of work–family conflict: A Sino-U.S. comparison of the effects of work and family demands. *Academy of Management Journal, 43,* 113–123. doi:10.2307/1556390

Critical Thinking

1. What appear to be the key factors related to how women with families achieve success as leaders?

2. What is the "culture of gender" and how does it influence women in different culture to achieve success in leadership?

3. How have older theories of leadership (such as trait and situation-based theories) yielded to new theories of leadership that incorporate culture and gender?

Create Central

www.mhhe.com/createcentral

Internet References

Gender neutral flexibility
www.nlcstrategies.com/home/topics-in-flexibility/gender-neutral-flexibility

The competitive agenda of family-friendly policies
http://pwc.blogs.com/gender_agenda

FANNY M. CHEUNG, Department of Psychology, The Chinese University of Hong Kong; **DIANE F. HALPERN,** Department of Psychology Claremont McKenna College.

Article   Prepared by: Eric Landrum, *Boise State University*

Self-Efficacy in the Workplace: Implications for Motivation and Performance

FRED C. LUNENBURG

Learning Outcomes

After reading this article, you will be able to:

- Articulate the definition of self-efficacy and understand how it applies to the workplace.

- Identify the four major factors thought to influence self-efficacy as presented by the author.

Mainly due to the work of Albert Bandura, self-efficacy has a widely acclaimed theoretical foundation (Bandura, 1986), an extensive knowledge base (Bandura, 1997; Maddux, 1995, 2002), and a proven record of application in the workplace (Bandura, 1997, 2004; Stajkovic & Luthans, 1998). Nine large-scale meta-analyses consistently demonstrate that the efficacy beliefs of organization members contribute significantly to their level of motivation and performance (Bandura & Locke, 2003).

Self-Efficacy Defined

Self-efficacy (also known as *social cognitive theory* or *social learning theory*) is a person's belief that she is capable of performing a particular task successfully (Bandura, 1977, 1997). Think of self-efficacy as a kind of self-confidence (Kanter, 2006) or a task-specific version of self-esteem (Brockner, 1988). Self-efficacy has three dimensions: *magnitude,* the level of task difficulty a person believes she can attain; *strength,* the conviction regarding magnitude as strong or weak; and *generality,* the degree to which the expectation is generalized across situations. An employee's sense of capability influences his perception, motivation, and performance (Bandura, 1997). We rarely attempt to perform a task when we expect to be unsuccessful.

Following is an example. One professor may believe that she can learn how to teach graduate courses online on her own. Another professor may have strong doubts about his ability to learn how to teach graduate courses online without taking some formal training. Self-efficacy has powerful effects on learning, motivation, and performance, because people try to learn and perform only those tasks that they believe they will be able to perform successfully. Self-efficacy affects learning and performance in three ways (Bandura, 1982):

1. *Self-efficacy influences the goals that employees choose for themselves.* Employees with low levels of self-efficacy tend to set relatively low goals for themselves. Conversely, an individual with high self-efficacy is likely to set high personal goals. Research indicates that people not only learn but also perform at levels consistent with their self-efficacy beliefs.
2. *Self-efficacy influences learning as well as the effort that people exert on the job.* Employees with high self-efficacy generally work hard to learn how to perform new tasks, because they are confident that their efforts will be successful. Employees with low self-efficacy may exert less effort when learning and performing complex tasks, because they are not sure the effort will lead to success.
3. *Self-efficacy influences the persistence with which people attempt new and difficult tasks.* Employees with high self-efficacy are confident that they can learn and perform a specific task. Thus, they are likely to persist in their efforts even when problems surface. Conversely, employees with low self-efficacy who believe they are incapable of learning and performing a difficult task are likely to give up when problems surface. In an extensive literature review on self-efficacy, Albert Bandura and Edwin Locke (2003) concluded that self-efficacy is a powerful determinant of job performance.

Sources of Self-Efficacy

Since self-efficacy can have powerful effects on organizations, it is important to identify its origin. Bandura (1997) has identified four principal sources of self-efficacy: past performance, vicarious experience, verbal persuasion, and emotional cues.

Past Performance

According to Bandura, the most important source of self-efficacy is past performance. Employees who have succeeded on job-related tasks are likely to have more confidence to complete similar tasks in the future (high self-efficacy) than employees who have been unsuccessful (low self-efficacy). Managers or supervisors can boost self-efficacy through careful hiring, providing challenging assignments, professional development and coaching, goal setting, supportive leadership, and rewards for improvement.

Vicarious Experience

A second source of self-efficacy is through vicarious experience. Seeing a co-worker succeed at a particular task may boost your self-efficacy. For example, if your co-worker loses weight, this may increase your confidence that you can lose weight as well. Vicarious experience is most effective when you see yourself as similar to the person you are modeling. Watching LeBron James dunk a basketball might not increase your confidence in being able to dunk the basketball yourself if you are 5 feet, 6 inches tall. But if you observe a basketball player with physical characteristics similar to yourself, it can be persuasive.

Verbal Persuasion

The third source of self-efficacy is through verbal persuasion. Essentially this involves convincing people that they have the ability to succeed at a particular task. The best way for a leader to use verbal persuasion is through the *Pygmalion effect*. The Pygmalion effect is a form of a self-fulfilling prophesy in which believing something to be true can make it true.

Rosenthal and Jacobson's (1968) classic study is a good example of the Pygmalion effect. Teachers were told by their supervisor that one group of students had very high IQ scores (when in fact they had average to low IQ scores), and the same teacher was told that another group of students had low IQ scores (when in fact they had high IQ scores). Consistent with the Pygmalion effect, the teachers spent more time with the students they *thought* were smart, gave them more challenging assignments, and expected more of them—all of which led to higher student self-efficacy and better student grades. A more recent experiment conducted by Harvard researchers in a ghetto community produced similar results (Rist, 2000). The Pygmalion effect also has been used in the workplace. Research has indicated that when managers are confident that their subordinates can successfully perform a task, the subordinates perform at a higher level. However, the power of the persuasion would be contingent on the leader's credibility, previous relationship with the employees, and the leader's influence in the organization (Eden, 2003).

Emotional Cues

Finally, Bandura argues that emotional cues dictate self-efficacy. A person who expects to fail at some task or finds something too demanding is likely to experience certain physiological symptoms: a pounding heart, feeling flushed, sweaty palms, headaches, and so on. The symptoms vary from individual to individual, but if they persist may become associated with poor performance.

Self-efficacy has been related to other motivation theories. Edwin Locke and Gary Latham suggest that goal-setting theory and self-efficacy theory complement each other. When a leader sets difficult goals for employees, this leads employees to have a higher level of self-efficacy and also leads them to set higher goals for their own performance. Why does this happen? Research has shown that setting difficult goals for people communicates confidence (Locke & Latham, 2002). For example, suppose that your supervisor sets a high goal for you. You learn that it is higher than the goal she has set for your colleagues. How would you interpret this? You would probably think that your supervisor believes you are capable of performing better than others. This sets in motion a psychological process in which you are more confident in yourself (higher self-efficacy) and then you set higher personal goals for yourself causing you to perform better. Self-efficacy also may be related to effort-performance relationships in expectancy theory (Vroom, 1964).

Implications of Self-Efficacy in the Workplace

Bandura devotes considerable attention to the workplace in his groundbreaking book, *Self-Efficacy: The Exercise of Control*. More recently, he provided an extensive review of the growing body of research dealing with the direct and indirect influence of self-efficacy on work-related personal and organizational effectiveness (Bandura, 2004). This research review of the impact of self-efficacy includes a wide range of topics such as training and development, teaming (i.e., collective efficacy), change and innovation, leadership, and stress. From this considerable body of theory and research on self-efficacy, the following managerial and organizational implications are provided (Ivancevich, Konopaske, & Matteson, 2011; Luthans, Yuussef, & Avolio, 2007):

Selection/Promotion Decisions

Organizations should select individuals who have high levels of self-efficacy. These people will be motivated to engage in the behaviors that will help them perform well in the workplace. A measure of self-efficacy can be administered during the hiring/promotion process.

Training and Development

Organizations should consider employee levels of self-efficacy when choosing among candidates for training and development programs. If the training budget is limited, then greater return (i.e., job performance) on training investment can be realized by sending only those employees high in self-efficacy. These people will tend to learn more from the training and, ultimately, will be more likely to use that learning to enhance their job performance.

Goal Setting and Performance

Organizations can encourage higher performance goals from employees who have high levels of self-efficacy. This will lead to higher levels of job performance from employees, which is critical for many organizations in an era of high competition.

Conclusion

Self-efficacy (beliefs about one's ability to accomplish specific tasks) influences the tasks employees choose to learn and the goals they set for themselves. Self-efficacy also affects employees' level of effort and persistence when learning difficult tasks. Four sources of self-efficacy are past performance, vicarious experience, verbal persuasion, and emotional cues. Managerial and organizational implications of self-efficacy in the workplace include hiring and promotion decisions, training and development, and goal setting.

References

Bandura, A. (1977). *Social learning theory.* Englewood Cliffs, NJ: Prentice Hall.

Bandura, A. (1982). Self-efficacy mechanism in human agency. *American Psychologist, 37,* 122–147.

Bandura, A. (1986). *Social foundations of thought and action.* Upper Saddle River, NJ: Prentice Hall.

Bandura, A. (1997). *Self-Efficacy: The exercise of control.* New York, NY: W.H. Freeman.

Bandura, A. (2004). Cultivate self-efficacy for personal and organizational effectiveness. In E. A. Locke (Ed.), *Handbook of principles of organizational behavior* (pp. 120–136). Malden, MA: Blackwell.

Bandura, A., & Locke, E. A. (2003). Negative self-efficacy and goal effects revisited. *Journal of Applied Psychology, 88*(1), 87–99.

Brockner, J. (1988). Self-esteem at work. Lexington, MA: Lexington Books.

Eden, D. (2003). Self-fulfilling prophecies in organizations. In J. Greenberg (Ed.), *Organizational behavior: The state of the science* (2nd ed.) (pp. 91–122). Mahwah, NJ: Erlbaum.

Ivancevich, J. M., Konopaske, R., & Matteson, M. T. (2011). *Organizational behavior and management* (9th ed.). New York, NY: McGraw-Hill.

Kanter, R. M. (2006). *Confidence: How winning and losing streaks begin and end.* New York, NY: Crown Publishing.

Locke, E. A., & Latham, G. P. (2002). Building a practically useful theory of goal setting and task motivation: A 35-year odyssey. *American Psychologist, 57*(9), 707–717.

Luthans, F., Youssef, C. M., & Avolio, B. J. (2007). *Psychological capital.* New York, NY: Oxford University Press.

Maddux, J. E. (1995). *Self-efficacy, adaptation and adjustment: Theory, research, and application.* New York, NY: Plenum Press.

Maddux, J. E. (2002). Self-efficacy. In C. R. Snyder & S. J. Lopez (Eds.), *Handbook of positive psychology* (pp. 277–287). New York, NY: Oxford University Press.

Rist, R. C. (2000). Student social class and teacher expectations: The self-fulfilling prophesy in ghetto education. *Harvard Educational Review, 70*(3), 266–301.

Rosenthal, R., & Jacobson, L. (1968). *Pygmalion in the classroom.* New York, NY: Holt, Rinehart, and Winston.

Stajkovic, A. D., & Luthans, F. (1988). Self-efficacy and work-related performance: A meta-analysis. *Psychological Bulletin, 124*(2), 240–261.

Vroom, V. H. (1994). *Work and motivation.* New York, NY: Wiley.

Critical Thinking

1. Thinking about your own work history—or the work you hope to have someday—what would be some of the factors or variables that will influence your self-efficacy (your belief that you can perform certain tasks successfully)?

2. Thinking about past performance, vicarious experience, verbal persuasion, and emotional cues, which of those do you think will influence you the most in a future job or career? Explain your answer.

Create Central

www.mhhe.com/createcentral

Internet References

Assessing the importance of building self-efficacy to impact motivation, performance levels, and team effectiveness
http://thesportdigest.com/archive/article/assessing-importance-building-self-efficacy-impact-motivation-performance-levels-and-team-e-0

Employee self-efficacy: How to identify, how to help
http://psychlearningjournal.wordpress.com/2012/03/26/employee-self-efficacy-how-to-identify-how-to-help

Lunenburg, Fred C. From *International Journal of Management, Business, and Administration,* vol. 14, no. 1, 2011, pp. 1–6. Copyright © 2011 by The International Journal of Business and Management Research. Reprinted by permission.

Article   Prepared by: R. Eric Landrum, *Boise State University*

Changing Faces: We Can Look More Trustworthy, but Not More Competent

NEW YORK UNIVERSITY

Learning Outcomes

After reading this article, you will be able to:

- Identify the features of a trustworthy face and a competent face.

- Appreciate the role that a series of experiments can play in helping to understand a complex phenomenon.

We can alter our facial features in ways that make us look more trustworthy, but don't have the same ability to appear more competent, a team of New York University (NYU) psychology researchers has found.

The study, which appears in the *Personality and Social Psychology Bulletin*, points to both the limits and potential we have in visually representing ourselves—from dating and career-networking sites to social media posts.

"Our findings show that facial cues conveying trustworthiness are malleable while facial cues conveying competence and ability are significantly less so," explains Jonathan Freeman, an assistant professor in NYU's Department of Psychology and the study's senior author. "The results suggest you can influence to an extent how trustworthy others perceive you to be in a facial photo, but perceptions of your competence or ability are considerably less able to be changed."

This distinction is due to the fact that judgments of trustworthiness are based on the face's dynamic musculature that can be slightly altered, with a neutral face resembling a happy expression likely to be seen as trustworthy and a neutral face resembling an angry expression likely to be seen as untrustworthy—even when faces aren't overtly smiling or angered. But perceptions of ability are drawn from a face's skeletal structure, which cannot be changed.

The study, whose other authors included Eric Hehman, an NYU post-doctoral researcher, and Jessica Flake, a doctoral candidate at the University of Connecticut, employed four experiments in which female and male subjects examined both photos and computer-generated images of adult males.

In the first, subjects looked at five distinct photos of 10 adult males of different ethnicities. Here, subjects' perceptions of trustworthiness of those pictured varied significantly, with happier-looking faces seen as more trustworthy and angrier-looking faces seen as more untrustworthy. However, the subjects' perceptions of ability, or competence, remained static—judgments were the same no matter which photo of the individual was being judged.

A second experiment replicated the first, but here, subjects evaluated 40 computer-generated faces that slowly evolved from "slightly happy" to "slightly angry," resulting in 20 different neutral instances of each individual face that slightly resembled a happy or angry expression. As with the first experiment, the subjects' perceptions of trustworthiness paralleled the emotion of the faces—the slightly happier the face appeared, the more likely he was seen to be trustworthy and vice versa for faces appearing slightly angrier. However, once again, perceptions of ability remained unchanged.

In the third experiment, the researchers implemented a real-world scenario. Here, subjects were shown an array of computer-generated faces and were asked one of two questions: which face they would choose to be their financial advisor (trustworthiness) and which they thought would be most likely to win a weightlifting competition (ability). Under this condition, the subjects were significantly more likely to choose as their financial advisor the faces resembling more positive, or happy, expressions. By contrast, emotional resemblance made no difference in subjects' selection of successful weight-lifters; rather, they were more likely to choose faces with a particular form: those with a comparatively wider facial structure, which prior studies have associated with physical ability and testosterone.

In the fourth experiment, the researchers used a "reverse correlation" technique to uncover how subjects visually represent a trustworthy or competent face and how they visually represent the face of a trusted financial advisor or competent weightlifting champion. This technique allowed the researchers to determine which of all possible facial cues drive these distinct perceptions without specifying any cues in advance.

Here, resemblance to happy and angry expressions conveyed trustworthiness and was more prevalent in the faces of an imagined financial advisor while wider facial structure conveyed ability and was more prevalent in the faces of an imagined weightlifting champion.

These results confirmed the findings of the previous three experiments, further cementing the researchers' conclusion that perceptions of trustworthiness are malleable while those for competence or ability are immutable.

Critical Thinking

1. If an actor wanted to portray trustworthiness, what facial expressions should be used and what facial expressions should be avoided? Why?

2. If you wanted to increase others' perception of your competence, according to the article and the research, what should you do? Why?

Internet References

7 things your face says about you

http://www.businessinsider.com/seven-things-your-face-says-about-you-2014-1

What's in a face?

https://www.psychologytoday.com/articles/201210/whats-in-face

Your facial bone structure has a big influence on how people see you

http://www.scientificamerican.com/article/your-facial-bone-structure-has-a-big-influence-on-how-people-see-you/

Article   Prepared by: R. Eric Landrum, *Boise State University*

Do Cholesterol Drugs Affect Aggression?

Study finds it's possible, but more research is suggested.

DENNIS THOMPSON

Learning Outcomes

After reading this article, you will be able to:

- Articulate how men and women are affected differently by statin drugs.

- Understand the cumulative effects that statins may have on many different aspects of behavior.

- Appreciate interactions, that is, when different levels of different independent variables have differential effects on the outcomes/dependent variables.

Cholesterol-lowering statin drugs might influence a person's aggressive behaviors, increasing or decreasing their irritability and violent tendencies, a new clinical trial suggests.

Men taking statins typically become less aggressive, while women on statins tend to become more aggressive, according to findings published July 1 in the journal *PLOS ONE*.

"Clinicians should be aware of this, and it's not bad for patients to be aware of it," said lead author Dr. Beatrice Golomb, a principal investigator at the University of California, San Diego School of Medicine. "If an individual develops a behavioral change, in my view medication should always be considered as a possibility."

However, the effect appears to be minimal and needs to be verified with follow-up studies, said one outside expert, Robert Geffner, founding president of the Institute on Violence, Abuse & Trauma at Alliant International University in San Diego.

"If I am reading their study right, it looks like they're dealing with really low levels of aggression to begin with," Geffner, a psychology professor at the University, said. "That's interesting, but I'm not sure how meaningful it is."

For the study, researchers randomly assigned more than 1,000 adult men and postmenopausal women to take either a statin medication or a placebo for six months.

The trial was aimed at clarifying a rather muddy picture that has emerged on the role that low blood cholesterol and statins might play in violent behavior, Golomb said.

Prior research has shown that low blood cholesterol levels can increase a person's aggressive behavior, increasing or decreasing the rate of violent death, violent crime, and suicide, she added.

Even though statins reduce blood cholesterol levels, the drugs theoretically should lower aggressive tendencies by reducing testosterone levels and improving the ability of cells to generate energy, Golomb continued. But statins also can alter a person's serotonin levels, causing sleep problems and increasing aggressive behavior, the researchers noted.

The participants' behavioral aggression was measured by tallying any aggressive acts they performed against other people, objects, or themselves in the previous week. Researchers looked for a change in aggression from the start of the study to the end.

They found that statins typically tended to increase aggression in postmenopausal women, with a significant effect on those older than 45. The increase appeared stronger in women who started out with lower levels of aggression, according to the study.

Analysis of the male participants proved trickier. Three men assigned to take statins had very large increases in aggression. When they were included in the review, statins had no effect one way or the other on average aggressive behavior.

But when the three outliers were removed from the group, researchers observed a significant decline in aggressive behavior for male statin users.

Statins' effect on hormone levels appeared to influence behavior, Golomb said. Those who experienced a decrease in testosterone due to statins also experienced a decrease in aggression.

Those who slept worse—possibly due to statins' effect on serotonin levels—experienced an increase in aggression.

The sleep finding helped account for the male outliers, as the two men with the biggest aggression increases both had developed much worse sleep problems, Golomb noted.

Geffner said that it's well-known that "hormones and neurotransmitters are definitely a player" in the way the brain functions.

But he questioned whether excluding the three aggressive male outliers was appropriate in the analysis, since this could be evidence of statins increasing violent behavior.

Geffner also noted that the study started out with 2,400 people, but that nearly 1,400 were left out because they either didn't meet the criteria for the study or declined to participate.

"I just have a lot more questions than answers at this point," he said. "I think there are interesting things to follow up on, but I have many questions."

Source

Beatrice Golomb, M.D., Ph.D., professor of medicine, University of California, San Diego School of Medicine; Robert Geffner, Ph.D., professor of psychology and founding president, Institute on Violence, Abuse & Trauma, Alliant International University, San Diego; July 1, 2015, *PLOS ONE*.

Critical Thinking

1. Explore the idea that there may be a relationship between low blood cholesterol and violent behavior. Why might that be the case? Explain.

2. The researchers in this study looked at changes in aggression from the beginning of the study to the end of the study. What are the advantages of this type of research approach?

3. When a study begins with 2,400 participants but eventually 1,400 participants are excluded, what concerns (if any) should there be about the remaining data? Explain.

Internet References

Cholesterol and your mood
http://www.healthcentral.com/cholesterol/c/59/45680/cholesterol-mood/
Lipitor rage
http://www.slate.com/articles/health_and_science/medical_examiner/2011/11/lipitor_side_effects_statins_and_mental_health_.html
Low cholesterol and suicide
https://www.psychologytoday.com/blog/evolutionary-psychiatry/201103/low-cholesterol-and-suicide

Unit 7

UNIT

Prepared by: Eric Landrum, *Boise State University*

Development

Two families—the Garcias and the Smiths—are brand new parents; in fact, they are still at the hospital with their newborns. When the babies are not in their mothers' rooms, both sets of parents wander down to the hospital's neonatal nursery where pediatric nurses care for both babies—José Garcia and Kimberly Smith. Kimberly is alert, active, and often cries and squirms when her parents watch her. On the other hand, José is quiet, often asleep, and less attentive to external commotion when his parents view him in the nursery.

Why are these babies so different? Are the differences gender related? Will these differences disappear as these children develop, or will they be expressed even more prominently? What role will parenting choices play in the development of each child? Will Kimberly excel at sports and José excel at art? Can Kimberly overcome her parents' poverty and succeed in a professional career? Will José become a doctor like his mother or a pharmacist like his father? Will both of these children avoid childhood disease, maltreatment, and the other misfortunes that sometimes occur with children? Developmental psychologists are concerned with all of the Kimberlys and Josés of our world. Developmental psychologists study age-related changes in language, motor and social skills, cognition, and physical health. Developmental psychologists are interested in the common skills shared by all children, as well as the differences among children, and the events that create these differences. And developmental psychologists are not only interested in child development, but our development over the lifespan from birth to death.

For just a moment, think back over your developmental path. What kind of person are you? What sorts of skills do you possess? Are you artistic? Are you athletic? Do you enjoy reading? Do you speak more than one language? Are you outgoing or shy? Do you have higher levels of self-control or lower levels of self-control? What about your personal values such as integrity and honor—how did you acquire these values? Did you have to work hard at becoming the person you are now, or did you just sort of become who you are naturally? Think now about the present and the future. How are you changing as a college student—is college shaping the way you think and challenging your values and beliefs? Will you ever stop developing or changing or growing or looking at the world in new ways?

In general, developmental psychologists are concerned with the forces that guide and direct development over the course of a lifetime. Some developmental theorists argue that the major forces that shape a child are found in the environment, such as social class, quality of available stimulation, parenting style, and so on. Other theorists insist that genetics and related physiological/biological factors such as hormones are the major forces that underlie human development. A third set of psychologists believe that a combination or interaction of both sets of factors (nature and nurture) are responsible for development. In this unit, we explore what developmental psychologists can tell us about human growth and change over the lifespan.

Article   Prepared by: Eric Landrum, *Boise State University*

Harnessing the Wisdom of the Ages

A volunteer program seeks to enhance minds young and old.

Amy Maxmen

Learning Outcomes

After reading this article, you will be able to:

- Describe the preliminary findings of the relationship observed between elderly individuals who volunteer and their cognitive capabilities.

- Understand the impact of continued executive functioning in later adulthood and its impact on physiological brain systems.

At age 63, Joyce Lawrence found that for the first time in her life, she had time on her hands. Her children had left her Baltimore home to raise their own families and she had retired from her job as a correction officer in prisons. Her duties were over, but she felt a growing urge to contribute to society in some other way.

"At our age, you're left alone a lot of the time and it's easy to just watch TV or watch cars go by because you feel no one needs you anymore," she says. "But that's not true. After you have that pity party, you need to find out how you're needed and go make yourself useful."

For Lawrence, the opportunity to be useful came through the Experience Corps, a nonprofit organization that brings retired volunteers as mentors to struggling students in needy schools. The program was the brainchild of psychologist and social reformer John Gardner, PhD, remembered for his push to improve education, eliminate poverty and promote equality. As Secretary of Health, Education and Welfare under President Lyndon Johnson in the 1960s, he launched Medicare and oversaw the passage of the Elementary and Secondary Education Act, which aimed to ensure quality education for poor and rich students alike. At 76 years old, he wrote a concept paper that served as the blueprint for the Experience Corps (http://www .experiencecorps.org/about_us/john_gardners_vision.cfm). In it, he argues that sending seniors out to pasture does a disservice to them as well as to society, and that a program like Experience Corps could capitalize on the wisdom of the elderly.

"We believe," he wrote, "that the large numbers of us over age 65 constitute a rich reservoir of talent, experience and commitment potentially available to society."

The Experience Corps now include about 2,000 seniors nationwide, who mentor elementary school students for at least 15 hours each week, especially in low-income neighborhoods where class sizes swell. Student attendance and reading comprehension appear to improve in classes supported by volunteers. And based on testimonials, the volunteers enjoy the program.

However, anecdotes may not be enough to keep the program afloat when education and public health budgets are strained. At the moment, the program relies on federal funding through AmeriCorps (the Corporation for National and Community Service), as well as state and local public and private funds, and foundations including the Atlantic Philanthropies. To examine whether the cost of the program is justified, Linda Fried, MD, MPH, the dean of Columbia's Mailman School of Public Health, has solicited help from an interdisciplinary group of colleagues to assess its impact on the students and elderly volunteers. Together with the Johns Hopkins Center on Aging and Health, she's developed a research-community partnership with the Greater Homewood Community Corporation to conduct trials assessing the program.

Quantifying Cognition

Michelle Carlson, PhD, an associate professor of psychology at Johns Hopkins, says her preliminary findings suggest that the cognitive capabilities of elderly volunteers in the Experience Corps improve. Small teams of Experience Corps volunteers cooperate with teachers to help children who struggle with reading and learning. Beyond aiding kids with their studies, the volunteers provide the individual encouragement often lacking in crowded classrooms.

"Every child has different needs, so that means the volunteers must solve problems, multitask and exercise their executive abilities on a broad level," says Carlson. After 32 hours of training, participants volunteer for at least 15 hours per week within schools, where they assist classroom teachers and librarians by helping students read, recommending books, and providing one-on-one encouragement to children who've struggled with their lessons.

Those executive abilities—planning, abstract thinking and filtering relevant sensory information—are also crucial for driving, shopping, cooking and other activities necessary for independent living, and so strengthening those abilities can help seniors stay independent longer. Carlson says the intellectual and social engagement, and the physical activity, which volunteering in schools requires, might have that effect, but it's difficult to prove causation. After all, seniors who retain their cognitive faculties longer might volunteer more often—and might fare equally well if they didn't.

To demonstrate causality, Carlson and her colleagues analyzed functional magnetic resonance imaging (fMRI) data for signs of improvement or at least maintenance in the prefrontal brain region that supports executive function, in Experience Corps volunteers and in elderly people not involved in the program. In two pilot studies published in 2008 and 2009 in *The Gerontologist* and the *Journal of Gerontology,* the team reported gains in executive function, according to cognitive tests and increased activity in the prefrontal regions of volunteers compared with controls. She and her colleagues have increased the number of participants to 702 in a trial that began in 2005. If participants who have been active in the program for two years show cognitive benefits or cognitive stability that accrues beyond one year of exposure or less, Carlson and colleagues can check off a critical element in proving causality—a dose-dependent effect.

"Even if the program simply maintains brain function over two years, that implies we can delay an individual's progression to dementia, and that has huge personal and public health implications," says Carlson.

Importantly, the Experience Corps reaches a population of senior citizens who are at high risk for cognitive impairment—often those from lower economic classes with no college education. The majority of participants are African American. Carlson says that in her trials, she intentionally tries to reach this at-risk population, who traditionally do not volunteer for health promotion programs, but are willing to serve the community.

"These volunteers are not the 'worried well,'" says Carlson. They don't usually leap at treatments and tasks marketed as cognitive-enhancing, such as ginkgo biloba and Sudoku, she says, but many respond to "calls to service" to help youth in need.

Nonetheless, the program in Baltimore, with 292 volunteers, costs about $1.5 million a year. That cost includes stipends for the volunteers' food and travel expenses, yearly salaries for the directors, program administrator, entry personnel, a volunteer coordinator and the cost of the training sessions. So, the Experience Corps is far more expensive than Sudoku and ginkgo. But Carlson argues that quick fixes like these haven't been shown to translate into broad improvements in cognition, particularly in real-world measures of executive functioning, while her preliminary analyses suggest the Experience Corps does. The way in which the program's activities improve executive functioning, however, may be tough to untangle.

"The Experience Corps can't tell us the nitty-gritty details on mechanism," says Arthur Kramer, PhD, a professor of psychology at the University of Illinois at Urbana-Champaign, "but from a practical point of view, it doesn't matter a whole heck of a lot."

A Boost for Students

To complement the neuroscience research, Johns Hopkins health economist Kevin Frick, PhD, is leading an effort to compute the program's financial and health effects by looking at its impact on teachers, tutored students and elderly participants. In a 2004 pilot study in the Journal of Urban Health, Frick's team found that the immediate improvements in health gained by participants over two years don't balance out the program's cost. However, this equation might change if long-term studies find that the program staves off dementia, Frick says.

Moreover, it's too soon to tell if the program increases children's chances of graduating high school. If it does, the program would be well worth its price tag. The team determined that the annual cost of the Baltimore program would be offset by the higher salaries earned by people with high school diplomas, if graduation rates increase by just 0.5 percent, or 1 in 200, because of Experience Corps interventions early on. However, filling in variables like the rate of high school graduation and the time to dementia, which would decrease medical costs, may take up to a decade. "The biggest threat to an economic argument is people's impatience in waiting for a benefit," Frick says.

Finances aside, preliminary results support the notion that the program provides a meaningful ray of light for people in their golden years and in their dawn. And testimony from volunteers doesn't hurt the case. "I go for the mental stimulation, and I go because physically it's good to move around," says Barbara, a 77-year-old participant. "It's emotional, and I must say it's awfully spiritual to know I'm making a difference."

Critical Thinking

1. What is the Experience Corps program, and what are its goals?

2. What are some examples of executive abilities that are necessary for independent living?

3. What region of the brain is linked to the enhanced development of executive function and abilities?

Create Central

www.mhhe.com/createcentral

Internet References

Do we really get wiser with age?
    http://science.howstuffworks.com/life/inside-the-mind/human-brain/ wiser-with-age.htm
Researchers find that wisdom and happiness increase as people grow older
    www.washingtonpost.com/wp-dyn/content/article/2010/08/09/ AR2010080904177.html

AMY MAXMEN, is a writer in New York City.

Article   Prepared by: R. Eric Landrum, *Boise State University*

How a Newborn Baby Sees You

Kjerstin Gjengedal

Learning Outcomes

After reading this article, you will be able to:

- Comprehend the visual acuity of newborn infants.

- Appreciate the role of motion/movement in babies' early perception of the world.

- Understand the benefit of researchers from different fields being able to collaborate on and solve a problem.

A newborn infant can see its parents' expressions at a distance of 30 centimeters. For the first time researchers have managed to reconstruct infants visual perception of the world.

By combining technology, mathematics and previous knowledge of the visual perception of infants, researchers have finally succeeded in showing to an adult audience how much of its environment a newborn baby can actually see. The results tell us that an infant of 2 to 3 days old can percieve faces, and perhaps also emotional facial expressions, at a distance of 30 centimeters—which corresponds to the distance between a mother and her nursing baby. If the distance is increased to 60 centimeters, the visual image gets too blurred for the baby to perceive faces and expressions.

The study was conducted by researchers at the Institute of Psychology in collaboration with colleagues at the University of Uppsala and Eclipse Optics in Stockholm, Sweden.

Live Pictures

The study plugs a gap in our knowledge about infants' visual world, which was left open for several decades. It may also help explain claims that newborn babies can imitate facial expressions in adults during the first days and weeks of their lives, long before their vision is sufficiently developed to perceive details in their environments. The key word is motion.

"Previously, when researchers have tried to estimate exactly what a newborn baby sees, they have invariably used still photos. But the real world is dynamic. Our idea was to use images in motion," says professor emeritus Svein Magnussen from the Institute of Psychology.

Testing an Old Idea

Early in his career, Magnussen conducted research into the visual perception of humans. One day, about 15 years ago, he found himself discussing with colleagues the problem of testing whether newborn infants are really able to perceive facial expressions in people around them. The researchers agreed that if it were true that babies could see and imitate facial expressions, the reason might be that the faces were moving.

"Back then we had neither the equipment nor the technical competence to test our idea. We dug it out again only a year ago. So, our results are based on an old idea which nobody had tested in the meantime," he says.

What Makes Facial Expressions Intelligible?

In order to carry out the test, the researchers had to combine modern simulation techniques with previous insight into how infants' vision works. We have a great deal of information about young infants' contrast sensitivity and spatial resolution from behavioural studies conducted, for the most part, in the 1980s. At that time, it was discovered that presenting an infant with a figure against a uniformly grey background caused the infant to direct its gaze towards the figure.

"Figures made up of black and white stripes were used. By choosing a certain stripe width and frequency, the field would appear uniformly grey, and the child would not direct its gaze towards it. Changing the width and frequency to make up figures made it possible to determine the exact level of contrast and spatial resolution needed to make the infant direct its gaze towards the figure," Magnussen says.

In other words, the researchers had access to quite accurate information about newborn infants' vision. What was unknown to them, was the practical consequences of this information. Does it, for instance, mean that a newborn baby can see the expression in the face of an adult bending over the baby?

Movement Is Easier to See

It's easier to recognise something that moves, than a blurry still photo. The researchers made video recordings of faces that changed between several emotional expressions, and subsequently filtered out the information which we know is unavailable to newborn infants. Then they let adult participants see the videos. The idea was that if the adults were unable to identify a facial expression, then we can certainly assume that a newborn would also be unable to do so.

The adult participants correctly identified facial expressions in three out of four cases when viewing the video at a distance of 30 centimeters. When the distance was increased to 120 centimeters, the participants' rate of identification were about what one could expect from random responding. This means that the ability to identify facial expressions based on the visual information available to a newborn baby, reaches its limit at a distance of about 30 centimeters.

Filling a Gap in the Foundation Wall

"It's important to remember that we have only investigated what the newborn infant can actually see, not whether they are able to make sense of it," Magnussen points out.

Previous attempts to recreate the newborn baby's visual reality, for instance in students' textbooks, have usually relied on taking a normal photograph and blurring it. Magnussen confesses himself surprised that nobody before them have made use of the detailed information we possess about infants' visual perception. Hence this is the first time that we have a concrete estimate of the visual information available to the newborn baby.

Magnussen and his colleagues are happy to finally have been able to carry out an idea that had been on the back burner for 15 years. But as for developing their results further, they will leave that to others.

"All of us behind this study are really involved in different fields of research now. Our position is: Now a piece of the foundation is in place. If anyone else wants to follow up, that's up to them," says Magnussen.

Reference

Svein Magnussen et al. "Simulating newborn face perception", *Journal of Vision*, doi: 10.1167/14.13.16

Critical Thinking

1. The researchers suggest that newborn infants can see faces and perhaps emotional expressions within two to three days of birth. Why would that be an important skill to possess so early? Explain.

2. Why is movement such a key component to newborn infants' vision? Explain.

3. When a newborn infant "sees" something, does that also mean that they can make sense of what they are seeing? Why or why not?

Internet References

The world according to babies
  http://www.parents.com/baby/care/newborn/babies-world/

Your baby's eyes
  http://www.bausch.com/vision-and-age/infant-eyes/eye-development#.VgAv-PnF9g0

Your baby's hearing, vision, and other senses: 1 month
  http://kidshealth.org/parent/pregnancy_newborn/senses/sense13m.html

Article   Prepared by: R. Eric Landrum, *Boise State University*

One in Five Teens May Be Bullied on Social Media

Review found wide variations in prevalence, but victims were often females who were depressed.

RANDY DOTINGA

Learning Outcomes

After reading this article, you will be able to:

- Understand the difficulty of establishing causation, such as whether depression causes cyberbullying or cyberbullying causes depression.

- Appreciate the challenges in studying the long-term effects of cyberbullying on children.

A new review suggests that estimates of cyberbullying are all over the place, ranging as low as 5 percent and as high as 74 percent.

But some findings are consistent: Bullied kids are more likely to be depressed and to be female, and cyberbullying mostly arises from relationships.

"When children and youth are cyberbullied, they are often reluctant to tell anyone," said review author Michele Hamm, a research associate with the Alberta Research Center for Health Evidence at the University of Alberta in Edmonton, Canada.

"Prevention and management efforts are likely necessary at multiple levels, involving adolescents, parents, teachers, and health care professionals," Hamm said.

Researchers launched the review to get a better understanding of cyberbullying, which they defined as bullying via social media and not in private conversations by text messages or Skype.

"We wanted to find out whether there was evidence that social media could be harmful to kids and if so, be able to inform future prevention strategies," Hamm said.

The researchers looked at 36 studies, mostly from the United States. Of those, 17 reports examined how often cyberbullying occurred. The researchers found that a median of 23 percent of kids reported being bullied via social media. A median is not an average; it's the midpoint in a group of numbers.

The percentage is derived from studies that had a wide variety of definitions of when cyberbullying had to have occurred to count, Hamm said.

In some cases, researchers counted whether kids had ever been bullied; in other cases, bullying only counted if it was repeated, she said.

One expert thought 23 percent was probably an accurate assessment of the prevalence of cyberbullying.

"It would be easy, just from watching the news, to conclude that virtually every child in America is a victim of bullying," said Robert Faris, an associate professor of sociology at the University of California, Davis.

"The prevalence of cyber- and traditional bullying will always vary based on the way they are defined, how the questions are asked and the time period in question," Faris explained. "But regardless of these issues, only a minority of kids can be considered victims. So, the overall estimate is actually in line with other estimates of traditional bullying."

The researchers also found an association between depression and cyberbullying, although it's not clear if one causes the other.

"The associations between cyberbullying and anxiety and self-harm were inconsistent," Hamm added. "Except for one, all of the studies that we found were only looking at relationships at one point in time, so it isn't known whether there is a long-term impact of cyberbullying on kids' mental health."

However, Faris believes cyberbullying by social media poses a special threat to kids and is "probably a lot more damaging to targets" than other forms of bullying. "Harassing messages can be blocked, but public humiliation can't be halted by victims," he said. "And, of course, it involves a much wider audience."

As for helping kids who are bullied, review author Hamm said, "Adolescents are often unaware that anything can be done about cyberbullying, so efforts should be made to increase education regarding how to address it and who to tell, focusing on both recipients and bystanders."

Rachel Annunziato, an assistant professor of clinical psychology at Fordham University in New York City, said, "The best advice we can give parents is to frequently monitor their children's Internet use ... We are in a position to spot and stop this behavior or help our children if they are recipients of cyberbullying. Another thing we can do is ask about cyberbullying. Our children may not realize that we are aware of this."

Faris agreed that parents must play a role.

"Kids do not tell adults about bullying. Not teachers, not coaches, not parents," he said. "This is largely because they feel adults will not help and can make things worse. So, one crucial lesson is that parents should really monitor what their kids are doing online and on social media, and also ask pressing questions about how things are going at school and with friends."

Source

Michele Hamm, Ph.D., research associate, Alberta Research Center for Health Evidence, department of pediatrics, University of Alberta, Edmonton, Canada; Robert Faris, Ph.D., associate professor, sociology, University of California, Davis; Rachel Annunziato, Ph.D., assistant professor, clinical psychology, Fordham University, New York City; June 22, 2015, *JAMA Pediatrics*, online

Critical Thinking

1. What is the typical response by a bullied child? Describe it, and discuss why you think the response is what it is.

2. In a research study, why is it important to define what "social media" are, and what they are not? Explain.

Internet References

Cyberbullying statistics
http://www.internetsafety101.org/cyberbullyingstatistics.htm

Teen depression and how social media can help or hurt
http://www.cnn.com/2015/08/05/health/teen-depression-social-media/

Teens, kindness and cruelty on social network sites
http://www.pewinternet.org/2011/11/09/teens-kindness-and-cruelty-on-social-network-sites/

Article   Prepared by: R. Eric Landrum, *Boise State University*

How Do Smartphones Affect Childhood Psychology?

AMY WILLIAMS

Learning Outcomes

After reading this article, you will be able to:

- Appreciate the prevalence and widespread use of cellular phones.

- Understand how the use of brain scans can be a research tool to help understand the progress being made in a developing child's brain.

- Comprehend the effect of increased screen time on brain development.

Have you noticed what seems like an epidemic of people who are glued to their smartphone's soft glow? Unfortunately, you are not alone. Over 1.8 billion people own smartphones and use their devices on a daily basis. Some studies estimate that an average person checks their screen 150 times a day.

This widespread use of technology trickles down to the youngest members of our society. Data from Britain shows almost 70 percent of "11- to 12-year-olds use a mobile phone and this increases to close to 90 percent by the age of 14."

In a recent publication, it was noted that 56 percent of children between the ages of 10 to 13 own a smartphone. While that fact alone may come as a shock, it is estimated that 25 percent of children between the ages of 2 and 5 have a smartphone.

It should come as no surprise that smartphones and tablets have now replaced basketballs and baby dolls on a child's wish list. Elementary school-aged children start asking, or let's say begging, for these forms of technology before they can even tie their shoes.

This raises the question of how mobile technology, typically found in smartphones, affects childhood brain development.

This topic has been creating a lot of debate among parents, educators, and researchers. Unfortunately, smartphones are relatively new and a lot of the gathered evidence is unclear or inconsistent.

That means that it is important for parents to consider the potential effects smartphones can have on childhood psychology and development.

A lot of research has been conducted over the years to understand how children learn. There are many theories circulating, but Jean Piaget might be the most respected in the education field. He was one of the first people to study how a child's brain develops.

His cognitive development theory basically explains how learning is a mental process that reorganizes concepts based on biology and experiences. He deduced that children learn the same way—their brains grow and function in similar patterns, moving through four universal stages of development.

Educators have been implementing a variety of techniques and methods into their lessons that build on Piaget's principles. Children need to experience the world around them to accommodate new ideas. Children "construct an understanding of the world around them" and try to understand new ideas based on what they already know and discover.

For children, face-to-face interactions are the primary ways they gain knowledge and learn.

Dr. Jenny Radesky of Boston Medical Center, became concerned when she noticed the lack of interaction between parents and children. She had observed that smartphones and handheld devices were interfering with bonding and parental attention.

Radesky said, "They (children) learn language, they learn about their own emotions, they learn how to regulate them. They learn by watching us how to have a conversation, how to read other people's facial expressions. And if that's not happening, children are missing out on important development milestones."

Screen time takes away from learning and physically exploring the world through play and interactions. It can be noted that doctors and educators are worried how the overexposure to touch-screen technology can impact developing brains.

Radiation from cellphones has long been a primary fear of how smartphones can affect a brain. However, the radiation theory hasn't been proven and many professionals claim cellphones do not expose us to enough radiation to cause harm. That may provide parents a little relief, but it appears that the radio frequencies emitted from a smartphone might actually harm a developing brain.

The temporal and frontal lobes of the brain are still developing in a teen and they are closest to the part of the ear where teens tend to hold their device. In fact, "research has shown that both the temporal and frontal are actively developing during adolescence and are instrumental in aspects of advanced cognitive functioning."

Besides exposing developing brains to radio waves or harmful radiation, researchers are looking into how smartphones and the Internet can hinder or enrich brain function. Dr. Gary Small, head of UCLA's memory and aging research center, performed an experiment that demonstrates how people's brains change in response to Internet use.

He used two groups: those with a lot of computer savvy and those with minimal technology experience. With brain scans, he discovered that the two groups had similar brain functions while reading text from a book. However, the tech group showed "broad brain activity in the left-front part of the brain known as the dorsolateral prefrontal cortex, while the novices showed little, if any, activity in this area."

As a child ages it often feels like they need to practice technology to stay on top of the modern advancements. However, Dr. Small's experiment shows that after a few days of instruction, the novices were soon showing the same brain functions as the computer-savvy group.

Technology and screen time had rewired their brains. It appears that increased screen time neglects the circuits in the brain that control more traditional methods for learning. These are typically used for reading, writing, and concentration.

Smartphones and the Internet also affect communication skills and the emotional development of humans. If a child relies on electronics to communicate, they risk weakening their people skills. Dr. Small suggests that children can become detached from others' feelings.

If a human's mind can be easily molded, imagine the connections and wiring that is happening in a brain still developing.

However, there is no concrete proof that mobile technology is linked to adverse outcomes. Smartphones and technology do offer benefits to our children. Here is a quick rundown of the benefits technology can offer our youth:

- A child is more capable of: handling rapid cybersearches, making quick decisions, developing visual acuity, and multitasking.

- Games help develop peripheral vision.
- Visual motor tasks like tracking objects or visually searching for items is improved.
- Internet users tend to use decision-making and problem-solving brain regions more often.

Many experts and educators feel that interactive media has a place in a child's life. Smartphones and tablets can foster learning concepts, communication, and camaraderie.

Here are a few recommendations to make the most of time spent on a smartphone:

- Children under two should not be using screens or electronic devices.
- Play alongside your children and interact with them face-to-face.
- Make sure smartphones don't interfere with opportunities for play and socializing.
- Limit screen use to one or two hours a day. This includes smartphones, TV, computers, etc.
- It is all right to use a smartphone as an occasional treat.
- Model positive smartphone use.
- Encourage family meals and communication.
- Look for quality apps that promote building vocabulary, mathematical, literacy, and science concepts.
- Keep smartphones out of the bedrooms.

Health officials seem unable to agree on the impact smartphones and similar devices have on developing brains. Studies contradict each other and new benefits to technology are uncovered regularly.

Obviously, parents do need to stay informed. They should be aware of the possible side effects a smartphone can harbor. All of this inconclusive evidence can lead a parent to question when they should allow their children access to smartphones or technology. However, one thing all the experts seem to agree on is that moderation is key.

References

Babycentre. Is screen time good or bad for babies and children? BabyCentre. Retrieved from http://www.babycentre.co.uk/a25006035/is-screen-time-good-or-bad-for-babies-and-children#ixzz3MIEeZN84

Ballve, M. (2013). How Much Time Do We Really Spend On Our Smartphones Every Day? *Business Insider*. Retrieved from http://www.businessinsider.com.au/how-much-time-do-we-spend-on-smartphones-2013-6

Chapman, G.D., & Pellicane, A. (2014). Growing Up Social: Raising Relational Kids in a Screen-Driven World. Retrieved from http://www.amazon.com/Growing-Up-Social-Relational-Screen-Driven-ebook/dp/B00J48B03K

Glatter, R. M.D. (2014). Can Smartphones Adversely Affect Cognitive Development In Teens? *Forbes*. Retrieved from http://www.forbes.com/sites/robertglatter/2014/05/19/can-smartphones-adversely-affect-cognitive-development-in-teens/

Howley, D.P. (2013). Children and Smartphones: What's the Right Age? Laptop Part of Tom's Guide. Retrieved from http://blog.laptopmag.com/kids-smartphones-right-age

McLeod, S. (2009). Jean Piaget. Simply Psychology. Retrieved from http://www.simplypsychology.org/piaget.html

Neighmond, P. (2014). For The Children's Sake, Put Down That Smartphone. *NPR*. Retrieved from http://www.npr.org/blogs/health/2014/04/21/304196338/for-the-childrens-sake-put-down-that-smartphone

Williams, A. (2014). 7 Steps to Ease Your Tween into a Smartphone. *TeenSafe*. Retrieved from http://www.teensafe.com/blog/smartphones/7-steps-ease-tween-smartphone/

Critical Thinking

1. The author reported the estimate that the average person checks their cellphone screen 150 times a day. What type of impact, overall, do you think this behavior has on other behaviors? Explain.

2. The lack of interaction between parents and developing children is a concern to some researchers. What strategies might be used to reverse this trend? Be specific.

3. Based on the recommendations offered in the article, which of those recommendations are the most important to implement immediately, and why?

Internet References

Babies don't need smartphones

http://www.usatoday.com/story/opinion/2015/05/08/technology-babies-speech-development-toddler-column/70940608/

Pacifying toddlers with tablets, smartphones may hurt development, scientists speculate

http://www.thestar.com/life/2015/02/06/pacifying-toddlers-with-tablets-smartphones-may-hurt-development-scientists-speculate.html

Researchers: Using an iPad or smartphone can harm a toddler's learning and social skills

http://www.washingtonpost.com/news/morning-mix/wp/2015/02/02/using-an-ipad-or-smartphone-can-harm-a-toddlers-brain-researchers-says/

Unit 8

UNIT

Prepared by: Eric Landrum, *Boise State University*

Personality Processes

Sabrina and Sadie are identical twins. When the girls were young, their parents tried very hard to treat them equally. They dressed them the same, fed them same meals, and allowed them to play with the same toys. Each had a kitten from the same litter. Whenever Sabrina received a present, Sadie received one, too, and vice versa. Both girls attended dance school and completed early classes in ballet and tap dance. For elementary school, the twins were both placed in the same class with the same teacher. The teacher also tried to treat them the same. In junior high school, Sadie became a tomboy. She loved to play rough-and-tumble sports with the neighborhood boys. On the other hand, Sabrina remained indoors and practiced the piano. Sabrina was keenly interested in hobbies such as painting, needlepoint, and sewing. Sadie was more interested in reading novels, especially science fiction, and watching action movies on television.

As the twins matured, they decided it would be best to attend different colleges. Sabrina went to a small, quiet college in a rural setting, and Sadie entered a large public university. Sabrina majored in English, with a specialty in poetry; Sadie switched majors several times and finally decided on a psychology major. Why, when these twins were exposed to the same childhood environment, did their interests, personalities, and paths diverge later? What makes people—even identical twins—so unique and so different from one another? The study of individual differences resides in the domain of personality psychology.

The psychological study of personality includes two major thrusts. The first has focused on the search for the commonalties of human behavior and personality. Its major question is "How are humans, especially their personalities, affected by specific events or activities?" The second has focused on discovering the bases on which individuals differ in their responses to events, such as the self-control exhibited by Sadie and Sabrina as they went off to college. In its early history, this specialty was called genetic psychology because most people assumed that individual differences resulted from differences in inheritance. By the 1950s, the term *genetic psychology* had given way to the more current terminology: the psychology of individual differences.

Today, most psychologists accept the principle that both genes and the environment are important determinants of any type of behavior, whether it be watching adventure movies or sitting quietly and reading or caring for the elderly. Modern researchers devote much of their efforts to discovering how the two sources of influence (nature and nurture) interact to produce a unique individual. Thus, the focus of this unit is on personality characteristics and the differences and similarities among individuals, with these fascinating differences ranging from cultural expectations and stereotypes to the development of political attitudes.

Article   Prepared by: Eric Landrum, *Boise State University*

Evolutionary Psychology and Intelligence Research

Satoshi Kanazawa

Learning Outcomes

After reading this article, you will be able to:

- Evaluate the contribution of evolutionary psychology to the study of intelligence.

- Define and explain the Savanna Principle and how it relates to intelligence research.

Evolutionary psychology and intelligence research have largely stood separately despite the fact that both of these subfields of psychology take biological and genetic influences on human behavior and cognition seriously. In some sense, this is understandable. Evolutionary psychology focuses on universal human nature, which is shared by all humans, or on sex-specific male human nature and female human nature, which are shared by all men and all women, respectively. In contrast, intelligence research (psychometrics) is part of differential psychology, which focuses on what makes individuals different from each other. Psychometrics is concerned with accurate measurement of intelligence precisely because individuals vary in their level of intelligence largely (though not entirely) because of their different genetic makeup.

Yet, as Tooby and Cosmides (1990a) articulated, the concept of universal human nature is not inimical to or incompatible with individual differences (in intelligence or other traits). Although individual differences have yet to be fully integrated into evolutionary psychology (Buss, 1995; Nettle, 2006), some evolutionary psychologists have incorporated heritable or reactively heritable (Tooby & Cosmides, 1990a) individual differences in personality (Buss, 1991; MacDonald, 1995; Nettle, 2005), sociosexuality (Gangestad & Simpson, 1990, 2000), and attachment and reproductive strategies (Belsky, Steinberg, & Draper, 1991; Buss & Greiling, 1999). Scarr (1995), and J. M. Bailey (1998) called for the incorporation of behavior genetics into evolutionary psychology in order to emphasize heritable individual and group differences and provide a fuller explanation of human behavior.

In this article, I follow the lead of earlier evolutionary psychologists who have attempted to incorporate individual differences. I seek to integrate evolutionary psychology, on the one hand, and intelligence research in particular and differential psychology in general, on the other. I aim to incorporate individual differences in general intelligence and other traits into universal human nature. I suggest how and when evolutionary constraints on the human brain, universally shared by all humans, may interact with general intelligence, such that more intelligent individuals have fewer such constraints than less intelligent individuals. I suggest that general intelligence is both a domain-specific evolved psychological mechanism *and* an individual-difference variable. I derive a novel hypothesis, called the Savanna–IQ Interaction Hypothesis, from the intersection of evolutionary psychology and intelligence research and discuss its implications. Among other things, this hypothesis suggests one possible explanation for why general intelligence is correlated with the Big Five personality factor Openness to Experience; at the same time, it calls for a refinement of the concept of novelty. I conclude with several illustrations of how and when more intelligent individuals are more likely than less intelligent individuals to acquire and espouse evolutionarily novel values.

The Savanna Principle

Adaptations, physical or psychological, are designed for and adapted to the conditions of the environment of evolutionary adaptedness, not necessarily to the current environment (Tooby & Cosmides, 1990b). This is easiest to see in the case of physical adaptations, such as the vision and color recognition system.

What color is a banana? A banana is yellow in the sunlight and in the moonlight. It is yellow on a sunny day, on a cloudy day, and on a rainy day. It is yellow at dawn and at dusk. The color of a banana appears constant to the human eye under all these conditions despite the fact that the actual wavelengths of the light reflected by the surface of the banana under these varied conditions are different. Objectively, bananas are not the same color all the time. However, the human eye and color recognition system can compensate for these varied conditions because they all occurred during the course of the evolution of the human vision system, and humans can perceive the objectively varied colors as constantly yellow (Cosmides & Tooby, 1999, pp. 17–19; Shepard, 1994).

So a banana looks yellow under all conditions *except in a parking lot at night.* Under the sodium vapor lights commonly used to illuminate parking lots, a banana does not appear natural yellow. This is because the sodium vapor lights did not exist in the ancestral environment, during the course of the evolution of the human vision system, and the visual cortex is therefore incapable of compensating for them.

The same principle holds for psychological adaptations. Pioneers of evolutionary psychology (Crawford, 1993; Symons, 1990; Tooby & Cosmides, 1990b) all recognized that the evolved psychological mechanisms are designed for and adapted to the conditions of the environment of evolutionary adaptedness, not necessarily to the conditions of the current environment. I systematized these observations into what I called the *Savanna Principle* (Kanazawa, 2004a): The human brain has difficulty comprehending and dealing with entities and situations that did not exist in the ancestral environment. Burnham and Johnson (2005, pp. 130–131) referred to the same observation as the *evolutionary legacy hypothesis,* whereas Hagen and Hammerstein (2006, pp. 341–343) called it the *mismatch hypothesis.*

The Savanna Principle can explain why some otherwise elegant scientific theories of human behavior, such as the subjective expected utility maximization theory or game theory in microeconomics, often fail empirically, because they posit entities and situations that did not exist in the ancestral environment. For example, nearly half the players of one-shot Prisoner's Dilemma games make the theoretically irrational choice to cooperate with their partner (Sally, 1995). The Savanna Principle suggests that this may possibly be because the human brain has difficulty comprehending completely anonymous social exchange and absolutely no possibility of knowing future interactions (which together make the game truly one-shot; Kanazawa, 2004a, pp. 44–45). Neither of these situations existed in the ancestral environment; however, they are crucial for the game-theoretic prediction of universal defection.

Fehr and Henrich (2003) suggested that one-shot encounters and exchanges might have been common in the ancestral environment. In their response to Fehr and Henrich, Hagen and Hammerstein (2006) pointed out that even if one-shot encounters were common in the ancestral environment, anonymous encounters could not have been common, and the game-theoretic prediction of defection in one-shot games requires both noniteration and anonymity. A lack of anonymity can lead to reputational concerns even in nonrepeated exchanges.

As another illustration of the Savanna Principle, individuals who watch certain types of TV shows are more satisfied with their friendships, just as they would be if they had more friends or socialized with them more frequently (Derrick, Gabriel, & Hugenberg, 2009; Kanazawa, 2002). This may possibly be because realistic images of other humans, such as found in television, movies, videos, and photographs, did not exist in the ancestral environment, where all realistic images of other humans *were* other humans. As a result, the human brain may have implicit difficulty distinguishing "TV friends" (the characters repeatedly seen on TV shows) and real friends.

Most evolutionary psychologists and biologists concur that humans have not undergone significant evolutionary changes in the last 10,000 years, since the end of the Pleistocene Epoch, because the environment during this period has not provided a stable background against which natural and sexual selection can operate over many generations (A. S. Miller & Kanazawa, 2007, pp. 25–28). This is the assumption behind the Savanna Principle. More recently, however, some scientists have voiced opinions that human evolution has continued and even accelerated during the Holocene Epoch (Cochran & Harpending, 2009; Evans et al., 2005). Although these studies conclusively demonstrate that new alleles have indeed emerged in the human genome since the end of the Pleistocene Epoch, the implication and importance of such new alleles for evolutionary psychology are not immediately obvious. In particular, with the sole exception of lactose tolerance, it is not clear whether these new alleles have led to the emergence of new evolved psychological mechanisms in the last 10,000 years.

The Evolution of General Intelligence

General intelligence refers to the ability to reason deductively or inductively, think abstractly, use analogies, synthesize information, and apply it to new domains (Gottfredson, 1997; Neisser et al., 1996). The *g* factor, which is often used synonymously with general intelligence, is a latent variable that emerges in a factor analysis of various cognitive (IQ) tests. They are not exactly the same thing. *g* is an *indicator* or *measure* of general intelligence; it is not general intelligence itself. As a measure of reasoning ability, general intelligence is what Cattell (1971) called "fluid intelligence" (*Gf*), not what he called "crystallized intelligence" (*Gc*), which, while influenced by general intelligence, is a measure of acquired knowledge.

The concept of general intelligence poses a problem for evolutionary psychology (Chiappe & MacDonald, 2005; Cosmides & Tooby, 2002; G. F. Miller, 2000a). Evolutionary psychologists contend that the human brain consists of domain-specific evolved psychological mechanisms, which evolved to solve specific adaptive problems (problems of survival and reproduction) in specific domains. If the contents of the human brain are domain specific, how can evolutionary psychology explain general intelligence?

In contrast to views expressed by G. F. Miller (2000b); Cosmides and Tooby (2002), and Chiappe and MacDonald (2005), I proposed that what is now known as general intelligence may have originally evolved as a domain-specific adaptation to deal with evolutionarily novel, nonrecurrent problems (Kanazawa, 2004b). The human brain consists of a large number of domain-specific evolved psychological mechanisms to solve recurrent adaptive problems. In this sense, our ancestors did not really have to *think* in order to solve such recurrent problems. Evolution has already done all the thinking, so to speak, and equipped the human brain with the appropriate psychological mechanisms, which engender preferences, desires, cognitions, and emotions and motivate adaptive behavior in the context of the ancestral environment.

Even in the extreme continuity and constancy of the ancestral environment, however, there were likely occasional problems that were evolutionarily novel and nonrecurrent, problems that required our ancestors to think and reason in order to solve. Such problems may have included, for example, the following:

1. Lightning has struck a tree near the camp and set it on fire. The fire is now spreading to the dry underbrush. What should I do? How can I stop the spread of the fire? How can I and my family escape it? (Since lightning never strikes the same place twice, this is guaranteed to be a nonrecurrent problem.)

2. We are in the middle of the severest drought in a hundred years. Nuts and berries at our normal places of gathering, which are usually plentiful, are not growing at all, and animals are scarce as well. We are running out of food because none of our normal sources of food are working. What else can we eat? What else is safe to eat? How else can we procure food?

3. A flash flood has caused the river to swell to several times its normal width, and I am trapped on one side of it while my entire band is on the other side. It is imperative that I rejoin them soon. How can I cross the rapid river? Should I walk across it? Or should I construct some sort of buoyant vehicle to use to get across it? If so, what kind of material should I use? Wood? Stones?

To the extent that these evolutionarily novel, nonrecurrent problems happened frequently enough in the ancestral environment (a different problem each time) and had serious enough consequences for survival and reproduction, then any genetic mutation that allowed its carriers to think and reason would have been selected for, and what we now call "general intelligence" could have evolved as a domain-specific adaptation for the domain of evolutionarily novel, nonrecurrent problems, which did not exist in the ancestral environment and for which there are therefore no dedicated modules.

From this perspective, general intelligence may have become universally important in modern life (Gottfredson, 1997; Herrnstein & Murray, 1994; Jensen, 1998) only because our current environment is almost entirely evolutionarily novel. The new theory suggests, and empirical data confirm, that more intelligent individuals are better than less intelligent individuals at solving problems only if they are evolutionarily novel. More intelligent individuals are not better than less intelligent individuals at solving evolutionarily familiar problems, such as those in the domains of mating, parenting, interpersonal relationships, and wayfinding (Kanazawa, 2004b, 2007), unless the solution involves evolutionarily novel entities. For example, more intelligent individuals are no better than less intelligent individuals in finding and keeping mates, but they may be better at using computer dating services. Three recent studies, employing widely varied methods, have all shown that the average intelligence of a population appears to be a strong function of the evolutionary novelty of its environment (Ash & Gallup, 2007; D. H. Bailey & Geary, 2009; Kanazawa, 2008).

My theory (Kanazawa, 2004b) builds on and shares common themes with earlier evolutionary theories of intelligence, which posit climatic, ecological, and social novelties as the main forces behind the evolution of intelligence. Jerisen (1973) employed the concept of the encephalization quotient (EQ) to explain the evolution of intelligence of species as a function of the novelty of their ecological niches. Dunbar's (1998) and Humphrey's (1976) social brain hypothesis and Byrne and Whiten's (1988) machiavellian intelligence hypothesis both explain the evolution of intelligence as a consequence of having to deal with and potentially deceive a large number of conspecifics in the group. Geary's (2005) motivation-to-control theory explains the expansion of the human brain as a result of the human need to control, first its physical environment and then the social environment of fellow humans. Gottfredson (1997) argued that other humans provide the greatest complexities in social life, which select for greater intelligence. Social relationships, while themselves evolutionarily familiar and recurrent, may occasionally add novelty and complexity that requires general intelligence to deal with.

"Intelligences"

In recent years, psychologists have discussed various forms of intelligence or "intelligences," such as emotional intelligence (Mayer, Salovey, & Caruso, 2008; Salovey & Mayer, 1990), social intelligence (Kihlstrom & Cantor, 2000; Marlowe, 1986), mating intelligence (Geher & Miller, 2007), and Gardner's (1983) notion of multiple intelligences, which include linguistic, logical-mathematical, bodily-kinesthetic, spatial, musical, interpersonal, and intrapersonal intelligences. There is no question that these are all important intrapersonal and interpersonal skills and abilities that individuals need in their daily lives. Further, it seems reasonable to suggest that there are individual differences in such skills and abilities in the realm of interpersonal relations.

However, it is not at all clear what we gain by referring to such skills, competences, and abilities as "intelligences." The concept of intelligence in its historical origin in psychology was purely cognitive (Spearman, 1904). I personally would have preferred to keep it that way; however, the tide appears to have turned against my purist position. Whether to call these intrapersonal and interpersonal competencies "intelligences" or "skills," however, is a purely semantic matter without any necessary substantive implications. At any rate, in this article, I focus exclusively on purely cognitive general intelligence and not on other forms of intelligence, for two reasons. First, this is how most intelligence researchers and psychometricians define the concept of intelligence. Although educational, social, clinical, and industrial/organizational psychologists may refer to other "intelligences" as predictors of individual performance, intelligence researchers are nearly unanimous in their exclusive focus on cognitive general intelligence (Jensen, 1998). Second, as mentioned above, the concept of *general* intelligence presents a particular theoretical problem for evolutionary psychology's modular view of the human brain. Such a modular view can easily accommodate other "intelligences" as separate domain-specific modules, but it has more difficulty incorporating *general* intelligence with its seeming domain generality.

Other people and interactions with them (including mating) are "entities and situations" that we are certain existed during the entire period of human evolution. The theory of the evolution of general intelligence would therefore predict that general intelligence would not increase or correlate with emotional intelligence, social intelligence, or mating intelligence, each of which independently evolved to solve evolutionarily familiar problems in a given domain (Mayer, Salovey, Caruso, & Sitarenios, 2001, pp. 236–237). Several studies demonstrate that general intelligence is uncorrelated (or sometimes even negatively correlated) with measures of emotional, social, and mating intelligence (Davies, Stankov, & Roberts, 1998; Derksen, Kramer, & Katzko, 2002; Ford & Tisak, 1983; Fox & Spector, 2000; Kanazawa, 2007; Marlowe & Bedell, 1982).

There is some contrary evidence, however. Mayer, Roberts, and Barsade (2009) explicitly defined emotional intelligence as an application of general intelligence to the domain of emotions, and Roberts, Zeidner, and Matthews's (2001) study shows that measures of emotional intelligence are significantly and moderately *positively* correlated with general intelligence (as measured by the Air Force Qualifying Test). The question of whether emotional, social, and mating intelligences are "really" intelligences and how cognitive they are is difficult to answer definitively because, as Mayer et al. (2008) noted, there is a very wide spectrum of approaches to these other "intelligences." Some of them take cognitive intelligence seriously, others do not.

Is Evolutionary Novelty a Domain?

The theory of the evolution of general intelligence as a domain-specific adaptation is subject to two contradictory criticisms. The first criticism is that the domain of evolutionary novelty, which encompasses all entities and situations that did not exist in the ancestral environment, is too large and undefined, and thus a set of potentially indefinite evolutionarily novel problems presents the same "frame problem" that inspired Tooby and Cosmides (1992) to advocate the domain-specific view of the human mind. The second criticism is that evolutionarily novel problems in the ancestral environment and throughout human evolutionary history have by definition been few and far between, and thus they could not have exerted sufficient selection pressure to lead to the evolution of general intelligence as a domain-specific adaptation.[1]

Is the Domain of Evolutionary Novelty Too Large?

Evolutionarily novel problems have two characteristics in common: They are unanticipated by evolution (and thus there are no dedicated modules to solve them), and they are solvable by logical reasoning. Technically, all adaptive problems, evolutionarily novel or otherwise, are in principle logically solvable. Given sufficient time and data, for example, men, collectively and over time, can eventually figure out that women with symmetrical facial features are genetically healthier and that those with low waist-to-hip ratios are more fecund, so they should find them more desirable as mates. However, for such evolutionarily familiar and recurrent problems like mate selection, evolution short-circuits the long process of trial and error and

simply equips men with the module that inclines them to find women with symmetrical features and low waist-to-hip ratios sexually attractive without really knowing why. For other, evolutionarily novel, nonrecurrent problems, however, evolution has not had time or opportunity to equip humans with such dedicated modules, and they therefore have to "figure out" the problems anew and on their own by logic and reason.

What defines the domain of evolutionarily novel problems, along with their being novel and unanticipated by evolution, is their logical solvability, and it is therefore no larger nor any less defined than other domains, such as cheater detection, language acquisition, and face recognition. After all, potential cheaters may be any kind of exchange partner, and potential deception may occur in any situation. But cheaters all have one thing in common: violation of social contract. Similarly, potential first language to be acquired by a newborn baby may come in any form; there are a nearly infinite number of natural human languages. Yet they all have key features in common, what Chomsky (1957) calls the deep structure of grammar. Hence a developmentally normal human baby, equipped with the language acquisition device, can acquire any human language as its native language, however diverse and varied on the surface such languages may be. Similarly, all evolutionarily novel problems, infinite though they may be in potential number, have certain features in common that define them, chief among which is their logical solvability.

It is not that evolution can anticipate a whole host of evolutionarily novel problems in the future (any more than it could have anticipated the emergence of new human languages such as English or German). It is just that people who have been able to solve (rare and nonrecurrent) evolutionarily novel problems in the past genetically pass on the same ability to their descendants, who can then use it to solve other evolutionarily novel problems in the future, because all evolutionarily novel problems share the common characteristic of logical solvability.

All evolved psychological mechanisms (or modules) are content rich (Tooby & Cosmides, 1992). The contents of general intelligence as a domain-specific adaptation are a set of tools that allow its possessors to arrive at logical conclusions. Such a set of logical tools may include the principle of transitivity (If A then B, and if B then C, then it follows that if A then C); what is now known as Mills's methods of induction (such as the method of difference and the method of concomitant variation); syllogism and deductive reasoning (although deduction begins with a universally true major premise, which is unlikely to have been available to our ancestors); analogy; abstraction, and so forth. In general, intelligent people are those who can use these logical tools and reason correctly and efficiently.

Is the Domain of Evolutionary Novelty Too Small?

A second criticism of the theory avers that evolutionarily novel, nonrecurrent problems could not have arisen frequently enough in the ancestral environment to exert sufficient selection pressure to lead to the evolution of general intelligence or any other adaptation. Selection pressure, however, is a multiplicative function of the frequency of the problem and the magnitude of the selective force. Even a very weak selective force could lead to an evolved adaptation if the adaptive problem in question happens frequently enough over the course of human evolution to accumulate its small effects. Conversely, even a very infrequent adaptive problem can exert sufficient selection pressure if the magnitude of the selective force (the negative consequences of failing to solve the adaptive problem) is sufficiently great.

To take an extreme example for illustrative purposes, suppose a widespread drought or massive flash flood (of a kind used in the examples of evolutionarily novel problems above) on average happens once a century (roughly five generations), but, every time it happens, it kills everyone below the median in logical thinking and reasoning ability. So the adaptive problem happens very infrequently, but the selective force is very strong. In this scenario, in only one millennium (a blink of an eye on the evolutionary time scale), the average intelligence of the population becomes greater than the top 0.1% of the original population. This is equivalent to the current population of the United States, with the mean IQ of 100, changing to a new population 10 centuries later with a mean IQ of 146. From our current perspective, the average person then will be a genius. Even if the selective force was much weaker (one tenth of the original scenario above) and the adaptive problem only wiped out the bottom 5% in logical reasoning (allowing the top 95% of the population to survive each drought or flood every century), it would still take only 13,500 years to achieve a comparable effect on the average intelligence of the population and shift it upward by more than three standard deviations.

It would therefore appear that even an infrequent adaptive problem can produce sufficient selection pressure if the selective force is sufficiently strong. It would not be unreasonable to speculate that *some* (different) novel and nonrecurrent problem happened once a century during the evolutionary past that required our ancestors to think and reason to solve and that killed off the bottom 5% of the population in such an ability. General intelligence as a domain-specific adaptation would then have evolved relatively rapidly, in less than 15,000 years.

Is General Intelligence a Domain-Specific Adaptation or an Individual-Difference Variable?

Some critics (Borsboom & Dolan, 2006) contend that general intelligence could not be an adaptation because it is an individual-difference variable. Adaptations are universal and constant features of a species shared by all its members; in contrast, there are obviously heritable individual differences in general intelligence, whereby some individuals are more intelligent than others. These critics argue that adaptations and heritable individual differences are mutually exclusive.

These criticisms betray profound misunderstanding of the nature of adaptations. A trait could simultaneously be an evolved adaptation and an individual-difference variable. In fact, *most adaptations exhibit individual differences.* Full-time bipedalism is a uniquely human adaptation, yet some individuals walk and run faster than others. The eye is a complex adaptation, yet some individuals have better vision than others. Language is an adaptation, yet some individuals learn to speak their native language at earlier ages and have greater linguistic facility than others.

Individual differences in general intelligence and other adaptations are what Tooby and Cosmides (1990a) called random quantitative variation on a monomorphic design. "Because the elaborate functional design of individuals [e.g., general intelligence as a domain-specific adaptation] is largely monomorphic [shared by all members of a species], our adaptations do not vary in their architecture from individual to individual (*except quantitatively* [emphasis added])" (Tooby & Cosmides, 1990a, p. 37).

Intraspecific (interindividual) differences in such traits pale in comparison to interspecific differences. Carl Lewis and I run at a virtually identical speed compared with cheetahs or sloths. Similarly, Einstein and I have virtually identical intelligence compared with cheetahs or sloths. It is therefore possible for a trait to be both universal and species-typical (exhibiting virtually no variation in the architecture in a cross-species comparison) *and* to manifest vast individual differences in quantitative performance among members of a single species. General intelligence may be one such trait.

Tooby and Cosmides (1990a, pp. 38–39) made this exact point, using "a complex psychological mechanism regulating aggression" (p. 38) as their example. They contended that this mechanism is an adaptation, even though there are heritable individual differences in the mechanism's threshold of activation (i.e., whether one has a "short fuse" or not). Tooby and Cosmides suggested that a complex psychological mechanism regulating aggression "is (by hypothesis) universal and therefore has zero heritability" (p. 38) even though "the *variations* in the exact level at which the threshold of activation is set are probably not adaptations" (p. 39).

The ability to run bipedally, faster than a sloth but slower than a cheetah, is a trait that is universally shared by all normally developing humans; it is a species-typical adaptation with zero heritability. But the exact speed at which a human can run is a heritable individual-difference variable and is therefore not an adaptation. Similarly, I propose that general intelligence is an adaptation and has zero heritability (in the sense that all humans have the ability to think and reason), even though the exact level of an individual's general intelligence ("IQ") is not an adaptation and is a highly heritable individual-difference variable. And Tooby and Cosmides (1990a, p. 57) contended that "nonadaptive, random fluctuations in the monomorphic design of a mental organ can give rise to heritable individual differences *in nearly every manifest feature of human psychology* [emphasis added]." One would therefore expect some individual differences in general intelligence as a domain-specific adaptation.

Explicitly recognizing that general intelligence can simultaneously be a domain-specific, species-typical adaptation *and* an individual-difference variable allows us to integrate evolutionary psychology—the study of species-typical evolved psychological mechanisms—and intelligence research—the study and measurement of heritable individual differences in general intelligence. Further, Tooby and Cosmides's (1990a) notion of the random quantitative (but heritable) variations on a monomorphic design would allow us to study individual differences in other evolved psychological mechanisms.

For example, the cheater detection module was among the first evolved psychological mechanisms to be discovered (Cosmides, 1989). It is clearly an adaptation, in that all human beings have the evolutionarily given and innate ability to detect when they might be cheated out of a fair exchange in a social contract. But are there individual differences in how well individuals can detect cheaters? Are some individuals inherently better at it than others? If so, are such individual differences heritable? Are some individuals genetically predisposed to fall victim to cons and scams?

Theory of mind is another evolved psychological mechanism; adult humans have the ability to infer the mental states of others. However, we already know that some individuals with pathological conditions (autism, Asperger's syndrome) have a weakened or absent capacity for theory of mind (Baron-Cohen, 1995). Can developmentally typical individuals also vary in their theory of mind? Dunbar (2005) suggested that there are individual differences in higher order theory of mind ("I think that you think that Sally thinks that Anne thinks that . . .") and that good writers like Shakespeare are rare because great dramas like *Othello* require writers to possess a sixth-order theory of mind. If individuals can vary in their capacity for higher order theory of mind, it seems reasonable to suggest that they might also vary in their capacity for first-order theory of mind, with some being better than others at accurately inferring the mental states of another person. If so, can such individual differences in the evolved psychological mechanism of theory of mind be heritable, since we already know that autism and Asperger's syndrome may be heritable (A. Bailey et al., 1995; Folstein & Rutter, 1988)?

Incorporating individual differences, not only in general intelligence but in other evolved psychological mechanisms, will allow us to pursue these and other questions at the new frontier where evolutionary psychology meets differential psychology.

How General Intelligence Modifies the Evolutionary Limitations of the Human Brain

The logical conjunction of the Savanna Principle and the theory of the evolution of general intelligence suggests a qualification of the Savanna Principle. If general intelligence evolved to deal with evolutionarily novel problems, then the human brain's difficulty in comprehending and dealing with entities and situations that did not exist in the ancestral environment (proposed in the Savanna Principle) should interact with general intelligence such that the Savanna Principle will hold stronger among less intelligent individuals than among more intelligent individuals. More intelligent individuals should be better able than less intelligent individuals to comprehend and deal with evolutionarily novel (but *not* evolutionarily familiar) entities and situations.

Thus, the Savanna–IQ Interaction Hypothesis (Kanazawa, 2010) suggests that less intelligent individuals have greater difficulty than more intelligent individuals with comprehending and dealing with evolutionarily novel entities and situations that did not exist in the ancestral environment; in contrast, general intelligence does not affect individuals' ability to comprehend and deal with evolutionarily familiar entities and situations that existed in the ancestral environment.

Evolutionarily novel entities that more intelligent individuals are better able to comprehend and deal with may include ideas and lifestyles, which form the basis of their values and preferences; it would be difficult for individuals to prefer or value something that they cannot truly comprehend. Hence, applied to the domain of preferences and values, the Savanna–IQ Interaction Hypothesis suggests that more intelligent individuals are more likely than less intelligent individuals to acquire and espouse evolutionarily novel preferences and values that did not exist in the ancestral environment but that general intelligence has no effect on the acquisition and espousal of evolutionarily familiar preferences and values that existed in the ancestral environment (Kanazawa, 2010).

General Intelligence and Openness to Experience

Research in personality psychology has shown that one of the five-factor personality model factors—Openness to Experience—is significantly positively (albeit moderately) correlated with intelligence (Ackerman & Heggestad, 1997). The similarity and overlap between intelligence and openness are apparent from the fact that some researchers call this personality factor "intellect" rather than "openness" (Goldberg, 1992; McRae, 1994). Although it is widely accepted by personality psychologists that intelligence and openness covary across individuals, it is not known why (Chamorro-Premuzic & Furnham, 2006). The Savanna–IQ Interaction Hypothesis can potentially provide one explanation for why more intelligent individuals are more open to new experiences and are therefore more prone to seek novelty. It is instructive to note from this perspective that only the actions, ideas, and values facets of openness to experience are significantly correlated with general intelligence, not the fantasy, esthetics, and feelings facets (Gilles, Stough, & Loukomitis, 2004; Holland, Dollinger, Holland, & MacDonald, 1995).

At the same time, the Savanna–IQ Interaction Hypothesis suggests a possible need to refine the concept of novelty and to distinguish between *evolutionary novelty* (entities and situations that did not exist in the ancestral environment) and *experiential novelty* (entities and situations that individuals have not personally experienced in their own lifetimes). Although the five-factor personality model does not specify the type of novelty that open individuals are more likely to seek, the Savanna–IQ Interaction Hypothesis suggests that more intelligent individuals are more likely to seek only evolutionary novelty, not necessarily experiential novelty.

For example, all those who are alive in the United States today have lived their entire lives in a strictly monogamous society, and despite recent news events, very few contemporary Americans have any personal experiences with polygyny. Therefore monogamy is experientially familiar for most Americans, whereas polygyny is experientially novel. The five-factor model may therefore predict that more intelligent individuals are more likely to be open to polygyny as an experientially novel idea or action.

In contrast, humans have been mildly polygynous throughout their evolutionary history (Alexander, Hoogland, Howard, Noonan, & Sherman, 1979; Leutenegger & Kelly, 1977), and socially imposed monogamy is a relatively recent historical phenomenon (Kanazawa & Still, 1999). Therefore polygyny is evolutionarily familiar, whereas monogamy is evolutionarily novel. The Savanna–IQ Interaction Hypothesis would therefore predict that more intelligent individuals are more likely to be open to monogamy and less open to polygyny. In fact, the evidence suggests that more intelligent men are more likely to value monogamy and sexual exclusivity than are less intelligent men (Kanazawa, 2010).

As another example, for most contemporary Americans, traditional names derived from the Bible, such as John and Mary, are experientially more familiar than untraditional names such as OrangeJello and LemonJello (Levitt & Dubner, 2005). So the five-factor model may predict that more intelligent individuals are more likely to give their children untraditional names such as Orange Jello and LemonJello than are less intelligent individuals. From the perspective of the Savanna–IQ Interaction Hypothesis, however, both John and OrangeJello are equally evolutionarily novel (because the Bible itself and all the traditional names derived from it are evolutionarily novel), so it would not predict that more intelligent individuals are more likely to give their children untraditional names. In fact, there is no evidence at all that more intelligent individuals are more likely to prefer untraditional names for their children (Fryer & Levitt, 2004; Lieberson & Bell, 1992).

The Savanna–IQ Interaction Hypothesis underscores the need to distinguish between evolutionary novelty and experiential novelty. It can potentially explain why more intelligent individuals are more likely to seek evolutionary novelty but not necessarily experiential novelty. It further suggests that the established correlation between openness and intelligence may be limited to the domain of evolutionary novelty, not necessarily experiential novelty, but the current measures of openness do not adequately address this proposal.

Empirical Illustrations

The Savanna–IQ Interaction Hypothesis, derived from the intersection of evolutionary psychology and intelligence research, suggests one potential way to account for some known individual differences. I discuss just a few of them here for illustrative purposes.

TV Friends

Consistent with the Savanna Principle, I (Kanazawa, 2002) and Derrick et al. (2009) showed that individuals who watch certain types of TV shows are more satisfied with their friendships,

which suggests that they may possibly have implicit difficulty distinguishing evolutionarily novel realistic images of actors they repeatedly see on TV and their real friends. My reanalysis of the same data from the General Social Surveys shows, however, that this seeming difficulty in distinguishing between "TV friends" and real friends appears to be limited to men and women with below-median intelligence (Kanazawa, 2006). Those who are above the median in intelligence do not report greater satisfaction with friendships as a function of watching more TV; only those below the median in intelligence do. This finding seems to suggest that the evolutionary constraints on the brain suggested by the Savanna Principle, whereby individuals have implicit difficulty recognizing realistic electronic images on TV for what they are, appear to be weaker or altogether absent among more intelligent individuals.

Political Attitudes

It is difficult to define a whole school of political ideology precisely, but one may reasonably define *liberalism* (as opposed to *conservatism*) in the contemporary United States as the genuine concern for the welfare of genetically unrelated others and the willingness to contribute larger proportions of private resources for the welfare of such others. In the modern political and economic context, this willingness usually translates into paying higher proportions of individual incomes in taxes toward the government and its social welfare programs.

Defined as such, liberalism is evolutionarily novel. Humans (like other species) are evolutionarily designed to be altruistic toward their genetic kin (Hamilton, 1964a, 1964b), their repeated exchange partners (Trivers, 1971), and members of their deme (a group of intermarrying individuals) or ethnic group (Whitmeyer, 1997). They are not designed to be altruistic toward an indefinite number of complete strangers whom they are not likely ever to meet or exchange with. This is largely because our ancestors lived in small bands of 50–150 genetically related individuals, and large cities and nations with thousands and millions of people are themselves evolutionarily novel.

An examination of the 10-volume compendium *The Encyclopedia of World Cultures* (Levinson, 1991–1995), which describes *all* human cultures known to anthropology (more than 1,500) in great detail, as well as extensive primary ethnographies of traditional societies (Chagnon, 1992; Cronk, 2004; Hill & Hurtado, 1996; Lee, 1979; Whitten, 1976), reveals that liberalism as defined above is absent in these traditional cultures. Although sharing of resources, especially food, is quite common and often normatively prescribed among hunter-gatherer tribes, and although trade with neighboring tribes often takes place (Ridley, 1996), there is no evidence that people in contemporary hunter-gatherer bands *freely* share resources with *members of other tribes*. Because all members of a hunter-gatherer tribe are genetic kin or at the very least repeated exchange partners (friends and allies for life), sharing of resources among them does not qualify as an expression of liberalism as defined above. Given its absence in the contemporary hunter-gatherer tribes, which are often used as modern-day analogs of our ancestral life, it may be reasonable to infer that sharing of resources with total strangers that one has never met or is not ever likely to meet—liberalism—was not part of our ancestral life. Liberalism may therefore be evolutionarily novel, and the Savanna–IQ Interaction Hypothesis would predict that more intelligent individuals are more likely to espouse liberalism as a value than are less intelligent individuals.

Analyses of large representative American samples from the National Longitudinal Study of Adolescent Health (Add Health) and the General Social Surveys confirm this prediction (Kanazawa, 2010). Net of age, sex, race, education, earnings, and religion, more intelligent individuals are more liberal than their less intelligent counterparts. For example, among the Add Health respondents, those who identify themselves as "very liberal" in early adulthood have a mean childhood IQ of 106.4, whereas those who identify themselves as "very conservative" in early adulthood have a mean childhood IQ of 94.8. Even though past studies show that women are more liberal than men (Lake & Breglio, 1992; Shapiro & Mahajan, 1986; Wirls, 1986), and Blacks are more liberal than Whites (Kluegel & Smith, 1986; Sundquist, 1983), the analyses show that the effect of intelligence on liberalism is twice as large as the effect of sex or race.

Choice within Genetic Constraints: Circadian Rhythms

Choice is not incompatible with or antithetical to genetic influence. As long as heritability (h^2) is less than 1.0, individuals can still exercise some choice within broad genetic constraints. For example, political ideology has been shown to be partially genetically influenced; some individuals are genetically predisposed to be liberal or conservative (Alford, Funk, & Hibbing, 2005; Eaves & Eysenck, 1974). Nonetheless, individuals can still choose to be liberal or conservative within broad genetic constraints, and, as discussed above, more intelligent individuals are more likely to choose to be liberal than are less intelligent individuals.

Another example of choice within genetic constraints is circadian rhythms—whether one is a morning person or a night person. Virtually all species in nature, from single-cell organisms to mammals, including humans, exhibit a daily cycle of activity called circadian rhythm (Vitaterna, Takahashi, & Turek, 2001). The circadian rhythm in mammals is regulated by two clusters of nerve cells called the suprachiasmatic nuclei (SCN) in the anterior hypothalamus (Klein, Moore, & Reppert, 1991). Geneticists have by now identified a set of genes that regulate the SCN and thus the circadian rhythm among mammals (King & Takahashi, 2000). "Humans, however, have the unique ability to cognitively override their internal biological clock and its rhythmic outputs" (Vitaterna et al., 2001, p. 90).

Although there are some individual differences in the circadian rhythm, whereby some individuals are more nocturnal than others, humans are basically a diurnal (as opposed to nocturnal) species. Humans rely very heavily on vision for navigation but, unlike genuinely nocturnal species, cannot see in the dark or under little lighting, and our ancestors did not have artificial lighting during the night until the domestication of fire. Any human in the ancestral environment up and about during

the night would have been at risk of predation by nocturnal predators.

Once again, ethnographic evidence from traditional societies available in *The Encyclopedia of World Cultures* (Levinson, 1991–1995) and extensive ethnographies (Chagnon, 1992; Cronk, 2004; Hill & Hurtado, 1996; Lee, 1979; Whitten, 1976) suggest that people in traditional societies usually rise shortly before dawn and go to sleep shortly after dusk in order to take full advantage of the natural light provided by the sun. There is no indication that there are any sustained nocturnal activities, other than occasional conversations and singing, in these tribes. It is therefore reasonable to infer that our ancestors must also have limited their daily activities to daylight, and sustained nocturnal activities are largely evolutionarily novel. The Savanna–IQ Interaction Hypothesis would therefore predict that more intelligent individuals are more likely to be nocturnal than are less intelligent individuals.

Analysis of a large representative sample from Add Health confirms this prediction (Kanazawa & Perina, 2009). Net of age, sex, race, marital status, parenthood, education, earnings, religion, current status as a student, and number of hours worked in a typical week, more intelligent children grow up to be more nocturnal as adults than do less intelligent children. Compared with their less intelligent counterparts, more intelligent individuals go to bed later on weeknights (when they have to get up at a certain time the next day) and on the weekend (when they do not), and they wake up later on weekdays (but not on the weekend, for which the positive effect of childhood IQ on nocturnality is not statistically significant). For example, those with childhood IQs of less than 75 go to bed around 11:42 p.m. on weeknights in early adulthood, whereas those with childhood IQs of over 125 go to bed around 12:30 a.m.

Conclusion

This article seeks to integrate evolutionary psychology—the study of universal human nature—and intelligence research—the study and measurement of individual differences in intelligence. Tooby and Cosmides's (1990a) notion of random quantitative variation on a monomorphic design allows us to view general intelligence as both a domain-specific evolved adaptation (monomorphic design) and an individual-difference variable (random quantitative variation). Such random quantitative variation can also be highly heritable.

Although I have focused on general intelligence and psychometrics in this article, the proposed approach can integrate evolutionary psychology and any aspect of differential psychology. Aggression, theory of mind, the cheater detection mechanism, and some personality traits could all simultaneously be evolved psychological mechanisms and individual-difference variables.

The Savanna–IQ Interaction Hypothesis, which derives from the intersection of evolutionary psychology and intelligence research, suggests that more intelligent individuals are better able to comprehend and deal with evolutionarily novel entities and situations than are less intelligent individuals, but general intelligence does not affect individuals' ability to comprehend and deal with evolutionarily familiar entities and situations. The hypothesis suggests a new way to view some individual differences, such as the extent to which individuals implicitly confuse "TV friends" and real friends, political attitudes on the liberal–conservative continuum, and circadian rhythms, even when these traits are under some genetic control. As long as heritability (h^2) is less than 1.0, there is room for some individual choice.

The general approach proposed in this article will allow genuine integration of evolutionary psychology, on the one hand, and intelligence research in particular and differential psychology in general, on the other. It would simultaneously allow evolutionary psychologists to study a much wider range of psychological traits than hitherto possible and intelligence researchers and differential psychologists to make use of the theories and concepts of evolutionary psychology.

Note

1. I thank Jeremy Freese and Todd K. Shackelford, respectively, for articulating these views to me.

References

Ackerman, P. L., & Heggestad, E. D. (1997). Intelligence, personality, and interests: Evidence for overlapping traits. *Psychological Bulletin, 121,* 219–245. doi:10.1037/0033–2909.121.2.219

Alexander, R. D., Hoogland, J. L., Howard, R. D., Noonan, K. M., & Sherman, P. W. (1979). Sexual dimorphisms and breeding systems in pinnipeds, ungulates, primates, and humans. In N. A. Chagnon & W. Irons (Eds.), *Evolutionary biology and human social behavior: An anthropological perspective* (pp. 402–435). North Scituate, MA: Duxbury Press.

Alford, J. R., Funk, C. L., & Hibbing, J. R. (2005). Are political orientations genetically transmitted? *American Political Science Review, 99,* 153–167.

Ash, J., & Gallup, G. G., Jr. (2007). Paleoclimatic variation and brain expansion during human evolution. *Human Nature, 18,* 109–124. doi:10.1007/s12110–007–9015-z

Bailey, A., Le Couteur, A., Gottesman, I., Bolton, P., Simonoff, E., Yuzda, E., & Rutter, M. (1995). Autism as a strongly genetic disorder: Evidence from a British twin study. *Psychological Medicine, 25,* 63–77. doi:10.1017/S0033291700028099

Bailey, D. H., & Geary, D. C. (2009). Hominid brain evolution: Testing climatic, ecological, and social competition models. *Human Nature, 20,* 67–79. doi:10.1007/s12110–008–9054–0

Bailey, J. M. (1998). Can behavior genetics contribute to evolutionary behavioral science? In C. Crawford & D. L. Krebs (Eds.), *Handbook of evolutionary psychology: Ideas, issues, and applications* (pp. 211–233). Mahwah, NJ: Erlbaum.

Baron-Cohen, S. (1995). *Mind blindness: An essay on autism and theory of mind.* Cambridge, MA: MIT Press.

Belsky, J., Steinberg, L., & Draper, P. (1991). Childhood experiences, interpersonal development, and reproductive strategy: An evolutionary theory of socialization. *Child Development, 62,* 647–670. doi:10.1111/j.1467–8624.1991.tb01558

Borsboom, D., & Dolan, C. V. (2006). Why *g* is not an adaptation: A comment on Kanazawa (2004). *Psychological Review, 113,* 433–437. doi:10.1037/0033–295X.113.2.433

Burnham, T. C., & Johnson, D. D. P. (2005). The biological and evolutionary logic of human cooperation. *Analyse & Kritik, 27,* 113–135.

Buss, D. M. (1991). Evolutionary personality psychology. *Annual Review of Psychology, 42,* 459–491. doi:10.1146/annurev.ps.42.020191.002331

Buss, D. M. (1995). Evolutionary psychology: A new paradigm for psychological science. *Psychological Inquiry, 6,* 1–30.

Buss, D. M., & Greiling, H. (1999). Adaptive individual differences. *Journal of Personality, 67,* 209–243. doi:10.1111/1467–6494.00053

Byrne, R., & Whiten, A. (1988). *Machiavellian intelligence: Social expertise and the evolution of intellect in monkeys, apes, and humans.* Oxford, England: Oxford University Press.

Cattell, R. B. (1971). *Abilities: Their structure, growth, and action.* Boston, MA: Houghton Mifflin.

Chagnon, N. (1992). *Yanomamö* (4th ed.). Fort Worth, TX: Harcourt Brace Jovanovich.

Chamorro-Premuzic, T., & Furnham, A. (2006). Intellectual competence and the intelligent personality: A third way in differential psychology. *Review of General Psychology, 10,* 251–267. doi:10.1037/1089–2680.10.3.251

Chiappe, D., & MacDonald, K. (2005). The evolution of domain-general mechanisms in intelligence and learning. *Journal of General Psychology, 132,* 5–40.

Chomsky, N. (1957). *Syntactic structures.* The Hague, The Netherlands: Mouton.

Cochran, G., & Harpending, H. (2009). *The 10,000 year explosion: How civilization accelerated human evolution.* New York, NY: Basic Books.

Cosmides, L. (1989). The logic of social exchange: Has natural selection shaped how humans reason? Studies with the Wason selection task. *Cognition, 31,* 187–276. doi:10.1016/0010–0277(89)90023–1

Cosmides, L., & Tooby, J. (1999). *What is evolutionary psychology?* Unpublished manuscript, Center for Evolutionary Psychology, University of California, Santa Barbara.

Cosmides, L., & Tooby, J. (2002). Unraveling the enigma of human intelligence: Evolutionary psychology and the multimodular mind. In R. J. Sternberg & J. C. Kaufman (Eds.), *The evolution of intelligence* (pp. 145–198). Mahwah, NJ: Erlbaum.

Crawford, C. B. (1993). The future of sociobiology: Counting babies or proximate mechanisms? *Trends in Ecology and Evolution, 8,* 183–186. doi:10.1016/0169–5347(93)90145-F

Cronk, L. (2004). *From Mukogodo to Maasai: Ethnicity and cultural change in Kenya.* Boulder, CO: Westview.

Davies, M., Stankov, L., & Roberts, R. D. (1998). Emotional intelligence: In search of an elusive construct. *Journal of Personality and Social Psychology, 75,* 989–1015. doi:10.1037/0022–3514.75.4.989

Derksen, J., Kramer, I., & Katzko, M. (2002). Does a self-report measure for emotional intelligence assess something different than general intelligence? *Personality and Individual Differences, 32,* 37–48. doi:10.1016/S0191–8869(01)00004–6

Derrick, J. L., Gabriel, S., & Hugenberg, K. (2009). Social surrogacy: How favored television programs provide the experience of belonging. *Journal of Experimental Social Psychology, 45,* 352–362. doi:101016/j.esp.2008.12.003

Dunbar, R. I. M. (1998). The social brain hypothesis. *Evolutionary Anthropology, 6,* 178–190.

Dunbar, R. I. M. (2005). Why are good writers so rare? An evolutionary perspective on literature. *Journal of Cultural and Evolutionary Psychology, 3,* 7–21. doi:10.1556/JCEP.3.2005.1.1

Eaves, L. J., & Eysenck, H. J. (1974). Genetics and the development of social attitudes. *Nature, 249,* 288–289. doi:10.1038/249288a0

Evans, P. D., Gilbert, S. L., Mekel-Bobrov, N., Vallender, E. J., Anderson, J. R., Vaez-Azizi, L. M., . . . Lahn, B. T. (2005, September 9). *Microcephalin,* a gene regulating brain size, continues to evolve adaptively in humans. *Science, 309,* 1717–1720. doi:10.1126/science.1113722

Fehr, E., & Henrich, J. (2003). Is strong reciprocity a maladaptation? On the evolutionary foundations of human altruism. In P. Hammerstein (Ed.), *Genetic and cultural evolution of cooperation* (pp. 55–82). Cambridge, MA: MIT Press.

Folstein, S. E., & Rutter, M. L. (1988). Autism: Familial aggregation and genetic implications. *Journal of Autism and Developmental Disorders, 18,* 3–30. doi:10.1007/BF02211815

Ford, M. E., & Tisak, M. S. (1983). A further search for social intelligence. *Journal of Educational Psychology, 75,* 196–206. doi:10.1037/0022–0663.75.2.196

Fox, S., & Spector, P. E. (2000). Relations of emotional intelligence, practical intelligence, general intelligence, and trait affectivity with interview outcomes: It's not all just 'G.' *Journal of Organizational Behavior, 21,* 203–220. doi:10.1002/(SICI)1099–1379(200003)21:2<203::AID-JOB38>3.0.CO;2-Z

Fryer, R. G., Jr., & Levitt, S. D. (2004). The causes and consequences of distinctly Black names. *Quarterly Journal of Economics, 119,* 767–805.

Gangestad, S. W., & Simpson, J. A. (1990). Toward an evolutionary history of female sociosexual variation. *Journal of Personality, 58,* 69–96. doi:10.1111/j.1467–6494.1990.tb00908

Gangestad, S. W., & Simpson, J. A. (2000). The evolution of human mating: Trade-offs and strategic pluralism. *Behavioral and Brain Sciences, 23,* 573–644. doi:10.1017/S0140525X0000337X

Gardner, H. (1983). *Frames of mind: The theory of multiple intelligences.* New York, NY: Basic Books.

Geary, D. C. (2005). *The origin of mind: Evolution of brain, cognition, and general intelligence.* Washington, DC: American Psychological Association.

Geher, G., & Miller, G. (Eds.). (2007). *Mating intelligence: Sex, relationships, and the mind's reproductive system.* Mahwah, NJ: Erlbaum.

Gilles, G. E., Stough, C., & Loukomitis, S. (2004). Openness, intelligence, and self-report intelligence. *Intelligence, 32,* 133–143.

Goldberg, L. R. (1992). The development of markers for the big-five factor structure. *Psychological Assessment, 4,* 26–42.

Gottfredson, L. S. (1997). Why g matters: The complexity of everyday life. *Intelligence, 24,* 79–132. doi:10.1016/S0160–2896(97)90014–3

Hagen, E. H., & Hammerstein, P. (2006). Game theory and human evolution: A critique of some recent interpretations of experimental games. *Theoretical Population Biology, 69,* 339–348. doi:101016/j.tpb.2005.09.005

Hamilton, W. D. (1964a). The genetical evolution of social behavior. I. *Journal of Theoretical Biology, 7,* 1–16. doi:10.1016/0022–5193(64)90038–4

Hamilton, W. D. (1964b). The genetical evolution of social behavior. II. *Journal of Theoretical Biology, 7,* 17–52. doi:10.1016/0022–5193(64)90039–6

Herrnstein, R. J., & Murray, C. (1994). *The bell curve: Intelligence and class structure in American life.* New York, NY: Free Press.

Hill, K., & Hurtado, A. M. (1996). *Ache life history: The ecology and demography of a foraging people.* New York, NY: Aldine.

Holland, D. C., Dollinger, S. J., Holland, C. J., & MacDonald, D. A. (1995). The relationship between psychometric intelligence and the five-factor model of personality in a rehabilitation sample. *Journal of Clinical Psychology, 51,* 79–88. doi:10.1002/1097–4679(199501)51:1<79::AID-JCLP2270510113>3.0CO;2-P

Humphrey, N. K. (1976). The social function of the intellect. In P. P. G. Bateson & R. A. Hinde (Eds.), *Growing points in ethology* (pp. 303–317). New York, NY: Cambridge University Press.

Jensen, A. R. (1998). *The g factor: The science of mental ability.* Westport, CT: Praeger.

Jerisen, H. (1973). *Evolution of the brain and intelligence.* New York, NY: Academic Press.

Kanazawa, S. (2002). Bowling with our imaginary friends. *Evolution and Human Behavior, 23,* 167–171. doi:10.1016/S1090–5138(01)00098–8

Kanazawa, S. (2004a). The Savanna Principle. *Managerial and Decision Economics, 25,* 41–54. doi:10.1002/mde.1130

Kanazawa, S. (2004b). General intelligence as a domain-specific adaptation. *Psychological Review, 111,* 512–523. doi:10.1037/0033–295X.111.2.512

Kanazawa, S. (2006). Why the less intelligent may enjoy television more than the more intelligent. *Journal of Cultural and Evolutionary Psychology, 4,* 27–36. doi:10.1556/JCEP.4.2006.1.2

Kanazawa, S. (2007). Mating intelligence and general intelligence as independent constructs. In G. Geher & G. Miller (Eds.), *Mating intelligence: Sex, relationships, and the mind's reproductive system* (pp. 283–309). Mahwah, NJ: Erlbaum.

Kanazawa, S. (2008). Temperature and evolutionary novelty as forces behind the evolution of general intelligence. *Intelligence, 36,* 99–108. doi:10.1016/j.intell.2007.04.001

Kanazawa, S. (2010). Why liberals and atheists are more intelligent. *Social Psychology Quarterly, 73,* 33–57. doi:10.1177/0190272510361602

Kanazawa, S., & Perina, K. (2009). Why night owls are more intelligent. *Personality and Individual Differences, 47,* 685–690. doi:10.1016/j.paid.2009.05.021

Kanazawa, S., & Still, M. C. (1999). Why monogamy? *Social Forces, 78,* 25–50.

Kihlstrom, J. F., & Cantor, N. (2000). Social intelligence. In R. J. Sternberg (Ed.), *Handbook of intelligence* (pp. 359–379). Cambridge, England: Cambridge University Press.

King, D. P., & Takahashi, J. S. (2000). Molecular genetics of circadian rhythms in mammals. *Annual Review of Neuroscience, 23,* 713–742. doi:10.1146/annurev.neuro.23.1.713

Klein, D. C., Moore, R. Y., & Reppert, S. M. (1991). *Suprachiasmatic nucleus: The mind's clock.* New York, NY: Oxford University Press.

Kluegel, J. R., & Smith, E. R. (1986). *Beliefs about inequality: Americans' view of what is and what ought to be.* New York, NY: Aldine.

Lake, C. C., & Breglio, V. J. (1992). Different voices, different views: The politics of gender. In P. Ries & A. J. Stone (Eds.), *The American woman, 1992–93: A status report* (pp. 178–201). New York, NY: Norton.

Lee, R. B. (1979). *The !Kung San: Men, women, and work in a foraging society.* Cambridge, England: Cambridge University Press.

Leutenegger, W., & Kelly, J. T. (1977). Relationship of sexual dimorphism in canine size and body size to social, behavioral, and ecological correlates in anthropoid primates. *Primates, 18,* 117–136. doi:10.1007/BF02382954

Levinson, D. (Ed.). (1991–1995). *Encyclopedia of world cultures* (Vols. *1–10*). Boston, MA: G. K. Hall.

Levitt, S. D., & Dubner, S. J. (2005). *Freakonomics: A rogue economist explores the hidden side of everything*. London, England: Penguin.

Lieberson, S., & Bell, E. O. (1992). Children's first names: An empirical study of social taste. *American Journal of Sociology, 98*, 511–554. doi:10.1086/230048

MacDonald, K. (1995). Evolution, the five-factor model, and levels of personality. *Journal of Personality, 63*, 525–567. doi:101111/j.1467–6494.1995.tb00505.x

Marlowe, H. A., Jr. (1986). Social intelligence: Evidence for multidimensionality and construct independence. *Journal of Educational Psychology, 78*, 52–58. doi:10.1037/0022–0663.78.1.52

Marlowe, H. A., & Bedell, J. R. (1982). Social intelligence: Further evidence for the independence of the construct. *Psychological Reports, 51*, 461–462.

Mayer, J. D., Roberts, R. D., & Barsade, S. G. (2009). Human abilities: Emotional intelligence. *Annual Review of Psychology, 59*, 507–536. doi:10.1146/annurev.psych.59.103006.093646

Mayer, J. D., Salovey, P., & Caruso, D. R. (2008). Emotional intelligence: New ability or eclectic traits? *American Psychologist, 63*, 503–517. doi:10.1037/0003–066X.63.6.503

Mayer, J. D., Salovey, P., Caruso, D. R., & Sitarenios, G. (2001). Emotional intelligence as a standard intelligence. *Emotion, 1*, 232–242. doi:10.1037/1528–3542.1.3.232

McRae, R. R. (1994). Openness to experience: Expanding the boundaries of Factor V. *European Journal of Personality, 8*, 251–272. doi:10.1002/per.2410080404

Miller, A. S., & Kanazawa, S. (2007). *Why beautiful people have more daughters*. New York, NY: Penguin.

Miller, G. F. (2000a). How to keep our metatheories adaptive: Beyond Cosmides, Tooby, and Lakatos. *Psychological Inquiry, 11*, 42–46.

Miller, G. F. (2000b). Sexual selection for indicators of intelligence. In G. R. Bock, J. A. Goode, & K. Webb (Eds.), *The nature of intelligence* (pp. 260–275). New York, NY: Wiley.

Neisser, U., Boodoo, G., Bouchard, T. J., Jr., Boykin, A. W., Brody, N., Ceci, S. J., . . . Urbina, S. (1996). Intelligence: Knowns and unknowns. *American Psychologist, 51*, 77–101. doi:10.1037/0003–066X.51.2.77

Nettle, D. (2005). An evolutionary approach to the extraversion continuum. *Evolution and Human Behavior, 26*, 363–373. doi:10.1016/j.evolhumbehav.2004.12.004

Nettle, D. (2006). The evolution of personality variation in humans and other animals. *American Psychologist, 61*, 622–631. doi:10.1037/0003–066X.61.6.622

Ridley, M. (1996). *The origins of virtue: Human instincts and the evolution of cooperation*. New York, NY: Viking Press.

Roberts, R. D., Zeidner, M., & Matthews, G. (2001). Does emotional intelligence meet traditional standards for an intelligence? Some new data and conclusions. *Emotion, 1*, 196–231. doi:10.1037/1528–3542.1.3.196

Sally, D. (1995). Conversation and cooperation in social dilemmas: A meta-analysis of experiments from 1958 to 1992. *Rationality and Society, 7*, 58–92. doi:10.1177/1043463195007001004

Salovey, P., & Mayer, J. D. (1990). Emotional intelligence. *Imagination, Cognition and Personality, 9*, 557–568.

Scarr, S. (1995). Psychology will be truly evolutionary when behavior genetics is included. *Psychological Inquiry, 6*, 68–71. doi:10.1207/s15327965pli0601_13

Shapiro, R. Y., & Mahajan, H. (1986). Gender differences in policy preferences: A summary of trends from the 1960s to the 1980s. *Public Opinion Quarterly, 50*, 42–61. doi:10.1086/268958

Shepard, R. N. (1994). Perceptual-cognitive universals as reflections of the world. *Psychonomic Bulletin & Review, 1*, 2–28.

Spearman, C. (1904). General intelligence, objectively determined and measured. *American Journal of Psychology, 15*, 201–293. doi:10.2307/1412107

Sundquist, J. L. (1983). *Dynamics of the party system* (Rev. ed.). Washington, DC: Brookings Institution.

Symons, D. (1990). Adaptiveness and adaptation. *Ethology and Sociobiology, 11*, 427–444. doi:10.1016/0162–3095(90)90019–3

Tooby, J., & Cosmides, L. (1990a). On the universality of human nature and the uniqueness of the individual: The role of genetics and adaptation. *Journal of Personality, 58*, 17–67.

Tooby, J., & Cosmides, L. (1990b). The past explains the present: Emotional adaptations and the structure of ancestral environments. *Ethology and Sociobiology, 11*, 375–424. doi:10.1016/0162–3095(90)90017-Z

Tooby, J., & Cosmides, L. (1992). The psychological foundations of culture. In J. H. Barkow, L. Cosmides, & J. Tooby (Eds.), *The adapted mind: Evolutionary psychology and the generation of culture* (pp. 19–136). New York, NY: Oxford University Press.

Trivers, R. L. (1971). The evolution of reciprocal altruism. *Quarterly Review of Biology, 46*, 35–57.

Vitaterna, M. H., Takahashi, J. S., & Turek, F. W. (2001). Overview of circadian rhythms. *Alcohol Research and Health, 25*, 85–93.

Whitmeyer, J. M. (1997). Endogamy as a basis for ethnic behavior. *Sociological Theory, 15*, 162–178. doi:10.1111/0735–2751.00030

Whitten, N. E., Jr. (1976). *Sacha Runa: Ethnicity and adaptation of Ecuadorian jungle Quichua*. Urbana: University of Illinois Press.

Wirls, D. (1986). Reinterpreting the gender gap. *Public Opinion Quarterly, 50*, 316–330.

Critical Thinking

1. What is the Savanna Principle?
2. Describe the way in which the Savanna Principle may be used to conduct research on intelligence
3. Describe two different theories about traits such as intelligence.

Create Central

www.mhhe.com/createcentral

Internet References

The hypothesis: Why do people want what they want?
www.psychologytoday.com/blog/the-scientific-fundamentalist/201003/the-hypothesis

Intelligence and liberalism
http://andreaskluth.org/2010/03/31/intelligence-and-liberalism

Article — Prepared by: Eric Landrum, *Boise State University*

Enough about You

When Christopher Lasch's landmark book The Culture of Narcissism: American Life in an Age of Diminishing Expectations *was first published in 1979, narcissism was not a term with much popular currency. The book played a large role in changing that, and in the decades since its publication the wide-ranging cultural critique at its core has been embraced by conservatives and liberals alike. While there are sections of* The Culture of Narcissism *that now seem dated—or at least a product of their time—much of the material in the original edition is so spot-on and even prophetic that it could have been written this year. What follows is a general sampling of particularly timely or prescient passages from a book that has become a sort of* Silent Spring *of America's psychological journey inward.* —The Editors

CHRISTOPHER LASCH

Learning Outcomes

After reading this article, you will be able to:

- Describe the characteristics of a narcissist and those conditions by which a narcissist can thrive.
- Define the concept of anxious self-scrutiny and the role it plays to help individuals deal with the demands of daily life.

This book describes a way of life that is dying—the culture of competitive individualism, which in its decadence has carried the logic of individualism to the extreme of a war of all against all, the pursuit of happiness to the dead end of a narcissistic preoccupation with the self.

Economic man . . . has given way to the psychological man of our times—the final product of bourgeois individualism. The new narcissist is haunted not by guilt but by anxiety. His sexual attitudes are permissive rather than puritanical, even though his emancipation from ancient taboos brings him no sexual peace. He extols cooperation and teamwork while harboring deeply antisocial impulses. He praises respect for rules and regulations in the secret belief that they do not apply to himself. Acquisitive in the sense that his cravings have no limits, he does not accumulate goods and provisions against the future, in the manner of the acquisitive individualist of 19th-century political economy, but demands immediate gratification and lives in a state of restless, perpetually unsatisfied desire.

Storm warnings, portents, hints of catastrophe haunt our times. The Nazi holocaust, the threat of nuclear annihilation, the depletion of natural resources, well-founded predictions of ecological disaster have fulfilled poetic prophecy, giving concrete historical substance to the nightmare, or death wish, that avant-garde artists were the first to express. Impending disaster has become an everyday concern, so commonplace and familiar that nobody any longer gives much thought to how disaster might be averted. People busy themselves instead with survival strategies, measures designed to prolong their own lives, or programs guaranteed to ensure good health and peace of mind.

The contemporary climate is therapeutic, not religious. People today hunger not for personal salvation, let alone for the restoration of an earlier golden age, but for the feeling, the momentary illusion, of personal well-being, health, and psychic security.

Notwithstanding his occasional illusions of omnipotence, the narcissist depends on others to validate his self-esteem. He cannot live without an admiring audience. [His insecurity can be] overcome only by seeing his "grandiose self" reflected in the attentions of others, or by attaching himself to those who radiate celebrity, power, and charisma. For the narcissist, the world is a mirror, whereas the rugged individualist saw it as an empty wilderness to be shaped to his own design.

Today Americans are overcome not by the sense of endless possibility but by the banality of the social order they have erected against it. People nowadays complain of an inability to feel. They cultivate more vivid experiences, seek to beat sluggish flesh to life, attempt to revive jaded appetites. Outwardly bland, submissive, and sociable, they seethe with an inner anger for which a dense, overpopulated bureaucratic society can devise few legitimate outlets.

The popularity of the confessional mode testifies, of course, to the new narcissism that runs all through American culture. Instead of working through their memories, many writers now rely on mere self-disclosure to keep readers interested, appealing not to their understanding but to their salacious curiosity about the private lives of famous people.

The mass media, with their cult of celebrity and their attempt to surround it with glamour and excitement, have made America a nation of fans and moviegoers. The media give substance to and thus intensify narcissistic dreams of fame and glory, encourage common people to identify themselves with the stars and to hate the "herd," and make it more and more difficult for them to accept the banality of everyday existence.

The modern propaganda of commodities and the good life has sanctioned impulse gratification and made it unnecessary for the id to apologize for its wishes or disguise their grandiose proportions. But this same propaganda has made failure and loss unsupportable.

The proliferation of recorded images undermines our sense of reality. We distrust our perceptions until the camera verifies them. Photographic images provide us with the proof of our existence, without which we would find it difficult even to reconstruct a personal history.

Medicine and psychiatry—more generally, the therapeutic outlook and sensibility that pervade modern society—reinforce the pattern created by other cultural influences, in which individuals endlessly examine themselves for signs of aging and ill health, for telltale symptoms of psychic stress, for blemishes and flaws that might diminish their attractiveness. . . . Modern medicine has conquered the plagues and epidemics that once made life so precarious, only to create new forms of insecurity. In the same way, bureaucracy has made life predictable and even boring while reviving, in a new form, the war of all against all. Our over-organized society, in which large-scale organizations predominate but have lost the capacity to command allegiance, in some respects more nearly approximates a condition of universal animosity than did the primitive capitalism on which Hobbes modeled his state of nature.

A society that fears it has no future is not likely to give much attention to the needs of the next generation, and the ever-present sense of historical discontinuity—the blight of our society—falls with particularly devastating effect on the family. The modern parent's attempt to make children feel loved and wanted fails to conceal an underlying coolness—the remoteness of those who have little to pass on to the next generation and who in any case give priority to their own right to self-fulfillment.

The weakening of social ties, which originates in the prevailing state of social warfare, at the same time reflects a narcissistic defense against dependence. A warlike society tends to produce men and women who are at heart antisocial. It should therefore not surprise us to find that although narcissists conform to social norms for fear of external retribution, they often think of themselves as outlaws.

The ethic of self-preservation and psychic survival is rooted, then, not merely in objective conditions of economic warfare, rising rates of crime, and social chaos but in the subjective experience of emptiness and isolation. It reflects the conviction—as much of a projection of inner anxieties as a perception of the way things are—that envy and exploitation dominate even the most intimate relations. The ideology of personal growth, superficially optimistic, radiates a profound despair and resignation. It is the faith of those without faith.

In an age of diminishing expectations, the Protestant virtues no longer incite enthusiasm. Inflation erodes investments and savings. Advertising undermines the horrors of indebtedness, exhorting the consumer to buy now and pay later. Self-preservation has replaced self-improvement as the goal of earthly existence. In earlier times, the self-made man took pride in his judgment of character and probity; today he anxiously scans the faces of his fellows not so as to evaluate their credit but in order to gauge their susceptibility to his own blandishments. He practices the classic arts of seduction with the same indifference to moral niceties, hoping to win your heart while picking your pocket. The happy hooker stands in place of Horatio Alger as the prototype of personal success.

Success in our society has to be ratified by publicity. It is well known that Madison Avenue packages politicians and markets them as if they were cereals or deodorants; but the art of public relations penetrates even more deeply into political life, transforming policy making itself. The modern prince does not much care that "there's a job to be done"—the slogan of American capitalism at an earlier and more enterprising stage of its development; what interests him is that "relevant audiences," in the language of the Pentagon Papers, have to be cajoled, won over, seduced.

The search for competitive advantage through emotional manipulation increasingly shapes not only personal relations but relations at work as well. Personal life, no longer a refuge from deprivations suffered at work, has become as anarchical, as warlike, and as full of stress as the marketplace itself. The cocktail party reduces sociability to social combat.

At the same time that public life and even private life take on the qualities of spectacle, a countermovement seeks to model spectacle, theater, all forms of life, on reality—to obliterate the very distinction between art and life. Both developments popularize a sense of the absurd, that hallmark of the contemporary sensibility. Overexposure to manufactured illusions soon destroys their representational power. The illusion of reality dissolves, not in a heightened sense of reality as we might expect, but in a remarkable indifference to reality.

A number of historical currents have converged in our time to produce not merely in artists but also in ordinary men and women an escalating cycle of self-consciousness—a sense of the self as a performer under the constant scrutiny of friends and strangers. . . . To the performing self, the only reality is the identity he can construct out of materials furnished by advertising and mass culture, themes of popular film and fiction, and fragments torn from a vast range of cultural traditions. In order to polish and perfect the part he has devised for himself, the new Narcissus gazes at his own reflection, not so much in admiration as in unremitting search of flaws, signs of fatigue, decay.

In our society, anxious self-scrutiny (not to be confused with critical self-examination) not only serves to regulate information signaled to others and to interpret signals received; it also establishes an ironic distance from the deadly routine of daily life. On the one hand, the degradation of work makes skill and competence increasingly irrelevant to material success and thus encourages the presentation of the self as a commodity; on the other hand, it discourages commitment to the job and drives people, as the only alternative to boredom and despair, to view work with self-critical detachment. When jobs consist of little more than meaningless motions, and when social routines, formerly dignified as ritual, degenerate into role playing, workers . . . seek to escape from the resulting sense of inauthenticity by creating an ironic distance from their daily routine. They take refuge in jokes, mockery, and cynicism. By demystifying daily life, they convey to themselves and others the impression that they have risen beyond it, even as they go through the motions and do what is expected of them. As more and more people find themselves working at jobs that are in fact beneath their abilities, as leisure and sociability themselves take on the qualities of work, the posture of cynical detachment becomes the dominant style of every-day intercourse.

Critical Thinking

1. What is competitive individualism?

2. What is the relationship between the psychological concepts of narcissism and self-esteem?

3. From a societal perspective, what role does anxious self-scrutiny play?

Create Central

www.mhhe.com/createcentral

Internet References

Emotional competency
www.emotionalcompetency.com/tyranny.htm

When narcissism meets addiction
www.theatlantic.com/health/archive/2013/07/where-narcissism
-meets-addiction/278195/

Article   Prepared by: R. Eric Landrum, *Boise State University*

What Your Facebook Use Reveals about Your Personality and Your Self-Esteem

AMY MORIN

Learning Outcomes

After reading this article, you will be able to:

- Appreciate some of the differences between extroverts and introverts, and how those differences manifest themselves on Facebook.

- Understand the definition of narcissism and the role that personality trait plays on Facebook postings.

- Comprehend that on Facebook, what we post reveals a great deal about personality traits.

Every day when Facebook asks, "What's on your mind?" around 400 million people respond with a status message. While some people take the opportunity to share about their latest meal, other people post photos or inspirational messages. Over the past few years, researchers have discovered the way people choose to present themselves on Facebook speaks volumes about their personality and self-image.

Understanding your behavior on social media could give you insight into your own personality as well as how others perceive you. Clearly, we may think we're presenting ourselves in a certain light only to discover other people view our behavior completely different.

Recognizing what Facebook reveals about personality could serve many benefits in the business world. A hiring manager could quickly gain insight into an interviewee's personality by taking a quick look at that person's Facebook profile. Or a salesperson who understands whether his customer is likely agreeable or narcissistic could tailor his approach accordingly and gain a competitive edge in closing a deal.

Here are seven things our Facebook interactions reveal about us:

1. **People with a lot of Facebook friends tend to have low self-esteem.** A 2012 study published in *Computers in Human Behavior* found that people with low self-esteem who worried about their public perception had the most Facebook friends. The researchers concluded that self-conscious people compensate for low self-esteem by trying to appear popular on Facebook.

2. **Extroverts upload photos and update their status more often than introverts.** Just like in real life, extroverts socialize more on social media, according to a 2014 study titled "Personality Traits and Self-Presentation at Facebook." The study found that extroverts use the like button more often and update their status more frequently than introverts.

3. **Conscientious people organize their photos carefully.** Conscientious people are self-disciplined hard-workers who spend the least amount of time on Facebook. A 2014 study published in *Computers in Human Behavior,* reports that when conscientious people do use Facebook, they do so in a very organized manner. For example, they may create neat folders to help share their photos with friends and family in a methodical and convenient way.

4. **Open people are likely to fill out their personal profiles most thoroughly.** A 2010 study called "Social Network Use and Personality," discovered that open people—described as artistic, imaginative, and creative—use the most features on Facebook and are most likely to complete the personal information sections. They also tend to post more "wall messages" when communicating with specific friends.

5. **Narcissists are most likely to make deeper self-disclosures that contain self-promotional content.** Narcissists—people with an inflated self-concept and a strong sense of uniqueness and superiority—seek attention and affirmation on Facebook. A 2014 study found that narcissists made more frequent posts about themselves in an attempt to attract likes and comments that fuel their beliefs about self-importance. Other studies have found that narcissistic people love to [take] selfies and they share the ones where they think they look most attractive in hopes of gaining admiration.

6. **Neurotic people post mostly photos.** A 2014 study titled "Capturing Personality from Facebook Photos and Photo-Related Activity" found that highly neurotic people—those most prone to stress and anxiety—seek acceptance by publishing photos. Since neurotic people struggle with communication and social skills, researchers believe they use photos on Facebook as a means to express themselves. Also, photos are less controversial than comments—which could lead to a lot of anxiety as they wait for other people's responses.

Neurotic people tend to have the most photos per album. Researchers believe this stems from their desire to present themselves positively. They may use photos to try and appear happier and to show they are able to keep up with their friends. Over time, however, the behavior of highly neurotic people tends to change. They're likely to imitate their friends' Facebook behavior in an attempt to seek acceptance and decrease feelings of loneliness.

7. **Agreeable people are tagged in other people's photos most often.** A 2012 study titled "Personality and Patterns of Facebook Usage," found that the higher a person ranks in personality scales for agreeableness, the more likely that person will be tagged in Facebook photos posted by other people. Since agreeable people tend to behave warm and friendly and less competitive, it's not surprising that their friends enjoy taking lighthearted pictures with them and sharing them on Facebook.

Although we may think we're masking our insecurities or portraying ourselves in the most favorable light, our behavior on social media reveals more than we might think. It's not just what we post on Facebook that reveals information about our personalities—it's also what we don't post that can be quite telling. It's likely that our personality profiles will continue to play a major role in how advertisers market to us and how companies will choose to hire people in the future.

Facebook not only reveals how we see ourselves—our profiles also provide insight into how others perceive us.

Critical Thinking

1. According to the research, what is the relationship between having many Facebook friends and one's level of self-esteem? Explain.

2. Who tends to post more "wall messages" on Facebook, and why?

3. Why would individuals with neurotic behavior patterns post more pictures than text? The article author suggested some reasons why; do you agree? Why or why not?

Internet References

Does Facebook know you better than your mother? Or roommate?
    http://www.newsweek.com/does-facebook-know-you-better-your-mother-or-roommate-299171

Facebook's dark side: Status updates reveal personality traits, whether you're a psychopath
    http://www.medicaldaily.com/facebooks-dark-side-status-updates-reveal-personality-traits-whether-youre-psychopath-264024

New Stanford research finds computers are better judges of personality than friends and family
    http://news.stanford.edu/news/2015/january/personality-computer-knows-011215.html

AMY MORIN is a psychotherapist and the author of the forthcoming book *13 Things Mentally Strong People Don't Do.*

Unit 9

UNIT

Prepared by: Eric Landrum, *Boise State University*

Social Processes

We humans are particularly social creatures, as are many of the other species with whom we share the planet. We tend to assemble in groups, some large and some small. We form friendships with all sorts of people. Many of these relationships develop naturally from shared interests and common goals. Some of these friendships are long-lasting and endure hardship. Other kinds of friendships are shorter-term that are often soon forgotten. We form highly unique relationships in which we fall in love with another person and decide to commit the rest of our lives, or at least a large chunk of it, to being this person's most intimate companion. And then there are families, perhaps the most interesting social unit full of fascinating dynamics that emerge as children are born, grow up, and form families of their own.

The responsibility for understanding the complicated facets of human social behavior falls to social psychologists. These psychologists, like most research-focused behavioral scientists, are trained to apply rigorous experimental methods to discovering, understanding, and explaining how people interact with one another. During the past century, social psychologists studied some of the most pressing and fascinating social behaviors of the day. For example, social psychologists examined, and continue to study discrimination and prejudice, conformity, and obedience to authority. In addition to these high-profile issues, social psychologists study the more positive side of human social behavior such as liking and loving, attitude formation and change, attributions, and group behavior and decision making. There are fascinating examples available of the impact of positive psychology, such as the effort of an entire country to invest in its own national happiness.

In the past few decades, psychologists have become more aware of the impact of culture on human social relationships and have turned their attention to exploring differences among cultures with respect to social development, social perception, social influence, and social change. As the world seems to become smaller and smaller, the demand for social psychologists to provide explanations for both positive and negative social behaviors that are impacted by cultural influences will only become greater. Interesting challenges and opportunites occur when individuals from different backgrounds have the chance to live and work together, and social psychologists can often offer advice and tips about how to learn and develop in these environments.

Thus, as you study social psychology in your introductory psychology course, apply the principles you are learning not just to better understanding your own social behavior, but also ask yourself how these principles might (or might not) generalize to the social behavior of individuals from different cultures. Doing so might put you in a better position to understand the whys and wherefores of social behavior that would seem (on the surface) to be so radically different from your own. In this unit, we explore the fascinating field of social psychology.

Article   Prepared by: Eric Landrum, *Boise State University*

Gross National Happiness in Bhutan: The Big Idea from a Tiny State That Could Change the World

ANNIE KELLY

Learning Outcomes

After reading this article, you will be able to:

- Understand the concept of gross national happiness and understand that it is an alternative to gross national product.

- Articulate the expected outcomes of the GNH project in Bhutan, and know about some of the preliminary outcomes to date.

A series of hand-painted signs dot the side of the winding mountain road that runs between the airport and the Bhutanese capital, Thimphu. Instead of commands to cut speed or check mirrors, they offer the traveller a series of life-affirming mantras. "Life is a journey! Complete it!" says one, while another urges drivers to, "Let nature be your guide." Another, standing on the edge of a perilous curve, simply says: "Inconvenience regretted."

It's a suitably uplifting welcome to visitors to this remote kingdom, a place of ancient monasteries, fluttering prayer flags and staggering natural beauty. Less than 40 years ago, Bhutan opened its borders for the first time. Since then, it has gained an almost mythical status as a real-life Shangri-La, largely for its determined and methodical pursuit of the most elusive of concepts—national happiness.

Since 1971, the country has rejected GDP as the only way to measure progress. In its place, it has championed a new approach to development, which measures prosperity through formal principles of gross national happiness (GNH) and the spiritual, physical, social and environmental health of its citizens and natural environment.

For the past three decades, this belief that wellbeing should take preference over material growth has remained a global oddity. Now, in a world beset by collapsing financial systems, gross inequity and wide-scale environmental destruction, this tiny Buddhist state's approach is attracting a lot of interest.

As world leaders prepare to meet in Doha on Monday for the second week of the UN climate change conference, Bhutan's stark warning that the rest of the world is on an environmental and economical suicide path is starting to gain traction. Last year the UN adopted Bhutan's call for a holistic approach to development, a move endorsed by 68 countries. A UN panel is now considering ways that Bhutan's GNH model can be replicated across the globe.

As representatives in Doha struggle to find ways of reaching a consensus on global emissions, Bhutan is also being held up as an example of a developing country that has put environmental conservation and sustainability at the heart of its political agenda. In the last 20 years Bhutan has doubled life expectancy, enrolled almost 100% of its children in primary school and overhauled its infrastructure.

At the same time, placing the natural world at the heart of public policy has led to environmental protection being enshrined in the constitution. The country has pledged to remain carbon neutral and to ensure that at least 60% of its landmass will remain under forest cover in perpetuity. It has banned export logging and has even instigated a monthly pedestrian day that bans all private vehicles from its roads.

"It's easy to mine the land and fish the seas and get rich," says Thakur Singh Powdyel, Bhutan's minister of education, who has become one of the most eloquent spokespeople for GNH. "Yet we believe you cannot have a prosperous nation in the long run that does not conserve its natural environment or take care of the wellbeing of its people, which is being borne out by what is happening to the outside world."

Powdyel believes the world has misinterpreted Bhutan's quest. "People always ask how can you possibly have a nation of happy people? But this is missing the point," he says. "GNH is an aspiration, a set of guiding principles through which we are navigating our path towards a sustainable and equitable society. We believe the world needs to do the same before it is too late."

Bhutan's principles have been set in policy through the gross national happiness index, based on equitable social development, cultural preservation, conservation of the environment and promotion of good governance.

At a primary school in Thimphu, the headteacher, Choki Dukpa, watches her students make their way to class. She says that she has seen huge changes to the children's emotional well-being since GNH principles were integrated into the education system four years ago. She admits that at first she had no idea what the government's policy to change all education facilities into "green schools" meant.

"It sounded good but I wasn't sure how it would work," she says. But after Unicef funded a "green schools" teacher training programme, things improved. "The idea of being green does not just mean the environment, it is a philosophy for life," says Dukpa.

Alongside maths and science, children are taught basic agricultural techniques and environmental protection. A new national waste management programme ensures that every piece of material used at the school is recycled.

The infusion of GNH into education has also meant daily meditation sessions and soothing traditional music replacing the clang of the school bell.

"An education doesn't just mean getting good grades, it means preparing them to be good people," says Dukpa. "This next generation is going to face a very scary world as their environment changes and social pressures increase. We need to prepare them for this."

Despite its focus on national wellbeing, Bhutan faces huge challenges. It remains one of the poorest nations on the planet. A quarter of its 800,000 people survive on less than $1.25 a day, and 70% live without electricity. It is struggling with a rise in violent crime, a growing gang culture and the pressures of rises in both population and global food prices.

It also faces an increasingly uncertain future. Bhutan's representatives at the Doha climate talks are warning that its gross national happiness model could crumble in the face of increasing environmental and social pressures and climatic change.

"The aim of staying below a global two-degree temperature increase being discussed here this week is not sufficient for us. We are a small nation, we have big challenges and we are trying our best, but we can't save our environment on our own," says Thinley Namgyel, who heads Bhutan's climate change division. "Bhutan is a mountainous country, highly vulnerable to extreme weather conditions. We have a population that is highly dependent on the agricultural sector. We are banking on hydropower as the engine that will finance our development."

In Paro, an agricultural region one hour out of the capital, Dawa Tshering explains how the weather is already causing him problems. The 53-year-old farmer grew up in Paro, surrounded by mountains and streams, but has found it increasingly difficult to work his two acres of rice paddy.

"The weather has changed a lot: there is no snow in winter, the rains come at the wrong times and our plants get ruined. There are violent storms," he says. Around 70% of Bhutan's people are smallholder farmers like Tshering.

"The temperature has got hotter so there are more insects in the fruit and grain. I don't understand it, but if it continues we're going to have many problems in growing food and feeding ourselves."

Bhutan is taking action to try to protect itself. Groundbreaking work is being done to try to reduce the flooding potential in its remote glacial lakes. Yet it cannot do it alone. Last week in Doha, campaigners pushed for more support to countries such as Bhutan that are acutely vulnerable to climate change.

"While the world is now starting to look to Bhutan as an alternative model of sustainable economics, all of its efforts could be undone if the world doesn't take action in Doha," says Stephen Pattison from Unicef UK.

"Small and developing countries like Bhutan must get more support, and the UK and other governments must start actually taking action, like pledging their share of money to the green climate fund and get it up and running as soon as possible."

In Paro, teenagers in school uniform heading home from lessons are well aware of the hard times ahead for Bhutan as it tries to navigate a path between preserving its sustainable agenda and the global realities it faces. All say they are proud to be Bhutanese. They want to be forest rangers, environmental scientists and doctors. At the same time they want to travel the world, listen to Korean pop music and watch *Rambo*.

"I want to be able to go out and see the world but then I want to come home to Bhutan and for it to be the same," says Kunzang Jamso, a 15-year-old whose traditional dress is offset with a hint of a boyband haircut. "I think we must keep the outside from coming here too much because we might lose our culture, and if you don't have that then how do you know who you are?"

Critical Thinking

1. How do you think a person can balance the taking from the environment vs. the giving to the environment? Even though countries attempt to do this, individuals are faced with this dilemma daily, even if it isn't thought about daily. How do you resolve this dilemma each day? Are you more of a taker or a giver? Explain.
2. Think about living in a culture where you live on $1.25 a day, and 70% of citizens live without electricity. List at least three ways in which your life would be fundamentally different than it is today.

Create Central

www.mhhe.com/createcentral

Internet References

Gross national happiness
www.grossnationalhappiness.com
Gross national happiness USA
www.gnhusa.org

Article   Prepared by: Eric Landrum, *Boise State University*

13 Practical Tips for Training in Other Countries

Growing global opportunities have prompted many workplace learning and development professionals to seek out cross-cultural training opportunities in other countries. While many businesspeople know enough to explore the niceties of business etiquette before entering a new culture, fewer people have developed sufficient cultural intelligence to be sensitive to more profound issues when they embark on efforts to enter, and conduct training in, other countries.

WILLIAM J. ROTHWELL

Learning Outcomes

After reading this article, you will be able to:

- Identify many strategies that are useful for providing education and training services in other countries.
- Understand the importance of doing your homework on the cultural and technological differences between your own country and the educational environment of other countries.

Learning professionals should be cautious when embarking on cross-cultural assignments. Drawing on research and my experiences, here are 13 practical tips for training in cross-cultural settings.

Be Sensitive to Other Cultures

Cultural sensitivity is important, as is realizing that human beings are more alike than they are different. When first working cross-culturally, people are usually tempted to notice cultural differences first. For example, when I visited Saudi Arabia for the first time, I was surprised to learn that men and women are not usually permitted to meet in the same room and that women wearing full-head black coverings cannot travel outside their homes without a male relative or husband as escort.

These rare exceptions aside, the reality is that human beings are pretty much alike everywhere. Most everyone wants a family, a good job, a nice home life, good food, some freedom to speak their minds, and respect and dignity. While modes of dress and beliefs about religion may differ, people are pretty much alike in what they want.

It is wrong to regard people through the narrow lenses of one's own values and cultural views about what is right and wrong. If you question people from other cultures about why they believe or behave as they do, you will find out that their beliefs make perfect sense in the contexts in which they live.

Do Your Homework

Before entering a new country, do some research. Fewer Americans by percentage travel abroad than many other nationalities. Thus, there is a need to teach Americans simple basics about foreign travel. For example, before you embark on a trip, be absolutely sure you know the rules about visas—which countries need them and how to get one. There are easy places to find that information, beginning with a simple web search.

Work your social network to find out if you know anyone who knows people from that country so that you can talk to them before you go. At least find out if there are laws that you may inadvertently break. For instance, be careful about taking prescription medication unless it is in a bottle with your name on the label. Some drugs, such as diet medication or even something as simple as a nicotine lozenge, may be illegal in certain countries.

Also take time to learn about local conditions. When conducting training in South Africa, I was told how much HIV/AIDS affects local business planning on the African continent, a fact that I had known but wish I had researched more fully before my arrival.

Work with Reliable Local Partners and Informants

Spend time to find the right people with whom to work. That can be difficult to do because it is not always easy to check the reputation of others from the United States. But check you must. If you do not, you risk doing the work—and then never getting paid because there are many criminals eager to get you to pony up work first and then give you nothing when it comes time for payment.

When working with a partner for a first time, always ask for money in advance. It is wise to always ask for half the funds due up front to avoid the problem of not being paid anything. Work with people who have a track record of respecting intellectual property, copyrights, and trademarks. Beware of people who wish to partner for the short term and who may be looking for quick and easy ways to steal your products, services, or ideas and use them to their own advantage.

You may have a signed contract, but are you prepared to sue people for nonpayment in foreign courts? Legal recourse may work in America—but not so well elsewhere where networks of informal agreements and personal relationships are far more important than written contracts.

Pay Attention to Marketing

Marketing principles for training and consulting can be different in other countries. In the United States, it is common to send out emails or to offer free webinars as a marketing effort for training. Such relatively impersonal approaches do not work so well with cultures in which who you know is more important than what you can do.

As just one example, I had an experience in which a Chinese partner tried an experiment. On the one hand, the partner invested $30,000 to market seminars in Greater China through classified newspaper advertising, email, and faxes. On the other hand, the same partner marketed directly to key decision makers (vice presidents of HR) by paying them personal visits for seminar sign-ups and by offering free breakfasts with a sample of the training content. The former approach did not work at all; the latter was most effective and resulted in much business.

Consider Language As Well As Cultural Issues

Not everyone speaks English. If you plan to market in other countries, you limit yourself if the market is restricted to English speakers only. But translators are not always equally good. The best translators are not United Nations-trained; rather, they are individuals from the particular country who have some education and experience in the subject matter or industry. They know how to translate for concept as well as for words, and may even be able to cite local examples of how an idea was put into practice.

Be aware that people of other cultures are more comfortable with people like themselves. When in a public seminar, foreign nationals prefer to talk to someone who can speak their language—and is perhaps even the same gender. A particularly powerful solution is to pair up a famous foreign presenter with a local person of a different gender. While that may cost more, it can pay big dividends in the impression it makes.

Recognize Differences in How People Participate

Americans often are quite willing to publicly pose embarrassing business questions directly to senior leaders such as CEOs. But not all cultures are so open. Before arriving to conduct a seminar in a foreign country, ask others who have been to that country what participation style is typical and what strategies might work to get more participation. Do not limit such requests to one person. Ask several because perceptions are sometimes simply erroneous.

The first time I visited China I was told by an experienced Chinese training director that I should use lecture-only methods. After the first hour, my audience had nearly gone to sleep. I started asking participants questions—and giving them small gifts, such as candy bars, when they answered. That worked.

On another occasion I tried to teach public-speaking skills to Chinese graduate students. MBA students, it turned out, were not accustomed to public speaking and were immune to all efforts to use eye contact. So, I told the class that I would wave a 100RMB note (worth about $16) in the back of the room at some point during their individual talks and would give the money to the presenters who saw it. In teaching more than 60 people, I gave away only four bills. I learned that I had to stand right behind aspiring public speakers and direct them to look in specific places to teach eye contact.

Be Prepared to Negotiate

There are two ways to negotiate money in the world. There is the American-style "take-it-or-leave-it" fixed-price approach. And then there is the back-and-forth negotiation style that is used in other countries.

Start higher than you really expect, but allow some room for negotiation. Expect that others will start far lower than you expect; do not be insulted by that. Be prepared to go several rounds before reaching a level of agreement. Before you begin negotiating prices and expenses, determine what your lowest acceptable rate would be.

Would you accept economy travel instead of the much more expensive business or first-class travel? Would you stay in a four-star rather than a five-star hotel? These questions are worth considering. Also be aware that you may have to price your products or services differently if you wish to compete in some foreign markets because they simply cannot afford what they regard as outrageous U.S. or European rates.

Be Sensitive to Different Communication Styles

Realize that people in other cultures don't always communicate as openly as in the United States. In many cultures, there is concern about hurting other people's feelings. It is said in Asia and in the Middle East that there are a thousand ways to say no and a thousand ways to say yes. In fact, if a business problem exists, in some cultures they do not want to share that bad news until the last possible moment for fear of "losing face" or feeling bad about themselves. Sensitivity to communication styles is a key issue when working cross-culturally and occasionally requires exceptional skills to pull out critical information when it is needed.

When training participants who understand English, do not be offended by their slow response times. That's because the people sometimes have to mentally translate what you said to their native language and then translate their answer back into English. People will sometimes apologize to me about their poor English, but I have learned to answer that "your English is much better than my [whatever their language is]."

Recognize the Importance of Personal Relationships

In developed economies, results are important. In developing economies, results also are important—but may be less so or even overshadowed by considerations other than immediate results.

For instance, I was told in South America that "we can predict when a young person joins our company how far he will go—even to the point that we know which 21-year-old will definitely become CEO because he comes from the right family, has the right connections with government officials, attended the right school, and has the right connections in other places."

Be Tenacious in Your Efforts

There is a saying in China that "you can get anything you want in China—if you are prepared to wait long enough." In huge economies, it is possible to make an impact over time. But the buccaneer mentality of "let's go in, make a quick killing, and leave" will usually fail. Local people are waiting to hand you your head if that is your attitude.

Success may depend on being patient and dedicated. That requires long-term investments of time, money, and effort to get results. In India, for example, there are numerous inexpensive training programs offered by well-qualified people who speak very good English. Making an impact takes time, visibility, the right partner, and the most clever marketing approaches possible.

Make Personal Safety the First Priority

Never take safety for granted when you're traveling. Global organizations often have learned to assign a local mentor to someone before he arrives so that foreigners will not end up renting an apartment in an unsafe neighborhood or traveling to unsafe places in a city. Even taking a taxi can turn into a nightmare if not managed properly.

If you are a solitary traveler, make sure that you know how to reach your contacts before you arrive (such as cell phones), who (if anyone) will pick you up at the airport and how you will recognize them, and where you are going. Take nothing for granted.

I once arrived in Pakistan late at night. I was the only Westerner onboard the airplane. Before my arrival I made sure to know who was picking me up—and what to do in case, for any reason, that person was not there. Some countries, such as the Philippines or Indonesia, may have U.S.-style airport screening just to get into a hotel lobby. That speaks volumes about the need to be careful.

On another occasion I traveled to South America to conduct training for a large bank. I told them before I arrived that I was concerned about safety. They did not tell me what they planned to do about it, and I did not ask. Upon my arrival, I was greeted late at night by a large group of burly men with automatic weapons. They asked me who I was. I was a little hesitant to say, but it turned out they were an armed security detachment sent by the bank to ensure my safety.

Be Cautious in What You Take for Granted

In developed economies, HR and training practice may be quite advanced. There may be certifications and even graduate degree programs to ensure professionalism. But in many developing economies, the opportunities to learn about the professions of HR or learning and development may not be so common. Practitioners learn by working in foreign companies and then transferring some of what they have learned into local practice by eventually moving to local companies. Bear that in mind as you consider training in other nations.

Avoid using terms that may seem common—such as training needs assessment, instructional systems design, or even something such as Kirkpatrick's four levels of evaluation. Strive for simple English that is jargon-free and readily transparent in meaning. Always define special terms immediately if you are forced to use them.

Don't Take Training Technology for Granted

Developed economies are in love with technology-assisted training. Everybody wants to try the latest fad or gizmo—whether it is mobile learning, iPad-based instruction, wikis, or even more elaborate approaches such as technology-based simulations or virtual worlds. But the practical reality is that, in many developing economies, either connection speeds are slower than in developed economies or the infrastructure is less reliable. (But it is also true that, in some countries, such as Korea, they make fun of the slow speeds of the Internet in the United States because their infrastructure is newer.) Fewer people have home-based Internet access.

Realize that even something such as offering a virtual meeting may require several rehearsals. I recently offered a virtual training session in Singapore using a popular brand of virtual meeting software. Even though we had two rehearsals, we still had trouble on the day of the training.

The lesson: Never take technology for granted when working abroad. Check and verify what they have, and how well it works, first.

Practical Realities

As globalization continues with the advent of more sophisticated technology and easy travel, more learning and development professionals will work in other countries. As they do, they need to be aware of some practical realities to achieved continued success.

Critical Thinking

1. Do you think you would like to travel abroad someday? Would you rather be a tourist, a worker, or both? Explore and explain your feelings about traveling and working abroad.

2. What are some of the key challenges in providing training abroad? Although your author provided 13 tips, which three do you think are most important, and why?

Create Central

www.mhhe.com/createcentral

Internet References

World business culture
www.worldbusinessculture.com/business-with-other-countries.html

7 tips for foreign business travel
www.inc.com/guides/201103/7-tips-for-foreign-business-travel.html

WILLIAM J. ROTHWELL is a professor of workforce education and development on the University Park campus of The Pennsylvania State University. He also is president of Rothwell & Associates.

Rothwell, William J. From *T+D*, vol. 66, no. 5, May 7, 2012, pp. 39–42. Copyright © 2012 by American Society for Training & Development. Reprinted by permission.

Article   Prepared by: R. Eric Landrum, *Boise State University*

The Third Wheel: the Impact of Twitter Use on Relationship Infidelity and Divorce

Russell B. Clayton

Learning Outcomes

After reading this article, you will be able to:

- Appreciate the research design utilized to study the impact of Twitter use on relationship status.

- Practice the interpretation of statistical results in order to draw conclusions about psychological ideas.

Introduction

The Introduction of Social Networking Sites (SNSs) such as MySpace, Facebook, and Twitter have provided a relatively new platform for interpersonal communication and, as a result, have substantially enhanced and altered the dynamics of interpersonal relationships.[1-7] Twitter, once deemed merely an "information network,"[8] is now considered one of the most popular SNSs, with more than 554 million active users, competing with Facebook, Google+, and LinkedIn.[9] Although Facebook and MySpace have received a great deal of empirical attention,[3,6] research investigating the effects of Twitter use on interpersonal relationships has been somewhat limited, despite Twitter's increasing popularity. Thus, the current study's aim is to examine the effects of Twitter use on romantic relationships.

Evolution of Twitter as a SNS

Since its creation in 2006, the microblogging site Twitter has accumulated more than 554 million active registered users with 58 million tweets per day.[10] Twitter provides users a communication platform to initiate and develop connections in real time with thousands of people with shared interests.[11] It is also a way to get to know strangers who share the details of their daily lives.[12] As Chen[13] notes, Twitter evolved from an online information network where users responded to a simple question: "What are you doing right now?" to a social network that provides a "new economy of info-sharing and connectivity" between people.[10] Johnson and Yang[14] found that those who have Twitter accounts use the site primarily to give and receive advice, gather and share information, and meet new people.

The primary source for providing and obtaining information on Twitter is by reading or communicating 140-character personal updates, now known as "tweets," to those who opt to "follow" the tweeter. Additional features allow users to retweet, abbreviated as RT, others' tweets and privately direct message, or DM, other users. Twitter users can also have public conversations with others by using "@replies" and can engage in larger conversations by hashtagging ("#") words or phrases. Tweets, RTs, @replies, and hashtags are sent to a public newsfeed viewable by others, unless the user designates his or her tweets as private. Twitter updates can be sent to the newsfeed using mobile phone text messaging from Twitter's mobile phone website, phone applications, and from a user's Twitter home web page.[8,14] Although users can access Twitter across many electronic devices,[8,14] Twitter user interactivity is still somewhat limited compared to other SNSs.

While other SNSs, such as Facebook, allow users to share information about their daily lives on their Facebook newsfeeds, or directly communicate with other users via online chat, Twitter does not provide users the same functionality. Twitter does, however, allow users to post photos, videos, and check-ins that display on the Twitter newsfeed through third-party sites, such as Instagram (photos/videos) and Foursquare (check-ins). Although the method of sharing information varies between Facebook and Twitter, the type of information that can be shared publicly is similar. Therefore, the researcher speculates that the effects of Twitter usage on relationships may parallel those of Facebook. For this reason, the researcher will briefly highlight recent literature pertaining to the effects of SNS use on romantic relationships.

SNSs' effects on romantic relationships

The evolution of SNSs, as well as their increasing popularity, has provided communication and psychology researchers with an avenue to investigate, more than ever, computer-mediated communication. As a result, scholars have compiled a body of research that has systematically investigated the dynamic, complex interactions between SNS use, health, and romantic relationship outcomes.[1,3–7,15–24] While SNSs may be beneficial in helping users keep in touch with others,[16] research has shown that excessive SNS use can be detrimental to romantic relationships.[3] As Tong[17] notes, relationships, both personal and impersonal, are social in nature, and therefore involve one's social networks. Since Twitter and Facebook use "maps on to one's social networks almost isomorphically, SNSs' potential role in the process of relationship maintenance and termination seems quite likely."[17(p1)]

In fact, several studies have found that Facebook-induced jealousy, partner survelliance, posting ambiguous information, compulsive Internet use, and online portrayal of intimate relationships can be damaging to romantic relationships.[18–21] Additionally, Lyndon[22] found that Facebook monitoring leads to negative relationship outcomes, such as online and offline relationship intrusion, which may induce jealousy among romantic partners.[23] Marshall[24] found that remaining friends on SNSs, specifically Facebook, after a breakup delays the healing process. One possible explanation for this delay could be due to romantic partners taking advantage of the information Facebook provides of their ex-partner.[17] This type of information visibility, which occurs not only on Facebook but also on Twitter, may lead to similar relationship outcomes for the latter SNS.

Since Twitter now allows users to interact in a similar way as Facebook (i.e., write posts and upload images, videos, and location check-ins), the researcher theorizes that the effects of Twitter use on interpersonal relationships are comparable to those associated with Facebook. Thus, one additional aim of this study is to examine if Twitter uses parallels that of Facebook with regard to negative relationship outcomes.[3]

The current study

The current study is grounded in the methodological framework of Clayton et al.'s[3] survey study examining the influence of Facebook use on romantic relationships. Clayton et al.'s[4] study of 205 Facebook users found that Facebook-related conflict mediated the relationship between Facebook use and negative relationship outcomes (i.e., cheating, breakup, and divorce). This indirect effect was more pronounced for those in relatively newer relationships of 3 years or less.[3] To understand the influence of Twitter usage on romantic relationships, this study used the same mediating variable, now termed "Twitter-related conflict," as well as the negative relationship outcome items.[3] The researcher conceptualized Twitter-related conflict as whether Twitter use increases relationship complications in intimate romantic relationships. Negative relationship outcomes were conceptualized as whether Twitter use influences the likelihood for emotional cheating, physical cheating, relationship breakup, and divorce. As a result, the researcher predicted that active Twitter use and negative relationship outcomes would be positively related and that Twitter-related conflict would mediate the relationship between active Twitter use and negative relationship outcomes.

Clayton et al.'s[3] study found a moderating effect on the mediational relationship for those who are, or have been, in relationships of 3 years or less. Therefore, the current study hypothesizes that the length of the romantic relationship will moderate the indirect effect on the relationship between active Twitter use and negative relationship outcomes. Based on this examination of the literature, the author hypothesizes the following:

H1: The relationship between active Twitter use and negative relationship outcomes will be positively related.

H2: Twitter-related conflict will mediate the relationship between active Twitter use and negative relationship outcomes.

H3: The indirect effect of active Twitter use on negative relationship outcomes through Twitter-related conflict will be greater for those who are, or have been, in shorter duration relationships.

Method
Participants

An online survey was created on qualtrics.com and distributed to Twitter users via the researcher's Twitter account, as well as *The Huffington Post*'s Twitter account. The survey was tweeted a total of 20 times to followers. The total number of users the survey link was tweeted to, not including possible retweets, exceeded 3.4 million Twitter users. The final number of participants was 581 Twitter users. All participants were 18 years of age or older. The participants' ages ranged from 18 to 67 years ($M = 29$, $SD = 8.9$). Most participants (62%) were Caucasian, 15% Asian, 12% Hispanic, 6% African American, and 5% Native American. The majority of participants (63%) were male. This study was approved by the university's Institutional Review Board.

Materials

Following Clayton's[3] methodology, a 20-question survey was designed using qualtrics.com. The survey included demographic questions, as well as questions about participants' perceived levels of Twitter use. Additionally, participants were asked if they had encountered relationship conflict with their current or former partner as a result of Twitter use. Participants were also asked if Twitter use had led to breakup or divorce, emotional cheating, and physical cheating with a current or former partner.

Relationships

The researcher asked the participants to indicate if their partner or former partner had a Twitter account. Those who indicated that their former partner or spouse did not have a Twitter account were not included in further analyses because some items pertained to participants' perceived levels of their current or former partner's Twitter use ($n = 67$). In order for the researcher to understand to whom the participants' answers were directed, the survey also instructed participants to answer the question, "Are you currently in a romantic relationship?" If the participants answered, "Yes," they were then asked to type how many months or years they had been in the relationship with their current partner. If participants answered "No," the researcher could analyze their data in connection with the participants' former partners. After screening participants' responses for initial criteria, the total number of participants included for analyses was 514. Of the 514 participants, 386 (75%) participants responded that they were in a romantic relationship, while 128 (25%) reported being single.

Active Twitter use

Following Rubin's[25] active audience construct and Chen's[13] Twitter use items, active Twitter use was measured by asking participants to rate the following five statements: "How often do you log in into Twitter?" "How often do you Tweet?" "How often do you @replies?" "How often do you direct message followers?" and "How often do you scroll the Twitter newsfeed?" Data were gathered using a Likert-type scale where A = "never," B = "monthly," C = "weekly," D = "daily," E = "hourly," and F = "more than hourly." The Cronbach's alpha for the scale was 0.90. To create a multiplicative index of Twitter use, participants indicated how many hours per day,

and how many days per week, they used Twitter. On average, participants used Twitter for 52 minutes per day ($SD = 66.3$), five days per week ($SD = 2.3$).

Twitter-related conflict

The current study adapted the items in Clayton et al.'s[3] Facebook-related conflict scale (Cronbach's $\alpha = 0.85$) to measure Twitter-related conflict. Such items included, "How often do you have an argument with your significant other as a result of excessive Twitter use?" and "How often do you have an argument with your significant other as a result of viewing friends' Twitter profiles?" The questions were answered using a Likert scale ranging from A = "never" to F = "always." The Cronbach's alpha for the scale was 0.94.

Negative relationship outcomes. The current study used Clayton et al.'s[3] negative relationship outcome questions (Kuder Richardson [KR-20] = 0.70) to measure the criterion variable. Such items included, "Have you emotionally cheated on your significant other with someone you have connected or reconnected with on Twitter?" "Have you physically cheated on your significant other with someone you have connected or reconnected with on Twitter?" and "Has Twitter led to a breakup/divorce?" The researcher condensed the answers into dichotomous yes/no answer choices. Once averaged, the KR-20 measure of reliability was 0.72 (see Table 1).

Results

To test the aforementioned hypotheses, moderation–mediation regression analyses using bootstrapping resampling methods were conducted according to the specifications set out by Andrew Hayes's PROCESS for SPSS using model four for simple mediation and model seven to test for moderation–mediation.[26] As Figure 1 shows, active Twitter use was entered

Table 1 Means, standard deviations, correlations, and alpha reliabilities[a] for variables

	M	**SD**	**1**	**2**	**3**
1. Active Twitter use	3.36	1.0	(0.90)		
2. Twitter-related conflict	2.77	1.4	0.52***	(0.94)	
3. Negative relationship outcomes	1.17	0.30	0.33***	0.53***	(0.72)

[a]On diagonal in parentheses.
*$p < 0.05$; **$p < 0.01$; ***$p < 0.001$.

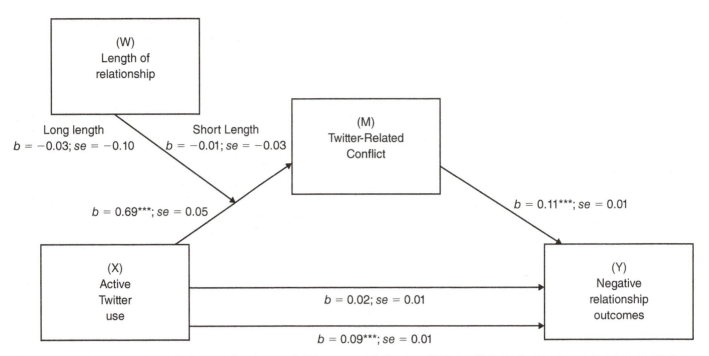

Figure 1 Andrew Hayes's mediation–moderation model 7 conceptual diagram. Path coefficients for simple moderation–mediation model analysis. *Note.* Model four is the same as model seven excluding the moderator variable (W). Dotted line denotes the effect of active Twitter use on negative relationship outcomes when Twitter-related conflict is not included as a mediator. *$p < 0.05$; **$p < 0.01$; ***$p < 0.001$.

as the independent variable (X), Twitter-related conflict as the mediator variable (M), length of romantic relationship as the moderator variable (W), and negative relationship outcomes was entered as the criterion variable (Y) in the model.

Mediation

As a test of simple mediation, Twitter-related conflict was entered as the mediator variable (M) in model four of Hayes's PROCESS[26] (see Figure 1). Data analysis using 1,000 bootstrap simulations[26] revealed that the total effect between active

Twitter use negative relationship outcomes was positively associated (*effect* = 0.09, *SE* = 0.01, $p < 0.001$ [95% CI 0.07, 0.12]), supporting H1 (see Table 2). Moreover, active Twitter use exerted an indirect effect on negative relationship outcomes through Twitter-related conflict (*effect* = 0.07, *SE* = 0.01, $p < 0.001$ [95% bias-corrected bootstrap CI 0.06, 0.09]), while the direct relationship between active Twitter use and negative relationship outcomes was not significant (*effect* = 0.02, *SE* = 0.01, $p = 0.082$ [95% CI −0.01, 0.05]), supporting H2 (see Table 2). This indirect effect is statistically different from zero,

Table 2 Total, direct, and indirect effects

	Negative relationship outcomes as criterion				
	Effect	**SE**	**t**	**LLCI**	**ULCI**
Total effect of active Twitter use	0.09	0.01	7.90***	0.07	0.12
Direct effect of active Twitter use	0.02	0.01	1.75	−0.01	0.05
	Effect	**Boot SE**		**BootLLCI**	**BootULCI**
Indirect effect of active Twitter use	0.07***	0.01	—	0.06	0.09

Note. Number of bootstrap samples for bias-corrected bootstrap confidence intervals: 1,000. Level of confidence for all confidence intervals: 95.

*$p < 0.05$; **$p < 0.01$; ***$p < 0.001$.

as revealed by a 95% bias-corrected bootstrap confidence interval,[26] and indicates that Twitter-related conflict mediates the relationship between active Twitter use and negative relationship outcomes.

Moderation

As a test of moderation–mediation, negative relationship outcomes was entered as the moderator variable (W) in model seven of Hayes's PROCESS[26] using 1,000 bootstrap simulations[26] (see Figure 1). The sample was divided based upon a median split (median = 18 months). Those participants who reported being in a relationship for 18 months or less were categorized in the shorter length group ($n = 194$), whereas those who reported being in relationships for more than 18 months were categorized in the longer length group ($n = 181$). The moderating effect on the indirect relationship between active Twitter use and negative relationship outcomes was not significant for the shorter length group (*effect* = 0.01, *SE* = 0.02, $p = 0.337$ [95% CI −0.02, 0.05]) or for the longer length group (*effect* = 0.02, *SE* = 0.03, $p = 0.454$ [95% CI −0.03, 0.08]). H3 was not supported.

Discussion

Although a number of variables can contribute to relationship infidelity and separation, the current study hypothesized that SNS use, specifically Twitter use, can contribute to negative relationship outcomes. Therefore, the purpose of this study was to investigate the relationship between active Twitter use and negative romantic relationship outcomes. Moreover, the researcher sought to examine whether the findings of Clayton et al.'s[3] recent study, which concluded that Facebook-related conflict fully mediated the relationship between Facebook use and negative relationship outcomes, were consistent with a different SNS platform—Twitter.

Since Twitter allows users to share similar types of information as Facebook, the researcher argued that Twitter outcomes may parallel those of Facebook regarding SNS use, romantic conflict, and negative relationship outcomes. The researcher theorized that if an individual who is in a romantic relationship is highly active on Twitter (e.g., tweeting, direct messaging others, check-ins, and posting images to the Twitter newsfeed), Twitter use could create conflict within the relationship. If high amounts of Twitter use does, indeed, lead to high amounts of Twitter-related conflict (i.e., arguments pertaining to a partner's Twitter use, etc.) among romantic partners, it is plausible to speculate that such conflict could lead to unfavorable relationship outcomes such as cheating, breakup, or divorce. The results from this study largely support these propositions. In contrast to recent findings,[3] the length of the relationship did

not moderate the mediational effect, suggesting that relationship maturity may not influence negative relationship outcomes in terms of Twitter use.

The results of this study partially replicate Clayton et al.'s[3] findings regarding Facebook use and negative relationship outcomes. Based on the findings from both[3] studies, Twitter and Facebook use can have damaging effects on romantic relationships. That is, when SNS use becomes problematic in one's romantic relationship, risk of negative relationship outcomes may follow. In contrast, recent reports have shown that SNS conflict can be reduced when partners share joint accounts.[27] Furthermore, recent SNS applications have been developed to facilitate interpersonal communication between partners by providing a private, secure, and organized environment for two people to share, such as the 2life app[28] for iPhone users. Whether this type of app reduces SNS-related conflict between romantic partners is yet to be determined.

Limitations and implications for further research

The current study has several limitations. The sample included participants who were told before starting the survey that they would be answering questions regarding Twitter use and romantic relationship outcomes, and this may have skewed the data. Additionally, some items were left to participants' interpretation, such as the word "excessive" when answering questions about Twitter-related conflict. Moreover, social desirability is an unavoidable issue when it comes to self-reported data, particularly when the issues under investigation are sensitive, as in the current study. Since the online survey link was distributed by the researcher's Twitter account and *The Huffington Post*'s Twitter account, the current study's sample is limited to only those who use Twitter and who follow the researcher or *The Huffington Post*'s profile on Twitter. This limitation significantly limits the generalizations of the findings. Future research should investigate if engaging in high levels of other SNS usage, such as Instagram and LinkedIn, also predicts negative relationship outcomes. Additional future research should explore other mediators in the current study's model, such as relationship quality and satisfaction.

Conclusion

The results from this study show that active Twitter use leads to greater amounts of Twitter-related conflict among romantic partners, which in turn leads to infidelity, breakup, and divorce. Results from the current study and Clayton et al.'s[3] study demonstrate that Twitter and Facebook use can have damaging effects on romantic relationships.

Author Disclosure Statement

No competing financial interests exist.

References

1. Boyd D, Ellison BN. Social network sites: definition, history, and scholarship. *Journal of Computer-Mediated Communication* 2007; 13.

2. Choi JH. (2008) Living in cyworld: contextualising cy-ties in South Korea. In Bruns A, Jacobs J, eds. *Uses of blogs.* New York: Peter Lang, pp. 173–186.

3. Clayton R, Nagurney A, Smith J. Cheating, breakup, and divorce: is Facebook use to blame? *Cyberpsychology, Behavior, & Social Networking* 2013; 16:717–720.

4. Ellison BN, Steinfield C, Lampe, C. The benefits of Facebook "friends": exploring the relationship between college students' use of online social networks and social capital. *Journal of Computer-Mediated Communication* 2007; 12:article 1.

5. Lampe C, Ellison BN, Steinfield C. Social capital, self-esteem, and use of online social network sites. *Journal of Applied Developmental Psychology* 2008; 29:434–445.

6. Raacke J, Bonds-Raacke J. MySpace and Facebook: applying the uses and gratifications theory to exploring friend-networking sites. *Individual Differences Research Group* 2008; 8:27–33.

7. Fox J, Warber K. Romantic relationship development in the age of Facebook: an exploratory study of emerging adults' perceptions, motives, and behaviors. *Journal of Cyberpsychology, Behavior, & Social Networking* 2013; 16:3–7.

8. About Twitter. https://twitter.com/about (accessed Jun. 20, 2013).

9. 2010 Best social networking site reviews and comparisons. http://social-networking-websites-review.toptenreviews.com (accessed Dec. 28, 2013).

10. Statistics Brain. Twitter statistics. www.statisticbrain.com/twitter-statistics/ (accessed Jun. 20, 2013).

11. Sarno D. On Twitter, mindcasting is the new lifecasting. Los Angeles Times, Mar. 11, 2009. http://latimesblogs.latimes.com/technology/2009/03/on-twitter-mind.html (accessed Jan. 12, 2014).

12. Thompson C. Brave new world of digital intimacy. The New York Times, Sep. 5, 2008. www.nytimes.com/2008/09/07/magazine/07awareness-t.html?_r=1&pagewanted=all (accessed Dec. 29, 2013).

13. Chen G. Tweet this: a uses and gratifications perspective on how active Twitter use gratifies a need to connect with others. *Journal of Computers in Human Behavior* 2011; 27:755–762.

14. Johnson P, Yang S-U. Uses and gratifications of Twitter: an examination of user motives and satisfaction of Twitter use. Paper presented at the Annual Convention of Association for Education in Journalism and Mass Communication in Boston, MA.

15. Clayton R, Osborne R, Miller B, et al. Loneliness, anxiousness, and substance use as predictors of Facebook use. *Computers in Human Behavior* 2013; 29:687–693.

16. Joinson AN. (2008) "Looking at," "looking up" or "keeping up with" people? Motives and uses of Facebook. In: *Proceedings of the 26th Annual SIGCHI Conference on Human Factors in Computing Systems (Florence, Italy, April 5–10, 2008), CHI'08.* New York: ACM Press, pp. 1027–1036.

17. Tong ST. Facebook use during relationship termination: uncertainty reduction and surveillance. *Cyberpsychology, Behavior, & Social Networking* 2013; 16:788–793.

18. Utz S, Beukeboom CJ. The role of social network sites in romantic relationships: effects on jealousy and relationship happiness. *Journal of Computer-Mediated Communication* 2011; 16:511–527.

19. Tokunaga RS. Social networking site or social surveillance site? Understanding the use of interpersonal electronic surveillance in romantic relationships. *Computers in Human Behavior* 2011; 27:705–713.

20. Kerkhof P, Finkenauer C, Muusses, LD. Relational consequences of compulsive internet use: a longitudinal study among newlyweds. *Human Communication Research* 2011; 37:147–173.

21. Papp LM, Danielewicz J, Cayemberg C. "Are we Facebook official?" Implications of dating partners' Facebook use and profiles for intimate relationship satisfaction. *Cyberpsychology, Behavior, & Social Networking* 2012; 15:85–90.

22. Lyndon A, Bonds-Raacke J, Cratty AD. College students' Facebook stalking of ex-partners. *Cyberpsychology, Behavior, & Social Networking* 2011; 14:711–716.

23. Muise A, Christofides E, Desmarais S. More information than you ever wanted: does Facebook bring out the green-eyed monster of jealousy? *Cyberpsychology & Behavior* 2009; 12:441–444.

24. Marshall T. Facebook surveillance of former romantic partners: associations with postbreakup recovery and personal growth. *Cyberpsychology, Behavior, & Social Networking* 2012; 15:521–526.

25. Rubin AM. (2009) Uses and gratifications: an evolving perspective on media effects. In Nabi RL, Oliver MB, eds. *The SAGE handbook of media processes and effect.* Washington, DC: Sage, pp. 147–159.

26. Hayes AF. (2013) *Introduction to mediation, moderation, and conditional process analysis: a regression-based approach.* New York: Guilford Press.

27. Buck S. (2013) When Facebook official isn't enough. Mashable.com. http://mashable.com/2013/08/04/social-media-couples/ (accessed Jan. 10, 2014).

28. 2 For Life Media Inc. (2013) 2Life App description. www.2life.io (accessed Sep. 28, 2013).

Critical Thinking

1. The development of social networking is developing rapidly and changing daily. Why is it important that this article was published in 2014 rather than in 2009? Explain.

2. Some fairly complex results appear in this journal article. What are the takeaway messages that you have after reading the complete article? What reservations might you have about the results and what they mean?

Internet References

Is constant texting good or bad for your relationship?
http://www.psychologytoday.com/blog/meet-catch-and-keep/201403/is-constant-texting-good-or-bad-your-relationship

The effect of technology on relationships
http://www.psychologytoday.com/blog/happiness-in-world/201006/the-effect-technology-relationships

Article   Prepared by: R. Eric Landrum, *Boise State University*

Rethinking One of Psychology's Most Infamous Experiments

CARI ROMM

Learning Outcomes

After reading this article, you will be able to:

- Understand that no real shocks were delivered during the Milgram experiments.

- Appreciate that the patterns of results found by Milgram in the 1960s also hold up today.

- Articulate the importance of the historical context which was in part the motivation for Milgram to carry out his series of experiments.

I n the 1960s, Stanley Milgram's electric-shock studies showed that people will obey even the most abhorrent of orders. But recently, researchers have begun to question his conclusions—and offer some of their own.

In 1961, Yale University psychology professor Stanley Milgram placed an advertisement in the *New Haven Register.* "We will pay you $4 for one hour of your time," it read, asking for "500 New Haven men to help us complete a scientific study of memory and learning."

Only part of that was true. Over the next two years, hundreds of people showed up at Milgram's lab for a learning and memory study that quickly turned into something else entirely. Under the watch of the experimenter, the volunteer—dubbed "the teacher"—would read out strings of words to his partner, "the learner," who was hooked up to an electric-shock machine in the other room. Each time the learner made a mistake in repeating the words, the teacher was to deliver a shock of increasing intensity, starting at 15 volts (labeled "slight shock" on the machine) and going all the way up to 450 volts ("Danger: severe shock"). Some people, horrified at what they were being asked to do, stopped the experiment early, defying their supervisor's urging to go on; others continued up to 450 volts, even as the learner pled for mercy, yelled a warning about his heart condition—and then fell alarmingly silent. In the most well-known variation of the experiment, a full 65 percent of people went all the way.

Until they emerged from the lab, the participants didn't know that the shocks weren't real, that the cries of pain were pre-recorded, and that the learner—railroad auditor Jim McDonough—was in on the whole thing, sitting alive and unharmed in the next room. They were also unaware that they had just been used to prove the claim that would soon make Milgram famous: that ordinary people, under the direction of an authority figure, would obey just about any order they were given, even to torture. It's a phenomenon that's been used to explain atrocities from the Holocaust to the Vietnam War's My Lai massacre to the abuse of prisoners at Abu Ghraib. "To a remarkable degree," Peter Baker wrote in *Pacific Standard* in 2013, "Milgram's early research has come to serve as a kind of all-purpose lightning rod for discussions about the human heart of darkness."

Others continued shocking even as the victim pled for mercy, yelled a warning about his heart condition—and then fell alarmingly silent.

In some ways, though, Milgram's study is also—as promised—a study of memory, if not the one he pretended it was.

More than five decades after it was first published in the *Journal of Abnormal and Social Psychology* in 1963, it's earned a place as one of the most famous experiments of the

20th century. Milgram's research has spawned countless spin-off studies among psychologists, sociologists, and historians, even as it's leapt from academia into the realm of pop culture. It's inspired songs by Peter Gabriel (lyrics: "We do what we're told/We do what we're told/Told to do") and Dar Williams ("When I knew it was wrong, I played it just like a game/I pressed the buzzer"); a number of books whose titles make puns out of the word "shocking"; a controversial French documentary disguised as a game show; episodes of *Law and Order* and *Bones;* a made-for-TV movie with William Shatner; a jewelry collection (bizarrely) from the company Enfants Perdus; and most recently, the biopic *The Experimenter,* starring Peter Sarsgaard as the title character—and this list is by no means exhaustive.

But as with human memory, the study—even published, archived, enshrined in psychology textbooks—is malleable. And in the past few years, a new wave of researchers have dedicated themselves to reshaping it, arguing that Milgram's lessons on human obedience are, in fact, misremembered—that his work doesn't prove what he claimed it does.

The problem is, no one can really agree on what it proves instead.

To mark the 50th anniversary of the experiments' publication (or, technically, the 51st), the *Journal of Social Issues* released a themed edition in September 2014 dedicated to all things Milgram. "There is a compelling and timely case for reexamining Milgram's legacy," the editors wrote in the introduction, noting that they were in good company: In 1964, the year after the experiments were published, fewer than 10 published studies referenced Milgram's work; in 2012, that number was more than 60.

It's a trend that surely would have pleased Milgram, who crafted his work with an audience in mind from the beginning. "Milgram was a fantastic dramaturg. His studies are fantastic little pieces of theater. They're beautifully scripted," said Stephen Reicher, a professor of psychology at the University of St. Andrews and a co-editor of the *Journal of Social Issues'* special edition. Capitalizing on the fame his 1963 publication earned him, Milgram went on to publish a book on his experiments in 1974 and a documentary, *Obedience,* with footage from the original experiments.

"His studies are fantastic little pieces of theater. They're beautifully scripted."

But for a man determined to leave a lasting legacy, Milgram also made it remarkably easy for people to pick it apart. The Yale University archives contain boxes upon boxes of papers, videos,

and audio recordings, an entire career carefully documented for posterity. Though Milgram's widow Alexandra donated the materials after his death in 1984, they remained largely untouched for years, until Yale's library staff began to digitize all the materials in the early 2000s. Able to easily access troves of material for the first time, the researchers came flocking.

"There's a lot of dirty laundry in those archives," said Arthur Miller, a professor emeritus of psychology at Miami University and another co-editor of the *Journal of Social Issues.* "Critics of Milgram seem to want to—and do—find material in these archives that makes Milgram look bad or unethical or, in some cases, a liar."

One of the most vocal of those critics is Australian author and psychologist Gina Perry, who documented her experience tracking down Milgram's research participants in her 2013 book *Behind the Shock Machine: The Untold Story of the Notorious Milgram Psychology Experiments.* Her project began as an effort to write about the experiments from the perspective of the participants—but when she went back through the archives to confirm some of their stories, she said, she found some glaring issues with Milgram's data. Among her accusations: that the supervisors went off script in their prods to the teachers, that some of the volunteers were aware that the setup was a hoax, and that others weren't debriefed on the whole thing until months later. "My main issue is that methodologically, there have been so many problems with Milgram's research that we have to start reexamining the textbook descriptions of the research," she said.

But many psychologists argue that even with methodological holes and moral lapses, the basic finding of Milgram's work, the rate of obedience, still holds up. Because of the ethical challenge of reproducing the study, the idea survived for decades on a mix of good faith and partial replications—one study had participants administer their shocks in a virtual-reality system, for example—until 2007, when ABC collaborated with Santa Clara University psychologist Jerry Burger to replicate Milgram's experiment for an episode of the TV show *Basic Instincts* titled "The Science of Evil," pegged to Abu Ghraib.

"For years I had heard from my students, 'Well, that was back in the 1960s. People have changed.'"

Burger's way around an ethical breach: In the most well-known experiment, he found, 80 percent of the participants who reached a 150-volt shock continued all the way to the end. "So what I said we could do is take people up to the 150-volt point, see how they reacted, and end the study right there," he said. The rest of the setup was nearly identical to Milgram's lab of the early 1960s (with one notable exception: "Milgram had a gray lab coat and I couldn't find a gray, so I got a light blue.")

At the end of the experiment, Burger was left with an obedience rate around the same as the one Milgram had recorded—proving, he said, not only that Milgram's numbers had been accurate, but that his work was as relevant as ever. "[The results] didn't surprise me," he said, "but for years I had heard from my students and from other people, 'Well, that was back in the 1960s, and somehow now we're more aware of the problems of blind obedience, and people have changed.'"

In recent years, though, much of the attention has focused less on supporting or discrediting Milgram's statistics, and more on rethinking his conclusions. With a paper published earlier this month in the *British Journal of Social Psychology*, Matthew Hollander, a sociology PhD candidate at the University of Wisconsin, is among the most recent to question Milgram's notion of obedience. After analyzing the conversation patterns from audio recordings of 117 study participants, Hollander found that Milgram's original classification of his subjects—either obedient or disobedient—failed to capture the true dynamics of the situation. Rather, he argued, people in both categories tried several different forms of protest—those who successfully ended the experiment early were simply better at resisting than the ones that continued shocking.

"Research subjects may say things like 'I can't do this anymore' or 'I'm not going to do this anymore,'" he said, even those who went all the way to 450 volts. "I understand those practices to be a way of trying to stop the experiment in a relatively aggressive, direct, and explicit way."

It's a far cry from Milgram's idea that the capacity for evil lies dormant in everyone, ready to be awakened with the right set of circumstances. The ability to disobey toxic orders, Hollander said, is a skill that can be taught like any other—all a person needs to learn is what to say and how to say it.

In some ways, the conclusions Milgram drew were as much a product of their time as they were a product of his research. At the time he began his studies, the trial of Adolf Eichmann, one of the major architects of the Holocaust, was already in full swing. In 1963, the same year that Milgram published his studies, writer Hannah Arendt coined the phrase "the banality of evil" to describe Eichmann in her book on the trial, *Eichmann in Jerusalem.*

The ability to disobey toxic orders is a skill that can be learned like any other—all a person needs to learn is what to say.

Milgram, who was born in New York City in 1933 to Jewish immigrant parents, came to view his studies as a validation of

Arendt's idea—but the Holocaust had been at the forefront of his mind for years before either of them published their work. "I should have been born into the German-speaking Jewish community of Prague in 1922 and died in a gas chamber some 20 years later," he wrote in a letter to a friend in 1958. "How I came to be born in the Bronx Hospital, I'll never quite understand."

And in the introduction of his 1963 paper, he invoked the Nazis within the first few paragraphs: "Obedience, as a determinant of behavior, is of particular relevance to our time," he wrote. "Gas chambers were built, death camps were guarded; daily quotas of corpses were produced . . . These inhumane policies may have originated in the mind of a single person, but they could only be carried out on a massive scale if a very large number of persons obeyed orders."

Though the term didn't exist at the time, Milgram was a proponent of what today's social psychologists call situationism: the idea that people's behavior is determined largely by what's happening around them. "They're not psychopaths, and they're not hostile, and they're not aggressive or deranged. They're just people, like you and me," Miller said. "If you put us in certain situations, we're more likely to be racist or sexist, or we may lie, or we may cheat. There are studies that show this, thousands and thousands of studies that document the many unsavory aspects of most people."

But continued to its logical extreme, situationism "has an exonerating effect," he said. "In the minds of a lot of people, it tends to excuse the bad behavior . . . it's not the person's fault for doing the bad thing, it's the situation they were put in." Milgram's studies were famous because their implications were also devastating: If the Nazis were just following orders, then he had proved that anyone at all could be a Nazi. If the guards at Abu Ghraib were just following orders, then anyone was capable of torture.

The latter, Reicher said, is part of why interest in Milgram's work has seen a resurgence in recent years. "If you look at acts of human atrocity, they've hardly diminished over time," he said, and news of the abuse at Abu Ghraib was surfacing around the same time that Yale's archival material was digitized, a perfect storm of encouragement for scholars to turn their attention once again to the question of what causes evil.

If the Nazis were just following orders, then he had just proved that anyone at all could be a Nazi.

He and his colleague Alex Haslam, the third co-editor of *The Journal of Social Issues*' Milgram edition and a professor of psychology at the University of Queensland, have come up with a different answer. "The notion that we somehow automatically obey authority, that we are somehow programmed, doesn't account for the variability [in rates of obedience] across conditions," he said; in some iterations of Milgram's study, the rate of compliance was close to 100 percent, while in others it was closer to zero. "We need an account that can explain the variability—when we obey, when we don't."

"We argue that the answer to that question is a matter of identification," he continued. "Do they identify more with the cause of science, and listen to the experimenter as a legitimate representative of science, or do they identify more with the learner as an ordinary person? . . . You're torn between these different voices. Who do you listen to?"

The question, he conceded, applies as much to the study of Milgram today as it does to what went on in his lab. "Trying to get a consensus among academics is like herding cats," Reicher said, but "if there is a consensus, it's that we need a new explanation. I think nearly everybody accepts the fact that Milgram discovered a remarkable phenomenon, but he didn't provide a very compelling explanation of that phenomenon."

What he provided instead was a difficult and deeply uncomfortable set of questions—and his research, flawed as it is, endures not because it clarifies the causes of human atrocities, but because it confuses more than it answers.

Or, as Miller put it: "The whole thing exists in terms of its controversy, how it's excited some and infuriated others.

People have tried to knock it down, and it always comes up standing."

Critical Thinking

1. It's unusual for a psychological study to inspire song lyrics. Given this, what do you think the overall impact of the results of the Milgram studies has been on culture? Explain.

2. Milgram classified the participants in his research as obedient or disobedient. What are the potential problems with this approach, and what type of alternative system might have been better employed? Why?

3. What is situationism, and why is this concept particularly important in attempting to understand Milgram's results? Explain.

Internet References

Electric schlock: Did Stanley Milgram's famous obedience experiments prove anything?
  http://www.psmag.com/books-and-culture/electric-schlock-65377

Milgram experiment—Obedience to authority
  https://explorable.com/stanley-milgram-experiment

Stanley Milgram and the uncertainty of evil
  https://www.bostonglobe.com/ideas/2013/09/28/stanley-milgram-and-uncertainty-evil/qUjame9xApiKc6evtgQRqN/story.html

Article   Prepared by: R. Eric Landrum, *Boise State University*

Ten Psychological Studies That Will Change What You Think You Know about Yourself

CAROLYN GREGOIRE

Learning Outcomes

After reading this article, you will be able to:

- Appreciate how the results of psychological studies can have a direct influence in helping us understand our own behaviors.

- Understand that psychologists are interested in important topics relevant to today's society, including power, guilt, loyalty, self-esteem, happiness, and more.

- Comprehend the powerful role that stereotypes can play in our culture.

Why do we do the things we do? Despite our best attempts to "know thyself," the truth is that we often know astonishingly little about our own minds, and even less about the way others think. As Charles Dickens once put it, "A wonderful fact to reflect upon, that every human creature is constituted to be that profound secret and mystery to every other."

Psychologists have long sought insights into how we perceive the world and what motivates our behavior, and they've made enormous strides in lifting that veil of mystery. Aside from providing fodder for stimulating cocktail-party conversations, some of the most famous psychological experiments of the past century reveal universal and often surprising truths about human nature.

Here are 10 classic psychological studies that may change the way you understand yourself.

We all have some capacity for evil.

Arguably the most famous experiment in the history of psychology, the 1971 Stanford prison study put a microscope on how social situations can affect human behavior. The researchers, led by psychologist Philip Zimbardo, set up a mock prison in the basement of the Stanford psych building and selected 24 undergraduates (who had no criminal record and were deemed psychologically healthy) to act as prisoners and guards. Researchers then observed the prisoners (who had to stay in the cells 24 hours a day) and guards (who shared eight-hour shifts) using hidden cameras.

The experiment, which was scheduled to last for two weeks, had to be cut short after just six days due to the guards' abusive behavior—in some cases they even inflicted psychological torture—and the extreme emotional stress and anxiety exhibited by the prisoners.

"The guards escalated their aggression against the prisoners, stripping them naked, putting bags over their heads, and then finally had them engage in increasingly humiliating sexual activities," Zimbardo told *American Scientist*. "After six days I had to end it because it was out of control—I couldn't really go to sleep at night without worrying what the guards could do to the prisoners."

We don't notice what's right in front of us.

Think you know what's going on around you? You might not be nearly as aware as you think. In 1998, researchers from Harvard and Kent State University targeted pedestrians on a college campus to determine how much people notice about their immediate environments. In the experiment, an actor came up to a pedestrian and asked for directions. While the pedestrian was giving the directions, two men carrying a large wooden door walked between the actor and the pedestrian, completely blocking their view of each other for several seconds. During that time, the actor was replaced by another actor, one of a different height and build, and with a different outfit, haircut, and voice. A full half of the participants didn't notice the substitution.

The experiment was one of the first to illustrate the phenomenon of "change blindness," which shows just how selective we are about what we take in from any given visual scene—and it seems that we rely on memory and pattern-recognition significantly more than we might think.

Delaying gratification is hard—but we're more successful when we do.

A famous Stanford experiment from the late 1960s tested preschool children's ability to resist the lure of instant gratification—and it yielded some powerful insights about willpower and self-discipline. In the experiment, four-year-olds were put in a room by themselves with a marshmallow on a plate in front of them, and told that they could either eat the treat now, or if they waited until the researcher returned 15 minutes later, they could have two marshmallows.

While most of the children said they'd wait, they often struggled to resist and then gave in, eating the treat before the researcher returned, *TIME* reports. The children who did manage to hold off for the full 15 minutes generally used avoidance tactics, like turning away or covering their eyes. The implications of the children's behavior were significant: Those who were able to delay gratification were much less likely to be obese, or to have drug addiction or behavioral problems by the time they were teenagers, and were more successful later in life.

We can experience deeply conflicting moral impulses.

A famous 1961 study by Yale psychologist Stanley Milgram tested (rather alarmingly) how far people would go to obey authority figures when asked to harm others, and the intense internal conflict between personal morals and the obligation to obey authority figures.

Milgram wanted to conduct the experiment to provide insight into how Nazi war criminals could have perpetuated

unspeakable acts during the Holocaust. To do so, he tested a pair of participants, one deemed the "teacher" and the other deemed the "learner." The teacher was instructed to administer electric shocks to the learner (who was supposedly sitting in another room, but in reality was not being shocked) each time they got questions wrong. Milgram instead played recordings which made it sound like the learner was in pain, and if the "teacher" subject expressed a desire to stop, the experimenter prodded him to go on. During the first experiment, 65 percent of participants administered a painful, final 450-volt shock (labeled "XXX"), although many were visibly stressed and uncomfortable about doing so.

While the study has commonly been seen as a warning of blind obedience to authority, *Scientific American* recently revisited it, arguing that the results were more suggestive of deep moral conflict.

"Human moral nature includes a propensity to be empathetic, kind and good to our fellow kin and group members, plus an inclination to be xenophobic, cruel and evil to tribal others," journalist Michael Shermer wrote. "The shock experiments reveal not blind obedience but conflicting moral tendencies that lie deep within."

Recently, some commenters have called Milgram's methodology into question, and one critic noted that records of the experiment performed at Yale suggested that 60 percent of participants actually disobeyed orders to administer the highest-dosage shock.

We're easily corrupted by power.

There's a psychological reason behind the fact that those in power sometimes act towards others with a sense of entitlement and disrespect. A 2003 study published in the journal *Psychological Review* put students into groups of three to write a short paper together. Two students were instructed to write the paper, while the other was told to evaluate the paper and determine how much each student would be paid. In the middle of their work, a researcher brought in a plate of five cookies. Although generally the last cookie was never eaten, the "boss" almost always ate the fourth cookie—and ate it sloppily, mouth open.

"When researchers give people power in scientific experiments, they are more likely to physically touch others in potentially inappropriate ways, to flirt in more direct fashion, to make risky choices and gambles, to make first offers in negotiations, to speak their mind, and to eat cookies like the Cookie Monster, with crumbs all over their chins and chests," psychologist Dacher Keltner, one of the study's leaders, wrote in an article for UC Berkeley's Greater Good Science Center.

We seek out loyalty to social groups and are easily drawn to intergroup conflict.

This classic 1950s social psychology experiment shined a light on the possible psychological basis of why social groups and countries find themselves embroiled in conflict with one another—and how they can learn to cooperate again.

Study leader Muzafer Sherif took two groups of 11 boys (all age 11) to Robbers Cave State Park in Oklahoma for "summer camp." The groups (named the "Eagles" and the "Rattlers") spent a week apart, having fun together and bonding, with no knowledge of the existence of the other group. When the two groups finally integrated, the boys started calling each other names, and when they started competing in various games, more conflict ensued and eventually the groups refused to eat together. In the next phase of the research, Sherif designed experiments to try to reconcile the boys by having them enjoy leisure activities together (which was unsuccessful) and then having them solve a problem together, which finally began to ease the conflict.

We only need one thing to be happy.

The 75-year Harvard Grant study—one of the most comprehensive longitudinal studies ever conducted—followed 268 male Harvard undergraduates from the classes of 1938–1940 (now well into their 90s) for 75 years, regularly collecting data on various aspects of their lives. The universal conclusion? Love really *is* all that matters, at least when it comes to determining long-term happiness and life satisfaction.

The study's longtime director, psychiatrist George Vaillant, told *The Huffington Post* that there are two pillars of happiness: "One is love. The other is finding a way of coping with life that does not push love away." For example, one participant began the study with the lowest rating for future stability of all the subjects and he had previously attempted suicide. But at the end of his life, he was one of the happiest. Why? As Vaillant explains, "He spent his life searching for love."

We thrive when we have strong self-esteem and social status.

Achieving fame and success isn't just an ego boost—it could also be a key to longevity, according to the notorious Oscar winners study. Researchers from Toronto's Sunnybrook and Women's College Health Sciences Centre found that Academy Award-winning actors and directors tend to live longer than those who were nominated but lost, with winning actors and actresses outliving their losing peers by nearly four years.

"We are not saying that you will live longer if you win an Academy Award," Donald Redelmeier, the lead author of the study, told ABC News. "Or that people should go out and take acting courses. Our main conclusion is simply that social factors are important . . . It suggests that an internal sense of self-esteem is an important aspect to health and health care."

We constantly try to justify our experiences so that they make sense to us.

Anyone who's taken a freshman Psych 101 class is familiar with cognitive dissonance, a theory which dictates that human beings have a natural propensity to avoid psychological conflict based on disharmonious or mutually exclusive beliefs. In an often-cited 1959 experiment, psychologist Leon Festinger asked participants to perform a series of dull tasks, like turning pegs in a wooden knob, for an hour. They were then paid either $1 or $20 to tell a "waiting participant" (aka a researcher) that the task was very interesting. Those who were paid $1 to lie rated the tasks as more enjoyable than those who were paid $20. Their conclusion? Those who were paid more felt that they had sufficient justification for having performed the rote task for an hour, but those who were only paid $1 felt the need to justify the time spent (and reduce the level of dissonance between their beliefs and their behavior) by saying that the activity was fun. In other words, we commonly tell ourselves lies to make the world appear a more logical, harmonious place.

We buy into stereotypes in a big way.

Stereotyping various groups of people based on social group, ethnicity, or class is something nearly all of us do, even if we make an effort not to—and it can lead us to draw unfair and potentially damaging conclusions about entire populations. NYU psychologist John Bargh's experiments on "automaticity of social behavior" revealed that we often judge people based on unconscious stereotypes—and we can't help but act on them. We also tend to buy into stereotypes for social groups that we see ourselves being a part of. In one study, Bargh found that a group of participants who were asked to unscramble words related to old age—"Florida," "helpless," and "wrinkled"—walked significantly slower down the hallway after the experiment than the group who unscrambled words unrelated to age. Bargh repeated the findings in two other comparable studies that enforced stereotypes based on race and politeness.

"Stereotypes are categories that have gone too far," Bargh told *Psychology Today*. "When we use stereotypes, we take in the gender, the age, the color of the skin of the person before us, and our minds respond with messages that say hostile, stupid, slow, weak. Those qualities aren't out there in the environment. They don't reflect reality."

Critical Thinking

1. It is often debated whether the "Stanford Prison Experiment" was actually an experiment at all? What is your opinion about this, and why?

2. Why is the marshmallow study still so relevant today, and how might these results help explain current patterns of behavior? Explain.

3. According to longitudinal research, what are the two key factors that are linked to happiness?

Internet References

10 of the most surprising findings from psychological studies

http://io9.com/5894500/10-of-the-most-surprising-findings-from-psychological-studies

10 ways we get the odds wrong

https://www.psychologytoday.com/articles/200712/10-ways-we-get-the-odds-wrong

How thinking works: 10 brilliant cognitive psychology studies everyone should know

http://www.spring.org.uk/2014/01/how-thinking-works-10-brilliant-cognitive-psychology-studies-everyone-should-know.php

Unit 10

UNIT

Prepared by: Eric Landrum, *Boise State University*

Psychological Disorders

Jay and Harry are two brothers who own a service station. Harry and Jay have a good working relationship. Harry is the "up-front" man. Taking customer orders, accepting payments, and working with parts distributors, Harry deals directly with the public, delivery personnel, and other people visiting the station. Jay works behind the scenes. Although Harry makes the mechanical diagnoses, Jay is the mastermind who does the corrective work. Some of his friends think Jay is a veritable mechanical genius; he can fix anything. Preferring to spend time by himself, Jay has always been a little odd and a bit of a loner. Jay's friends think his emotions have always been inappropriate and more intense than other people, but they pass it off as part of his eccentric talent. On the other hand, Harry is the stalwart of the family. He is the acknowledged leader and decision maker when it comes to family finances.

One day, Jay did not show up for work on time. When he finally did appear, he was dressed in the most garish outfit and was laughing hysterically and talking to himself. At first, Harry suspected that his brother was high. However, Jay's condition persisted and, in fact, worsened. Out of concern, his family took him to their physician, who immediately sent Jay and his family to a psychiatrist. After several visits, the doctor informed the family that Jay suffers from schizophrenia. Jay's maternal uncle had also been schizophrenic. The family somberly left the psychiatrist's office and went to the local pharmacy to fill a prescription for anti-psychotic medication.

What caused Jay's drastic change in mental health? Was Jay destined to be schizophrenic because of his family tree? Did competitiveness with his brother and the feeling that he was less revered than Harry cause his descent into mental disorder? How do psychiatrists and clinical psychologists make accurate diagnoses? Once a diagnosis of mental disorder is made (such as schizophrenia), can the individual ever completely recover? Mental disorders affect millions of people throughout the world. Mental disorders impact every aspect of an individual's life, but work, family, and friendships are especially impacted. Because of their detrimental effect on the individual, mental disorders have been a focal point of psychological research for decades. This important work has revealed the likely origins or causes of mental disorders and has led to breakthroughs in the care and treatment of people with mental disorders. This unit emphasis the questions that psychologists have attempted to address in their quest to understand the nature of mental illness.

Article   Prepared by: Eric Landrum, *Boise State University*

Bringing Life into Focus

A generation of adults who came of age too early to be diagnosed with childhood ADHD is finding that later-in-life treatment can bring great rewards.

BRENDAN L. SMITH

Learning Outcomes

After reading this article, you will be able to:

- Review some of the effects that ADHD can have on adults.

- Describe some of the treatment options for those adults diagnosed with ADHD.

When he was attending law school at Wake Forest University in the 1980s, E. Clarke Dummit couldn't study in the library. It was just too quiet.

"I got in the habit of hanging out at a Krispy Kreme doughnut shop and drinking coffee while I studied my law books," he says. "I needed constant noise around me and a stimulant to focus."

Another decade would pass before Dummit saw a psychologist and was diagnosed with attention-deficit hyperactivity disorder. The diagnosis came as a revelation, and it helped him to fit together some of the jigsaw pieces of his life.

"It was fascinating. I've always had learning disabilities and had to work my way around them," says Dummit, now a 50-year-old criminal defense attorney with his own firm in Winston-Salem, N.C. "I have focus when I really need to for a short period, but then my brain has to relax for a certain amount of time."

Dummit and other adults with ADHD also have to battle a stereotype that ADHD is a childhood mental disorder that doesn't affect adults. Most research on ADHD has focused on children, and the fourth edition of the Diagnostic and Statistical Manual of Mental Disorders (DSM-IV) lists symptoms for ADHD that apply mainly to children, such as losing toys or climbing on things. But a growing body of research is examining the effects of ADHD on adults and documenting that the disorder can have lifelong consequences.

ADHD can cause serious disruptions for adults in their careers, personal relationships and higher education, says J. Russell Ramsay, PhD, an associate professor of psychology and co-director of the Adult ADHD Treatment and Research Program at the University of Pennsylvania School of Medicine. "Society in general values good self-regulation, being able to follow through on things, being reliable, completing tasks on deadline. These skills are important at school and work, and they are equated with good character," Ramsay says. "An individual going through life with ADHD often ends up saying, 'I must not be good enough. I must be lazy. I must be stupid.' These negative beliefs get reactivated and strengthened and may lead people to start giving up or limiting themselves."

Several studies have shown that more than half of children with ADHD will continue to have full symptoms as adults, while some level of impairment may affect up to 80 percent or 90 percent, says Ramsay, who has researched ADHD for more than a decade. "Many adults aren't growing out of ADHD. They're actually just growing out of the childhood definition of ADHD, such as running around and climbing on things," he says. "Adult ADHD research has been hampered because the current symptoms were designed for childhood and adolescence."

Diagnosing Adult ADHD

Many middle-aged and elderly adults grew up at a time when children with ADHD were just considered to be hyperactive or poor learners. ADHD first appeared in DSM-II in 1968, when it was called "hyperkinetic reaction of childhood (or adolescence)." The symptoms included "overactivity, restlessness, distractibility and short attention span, especially in young children."

When Dummit was growing up in the 1960s in Columbia, Tenn., he had trouble focusing in school so his parents took him to Nashville for an evaluation at the Peabody College of Education and Human Development, now part of Vanderbilt University. "No one diagnosed me with ADHD," Dummit says with a laugh. "They said my father was being overbearing and too demanding. My dad said, 'You're damn right,' and we marched out of there."

Today, in contrast, more than 5 million children have been diagnosed with ADHD in the United States, and the percentage of children who are diagnosed has increased each year over the past decade. But for Dummit's generation, who missed the chance to be diagnosed as children, psychologists and psychiatrists must devise a way to identify ADHD in adults.

And even today, some people may not realize the extent of their ADHD symptoms until later in life. ADHD symptoms can sometimes be masked until adulthood because childhood often is structured by parents, school and other activities, says Stephen Faraone, PhD, a clinical psychologist and psychiatry professor at the State University of New York's Upstate Medical University.

"ADHD is a disorder characterized by the inability to regulate one's behavior, emotions and attention. As we get older, we have fewer people telling us what to do," Faraone says. "When we get to college or a job, we're expected to show up without having someone tell us what to do."

Paul Wender, MD, a pioneer in ADHD research, developed one of the first rating scales for measuring ADHD in adults—the Wender Utah Rating Scale—in the 1990s, when he was a psychiatry professor at the University of Utah School of Medicine. The questionnaire, published in the *American Journal of Psychiatry* in 1993, helped retrospectively diagnose adults with ADHD based on their childhood symptoms.

"The diagnosis of ADHD in adults has occurred more and more frequently in recent years, and it has improved dramatically over the past decade," says Wender, now a psychiatrist in private practice in Andover, Mass.

While the DSM-IV lists symptoms for ADHD that are mostly geared toward children, the upcoming fifth edition most likely will contain symptoms that apply more readily to adults, such as having racing thoughts instead of racing around the room. "Adults obviously aren't on top of their desks, but they are restless and unable to sit still," Wender says. Several other scales have been developed to help diagnose ADHD in adults since Wender's work. Faraone helped develop a self-reporting screening scale that was adopted by the World Health Organization. Published in *Psychological Medicine* in 2005, the 18-question survey translates childhood ADHD symptoms from the DSM-IV into adult situations.

In a nationwide telephone survey of 966 adults, published in the *Journal of Attention Disorders* in 2005, almost 3 percent of respondents reported they often had ADHD symptoms, while almost 16 percent reported occasional symptoms. The study by Faraone and Harvard Medical School researcher Joseph Biederman showed that individuals who reported ADHD symptoms were less likely to graduate from high school or college than those who reported no symptoms. Individuals who reported more severe ADHD symptoms were almost three times more likely to be unemployed than adults with no symptoms.

"In the workplace, we know from studies of work productivity and income that adults with ADHD are not likely to achieve as well as their peers," Faraone says. "The estimates range into billions of dollars each year in lost productivity related to adult ADHD."

'Playing Defense Every Day'

Drew Brody, a 39-year-old father with two young children in Santa Monica, Calif., says he used to struggle through his daily routine because of ADHD. As a high-school tutor, he would lose track of time, miss deadlines and feel overwhelmed. "You're walking around with a fog around your brain. Just getting through normal daily behavior is hard, getting up, getting dressed, getting shaved, getting out the door on time," he says. "All of that stuff is 10 times harder than it should be."

Brody was diagnosed with ADHD about seven years ago after his wife, a middle-school vice principal, suggested that he be evaluated. Brody began cognitive-behavioral therapy with a psychologist to identify coping mechanisms, such as time management skills, exercise and a healthy diet. But his persistent symptoms interfered with the therapy. "After a year, I never really got my act together to do any of the improvements on a regular basis," he says.

Brody then was prescribed Concerta, the extended-release version of methylphenidate (Ritalin), and his life changed. He was able to start his own tutoring company, The Scholar Group, which now has 16 tutors who help students in more than 40 academic subjects and on standardized tests such as the SAT.

"It was a revelation," he says. "I don't think I would have created my business if I hadn't started taking Concerta on a daily basis. It's made a substantial change in my life. For bigger life decisions, I am able to think more clearly and work through the steps on how to get there."

His problems from ADHD haven't disappeared, but Brody says his symptoms are more manageable now than they were in the past. "Life with ADHD is like playing defense every day. Things happen to you and you have to address them," he says. "You're not proactively dealing with life. You're waiting to be late or to get in trouble because you can't get ahead."

Brody's experience is common for adults with ADHD who try cognitive-behavioral therapy without medication, says Ramsay, who wrote the 2010 book *"Nonmedication Treatments for Adult ADHD."* Therapy can be very helpful in teaching time management and organization skills, but ADHD symptoms can lead to late or missed appointments, failure to complete homework, and little progress on a treatment plan. Medication in conjunction with therapy can help bring ADHD symptoms under control through life coaching skills and counseling for underlying negative thoughts that can lead to procrastination and frustration, Ramsay says.

The public controversy about overmedication and overdiagnosis of ADHD is really a problem of misdiagnosis, which can result from quick visits to primary-care physicians, Ramsay says. "Some patients may get a diagnosis based on an all-too-brief evaluation and therefore may start treatment with a medication when maybe their symptoms are not a result of ADHD," he says. "Other people with ADHD may be misdiagnosed with some other mental disorder."

Stimulants on Campus

Several studies have shown that stimulants such as Ritalin or amphetamine salts (Adderall) are effective in treating ADHD in adults, but the drugs also can be abused, especially by college students who believe stimulants will boost their academic performance. In a survey of more than 1,800 students at the University of Kentucky, a third of the students reported they had illegally used ADHD stimulants, mainly by obtaining pills from fellow students with prescriptions. Most of the illegal users said the stimulants helped them stay up late and cram for exams, and they believed the drugs increased their reading comprehension, attention and memory. The study was published in 2008 in the Journal of American College Health.

Every college in the United States faces problems with misuse of ADHD stimulants, but most students with ADHD are not faking their symptoms to get medication, says Lorraine Wolf, PhD, a neuropsychologist and director of the Office of Disability Services at Boston University. "Most students with ADHD are serious, hard-working young people who struggle in a college environment, but with accommodations and support they are very successful," says Wolf, an assistant psychiatry professor who researches adult ADHD.

Wolf's office offers time management skills for students with ADHD and provides academic accommodations, including extra time on tests and computer use during exams to help with spelling and grammar. Students must provide extensive documentation of severe ADHD symptoms before accommodations will be granted, Wolf says. "People who come to college with symptoms are pretty much going to have ADHD for the rest of their lives," Wolf says. "People become more refined in how they deal with it. They just get better at handling ADHD."

Almost 5 percent of teenagers in the United States were prescribed stimulants to treat ADHD in 2008, compared with just 2.3 percent in 1996, suggesting that many children aren't outgrowing their symptoms, according to a study by the National Institutes of Health and the Agency for Healthcare Research and Quality. The study was published online in September in the American Journal of Psychiatry.

Some college students who illegally use stimulants may have undiagnosed ADHD, according to a study of 184 college students in northern Virginia, published this year in the Journal of Attention Disorders. The study found that 71 percent of the respondents who misused stimulants also screened positive for ADHD symptoms. Students who illegally used stimulants were seven times more likely to have ADHD symptoms than those who didn't misuse the drugs.

Meanwhile, those symptoms aren't always entirely bad. ADHD can have some beneficial aspects, including the ability to multi-task, solve problems quickly and work with people, Wolf says.

Dummit, the criminal defense attorney in North Carolina, says he has embraced his ADHD and believes it helps him hyperfocus on detailed projects for short periods. He only takes a stimulant medication when he needs to concentrate for long stretches, such as during a trial. "I don't accept ADHD as an excuse for bad behavior, but I do try to talk openly about my strengths and weaknesses," he says.

Critical Thinking

1. What are some of the stereotypes that continue to persist concerning attention deficit hyperactivity disorder (ADHD)?

2. What is the linkage between someone having ADHD as a children but then also having ADHD as an adult?

3. What percentages of adults in the general population report that they experience ADHD symptoms?

Create Central

www.mhhe.com/createcentral

Internet References

10 problems that could mean adult ADHD
  www.webmd.com/add-adhd/10-symptoms-adult-adhd

Attention Deficit Disorder (ADD/ADHD) test
  http://psychcentral.com/addquiz.htm

BRENDAN L. SMITH is a writer in Washington, D.C.

Article   Prepared by: Eric Landrum, *Boise State University*

The Roots of Mental Illness

How much of mental illness can the biology of the brain explain?

KIRSTEN WEIR

Learning Outcomes

After reading this article, you will be able to:

- Understand the ongoing research that is linking the existence of mental illness to the malfunctioning of specific centers of the brain.

- Describe the risk of placing too much emphasis on the hardware (brain) rather than the software (mental processes) in the development of mental illness.

D iagnosing mental illness isn't like diagnosing other chronic diseases. Heart disease is identified with the help of blood tests and electrocardiograms. Diabetes is diagnosed by measuring blood glucose levels. But classifying mental illness is a more subjective endeavor. No blood test exists for depression; no X-ray can identify a child at risk of developing bipolar disorder. At least, not yet.

Thanks to new tools in genetics and neuroimaging, scientists are making progress toward deciphering details of the underlying biology of mental disorders. Yet experts disagree on how far we can push this biological model. Are mental illnesses simply physical diseases that happen to strike the brain? Or do these disorders belong to a class all their own?

Eric Kandel, MD, a Nobel Prize laureate and professor of brain science at Columbia University, believes it's all about biology. "All mental processes are brain processes, and therefore all disorders of mental functioning are biological diseases," he says. "The brain is the organ of the mind. Where else could [mental illness] be if not in the brain?"

That viewpoint is quickly gaining supporters, thanks in part to Thomas R. Insel, MD, director of the National Institute of Mental Health, who has championed a biological perspective during his tenure at the agency.

To Insel, mental illnesses are no different from heart disease, diabetes or any other chronic illness. All chronic diseases have behavioral components as well as biological components, he says. "The only difference here is that the organ of interest is the brain instead of the heart or pancreas. But the same basic principles apply."

A New Toolkit

Take cardiology, Insel says. A century ago, doctors had little knowledge of the biological basis of heart disease. They could merely observe a patient's physical presentation and listen to the patient's subjective complaints. Today they can measure cholesterol levels, examine the heart's electrical impulses with EKG, and take detailed CT images of blood vessels and arteries to deliver a precise diagnosis. As a result, Insel says, mortality from heart attacks has dropped dramatically in recent decades. "In most areas of medicine, we now have a whole toolkit to help us know what's going on, from the behavioral level to the molecular level. That has really led to enormous changes in most areas of medicine," he says.

Insel believes the diagnosis and treatment of mental illness is today where cardiology was 100 years ago. And like cardiology of yesteryear, the field is poised for dramatic transformation, he says. "We are really at the cusp of a revolution in the way we think about the brain and behavior, partly because of technological breakthroughs. We're finally able to answer some of the fundamental questions."

Indeed, in recent years scientists have made many exciting discoveries about the function—and dysfunction—of the human brain. They've identified genes linked to schizophrenia and discovered that certain brain abnormalities increase a person's risk of developing post-traumatic stress disorder after a distressing event. Others have zeroed in on anomalies associated with autism, including abnormal brain growth and underconnectivity among brain regions.

Researchers have also begun to flesh out a physiological explanation for depression. Helen Mayberg, MD, a professor of psychiatry and neurology at Emory University, has been actively involved in research that singled out a region of the brain—Brodmann area 25—that is overactive in people with depression. Mayberg describes area 25 as a "junction box" that interacts with other areas of the brain involved in mood, emotion and thinking. She has demonstrated that deep-brain stimulation of the area can alleviate symptoms in people with treatment-resistant depression (Neuron, 2005).

Maps of depression's neural circuits, Mayberg says, may eventually serve as a tool both for diagnosis and treatment.

Understanding the underlying biology, she adds, could help therapists and psychopharmacologists decide which patients would benefit from more intensive therapy, and which aren't likely to improve without medication. That would be a welcome improvement, she says. "Syndromes are so nonspecific by our current criteria that the best we can do now is flip a coin. We don't do that for any other branch of medicine," she says.

Yet despite the progress and promise of her research, Mayberg isn't ready to concede that all mental illnesses will one day be described in purely biological terms. "I used to think you could localize everything, that you could explain all the variants by the biology," she says. "I think in a perfect world you could, but we don't have the tools to explain all those things because we can't control for all of the variables."

One of the biggest problems, she says, is that mental illness diagnoses are often catchall categories that include many different underlying malfunctions. Mental illnesses have always been described by their outward symptoms, both out of necessity and convenience. But just as cancer patients are a wildly diverse group marked by many different disease pathways, a depression diagnosis is likely to encompass people with many unique underlying problems. That presents challenges for defining the disease in biological terms. "Depression does have patterns," Mayberg says. "The caveat is different cohorts of patients clearly have different patterns—and likely the need for different specific interventions."

Software Malfunction

When it comes to mental illness, a one-size-fits-all approach does not apply. Some diseases may be more purely physiological in nature. "Certain disorders such as schizophrenia, bipolar disorder and autism fit the biological model in a very clearcut sense," says Richard McNally, PhD, a clinical psychologist at Harvard University and author of the 2011 book *"What is Mental Illness?"* In these diseases, he says, structural and functional abnormalities are evident in imaging scans or during postmortem dissection.

Yet for other conditions, such as depression or anxiety, the biological foundation is more nebulous. Often, McNally notes, mental illnesses are likely to have multiple causes, including genetic, biological and environmental factors. Of course, that's true for many chronic diseases, heart disease and diabetes included. But for mental illnesses, we're particularly long way from understanding the interplay among those factors.

That complexity is one reason that experts such as Jerome Wakefield, PhD, DSW, a professor of social work and psychiatry at New York University, believe that too much emphasis is being placed on the biology of mental illness at this point in our understanding of the brain. Decades of effort to understand the biology of mental disorders have uncovered clues, but those clues haven't translated to improvements in diagnosis or treatment, he believes. "We've thrown tens of billions of dollars into trying to identify biomarkers and biological substrates for mental disorders," Wakefield says. "The fact is we've gotten very little out of all of that."

To be sure, Wakefield says, some psychological disorders are likely due to brain dysfunction. Others, however, may stem from a chance combination of normal personality traits. "In the unusual case where normal traits come together in a certain configuration, you may be maladapted to society," he says. "Call it a mental disorder if you want, but there's no smoking-gun malfunction in your brain."

You can think of the brain as a computer, he adds. The brain circuitry is equivalent to the hardware. But we also have the human equivalent of software. "Namely, we have mental processing of mental representations, meanings, conditioning, a whole level of processing that has to do with these psychological capacities," he says. Just as software bugs are often the cause of our computer problems, our mental motherboards can be done in by our psychological processing, even when the underlying circuitry is working as designed. "If we focus only at the brain level, we are likely to miss a lot of what's going on in mental disorders," he says.

The danger in placing too much attention on the biological is that important environmental, behavioral and social factors that contribute to mental illness may be overlooked. "By over-focusing on the biological, we are doing patients a disservice," Wakefield says. He sees a red flag in a study by Steven Marcus, PhD, and Mark Olfson, MD, that found the percentage of patients who receive psychotherapy for depression declined from 53.6 percent in 1998 to 43.1 percent in 2007, while rates of antidepressant use stayed roughly the same (*Archives of General Psychiatry*, 2010).

A Nuanced View

The emerging area of epigenetics, meanwhile, could help provide a link between the biological and other causes of mental illness. Epigenetics research examines the ways in which environmental factors change the way genes express themselves. "Certain genes are turned on or turned off, expressed or not expressed, depending on environmental inputs," McNally says.

One of the first classic epigenetics experiments, by researchers at McGill University, found that pups of negligent rat mothers were more sensitive to stress in adulthood than pups that had been raised by doting mothers (Nature Neuroscience, 2004). The differences could be traced to epigenetic markers, chemical tags that attach to strands of DNA and, in the process, turn various genes on and off. Those tags don't just affect individuals during their lifetime, however; like DNA, epigenetic markers can be passed from generation to generation. More recently, the McGill team studied the brains of people who committed suicide, and found those who had been abused in childhood had unique patterns of epigenetic tags in their brains (*Nature Neuroscience*, 2009). "Stress gets under the skin, so to speak," McNally says.

In McNally's view, there's little danger that mental health professionals will forget the importance of environmental factors to the development of mental illness. "I think what's happening is not a battle between biological and non-biological approaches, but an increasingly nuanced and sophisticated appreciation for the multiple perspectives that can illuminate the etiology of these conditions," he says.

Still, translating that nuanced view to improvements in diagnosis and treatment will take time. Despite decades of research on the causes and treatments of mental illness, patients are still suffering. "Suicide rates haven't come down. The rate of prevalence for many of these disorders, if anything, has gone up, not down. That tells you that whatever we've been doing is probably not adequate," Insel says.

But, he adds, there's good reason to hold out hope. "I think, increasingly, we'll understand behavior at many levels, and one of those will be physiological," Insel says. "That may take longer to translate into new therapies and new opportunities for patients, but it's coming."

In the meantime, according to Insel and Kandel, patients themselves are clamoring for better biological descriptions of mental disorders. Describing mental illnesses as brain malfunctions helps minimize the shame often associated with them, Kandel says. "Schizophrenia is a disease like pneumonia. Seeing it as a brain disorder destigmatizes it immediately."

Certainly, Kandel adds, social and environmental factors are undeniably important to understanding mental health. "But they do not act in a vacuum," he says. "They act in the brain."

It's too soon to say whether we'll someday have a blood test for schizophrenia or a brain scanning technique that identifies depression without any doubt. But scientists and patients agree: The more we understand about our brain and behavior, the better. "We have a good beginning of understanding of the brain," says Kandel, "but boy, have we got a long way to go."

Critical Thinking

1. If you believe that "all mental disorders are biological diseases," how might that influence your approach to treatment?

2. How does a biological model to mental illness help to describe conditions such as schizophrenia, bipolar disorder, and autism?

3. What is epigenetics, and how does its study contribute to our understanding of mental illness?

Create Central

www.mhhe.com/createcentral

Internet References

Five major mental disorders share genetic roots
   www.nimh.nih.gov/news/science-news/2013/five-major-mental-disorders-share-genetic-roots.shtml
Origins of mental illness
   www.minddisorders.com/Ob-Ps/Origin-of-mental-illnesses.html

---

KIRSTEN WEIR is a freelance writer in Minneapolis.

Weir, Kirsten. From *Monitor on Psychology*, vol 43, no. 6, June 2012. Copyright © 2012 by American Psychological Association. Reproduced with permission. No further reproduction or distribution without written permission from the American Psychological Association.

Article   Prepared by: R. Eric Landrum, *Boise State University*

A Mad World

A diagnosis of mental illness is more common than ever—did psychiatrists create the problem, or just recognise it?

JOSEPH PIERRE

Learning Outcomes

After reading this article, you will be able to:

- Understand how the role of psychiatry has changed in the past century.

- Appreciate the modern techniques that psychiatrists employ to treat a vast array of psychological issues and problems.

- Articulate "caseness" and the role it plays in psychiatrist's abilities to help individuals.

When a psychiatrist meets people at a party and reveals what he or she does for a living, two responses are typical. People either say, 'I'd better be careful what I say around you,' and then clam up, or they say, 'I could talk to you for hours,' and then launch into a litany of complaints and diagnostic questions, usually about one or another family member, in-law, co-worker or other acquaintance. It seems that people are quick to acknowledge the ubiquity of those who might benefit from a psychiatrist's attention, while expressing a deep reluctance ever to seek it out themselves.

That reluctance is understandable. Although most of us crave support, understanding, and human connection, we also worry that if we reveal our true selves, we'll be judged, criticised, or rejected in some way. And even worse—perhaps calling upon antiquated myths—some worry that, if we were to reveal our inner selves to a psychiatrist, we might be labelled crazy, locked up in an asylum, medicated into oblivion or put into a straitjacket. Of course, such fears are the accompaniment of the very idiosyncrasies, foibles, and life struggles that keep us from unattainably perfect mental health.

As a psychiatrist, I see this as the biggest challenge facing psychiatry today. A large part of the population—perhaps even the majority—might benefit from some form of mental health care, but too many fear that modern psychiatry is on a mission to pathologise normal individuals with some dystopian plan fuelled by the greed of the pharmaceutical industry, all in order to put the populace on mind-numbing medications. Debates about psychiatric overdiagnosis have amplified in the wake of last year's release of the newest edition of the *Diagnostic and Statistical Manual of Mental Disorders* (*DSM*-5), the so-called 'bible of psychiatry', with some particularly vocal critics coming from within the profession.

It's true that the scope of psychiatry has greatly expanded over the past century. A hundred years ago, the profession had a near-exclusive focus on the custodial care of severely ill asylum patients. Now, psychiatric practice includes the office-based management of the 'worried well.' The advent of psychotherapy, starting with the arrival of Sigmund Freud's psychoanalysis at the turn of the 20th century, drove the shift. The ability to treat less severe forms of psychopathology—such as anxiety and so-called adjustment disorders related to life stressors— with the talking cure has had profound effects on mental health care in the United States.

Early forms of psychotherapy paved the way for the Mental Hygiene Movement that lasted from about 1910 through the 1950s. This public health model rejected hard boundaries of mental illness in favour of a view that acknowledged the potential for some degree of mental disorder to exist in nearly everyone. Interventions were recommended not just within a psychiatrist's office, but broadly within society at large; schools and other community settings were all involved in providing support and help.

A new abundance of 'neurotic' symptoms stemming from the trauma experienced by veterans of the First and Second World Wars reinforced a view that mental health and illness existed on a continuous spectrum. And by the time *DSM* was first published in 1952, psychiatrists were treating a much wider swath of the population than ever before. From the first *DSM* through to the most recent revision, inclusiveness and clinical usefulness have been guiding principles, with the profession erring on the side of capturing all of the conditions that bring people to psychiatric care in order to facilitate evaluation and treatment.

In the modern era, psychotherapy has steered away from traditional psychoanalysis in favour of more practical, shorter-term therapies: for instance, psychodynamic therapy explores unconscious conflicts and underlying distress on a weekly basis for as little as a few months' duration, and goal-directed cognitive therapy uses behavioural techniques to correct disruptive distortions in thinking. These streamlined psychotherapeutic techniques have widened the potential consumer base for psychiatric intervention; they have also expanded the range of clinicians who can perform therapy to include not only psychiatrists, but primary care doctors, psychologists, social workers and marriage and family therapists.

In a similar fashion, newer medications with fewer side effects are more likely to be offered to people with less clear-cut psychiatric illnesses. Such medications can be prescribed by a family physician or, in some states, a psychologist or nurse practitioner.

Viewed through the lens of the *DSM*, it is easy to see how extending psychiatry's helping hand deeper into the population is often interpreted as evidence that psychiatrists think more and more people are mentally ill. Recent epidemiological studies based upon *DSM* criteria have suggested that half or more of the US population will meet the threshold for mental disorder at some point in their lives. To many, the idea that it might be normal to have a mental illness sounds oxymoronic at best and conspiratorially threatening at worst. Yet the widening scope of psychiatry has been driven by a belief—on the parts of both mental health consumers and clinicians alike—that psychiatry can help with an increasingly large range of issues.

The diagnostic creep of psychiatry becomes more understandable by conceptualising mental illness, like most things in nature, on a continuum. Many forms of psychiatric disorder, such as schizophrenia or severe dementia, are so severe—that is to say, divergent from normality—that whether they represent illness is rarely debated. Other syndromes, such as generalised anxiety disorder, might more closely resemble what seems, to some, like normal worry. And patients might even complain of isolated symptoms such as insomnia or lack of energy that arise in the absence of any fully formed disorder. In this way, a continuous view of mental illness extends into areas that might

actually be normal, but still detract from optimal, day-to-day function.

While a continuous view of mental illness probably reflects underlying reality, it inevitably results in grey areas where 'caseness' (whether someone does or does not have a mental disorder) must be decided based on judgment calls made by experienced clinicians. In psychiatry, those calls usually depend on whether a patient's complaints are associated with significant distress or impaired functioning. Unlike medical disorders where morbidity is often determined by physical limitations or the threat of impending death, the distress and disruption of social functioning associated with mental illness can be fairly subjective. Even those on the softer, less severe end of the mental illness spectrum can experience considerable suffering and impairment. For example, someone with mild depression might not be on the verge of suicide, but could really be struggling with work due to anxiety and poor concentration. Many people might experience sub-clinical conditions that fall short of the threshold for a mental disorder, but still might benefit from intervention.

The truth is that while psychiatric diagnosis is helpful in understanding what ails a patient and formulating a treatment plan, psychiatrists don't waste a lot of time fretting over whether a patient can be neatly categorised in *DSM,* or even whether or not that patient truly has a mental disorder at all. A patient comes in with a complaint of suffering, and the clinician tries to relieve that suffering independent of such exacting distinctions. If anything, such details become most important for insurance billing, where clinicians might err on the side of making a diagnosis to obtain reimbursement for a patient who might not otherwise be able to receive care.

Though many object to psychiatry's perceived encroachment into normality, we rarely hear such complaints about the rest of medicine. Few lament that nearly all of us, at some point in our lives, seek care from a physician and take all manner of medications, most without need of a prescription, for one physical ailment or another. If we can accept that it is completely normal to be medically sick, not only with transient conditions such as coughs and colds, but also chronic disorders such as farsightedness, lower back pain, high blood pressure or diabetes, why can't we accept that it might also be normal to be psychiatrically ill at various points in our lives?

The answer seems to be that psychiatric disorders carry a much greater degree of stigma compared with medical conditions. People worry that psychiatrists think everyone is crazy because they make the mistake of equating any form of psychiatric illness with being crazy. But that's like equating a cough with tuberculosis or lung cancer. To be less stigmatising, psychiatry must support a continuous model of mental health instead of maintaining an exclusive focus on the mental disorders that make up the *DSM.* If general medicine can work within a continuous view of physical health and illness, there is no reason why psychiatry can't as well.

Criticism of this view comes from concern over the type of intervention offered at the healthier end of the continuum. If the scope of psychiatry widens, will psychiatric medications be vastly overprescribed, as is already claimed with stimulants such as methylphenidate (Ritalin) for attention deficit hyperactivity disorder (ADHD)? This concern is well worth fretting over, given the uncertain effectiveness of medications for patients who don't quite meet *DSM* criteria. For example, a 2008 study by the Harvard psychologist Irving Kirsch published in *PLOS Medicine* found that, for milder forms of depression, antidepressants are often no better than placebos. Likewise, recent research suggests that children at risk of developing psychosis—but not diagnosable just yet—might benefit more from fish oil or psychotherapy than antipsychotic drugs.

In the end, implementing pharmacotherapy for a given condition requires solid evidence from peer-reviewed research studies. Although by definition the benefit of medications decreases at the healthier end of a mental health continuum (if one isn't as sick, the degree of improvement will be less), we need not reject all pharmacotherapy at the healthier end of the spectrum, provided medications are safe and effective. Of course, medications aren't candy—most have a long list of potential side effects ranging from trivial to life-threatening. There's a reason such medications require a prescription from a physician and why many psychiatrists are sceptical of proposals to grant prescribing privileges to health practitioners with far less medical training.

Pharmacotherapy for healthier individuals *is* likely to increase in the future as safer medications are developed, just as happened after selective serotonin re-uptake inhibitors (SSRIs) supplanted tricyclic antidepressants (TCAs) during the 1990s. In turn, the shift to medicating the healthier end of the continuum paves a path towards not only maximising wellness but enhancing normal functioning through 'cosmetic' intervention. Ultimately, availability of medications that enhance brain function or make us feel better than normal will be driven by consumer demand, not the Machiavellian plans of psychiatrists. The legal use of drugs to alter our moods is already nearly ubiquitous. We take Ritalin, modafinil (Provigil), or just our daily cup of caffeine to help us focus, stay awake, and make that deadline at work; then we reach for our diazepam (Valium), alcohol, or marijuana to unwind at the end of the day. If a kind of anabolic steroid for the brain were created, say a pill that could increase IQ by an average of 10 points with a minimum

of side effects, is there any question that the public would clamour for it? Cosmetic psychiatry is a very real prospect for the future, with myriad moral and ethical implications involved.

In the final analysis, psychiatrists don't think that everyone is crazy, nor are we necessarily guilty of pathologising normal existence and foisting medications upon the populace as pawns of the drug companies. Instead, we are just doing what we can to relieve the suffering of those coming for help, rather than turning those people away.

The good news for mental health consumers is that clinicians worth their mettle (and you might have to shop around to find one) don't rely on the *DSM* as a bible in the way that many imagine, checking off symptoms like a computer might and trying to 'shrink' people into the confines of a diagnostic label. A good psychiatrist draws upon clinical experience to gain empathic understanding of each patient's story, and then offers a tailored range of interventions to ease the suffering, whether it represents a disorder or is part of normal life.

Critical Thinking

1. What role do you think the "bible of psychiatry"—the Diagnostic and Statistical Manual of Mental Disorders, 5th Edition—has to play in how both psychiatrists and clinical psychologists are perceived? Explain.

2. If you hold the belief that everyone in society has some sort of mental disorder, how might that belief affect everyday life? Explain.

3. What are some of the challenges for psychiatrists in the treatment of depression? Be specific.

Internet References

Normal or not? New psychiatric manual stirs controversy
http://www.livescience.com/34496-psychiatric-manual-stirs-controversy.html

Symptoms and treatments of mental disorders
http://psychcentral.com/disorders/

The problem with psychiatry, the 'DSM,' and the way we study mental illness
http://www.psmag.com/books-and-culture/real-problem-with-dsm-study-mental-illness-58843

JOSEPH PIERRE is a professor of psychiatry at the University of California, LA, and co-chief of the Schizophrenia Treatment Unit at the West Los Angeles VA Medical Center. He writes the Psych Unseen blog for *Psychology Today*.

Unit 11

UNIT

Prepared by: Eric Landrum, *Boise State University*

Psychological Treatments

Have you ever had the nightmare of being trapped in a dark, dismal place and no one lets you out? Your pleas for freedom go unanswered and, in fact, are suppressed or ignored by domineering authority figures around you. You keep begging for mercy but to no avail.

You are fortunate to awake to the normal realities of your daily life. Have you ever wondered what would happen if we took perfectly normal individuals and institutionalized them in such a dark, dismal place? In one well-known and remarkable study, that is exactly what happened.

In 1973, eight individuals, including a pediatrician, a psychiatrist, and some psychologists, presented themselves to psychiatric hospitals. Each claimed that he or she was hearing voices. The voices, they reported, seemed unclear but appeared to be saying "empty" or "thud." Each of these individuals was admitted to a mental hospital, and most were diagnosed as being schizophrenic. After admission to the hospital, the "pseudopatients" or fake patients gave truthful information and thereafter acted like their usual, normal selves.

Their hospital stays lasted anywhere from 7 to 52 days. The nurses, doctors, psychologists, and other staff members treated them as if they were schizophrenic and never saw through their trickery. Some of the real patients in the hospital, however, recognized that the pseudopatients were perfectly normal. After their discharge, almost all of the pseudopatients received the diagnosis of "schizophrenic in remission," meaning that they were still diagnosed as schizophrenic, but they weren't exhibiting any of the symptoms at the time of release.

What does this classic study demonstrate about the diagnosis and treatment of mental illness? Is genuine mental illness readily detectable? If we can't always pinpoint mental disorders, how can we treat them appropriately? What treatments are available, and which treatments work better for various diagnoses? Although the diagnosis of schizophrenia is dramatic and often of interest to those studying psychology, what about the diagnosis and treatment of much more common disorders, such as depression or addiction?

The treatment of mental disorders is certainly challenging. As you probably know, not all individuals diagnosed as having a mental disorder are institutionalized. In fact, only a relatively small percentage of people suffering from one or more psychological disorders is confined to a mental institution. The most common treatments for mental disorders involve psychotherapy or counseling, medication, or some combination. Depending on the individual and the severity of his or her symptoms, the course of treatment may be relatively short (less than a year) or quite long (several years or more).

The array of available treatments is ever increasing and can be downright bewildering—and not just to the patient or client! Psychotherapists, clinical psychologists, and psychiatrists must weave their way through complicated sets of symptoms, identify the best diagnosis, and then suggest a course of treatment that seems to best address the client's problems in the context of complex healthcare delivery systems. In order to demystify and simplify your understanding of treatments and interventions for mental disorders, this unit presents some of these concepts.

Article   Prepared by: Eric Landrum, *Boise State University*

More Support Needed for Trauma Intervention

Treatment for child trauma works, but too often, children don't have access to it.

BETH AZAR

Learning Outcomes

After reading this article, you will be able to:

- Describe the consequences and characteristics of children who suffer from abuse.

- Explain the concept of evidence-based treatment and provide some examples of successful evidence-based treatments for those suffering from child abuse.

In the wake of the Penn State sexual abuse scandal, legislators are looking for ways to protect children from abuse. Less than two weeks after Penn State officials were charged with perjury and failing to report suspected child abuse, Sen. Robert Casey Jr. (D-Pa.) introduced legislation that would pressure states to have and enforce laws requiring all adults to report suspected child abuse and neglect.

Decades of research spell out the long-term consequences that abuse can have for children. The ongoing CDC "Study of Adverse Childhood Experiences," for example, shows that children who are abused and neglected have an increased risk of severe mental and physical health problems, including post-traumatic stress disorder (/topics/ptsd/index.aspx), depression (/topics/depress/index.aspx), suicide (/topics/suicide/index.aspx), substance abuse (/topics/addiction/index.aspx), chronic obstructive pulmonary disease, ischemic heart disease and liver disease.

But just as important as identifying cases of abuse is supporting treatments that help victims recover. Psychologists have developed evidence-based interventions that can reduce the harmful effects of child abuse. The key is ensuring that all individuals who experience abuse have access to these evidence-based treatments, so they don't become victims for life, says psychologist Anthony Mannarino, PhD, vice chair of the department of psychiatry, Allegheny General Hospital, Pittsburgh, and professor of psychiatry at Drexel University College of Medicine.

"With treatment, these kids can have the resilience to overcome their experience," says Mannarino, who through APA submitted written testimony to a Dec. 13 hearing on child abuse held by the Senate Health, Education, Labor and Pensions Subcommittee on Children and Families. "Being a victim doesn't have to become who they are or how they define themselves. But if they don't get help and their families don't participate, they can have long-standing difficulties."

Scope of the Problem

The Penn State case serves to remind the public that child abuse is all too common in the United States. Although estimates vary greatly depending on the source, the Fourth National Incidence Study of Child Abuse and Neglect, released in 2010, found that in 2005–06, one child in 25 in the United States, or 2.9 million children, experienced some kind of abuse or neglect. Most of those children—77 percent—were neglected. Of the 29 percent of those children who were abused, 57 percent were physically abused, 36 percent were emotionally abused and 22 percent were sexually abused.

Estimates of the percentage of abused children who will suffer long-term consequences vary widely. One review of research on child maltreatment—including physical and sexual abuse as well as neglect—published in the 2004 "Post-traumatic Stress Disorder In Children and Adolescents: Handbook," found that PTSD rates ranged from 20 percent to 63 percent. In her studies, psychologist Sheree Toth, PhD, director of the Mt. Hope Family Center in Rochester, N.Y., and associate professor at the University of Rochester, finds that as many as 90 percent of maltreated infants have insecure or disorganized attachment. "The bright side is that there are evidence-based treatments that can dramatically improve the prognosis for these kids," says Toth. "We've shown that with intervention we can greatly decrease rates of insecure and disorganized attachment."

Interventions That Work

A study published in 2006 in Development and Psychopathology by Toth and her colleagues showed that before intervention, 90 percent of a group of 137 maltreated infants had disorganized attachment and only one infant had secure attachment. Of the 50 infants who subsequently received one of two evidence-based therapies—infant-parent psychotherapy or a psychoeducational parenting intervention—58 percent had secure attachment a year later. In comparison, only one child among the 54 who received the standard treatment available in the community had secure attachment a year later.

Other researchers have shown positive results using evidence-based treatments to decrease the incidence of PTSD, depression, aggression and other behavioral problems seen in abused children. Mannarino, for example, has spent more than 25 years developing and testing an intervention called Trauma-Focused Cognitive Behavioral Therapy (TFCBT) to treat children age 3 and older who have post-traumatic stress symptoms from abuse. In 12 to 16 sessions, children and their non-offending parents or caregivers learn about the specific effects trauma can have on emotions and behavior, and develop skills to manage their emotional distress, including relaxation techniques and how to use words to express their feelings.

In addition, the therapists help the children construct a narrative about their experience. "We talk about the idea of making the unspeakable speakable," says Mannarino. "By showing them that it's OK to talk about it, it makes the experience less overwhelming."

Many child abuse experts agree that, to date, TF-CBT has a strong base of empirical support as an intervention to treat trauma in children, with 10 randomized controlled trials, all showing its effectiveness. The studies show that as many as 85 percent of children treated with TF-CBT get markedly better on measures of shame, PTSD and depression, says Mannarino. Parents improve as well, showing less depression and emotional distress, better parenting skills and having a better outlook for the future.

Another highly regarded intervention is Alternatives for Families: A Cognitive Behavioral Therapy (AF-CBT), whose senior developer is David Kolko, PhD, professor of psychiatry, psychology and pediatrics at the University of Pittsburgh School of Medicine. AFCBT is designed to address individual and family involvement in conflict, coercion and aggression, including hostility and anger, mild physical force and child physical abuse. Its focus on physical abuse includes joint and individual work involving the alleged perpetrator—in most cases abusing parents or caregivers—and the child at various times throughout treatment. Working with the adult offender makes treatment complicated clinically, says Kolko, and may require additional time, but his team sees good results from this integrated approach.

Kolko also directs a program that provides services to the adolescent sexual offender, called Services for Adolescent and Family Enrichment. His program—which is funded by the local court system—has kept data on more than 250 cases and finds a two-year recidivism rate of only 1.5 percent, he says.

Unfortunately, access to these evidence-based treatments for child abuse is "pitiful," says Toth. Because researchers have developed them in university settings, they're mostly available near big medical centers. In addition, only 45 percent of graduate programs and 51 percent of internships that train psychology students to treat abused or otherwise traumatized children use TFCBT, according to two studies published in December in *Psychological Trauma:* Theory, Research, Practice, and Policy and Training and Education in Professional Psychology.

That's why Mannarino is putting much of his efforts these days into training and dissemination of TF-CBT around the country.

"Despite our ability to treat these kids, the real truth is that most kids who are abused are never properly treated," says Mannarino. "They grow up bearing the scars of unfortunate victimizations and wind up having serious adult problems, including depression, psychiatric hospitalizations and a general overuse of health services because they didn't get the help they needed."

Critical Thinking

1. What are some of the long-term consequences for abused children?
2. Describe the role that resilience can play in providing effective treatment for child abuse victims.
3. When child abuse victims are not treated as children, what are some of the potential long-term problems due to lack of treatment?

Create Central

www.mhhe.com/createcentral

Internet References

Treatment for traumatized children, youth, and families
www.childwelfare.gov/responding/treatment.cfm
Grief and trauma intervention for children
www.nrepp.samhsa.gov/ViewIntervention.aspx?id=259

BETH AZAR is a writer in Portland, Ore.

Article   Prepared by: Eric Landrum, *Boise State University*

Yes, Recovery Is Possible

APA is participating in a new federally funded initiative designed to spread the word that people can—and do—recover from mental illnesses.

REBECCA A. CLAY

Learning Outcomes

After reading this article, you will be able to:

- Differentiate between the typical recovery expectations from individuals who suffer from a heart attack (or other chronic illness) vs. those who suffer from the onset of a mental illness.

- Describe how the focus on a wellness or recovery approach differs from the current traditional treatment approach exhibited by psychologists.

Peter Ashenden was determined not to let his severe depression keep him from finishing his college degree and getting a job. The clinical staff at the day facility where he was receiving treatment in the 1980s had a different idea: a sheltered workshop for people with disabilities. "The workshop was putting caps on lipstick tubes for six hours a day," remembers Ashenden, who now directs consumer and family affairs at the insurance company Optum Health.

To Ashenden, that's a perfect example of what happens when a mental health system hasn't embraced the idea that people can recover from mental illnesses. Now, as part of a team at APA devoted to an initiative called Recovery to Practice, he's working to ensure that psychologists get the training they need to help people with mental health conditions live meaningful lives in the community and achieve their full potential.

Funded by the Substance Abuse and Mental Health Services Administration (SAMHSA), the five-year initiative has a dual mission: to create an online repository of resources on recovery principles and practices and to develop recovery-focused training for mental health professionals.

APA is one of five national mental health organizations to partner with SAMHSA; the other grantees include the American Psychiatric Association, American Psychiatric Nurses Association, Council on Social Work Education and National Association of Peer Specialists. Like the other organizations, APA will share resources and develop a recovery-oriented curriculum that will be used to train its constituency.

"SAMHSA has made Recovery to Practice a priority, and I am pleased that APA is one of the organizations involved in moving this initiative forward," says Gwendolyn P. Keita, PhD, executive director of APA's Public Interest Directorate (/pi/index.aspx). "Recovery is a growing movement, and it is important that psychologists are involved."

Research Changes Minds

"Until fairly recently, it was assumed that people with serious mental illness would never recover," says Mary A. Jansen, PhD, who chairs APA's Task Force on Serious Mental Illness and Severe Emotional Disturbance and is a member of the Recovery Advisory Committee that guides APA's Recovery to Practice initiative. "Individuals were often warehoused in state mental institutions."

When new medications allowed many of those people to return to their communities, most psychologists and other mental health practitioners still believed they would never regain full functioning, says Jansen, director of Bayview Behavioral Consulting in Vancouver. Then research by psychologists and others in the 1970s began to show that people could recover, and individuals with serious mental illnesses began to advocate for services that would help them achieve recovery.

By 2003, mental health recovery had become the overarching goal of President George W. Bush's New Freedom Commission on Mental Health. The commission's 2003 report, *Achieving the Promise: Transforming Mental Health Care in America,* argued that the nation's mental health system was broken and identified the major flaw as the lack of a vision of recovery. The commission also laid out a challenge: "We envision a future when everyone with a mental illness will recover, a future when mental illnesses can be prevented or cured, a future when mental illnesses are detected early and a future when everyone with a mental illness at any stage of life has access to effective treatment and supports—essentials for living, working, learning and participating fully in the community."

Now the Recovery to Practice initiative is working to make that vision a reality.

"It's really no different than if you have a heart attack or another chronic illness," says Jansen. "Once you recover from the acute stage, you generally begin a recovery process, with a team of professionals and interventions all working toward helping you get back to the highest level of functioning you can achieve." Now the push is on to get that same focus on rehabilitation into the mental health field and into the mainstream of psychology, says Jansen.

"In the late 1970s into the 1990s, interventions were specifically designed for people with serious mental illnesses, many of whom had lost considerable functioning in part because they had languished in environments where no one believed they could do anything," she says.

In the same way that cardiologists might encourage heart attack patients to stop smoking, start exercising and work on lowering their cholesterol, she says, psychologists and others committed to a recovery-oriented approach now use psychosocial rehabilitation interventions to assist people with mental health conditions. These services, says Jansen, are designed to involve individuals in a partnership with professionals as they try to gain—or regain—a meaningful life, however they define it.

That recovery-oriented approach shouldn't just be used with people who have severe depression, schizophrenia, bipolar disorder and other serious mental illnesses, adds Jansen. It's also useful for any mental health condition that keeps someone from functioning as well as he or she could.

In 2009, APA's Council of Representatives passed a resolution endorsing the concept of recovery for people with serious mental illness. "This resulted from a commitment by APA's Committee for the Advancement of Professional Practice (CAPP) (/practice/leadership/capp/index.aspx) to place increased emphasis on recovery within psychology practice," says Katherine C. Nordal, PhD, executive director for APA's Practice Directorate.

But the recovery movement hasn't become well integrated into psychology yet, says Andrew T. Austin Daily, the APA staffer who directs the association's Recovery to Practice project.

An analysis by APA staff, the Recovery Advisory Committee and APA's Committee for Assessment and Training in Recovery revealed multiple economic, political, social and technological barriers to integrating recovery into psychology. One obstacle is inadequate reimbursement for providing recovery-related services. Some psychologists are reluctant to change their practice orientation; others may fear people with serious mental illnesses. There's a shortage of affordable housing options, supported employment programs and other services that psychologists can point patients to as they begin re-integrating into their communities. And because few training standards and best practices exist, psychologists simply may not know how to use this orientation to facilitate their clients' recovery.

"The big challenge is addressing psychologists' perceptions of recovery and how it impacts their work," says APA 2011 President Melba J.T. Vasquez, PhD. "But another challenge that APA really cares about is getting recovery into education and training: It's important for both our students in graduate doctoral programs but also for our current providers to learn these recovery concepts and principles and put them into practice."

Working with a recovery mindset is very different from what psychologists traditionally do, adds Vasquez. For example, in therapy sessions with the mother of a son with serious mental illness, Vasquez didn't just focus on helping to ease her distress. She also reached out to a social worker and others in the community to help the woman find housing and a job for her son. "Working collaboratively with others in the community is important," says Vasquez, "and we're not usually trained to work that way."

Training Materials

To help psychologists get that training, APA's Recovery to Practice team is developing a curriculum for doctoral psychology training programs that emphasizes recovery outcomes and explains recovery-related principles and practices.

"This process should be greatly facilitated by the tremendous work of CAPP's Task Force on Serious Mental Illness and Severe Emotional Disturbance, which spent years developing and revising the *Catalog of Clinical Training Opportunities: Best Practices for Recovery and Improved Outcomes for People with Serious Mental Illness,*" says Nordal.

Still in draft form, the curriculum features more than a dozen modules on such topics as the recovery movement's history, the scientific foundations of recovery, health disparities, ethics and how to incorporate recovery principles into such tasks as clinical assessment, treatment planning and interventions.

The APA team will spend the next year developing the curriculum and plans to have it ready for pilot testing by the end of next summer. The hope is to have three or four graduate training directors incorporate the curriculum into their programs and provide feedback. The Recovery to Practice team will then modify the curriculum as needed and either do another round of pilot testing or move ahead with working with the psychology training councils on dissemination and marketing.

APA also plans to go beyond the SAMHSA-funded project in its efforts to spread the word on recovery. In addition to the curriculum for graduate students, APA will develop versions for use in internship programs as well as continuing-education programs for psychologists already in practice.

For Jansen, the focus on recovery is especially timely given the roll-out of health-care reform.

"Health-care reform is all about promoting wellness: getting people to be as healthy and productive members of society as they can be," she says, adding that this will ultimately reduce costs. "If psychology as a profession doesn't embrace the notion of recovery and the need to train psychologists in the rehabilitative interventions needed to assist people to recover, psychology will likely be left behind."

Critical Thinking

1. If you don't believe that individuals can recover from mental illness, what are some of the ramifications of that belief for those with mental illness? What are their life prospects under that scenario?

2. How might the mindset of a psychologist differ when working toward a treatment goal vs. a recovery goal?
3. How might the education and training of current psychology graduate students be modified to encourage more of a recovery/wellness orientation?

Create Central

www.mhhe.com/createcentral

Internet References

Psychology is a behavioral and mental health profession
www.apa.org/about/gr/issues/health-care/profession.aspx

Discover and recover: Resources for mental and overall wellness
http://discoverandrecover.wordpress.com/mental-health-freedom-and-recovery-act

REBECCA A. CLAY, is a writer in Washington, D.C.

Article   Prepared by: Eric Landrum, *Boise State University*

Addiction Interaction, Relapse and Recovery

CHERYL KNEPPER

Learning Outcomes

After reading this article, you will be able to:

- Articulate the definition of an addiction.

- Identify some of the potential screening tools in identifying addictions.

Substance abuse and dependence rarely occur in a vacuum. Today's addict is faced with a multitude of issues that may co-exist and compromise recovery. Co-existing addictions/compulsive behaviors such as drugs and alcohol, pathological gambling, sex, food, work, internet and gaming can become chronic and progressive if left unidentified and untreated. Many of these addictions don't only coexist, but interact, reinforce and fuse together becoming part of a package known as Addiction Interaction. The term "Addiction Interaction Disorder" was introduced by Patrick Carnes PhD in 2011.

Caron Treatment Centers conducted a research study among adult patients with drug and alcohol addictions to determine what percentage may be at risk for sex and love addiction. The 485 participants were given the SAST-R (Sexual Addiction Screening Tool-Revised a 45 item forced choice (Yes/No) instrument) (Carnes, Green & Carnes, 2010). The findings of this study indicated that 21 percent of individuals being treated for primary substance dependence scored at risk. Another interesting finding from the study showed a higher percentage of cannabis, cocaine and amphetamine abuse or dependence diagnosis in the individuals that scored at-risk for sexual addiction. In addition, at-risk individuals had higher percentages of mood disorder, PTSD and eating disorder diagnoses.

ASAM's definition of addiction is a primary, chronic disease of the brain reward, motivation, memory and related circuitry. Dysfunction in these circuits leads to characteristic biological, psychological, social and spiritual manifestations. This is reflected in an individual pathologically pursuing reward and/or relief by substance use and other behaviors. The neural pathways are altered when drugs or other compulsive addictive behaviors exist. Changes in the neural plasticity occur which alters the brain wiring. Neurons that fuse together wire together which creates an interaction of addictions. When the pleasurable or reward-driven behavior stops, there is a decrease of dopamine (and possibly other neuro-transmitters depending on what the behavioral effect is), therefore causing a sensation of a "crash" or withdrawal, compelling the person to re-engage in the original euphoric behavior (Milkman & Sunderwirth, 1987).

Pleasurable, reward-driven behaviors can serve to self-medicate, fuse, or replace each other just like substances interact. For example, alcoholism is put into remission, and gambling addiction substitutes the absence of alcohol; this is known as "Replacement." This puts the individual at high risk for relapse back to drug of choice. Another process known as "Fusion" occurs when two or more addictive behaviors develop into one episode. For example, when sex and cocaine are combined, the individual cannot engage in either addictive behavior without the other addiction present. This cycle repeats over and over. Addictions can cycle back and forth in a patterned and systematic way, which leaves the co-addicted individual at higher risk for relapse.

The addictive behavior of one addiction can serve as a ritual pattern to engage another. Actions such as buying and preparing drugs can activate the pleasure center of the brain. Alterations in the reward center of the brain could lead to distorted perceptions about people, places, and things, as well as interfere with the brain's ability to process feelings. Furthermore, circuits in the brain found in the reward center have routes to the part of the brain that affect memory, judgment, and our intellect. If all of a patient's addictions are not addressed during treatment, their likelihood of relapsing is much greater. An integrated approach is best. This approach takes a thorough look at what other compulsive behaviors or addictions may be contributing to one's chemical addiction and provides the individual with a broader understanding of potential risk factors.

During a patient's stay at Caron, we use multiple screening tools such as the Minnesota Multiphasic Personality Inventory-2 Restructured Form (MMPI-2-RF), the Sexual Addiction Screening Test—Revised (SAST-R), Sexual Dependency Inventory—R 4 (SDI-R 4.0), South Oaks Gambling Screen-Revised (SOGS-R) and Eating Attitudes Test-26 (EAT-26). Patients are given these screens and assessments if they endorse certain behavioral questions during the psychosocial interview, but can be given a little further into treatment when patients start to be more honest and open about themselves. From these assessments, there is a clearer picture of the addictions and disorders from which the patient suffers.

Because of the interactive nature of multiple addictions, it is necessary to use an integrated multidisciplinary treatment approach. Caron has certified and licensed addictions experts from an array of disciplines: addictions counselors, psychologists, psychiatrists, spiritual counselors, nutritionists, medical team of nurses and physicians. The treatment philosophy at Caron is built on the foundation of the 12 Steps and evidence based practices; for example, CBT (Cognitive Behavioral Therapy), Mindfulness Practice and MI (Motivational Interviewing). In addition, patients are offered specialty groups such as Addiction Interaction groups and tasks, 12 Step lecture series, Family of Origin group, Seeking Safety group, Parenting, Body Image, Grief and Loss. While patient treatment will vary depending on each individual's circumstances, it is important to make them aware if multiple addictions co-exist. Additionally, psycho-education helps patients work through shame and "normalize" behavior based on their history. It is also essential to identify relapse triggers, high-risk situations, relapse signs and symptoms, repetitive patterns and relapse thinking and develop interventions to address these issues along with an integrated continuing care plan.

Patients and their family members are encouraged as part of the treatment process to attend the 5-day Family Education Program which is didactic and experiential in design. The goal is to educate and assist the family in understanding the disease of addiction while providing support and encouragement for their part of the recovery process.

The goal is to give the individual and their family the gift of Recovery for Life!

Critical Thinking

1. There are many different types of addictions beyond those we stereotypically think of, such as drug addiction and alcohol addiction. Can someone be addicted to the Internet? Can someone be addicted to swimming pools? Explain your answer to both of these questions.

2. What are the relationships between drug and alcohol addiction and sex and love addiction? If a person has one addiction, is he or she more likely to have another addiction? Explore this possibility and explain your answer.

Create Central

www.mhhe.com/createcentral

Internet References

A relapse prevention plan: The tools of recovery
www.addictionsandrecovery.org/relapse-prevention.htm

Is relapse a normal part of recovery?
www.familyrecoverysolutions.com/articles/relapse

Article

Prepared by: Eric Landrum, *Boise State University*

Post-Prozac Nation: The Science and History of Treating Depression

SIDDHARTHA MUKHERJEE

Learning Outcomes

After reading this article, you will be able to:

- Understand the effects of taking Prozac from the perspective of someone who has taken Prozac.

- Articulate the current status of the serotonin hypothesis of depression.

Few medicines, in the history of pharmaceuticals, have been greeted with as much exultation as a green-and-white pill containing 20 milligrams of fluoxetine hydrochloride—the chemical we know as Prozac. In her 1994 book *Prozac Nation,* Elizabeth Wurtzel wrote of a nearly transcendental experience on the drug. Before she began treatment with antidepressants, she was living in "a computer program of total negativity . . . an absence of affect, absence of feeling, absence of response, absence of interest." She floated from one "suicidal reverie" to the next. Yet, just a few weeks after starting Prozac, her life was transformed. "One morning I woke up and really did want to live. . . . It was as if the miasma of depression had lifted off me, in the same way that the fog in San Francisco rises as the day wears on. Was it the Prozac? No doubt."

Like Wurtzel, millions of Americans embraced antidepressants. In 1988, a year after the Food and Drug Administration approved Prozac, 2,469,000 prescriptions for it were dispensed in America. By 2002, that number had risen to 33,320,000. By 2008, antidepressants were the third-most-common prescription drug taken in America.

Fast forward to 2012 and the same antidepressants that inspired such enthusiasm have become the new villains of modern psychopharmacology—overhyped, overprescribed chemicals, symptomatic of a pill-happy culture searching for quick fixes for complex mental problems. In *The Emperor's New Drugs,* the psychologist Irving Kirsch asserted that antidepressants work no better than sugar pills and that the clinical effectiveness of the drugs is, largely, a myth. If the lodestone book of the 1990s was Peter Kramer's near-ecstatic testimonial, *Listening to Prozac,* then the book of the 2000s is David Healy's

Let Them Eat Prozac: The Unhealthy Relationship Between the Pharmaceutical Industry and Depression.

In fact, the very theory for how these drugs work has been called into question. Nerve cells—neurons—talk to one another through chemical signals called neurotransmitters, which come in a variety of forms, like serotonin, dopamine and norepinephrine. For decades, a central theory in psychiatry has been that antidepressants worked by raising serotonin levels in the brain. In depressed brains, the serotonin signal had somehow been "weakened" because of a chemical imbalance in neurotransmitters. Prozac and Paxil were thought to increase serotonin levels, thereby strengthening the signals between nerve cells—as if a megaphone had been inserted in the middle.

But this theory has been widely criticized. In *The New York Review of Books,* Marcia Angell, a former editor of *The New England Journal of Medicine,* wrote: "After decades of trying to prove [the chemical-imbalance theory], researchers have still come up empty-handed." Jonathan Rottenberg, writing in *Psychology Today,* skewered the idea thus: "As a scientific venture, the theory that low serotonin causes depression appears to be on the verge of collapse. This is as it should be; the nature of science is ultimately to be self-correcting. Ideas must yield before evidence."

Is the "serotonin hypothesis" of depression really dead? Have we spent nearly 40 years heading down one path only to find ourselves no closer to answering the question how and why we become depressed? Must we now start from scratch and find a new theory for depression?

Science may be self-correcting, but occasionally it overcorrects—discarding theories that instead need to be rejuvenated. The latest research suggests that serotonin is, in fact, central to the functioning of mood, although its mechanism of action is vastly more subtle and more magnificent than we ever imagined. Prozac, Paxil and Zoloft may never turn out to be the "wonder drugs" that were once advertised. But they have drastically improved our understanding of what depression is and how to treat it.

Our modern conception of the link between depression and chemicals in the brain was sparked quite by accident in the middle of the last century. In the autumn of 1951, doctors treating tubercular patients at Sea View Hospital on Staten Island with a new drug—iproniazid—observed sudden transformations in their patients' moods and behaviors. The wards—typically glum and silent, with moribund, lethargic patients—were "bright last week with the happy faces of men and women," a journalist wrote. Patients laughed and joked in the dining hall, as if a dark veil of grief had lifted. Energy flooded back and appetites returned. Many, ill for months, demanded five eggs for breakfast and then consumed them with gusto. When Life magazine sent a photographer to the hospital to investigate, the patients could no longer be found lying numbly in their beds: they were playing cards or dancing in the corridors.

If the men and women at Sea View were experiencing an awakening, then a few hundred miles south, others at Duke's hospital encountered its reverse. In 1954, a 28-year-old woman was prescribed Raudixin to control her blood pressure. A few months later, she returned to the hospital, complaining of crying spells, dullness and lethargy. She felt futile, guilty and hopeless, she told her doctors. A few months later, when she returned, the sense of futility had turned into hostility. A 42-year-old woman prescribed Raudixin told her doctor that "God would cause her to become insane" before she could repent. The "feeling blue," as another patient described it, persisted until the drug was discontinued. At another hospital, one patient treated with Raudixin attempted suicide. Several people had to be admitted to psychiatric wards and administered electroconvulsive therapy before the symptoms were alleviated.

Psychiatrists and pharmacologists were quick to note these bizarre case reports. How, they wondered, could simple, seemingly unrelated chemicals like Raudixin or iproniazid produce such profound and opposite effects on mood? It was around this same time that scientists were learning that the brain itself was immersed in a soup of chemicals. In the early part of the century, scientists wondered how nerve cells talked to one another. By the late 1960s, evidence suggested that signals between neurons were carried by several chemicals, including the neurotransmitter serotonin. Might iproniazid and Raudixin have altered the levels of some neurotransmitters in the brain, thereby changing brain signaling and affecting mood? Strikingly so, scientists found. Raudixin—the "feeling blue" drug—drastically lowered the concentration of serotonin and closely related neurotransmitters in the brain. Conversely, drugs known to increase euphoria, like iproniazid, increased those levels.

These early findings led psychiatrists to propose a radical new hypothesis about the cause and treatment of depression. Depression, they argued, was a result of a "chemical imbalance" of neurotransmitters in the brain. In the normal brain, serotonin shuttled between mood-maintaining neurons, signaling their appropriate function. In the depressed brain, this signal had somehow gone wrong. The writer Andrew Solomon once evocatively described depression as a "flaw in love"—and certainly, the doctors using Raudixin at Duke had seen that flaw emerge grimly in real time: flaws in self-love (guilt, shame, suicidal thoughts), love for others (blame, aggression, accusation), even the extinction of a desire for love (lethargy, withdrawal, dullness). But these were merely the outer symptoms of

a deeper failure of neurotransmitters. The "flaw in love" was a flaw in chemicals.

Powerful vindication for this theory came from the discovery of new medicines that specifically elevated serotonin concentrations. The first such drug, Zimelidine, was created by a Swedish researcher, Arvid Carlsson. Following Carlsson's lead, pharmaceutical chemists threw their efforts and finances into finding serotonin-enhancing drugs, and the new giants of the antidepressant world were born in rapid succession. Prozac was created in 1974. Paxil appeared in 1975, Zoloft in 1977 (the trade names were introduced years later).

In 2003, in Boston, I began treating a 53-year-old woman with advanced pancreatic cancer. Dorothy had no medical problems until she developed an ominous sign known to every cancer specialist: painless jaundice, the sudden yellowing of skin without any associated pinch of discomfort. Painless jaundice can have many causes, but the one that oncologists know best, and fear most, is pancreatic cancer.

In Dorothy's case, the mass in the pancreas turned out to be large and fist-shaped, with malignant extensions that reached backward to grip blood vessels, and a solitary metastasis in the liver. Surgical removal was impossible, chemotherapy the only option.

The suddenness of the diagnosis struck her like an intravenous anaesthetic, instantly numbing everything. As we started chemotherapy in the hospital, she spent her mornings in bed sleeping or staring out of the window at the river below. Most disturbing, I watched as she lapsed into self-neglect. Her previously well-kept hair grew into a matted coil. The clothes that she had worn to the hospital remained unchanged. There were even more troubling signs: tiny abrasions in the skin that were continuously picked at, food left untouched by the bedside table and a gradual withdrawal of eye contact. One morning, I walked into what seemed like a daily emotional flare-up: someone had moved a pillow on the bed, Dorothy had been unable to sleep and it was somehow her son's fault.

This grief, of course, was fully provoked by the somberness of her diagnosis—to *not* grieve would have been bizarre in these circumstances—but she recognized something troubling in her own reaction and begged for help. I contacted a psychiatrist. With her consent, we prescribed Prozac.

In the first weeks, we waited watchfully, and nothing happened. But when I saw her again in the clinic after a month and a half, there were noticeable changes. Her hair was clean and styled. Her cuts had disappeared, and her skin looked good. Yet she still felt sad beyond measure, she said. She spent her days mostly in bed. The drug certainly affected many of the symptoms of depression, yet had not altered the subjective "feeling" of it. It healed the flaws in her skin but not all the flaws in love.

Any sane reader of this case would argue that a serotonin imbalance was not the initiating cause of Dorothy's depression; it was, quite evidently, the diagnosis of a fatal disease. Should we be searching for a chemical cause and cure when the provocation of grief is so apparent?

Pause for a moment, though, to consider the physiology of a heart attack. A heart attack can be set off by a variety of causes—chronic high blood pressure or pathologically high levels of "bad" cholesterol or smoking. Yet aspirin is an effective treatment of a heart attack regardless of its antecedent cause. Why? Because a heart attack, however it might have been provoked, progresses through a common, final pathway: there must be a clot in a coronary artery that is blocking the flow of blood to the heart. Aspirin helps to inhibit the formation and growth of the clot in the coronary artery. The medicine is clinically effective regardless of what events led to the clot. "Aspirin," as a professor of mine liked to put it, "does not particularly care about your medical history."

Might major depression be like a heart attack, with a central common pathway and with serotonin as its master regulator? There was certainly precedent in the biology of the nervous system for such unifying pathways—for complex mental states triggered by simple chemicals. Fear, for instance, was found to involve a common hormonal cascade, with adrenaline as the main player, even though its initiators (bears, spiders or in-laws) might have little resemblance to one another.

But such a line of inquiry can't tell us whether the absence of serotonin *causes* depression. For that, we need to know if depressed men and women have measurably lower levels of serotonin or serotonin-metabolites (byproducts of serotonin breakdown), in their brains. In 1975, pathologists performed autopsies on depressed patients to measure serotonin levels. The initial findings were suggestive: depressed patients typically tended to have lower levels of brain serotonin compared with controls. But in 1987, when researchers in Scandinavia performed a similar experiment with newer tools to measure serotonin more accurately, serotonin levels were found to be higher in depressed patients. Further experiments only deepened these contradictions. In some trials, depressed patients were found to have decreased serotonin levels; in others, serotonin was increased; in yet others, there was no difference at all.

What about the converse experiment? In 1994, male subjects at McGill University in Montreal were given a chemical mixture that lowered serotonin. Doctors then measured the fluctuations in the mood of the men as serotonin levels dipped in the blood. Though serotonin was depleted, most of them experienced no significant alterations in their mood.

At first glance, these studies seem to suggest that there is no link between serotonin and depression. But an important fact stands out in the McGill experiment: lowering serotonin does not have any effect on healthy volunteers with no history of depression, but serotonin-lowering has a surprisingly brisk effect on people with a family history of depression. In these subjects, mood dipped sharply when serotonin levels dropped. An earlier version of this experiment, performed at Yale in 1990, generated even more provocative findings. When depressed patients who were already responding to serotonin-enhancing drugs, like Prozac, were fed the serotonin-lowering mixture, they became acutely, often profoundly, depressed. Why would serotonin depletion make such a difference in a patient's mood unless mood in these patients was, indeed, being controlled by serotonin?

Other experiments showed that though depressed patients generally didn't have consistently lower levels of serotonin, suicidal patients often did. Might contemplating suicide be the most extreme form of depression? Or is it a specific subtype of mood disorder that is distinct from all the other forms? And if so, might depression have multiple subtypes—some inherently responsive to treatment with serotonin-enhancing drugs and some inherently resistant?

We may not understand how serotonin-enhancing antidepressants work, but do we know whether they work at all?

In the late 1980s, studies examined the effect of Prozac on depressed subjects. Several of these trials showed Prozac reduced the symptoms of depression when compared with a placebo. Depression is usually assessed using a standardized rating scale of different symptoms. In general, some patients reported clinically meaningful improvements, although the effects were often small and varied from trial to trial. In real-world terms, such a change could be profound: a transformation in anxiety, the lifting of the ache of guilt, an end to the desire to commit suicide. But for other patients, the changes were marginal. Perhaps the most important number that emerged from these trials was the most subjective: 74 percent of the patients reported feeling "much" or "very much" better on antidepressants.

In 1997, a psychologist, Irving Kirsch, currently at the Harvard Medical School, set out to look at the placebo effect in relation to depression. In part, the placebo effect works because the psyche acutely modifies the perception of illness or wellness. Kirsch wondered how powerful this effect might be for drugs that treat depression—where the medical condition itself happens to involve an alteration of the psyche.

To measure this effect, Kirsch combined 38 trials that included patients who had been given antidepressants, placebos or no treatment and then applied mathematical reasoning to estimate how much the placebos contributed to the improvements in mood. The analysis revealed two surprises. First, when Kirsch computed the strength of the placebo effect by combining the trials, he found that 75 percent of an antidepressant's effect could have been obtained merely by taking the placebo. When Kirsch and his collaborators combined the published and unpublished studies of antidepressants (they obtained the unpublished data from the F.D.A. via the Freedom of Information Act), the effects of the antidepressants were even more diluted—in some cases, vanishingly so. Now, the placebo effect swelled to 82 percent (i.e., four-fifths of the benefit might have been obtained by swallowing an inert pill alone). Kirsch came to believe that pharmaceutical companies were exaggerating the benefits of antidepressants by selectively publishing positive studies while suppressing negative ones.

But there are problems in analyzing published and unpublished trials in a "meta-trial." A trial may have been unpublished not just to hide lesser effects but because its quality was poor—because patients were enrolled incorrectly, groups were assigned improperly or the cohort sizes were too small. Patients who are mildly depressed, for example, might have been lumped in with severely depressed patients or with obsessive-compulsives and schizophrenics.

In 2010, researchers revisited Kirsch's analysis using six of the most rigorously conducted studies on antidepressants.

The study vindicated Kirsch's conclusions but only to a point. In patients with moderate or mild depression, the benefit of an antidepressant was indeed small, even negligible. But for patients with the most severe forms of depression, the benefit of medications over placebo was substantial. Such patients might have found, as Andrew Solomon did, that they no longer felt "the self slipping out" of their hands. The most severe dips in mood were gradually blunted. Like Dorothy, these patients most likely still experienced sorrow, but they experienced it in ways that were less self-destructive or paralyzing. As Solomon wrote: "The opposite of depression is not happiness, but vitality, and my life, as I write this, is vital."

These slippery, seemingly contradictory studies converge on a surprisingly consistent picture. First, patients with severe depression tend to respond most meaningfully to antidepressants, while patients with moderate or mild depression do not. Second, in a majority of those who do respond, serotonin very likely plays an important role, because depleting serotonin in depressed patients often causes relapses. And third, the brain-as-soup theory—with the depressed brain simply lacking serotonin—was far too naïve.

As is often the case in science, a new theory emerged from a radically different line of inquiry. In the late 1980s, a neuroscientist named Fred Gage became interested in a question that seemed, at first, peripheral to depression: does the adult human brain produce new nerve cells?

The dogma in neurobiology at the time was that the adult brain was developmentally frozen—no new nerve cells were born. Once the neural circuits of the brain were formed in childhood, they were fixed and immutable. After all, if new neurons were constantly replacing old ones, wouldn't memories decay in that tide of growth? But Gage and other scientists revisited old findings and discovered that adult mice, rats and humans did, in fact, experience the birth of new neurons—but only in two very specific parts of the brain: in the olfactory bulb, where smells are registered, and in the hippocampus, a curl of tissue that controls memories and is functionally linked to parts of the brain that regulate emotion.

Could there be a connection between emotion and neuronal birth in the hippocampus? To find out, Gage and his collaborators began to study stressed mice. When mice are chronically stressed—by sudden changes in their living environments or by the removal of their bedding—they demonstrate behavioral symptoms like anxiety and lethargy and lose their sense of adventurousness, features that mimic aspects of human depression. Researchers found that in these mice, the burst of nerve cells in the hippocampus also diminished.

The converse turned out to be true as well. When mice are housed in an "enriched" environment—typically containing mazes, nesting materials and toys—they become more active and adventurous. They explore more; they learn faster; they seek pleasure. Enrichment, in short, acts behaviorally like an antidepressant. When Gage examined the brains of these enriched mice, he found that more neurons were being born in the hippocampus.

At Columbia University, another neuroscientist, René Hen, was intrigued by Gage's studies. Hen, working with other researchers, began to investigate the link between Prozac and nerve growth. The birth of neurons in the mice takes about two or three weeks—about the same time it takes for antidepressants to take effect. Might the psychiatric effects of Prozac and Paxil be related to the slow birth of neurons and not serotonin per se?

Hen began to feed his mice Prozac. Over the next few days, their behaviors changed: anxiety they had exhibited decreased, and the mice became more adventurous. They looked for food in novel environments and were quick to adopt newly learned behaviors. And newborn neurons appeared in the hippocampus in precisely the location that Gage found with the environmentally enriched mice. But when Hen selectively blocked the birth of neurons in the hippocampus, the adventurousness and the food-exploration instincts of the Prozac-fed mice vanished. Prozac's positive effects, in other words, depended on the birth of nerve cells in the hippocampi of these mice.

In 2011, Hen and his colleagues repeated these studies with depressed primates. In monkeys, chronic stress produces a syndrome with symptoms remarkably similar to some forms of human depression. Even more strikingly than mice, stressed monkeys lose interest in pleasure and become lethargic. When Hen measured neuron birth in the hippocampi in depressed monkeys, it was low. When he gave the monkeys antidepressants, the depressed symptoms abated and neuron birth resumed. Blocking the growth of nerve cells made Prozac ineffective.

Hen's experiments have profound implications for psychiatry and psychology. Antidepressants like Prozac and Zoloft, Hen suggested, may transiently increase serotonin in the brain, but their effect is seen only when new neurons are born. Might depression be precipitated by the death of neurons in certain parts of the brain? In Alzheimer's disease, areas of the brain involved in cognition degenerate, resulting in the characteristic dementia. In Parkinson's disease, nerve cells involved in coordinating movement degenerate, resulting in the characteristic trembling. Might depression also be a degenerative disease— an Alzheimer's of emotion, a dementia of mood? (Even our language begins to fail in this description. Dementia describes a breakdown of "mentation"—thinking—but we lack a similar word for a degeneration of mood: is it disaffection?)

And how, exactly, might the death of neurons in the tiny caul of the hippocampus (a part of the brain typically associated with the storage of memory) cause this disorder of mood? Traditionally, we think that nerve cells in the brain can form minuscule biological "circuits" that regulate behaviors. One set of nerve cells, for instance, might receive signals to move the hand and then relay these signals to the muscles that cause hand movement. It is easy to imagine that dysfunction of this circuit might result in a disorder of movement. But how does a circuit of nerves regulate mood? Might such a circuit store, for instance, some rules about adapting to stress: what to say or do or think when you are sick and nauseated and facing death and your son has moved a pillow? Did such a degeneration provoke a panic signal in the brain that goaded Wurtzel's deadly reverie: cellular death leading to thoughts of suicide.

And how, then, does the birth of cells heal this feeling? Are new circuits formed that restore vitality, regenerating behaviors that are adaptive and not destructive? Is this why Prozac or Zoloft takes two or three weeks to start working: to become "undepressed," do we have to wait for the slow rebirth of new parts of the brain?

If an answer to these questions exists, it may emerge from the work of Helen Mayberg, a neuroscientist at Emory University. Mayberg has been mapping anatomical areas of the brain that are either hyperactive or inactive in depressed men and women. Tracing such sites led her to the subcallosal cingulate, a minuscule bundle of nerve cells that sit near the hippocampus and function as a conduit between the parts of the brain that control conscious thinking and the parts that control emotion. Think of the subcallosal cingulate as a potential traffic intersection on the road between our cognitive and emotional selves.

When Mayberg stimulated this area of the brain with tiny bursts of electricity using probes in patients resistant to antidepressant therapy, she found remarkable response rates: about 75 percent of them experienced powerful changes in their moods during testing. Seconds after stimulation began, many patients, some of them virtually catatonic with depression, reported a "sudden calmness" or a "disappearance of the void." The stimulator can be implanted in patients and works like a depression pacemaker: it continues to relieve their symptoms for years. When the battery runs low, patients slowly relapse into depression.

At first glance, Mayberg's studies would appear to bypass the serotonin hypothesis. After all, it was electrical, not chemical, stimulation that altered mood. But the response to Mayberg's electrical stimulation also seemed to be linked to serotonin. The subcallosal cingulate is particularly rich in nerve cells that are sensitive to serotonin. Researchers found that if they blocked the serotonin signal in the brains of depressed rats, the pacemaker no longer worked.

A remarkable and novel theory for depression emerges from these studies. Perhaps some forms of depression occur when a stimulus—genetics, environment or stress—causes the death of nerve cells in the hippocampus. In the nondepressed brain, circuits of nerve cells in the hippocampus may send signals to the subcallosal cingulate to regulate mood. The cingulate then integrates these signals and relays them to the more conscious parts of the brain, thereby allowing us to register our own moods or act on them. In the depressed brain, nerve death in the hippocampus disrupts these signals—with some turned off and others turned on—and they are ultimately registered consciously as grief and anxiety. "Depression is emotional pain without context," Mayberg said. In a nondepressed brain, she said, "you need the hippocampus to help put a situation with an emotional component into context"—to tell our conscious brain, for instance, that the loss of love should be experienced as sorrow or the loss of a job as anxiety. But when the hippocampus malfunctions, perhaps emotional pain can be generated and amplified out of context—like Wurtzel's computer program of negativity that keeps running without provocation. The "flaw in love" then becomes autonomous and self-fulfilling.

We "grow sorrowful," but we rarely describe ourselves as "growing joyful." Imprinted in our language is an instinct that suggests that happiness is a state, while grief is a process. In a scientific sense too, the chemical hypothesis of depression has moved from static to dynamic—from "state" to "process." An antidepressant like Paxil or Prozac, these new studies suggest, is most likely not acting as a passive signal-strengthener. It does not, as previously suspected, simply increase serotonin or send more current down a brain's mood-maintaining wire. Rather, it appears to change the wiring itself. Neurochemicals like serotonin still remain central to this new theory of depression, but they function differently: as dynamic factors that make nerves grow, perhaps forming new circuits. The painter Cézanne, confronting one of Monet's landscapes, supposedly exclaimed: "Monet is just an eye, but, God, what an eye." The brain, by the same logic, is still a chemical soup—but, God, what a soup.

There are, undeniably, important gaps in this theory—and by no means can it claim to be universal. Depression is a complex, diverse illness, with different antecedent causes and manifestations. As the clinical trials show unequivocally, only a fraction of the most severely depressed patients respond to serotonin-enhancing antidepressants. Do these patients respond to Prozac because their depression involves cellular death in the hippocampus? And does the drug fail to work in mild to moderate depression because the cause of that illness is different?

The differences in responses to these drugs could also be due to variations in biological pathways. In some people, neurotransmitters other than serotonin may be involved; in yet others, there may be alterations in the brain caused by biological factors that are not neurotransmitters; in yet others, there may be no identifiable chemical or biological factors at all. The depression associated with Parkinson's disease, for instance, seems to have little to do with serotonin. Postpartum depression is such a distinct syndrome that it is hard to imagine that neurotransmitters or hippocampal neurogenesis play a primary role in it.

Nor does the theory explain why "talk therapies" work in some patients and not in others, and why the combination of talk and antidepressants seems to work consistently better than either alone. It is very unlikely that we can "talk" our brains into growing cells. But perhaps talking alters the way that nerve death is registered by the conscious parts of the brain. Or talking could release other chemicals, opening up parallel pathways of nerve-cell growth.

But the most profound implications have to do with how to understand the link between the growth of neurons, the changes in mood and the alteration of behavior. Perhaps antidepressants like Prozac and Paxil primarily alter *behavioral* circuits in the brain—particularly the circuits deep in the hippocampus where memories and learned behaviors are stored and organized—and consequently change mood. If Prozac helped Dorothy sleep better and stopped her from assaulting her own skin, might her mood eventually have healed as a response to her own alterations of behavior? Might Dorothy, in short, have created her own placebo effect? How much of mood is behavior anyway? Maybe your brain makes you "act" depressed, and then you "feel" depressed. Or you feel depressed in part because your brain is making you act depressed. Thoughts like these quickly transcend psychiatry and move into more unexpected and unsettling realms. They might begin with mood disorders, but they quickly turn to questions about the organizational order of the brain.

John Gribbin, a historian of science, once wrote that seminal scientific discoveries are inevitably preceded by technological inventions. The telescope, which situated the earth and the planets firmly in orbit around the sun, instigated a new direction in thinking for astronomy and physics. The microscope, taking optics in a different direction, ultimately resulted in the discovery of the cell.

We possess far fewer devices to look into the unknown cosmos of mood and emotion. We can only mix chemicals and spark electrical circuits and hope, indirectly, to understand the brain's structure and function through their effects. In time, the insights generated by these new theories of depression will most likely lead to new antidepressants: chemicals that directly initiate nerve growth in the hippocampus or stimulate the subcallosal cingulate. These drugs may make Prozac and Paxil obsolete—but any new treatment will owe a deep intellectual debt to our thinking about serotonin in the brain. Our current antidepressants are thus best conceived not as medical breakthroughs but as technological breakthroughs. They are chemical tools that have allowed us early glimpses into our brains and into the biology of one of the most mysterious diseases known to humans.

Critical Thinking

1. How did the early diagnosis of cases of depression influence the testing of new hypotheses? Explain.
2. What is a "meta-trial," and how does it work in advancing our understanding of depression and its treatments?

Create Central

www.mhhe.com/createcentral

Internet References

History of the treatment of depression
www.macalester.edu/psychology/whathap/UBNRP/depression05/history.html
Research on depression
http://psychcentral.com/disorders/depressionresearch.htm

SIDDHARTHA MUKHERJEE is an assistant professor of medicine in the division of medical oncology at Columbia University. He is the author of *Emperor of All Maladies: A Biography of Cancer.*

Article   Prepared by: R. Eric Landrum, *Boise State University*

Could Brain Scans Help Guide Treatment for OCD?

Small study suggests neural activity can point to patients who'll benefit most from psychotherapy.

MARY ELIZABETH DALLAS

Learning Outcomes

After reading this article, you will be able to:

- Understand the component behaviors of obsessive-compulsive disorder (OCD) and how certain beliefs lead to certain actions.

- Appreciate the prevalence of OCD in the United States.

- Comprehend why predicting the success of a treatment is important to an overall approach to improved mental health.

Psychotherapy can help some people avoid the disruptive behaviors linked to obsessive-compulsive disorder (OCD), and a new study suggests that brain scans can help spot those patients for whom the therapy will be most effective.

The treatment is called cognitive behavioral therapy (CBT). It works by placing patients in controlled situations where they are exposed to anxiety-causing stimuli, so that they gradually learn to deal better with these situations.

"Cognitive behavioral therapy is in many cases very effective, at least in the short term," said Dr. Jamie Feusner, an associate professor of psychiatry at University of California, Los Angeles (UCLA), and director of the Semel Institute's Adult OCD Program.

However, the treatment is "costly, time-consuming, difficult for patients and, in many areas, not available," Feusner noted in a UCLA news release. So, "if someone will end up having their symptoms return [after treatment], it would be useful to know before they get treatment," he reasoned.

His team wondered if certain patterns on brain scans might point to those patients who have the most to gain from CBT.

The notion has some merit, said one expert, especially since more reliable treatment is needed for people suffering from OCD.

"OCD is an illness in which patients experience obsessions and then act on them by performing compulsions," explained Dr. Alan Manevitz, a clinical psychiatrist at Lenox Hill Hospital in New York City.

Even though "the patient realizes that these obsessions and compulsions are unwanted, unreasonable, and excessive, he or she cannot stop listening to the thoughts and acting on them," he said.

According to Manevitz, one in every 40 Americans (2.5 percent) has clinical OCD, with symptoms bad enough to interfere with daily living, and another 10 percent have a lower-level form of the illness, where thoughts intrude but do not reach such a disruptive state.

"The past few decades, however, have seen the emergence of many effective treatments, both pharmacological and psychotherapeutic," including CBT, Manevitz said.

But who will gain the most from the psychotherapy? Feusner's team noted that although CBT may be very effective initially, not all patients see long-term benefits, and about 20 percent of patients suffer a relapse of their OCD symptoms.

In the UCLA study, brain scans known as fMRIs were used to study the brains of 17 people with OCD who ranged in age from 21 to 50.

The scans—which measure brain activity in real time—were performed before and after the patients completed intensive CBT.

The patients' symptoms were also monitored for one year.

According to Feusner, people with more efficient brain network "connectivity," as gauged by the brain scans, actually had *worse* long-term outcomes following CBT treatment.

The team also found that the intensity of OCD symptoms prior to treatment, or the patient's initial level of response to the therapy, was not a good predictor of long-term success.

Having a better understanding of which patients will not respond well to specific therapy long-term could help doctors develop a more effective treatment strategy.

The researchers were quick to point out that the study does not suggest that some patients with OCD are "beyond help" when it comes to psychotherapy. Instead, they believe that these patients may simply need longer CBT than the four weeks used in the study, or that they may be helped by medications as well.

"We are now starting to translate knowledge of the brain into useful information that in the future could be used by doctors and patients to make clinical decisions," Feusner said. "Although a brain scan may seem expensive, these scans only took about 15 minutes and thus the cost is not exceptionally high, particularly in comparison to medication or cognitive behavioral therapy treatments, which over time can cost many thousands of dollars."

However, Manevitz did have some reservations about the findings.

"The results are intriguing but this study has a very small sample size: 17 subjects," he said. Plus, those subjects appeared to be especially willing to undertake the rigors of CBT— something not every person with OCD might be amenable to, he said.

All of that "makes it harder to generalize [the findings] to the overall OCD population," Manevitz said. He also believes that while brain network "connectivity" may play a role in the effectiveness of psychotherapy for OCD, that remains only a theory.

The bottom line, according to Manevitz: "It is important to follow up this study with a larger group of participants."

Dr. Emily Stern is assistant professor of psychiatry and neuroscience at the Mount Sinai School of Medicine in New York City. She said that brain scans may have potential "to predict which patients will relapse [and] has the potential to identify those patients who may need further treatment or greater monitoring."

If the findings pan out, "brain network organization may provide a window into patient functioning that cannot be assessed through symptom measures alone," Stern said.

The study was funded by the U.S. National Institute of Mental Health and published recently in the journal *Frontiers in Psychiatry.*

Source

Alan Manevitz, M.D., clinical psychiatrist, Lenox Hill Hospital, New York City; Emily R. Stern, Ph.D. assistant professor, departments of psychiatry and neuroscience, Mount Sinai School of Medicine, New York City; University of California, Los Angeles, news release, June 23, 2015

Critical Thinking

1. Is psychotherapy effective in helping people with obsessive-compulsive disorder? Explain why or why not.

2. When the brains of OCD patients are scanned, what are the results? Explain.

Internet References

Causes of OCD
   http://www.anxietycare.org.uk/docs/ocdcauses.asp

Rewiring the brain to treat OCD
   http://discovermagazine.com/2013/nov/14-defense-free-will

What does an OCD brain look like?
   http://ocd.commons.yale.edu/ocdbrain/